CompTIA

CySA+ ™

CYBERSECURITY ANALYST

CERTIFICATION PASSPORT

(Exam CS0-002)

About the Author

Bobby Rogers is a cybersecurity professional with over 30 years in the information technology and cybersecurity fields. He currently works with a major engineering company in Huntsville, Alabama, helping to secure networks and manage cyber risk for its customers. Bobby's customers include the U.S. Army, NASA, the State of Tennessee, and private/commercial companies and organizations. His specialties are cybersecurity engineering, security compliance, and cyber risk management, but he has worked in almost every area of cybersecurity, including network defense, computer forensics and incident response, and penetration testing.

Bobby is a retired Master Sergeant from the U.S. Air Force, having served for over 21 years. He has built and secured networks in the U.S., Chad, Uganda, South Africa, Germany, Saudi Arabia, Pakistan, Afghanistan, and several other remote locations. His decorations include two Meritorious Service medals, three Air Force Commendation medals, the National Defense Service medal, and several Air Force Achievement medals. He retired from active duty in 2006.

Bobby has a Master of Science in Information Assurance and is currently writing his dissertation for a doctoral degree in cybersecurity. He also has a Bachelor of Science in Computer Information Systems (with a dual concentration in Russian Language) and two Associate of Science degrees. His many certifications include CISSP-ISSEP, CRISC, CySA+, CEH, and MCSE: Security.

He has narrated and produced over 30 computer training videos for several training companies, and currently produces them for Pluralsight (www.pluralsight.com). He is also the author of *CompTIA Mobility+ All-in-One Exam Guide (Exam MB0-001)*, *Certified in Risk and Information Systems Control (CRISC) All-in-One Certification Guide*, *Mike Meyers' CompTIA Security+ Certification Guide (Exam SY0-401)*, and contributing author/technical editor for the popular *CISSP All-in-One Exam Guide, Eighth Edition*, all from McGraw Hill.

About the Technical Editor

Dawn Dunkerley, Ph.D., CISSP®, CSSLP®, CRISC™, Security+®, is a leading cyberwarfare and cybersecurity researcher and author. She is an editor for the U.S. Army Cyber Institute's *Cyber Defense Review* and a Fellow of the America's Institute for Cybersecurity Leadership.

CompTIA

CySA+™

CYBERSECURITY ANALYST

CERTIFICATION PASSPORT

(Exam CS0-002)

Bobby Rogers

New York   Chicago   San Francisco   Athens
London   Madrid   Mexico City   Milan
New Delhi   Singapore   Sydney   Toronto

1 2 3 4 5 6 7 8 9   LCR   24 23 22 21 20

Library of Congress Control Number: 2020947644

ISBN   978-1-260-46226-5
MHID   1-260-46226-9

Sponsoring Editor Lisa McClain	**Acquisitions Coordinator** Emily Walters	**Proofreader** Rick Camp	**Composition** KnowledgeWorks Global Ltd.
Editorial Supervisor Patty Mon	**Technical Editor** Dawn Dunkerley	**Indexer** Ted Laux	**Illustration** KnowledgeWorks Global Ltd.
Project Manager Garima Poddar, KnowledgeWorks Global Ltd.	**Copy Editor** Bart Reed	**Production Supervisor** Pamela Pelton	**Art Director, Cover** Jeff Weeks

I'd like to dedicate this book to the cybersecurity professionals who tirelessly, and sometimes thanklessly, protect our information and systems from all who would do them harm. I also dedicate this book to the people who serve in uniform as military personnel, public safety professionals, police, firefighters, and medical professionals, sacrificing sometimes all that they are and have so that we may all live in peace, security, and safety.

Contents at a Glance

Contents

Acknowledgments

This book wasn't simply written by one person; so many people had key roles in the production of this guide, so I'd like to take this opportunity to acknowledge and thank them. First and foremost, I would like to thank the folks at McGraw Hill, and in particular Lisa McClain and Emily Walters. Both had the unenviable role of keeping me on track and leading me to see their vision of what this book is supposed to be. They are both awesome people to work with, and I'm grateful they had the faith to entrust this project to me!

I'd also like to thank Nicholas Lane for his great early work on the first three objectives of Domain 1.0; he did a great job in helping set the tone for the book and getting it off on the right track.

I owe a debt of thanks to the project manager, Garima Poddar of KnowledgeWorks Global Ltd, and Bart Reed, the copy editor. Both were great people to work with. Bart did a great job of turning my butchered attempts at style and grammar into a smooth-flowing, understandable book.

I also want to thank my family for their patience and understanding as I took time away from them to write this book. I owe them a great deal of time I can never pay back, and I am very grateful for their love and support.

And last, but certainly not least, I want to thank the technical editor, Dr. Dawn Dunkerley. Dawn has been my friend, partner-in-crime, and coworker at times for 14 years now. I've lost count of how many projects she has suffered through with me, yet she still immediately volunteers to work with me whenever I get a hairbrained idea to do another project that neither one of us appears to have the time or patience for. Dawn is truly the smartest person I know in cybersecurity, and this book is scores better for having her there to correct my mistakes, ask critical questions, make me do more research, and add a different and unique perspective to the process. Thank you, my friend!

Introduction

The Certification Passport Series

The Certification Passports are self-study certification guides that take an accelerated approach to reviewing the objectives and preparing to sit for the exam. The Passport series is designed to provide a concise review of the key information candidates need to know to pass the test, with learning elements that enables readers to focus their studies and quickly drill down into specific exam objectives.

In This Book

This Passport is divided into "Domains" that follow the exam domains. Each Domain is divided into "Objective" modules covering each of the top-level certification objectives.

We've created a set of learning elements that call your attention to important items, reinforce important points, and provide helpful exam-taking hints. Take a look at what you'll find in every module:

- Every domain and module begins with **Certification Objectives**—what you need to know in order to pass the section on the exam dealing with the module topic.
- The following elements highlight key information throughout the modules:

 EXAM TIP The Exam Tip element focuses on information that pertains directly to the test, such as a wording preference that is a hint to an answer. These helpful hints are written by authors who have taken the exam and received their certification—who better to tell you what to worry about? They know what you're about to go through!

 CAUTION These cautionary notes address common pitfalls or "real-world" issues as well as warnings about the exam.

KEY TERM This element highlights specific terms or acronyms that are essential to know in order to pass the exam.

 NOTE This element calls out any ancillary but pertinent information.

Cross-Reference

This element points to related topics covered in other Objective modules or Domains.

- **Tables** allow for a quick reference to help you quickly navigate quantitative data or lists of technical information.

Infrastructure	Advantages	Disadvantages
Cloud-based	Efficiency; cost savings; less required personnel and expertise; less required equipment, facilities, and resources; infrastructure is kept up to date, secure, and modern; some risk can be transferred to the cloud service provider.	Lack of control over asset and infrastructure; contract or SLA must be comprehensive and written to cover all possible issues; some liability, responsibility, and accountability cannot be transferred; the customer also sustains a vulnerability or attack suffered by the cloud service provider.
On-premises	Control over infrastructure and assets; visibility over how infrastructure is employed.	Cost; requires trained personnel; requires extensive equipment and facilities; incurs greater inherent risk that is not transferred.

- Each Objective module ends with a brief **Review**, which begins by repeating the official exam objective number and text, followed by a succinct and useful summary, geared toward quick review and retention.
- **Review Questions** are intended to be similar to those found on the exam. Explanations of the correct answer are provided.

Online Content

For more information on the practice exams included with the book, please see the "About the Online Content" appendix at the back of the book.

Introduction

Welcome to the *CompTIA CySA+™ Cybersecurity Analyst Certification Passport*! This book is focused on helping you pass CompTIA's CySA+ certification examination. The idea behind the Passport series is to give you a concise study guide for learning the key elements of the certification exam from the perspective of the required objectives published by CompTIA. This book is intended for mid-level cybersecurity analysts who have a few years of experience under their belt. While CompTIA has no specific mandatory experience or certification prerequisites, they do recommend that you have at least four years of hands-on experience in a technical cybersecurity job role, as well as the Security+ and Network+ certifications, or equivalent knowledge and experience.

I recommend you use this book for learning key terms and concepts as well as for studying in the final few days before your CySA+ exam, possibly after you've done all of your "deep" studying. This guide will help you memorize fast facts, as well as refresh you on topics you may not have studied for a while. This book is meant to be a "no fluff" concise guide with quick facts, definitions, memory aids, charts, and brief explanations, but nothing too in depth. This guide assumes you have already studied long and hard for your exam, and you just need a quick refresher before you test. Because it gives you the key concepts and facts, and not necessarily the in-depth explanations surrounding those facts, it should not be used as your only study source to prepare for the exam. There are numerous books you can use for your deep studying, such as the *CompTIA CySA+ Cybersecurity Analyst Certification All-in-One Exam Guide, Second Edition (Exam CS0-002)*, also from McGraw Hill.

This guide is organized around the most recent exam domains and objectives released by CompTIA as of the publishing date of this book. Keep in mind that CompTIA reserves the right to change or update the exam objectives at its sole discretion anytime without any prior notice, so you should check for the most recent objectives before you take the exam to make sure you are studying the most updated materials. CompTIA has published five domains for this exam; they are organized in numerical order in the book, with individual domain objectives also ordered by objective number in each domain. These domains are equivalent to regular book "chapters," so you have five considerably large chapters in the book with individual sections devoted to the objective numbers. Hopefully, this organization will help you learn and master each objective in a logical way. Because domain objectives can overlap sometimes, you may see a bit of redundancy in topics discussed throughout the book; where this is the case, we have tried to put the topic in its proper context within the domain objective where it resides and cross-reference it to the same topic discussed in other parts of the book in other objectives.

I hope this book is helpful to you, not only in studying for the exam but also as a quick reference guide you'll use in your professional life. Thanks for picking this book to help you study, and good luck on the exam!

Threat and Vulnerability Management

Domain Objectives

- **1.1** Explain the importance of threat data and intelligence.
- **1.2** Given a scenario, utilize threat intelligence to support organizational security.
- **1.3** Given a scenario, perform vulnerability management activities.
- **1.4** Given a scenario, analyze the output from common vulnerability assessment tools.
- **1.5** Explain the threats and vulnerabilities associated with specialized technology.
- **1.6** Explain the threats and vulnerabilities associated with operating in the cloud.
- **1.7** Given a scenario, implement controls to mitigate attacks and software vulnerabilities.

1

Objective 1.1 Explain the importance of threat data and intelligence

It is an unfortunate reality that cybercriminals have some advantages over their targets, chiefly with time and information. Like the white pieces in chess, attackers get to make the first move. In other words, *the attackers choose the targets; targets don't choose the attackers.* The hacker's first-move advantage gives them considerable time to research their target's security and people long before an attack takes place.

Meanwhile, unprepared organizations have no idea what's coming. Their security defenses will exist in a generalized state rather than aligning more strategically with potential and imminent threats. Compounding this cybersecurity imbalance is the fact that today's cybercriminals are considerably more numerous, intelligent, well-equipped, well-funded, and ambitious than ever before. Advantage bad guys.

 NOTE   Cybersecurity experts estimate that 75 percent of a hacker's overall attack effort is spent gathering target information. You can count on them knowing a great deal about your organization before striking. One of the oldest truisms of war remains as pertinent as ever—*know your enemy.*

Despite the challenges, organizations aren't helpless. Having recognized the rise in cybercriminal attacks, businesses are hiring cybersecurity analysts to reduce the time and information advantages afforded to attackers. Among other things, cybersecurity analysts spend a lot of time collecting and analyzing threat intelligence to identify threats that have, will, or are currently targeting their organization. While scouting out threats in the wild, these analysts are equally engaged in the continuous monitoring of their organization's in-house operations to identify any attacks in progress. Using this inside-out approach, organizations are deriving enough threat intelligence to better align their security defenses with probable threat tactics.

Ultimately, cybersecurity analysts share the same goal as other cybersecurity roles: help prevent, detect, and mitigate cybersecurity incidents. In doing so, organizations can focus on what's most important, and that is organizational objectives.

 NOTE   The modern era of targeted attacks must be met with targeted defenses. Although we can't expect to know all attacker specifics before an attack, we can narrow down the possibilities, which permits us to better align our defenses.

Having said that, you need to key in on the concept of *threat intelligence,* which we discuss in the upcoming sections. This includes several key concepts:

- Explain how we collect and analyze information from various intelligence sources.
- Explain how we assign confidence levels to intelligence findings.
- Explain how we use indicator management to share intelligence information with others in cybersecurity.
- Explain the different threat classifications and threat actors.
- Explain how intelligence cycles work.
- Explain how commodity malware works.
- Explain information sharing and analysis communities.

 KEY TERM **Cyber threat intelligence** is the collection and analysis of threat trends to identify potential or actual threats to the organization. As a result, organizations will be better prepared to create preventative and detective cybersecurity measures.

Although much of this book is about collecting information about the bad guys, we'll briefly highlight how hackers collect information about their victims. Unlike the two-hour hacking wizardry you see in movies, attackers prefer to take their time to perform some reconnaissance on their targets before the attack. This simultaneously maximizes their chances of success while minimizing the odds of being detected. The initial reconnaissance effort by the attackers is often called *footprinting*. Through footprinting, attackers attempt to collect as much information about targets as possible.

 EXAM TIP *Passive footprinting* collects information about the target without directly interacting with it. This typically involves combing through the target's website, job sites, forums, among other sites. *Active footprinting* collects information about the target through direct interaction, such as e-mailing, calling, and visiting the target's physical location.

Through various footprinting and network-scanning activities, attackers are likely to acquire several types of information:

- Organizational details (employee details, telephone numbers, location, organizational background, and so on)
- Network details (domains, subdomains, IP address ranges, WHOIS records, DNS records, and so on)
- Open ports

- Installed operating systems, services, and applications
- Hardware and software vulnerabilities
- Network map
- Usernames

Cross-References

Vulnerability scanning will be covered in more detail in Objectives 1.3 and 1.4.

Having discussed some of the basics of hackers footprinting their targets, we'll now direct our focus to the types of intelligence sources and how they can help us prepare for cybercriminal activities.

Intelligence Sources

To stay abreast of the latest security threats, threat actors, and vulnerabilities, cybersecurity analysts are tethered to accurate and up-to-date intelligence sources. They use a variety of security tools and web browsers to harvest this threat data via multiple open-source and closed-source intelligence feeds. Keep in mind, however, that the goal isn't simply to collect as much threat data as possible; instead, they must focus on acquiring data that is relevant, accurate, timely, and presented to the organization in a useful way.

Although terms like *threat data* and *threat intelligence* are often used interchangeably, they're not identical. Threat data is merely raw information about known malicious domains, URLs, IP addresses, and hash values. No context is provided. Think of them as individual puzzle pieces—important yet generic on their own. In contrast, threat intelligence is the enhanced version of threat data that has been analyzed, refined, and, by extension, creates the crucial context that organizations need to understand the threat landscape. Threat intelligence is the outcome of puzzle pieces connected to form a partial or complete picture of the puzzle.

This section goes through multiple intelligence sources, so you'll have a better idea of how cybersecurity analysts gather information about threats.

Open-Source Intelligence

If attackers are using *open-source intelligence* (OSINT) to learn about us, we'd be wise to follow suit. OSINT involves the collection of any information available on public sources. For example, you can learn a lot about CompTIA via its website and social media channels. Although cybersecurity analysts and hackers utilize OSINT, the information desired by both camps will be quite different. For instance, hackers collect information about their organizational targets from the following sources:

- **Google hacking**   Advanced Google searches to find target data
- **Internet registries**   ARIN, AFRINIC, APNIC, LACNIC, RIPE NCC
- **Job sites**   Monster, LinkedIn, Indeed, CareerBuilder

| TABLE 1.1-1 | OSINT Sources |

OSINT Categories	Types
Public media sources	TV, books, magazines, radio channels
Internet	Website threat feeds, social media networks, Google hacking, Shodan, Censys, forums, blogs, YouTube, WHOIS records, wikis
Public government data	Government website announcements, directories, records, hearings
Specialized publications	Academic thesis, dissertations, journals, conferences
Geospatial	Maps, images, metadata tags

- **Social media**   LinkedIn, Facebook, Twitter, YouTube
- **WHOIS**   IP address range, company contact, company address, phone number, e-mail address

Except for social media channels, cybersecurity analysts won't learn much, if anything, about potential attackers via these sources. Instead, they'll need to utilize various "good guy" OSINT sources listed in Table 1.1-1.

Not surprisingly, cybersecurity analysts will concentrate on *threat feeds* found throughout the Internet. Threat feeds are real-time data streams that publish large volumes of potential and actual threats. These feeds are typically hosted on security vendor websites and also shared by a global community of independent threat researchers and security professionals. Unlike closed-source intelligence feeds, OSINT feeds contain free-to-use information. Shown next are just a few good examples of organizations with public threat feeds:

- AT&T Cybersecurity (formerly AlienVault)
- Department of Homeland Security: Automated Indicator Sharing
- FBI: InfraGard
- MITRE Corporation ATT&CK
- SANS: Internet Storm Center
- The U.S. Computer Emergency Readiness Team (US-CERT), which was recently absorbed into the U.S. Cybersecurity and Infrastructure Security Agency (CISA): VirusShare and VirusTotal

 CAUTION   Cybersecurity analysts often drown in threat data. If your security tools are collecting threat data from multiple OSINT sources, super repositories may be created. If you're unable to isolate useful threat data and generate intelligence from it, you're more likely to miss true threats (known as false negatives) and to label benign traffic as a threat (a false positive).

The types of data to keep an eye out for in OSINT sources can be found in Table 1.1-2.

| TABLE 1.1-2 | Threat Data Types |

Threat Data Type	Description
Advanced persistent threats (APTs)	A threat actor, typically state-sponsored, that gains long-term unauthorized access to a network or system to continuously steal sensitive information
Exploits	A piece of code used by threat actors to take advantage of a vulnerability in a target system
General malware	Malware (with hashes) such as viruses, worms, Trojans, spyware, greyware, rootkits, adware, and logic bombs
Zero-day threats	A type of threat that attacks a vulnerability for which a solution has not yet been created by the hardware or software vendor
Ransomware	A type of malware that demands payment from a victim to prevent their files from being perpetually encrypted or published online (doxed)

Proprietary and Closed-Source Intelligence

Often superior to its OSINT counterpart, closed-source intelligence involves the collection of information from restricted, covert, or fee-based sources. In other words, the information found in these sources is *not* available to the general public. These closed sources can range from "underground" dark web sites to classified government systems, which are only accessible to individuals with security clearances.

 NOTE A good example of a fee-based closed source comes from FireEye, a leading cybersecurity and threat intelligence organization. FireEye provides various subscription-based threat intelligence services.

Although not always the case, OSINT threat feeds tend to share threat *data* as opposed to threat *intelligence*. Closed-source intelligence groups will generally review the accuracy and authenticity of threat data, plus enhance it wherever possible, before posting it online. The following are some closed-source intelligence sources:

- Threat intelligence platforms
- Classified government systems
- Dark web materials only available to "black market" customers
- Private intelligence sharing communities

Whereas closed-source intelligence focuses on data not being available to the general public, proprietary data refers to the more secretive or confidential nature of business data that, if unlawfully disclosed, could severely damage an organization's competitive edge. For example, research and development departments often have proprietary data in the form of technical and performance specifications, product plans, code names, and technical reports.

Timeliness

In the context of threat intelligence, *timeliness* is described as a relationship between the time that threat data is collected, organized, and finally reported. Since most threat data loses value over time, data must be quickly received and acted upon to make a difference. Yet, data collected too early or too late will either tell the wrong story or tell an old one. In either case, the lack of timeliness of data will likely result in ineffective decision making and, by extension, threat mitigations. Given the importance of timeliness, here are a few questions to keep in mind regarding the determination of timeliness requirements?

- How is the threat data delivered to ensure efficient use?
- How much time passes between threat detection and customer notification?
- Is threat data delivered immediately for expediency or eventually for completeness? Some customers may prefer one over the other.

EXAM TIP   Organizations should develop a well-defined schedule for data collection and reporting frequencies, in addition to prioritizing urgent data types that have time sensitivities.

Relevancy

Not every organization is at risk for the same kinds of threats. For example, if your organization doesn't use Mozilla Firefox, don't collect threat data about it. With organizations already full to bursting with data, be sure to exercise data frugality. We should concentrate on only collecting data that enlightens us into the probabilities and impacts of threats against actual technologies used at our companies.

Efforts to collect threat data will be hampered if businesses lack understanding about their hardware and software. Updating inventories would certainly help, but it's also important for cybersecurity teams to conduct comprehensive risk assessments on those inventoried assets to ensure appropriate technologies are incorporated into threat intelligence efforts.

EXAM TIP   Threat data is best obtained from intelligence sources that align with your sector, industry, and organization. Yet, priority should be granted to internally sourced threat data since it will represent former, actual, and potential indicators of compromise (IOCs) coming from *within the organization itself*.

Accuracy

In some cases, inaccurate threat data can be worse than no threat data. Inaccuracy usually takes the form of threat data corruption, spoofing, or improper analysis, and one should not ignore the role played by false positives. False positives are inevitable, but too many indicate an ineffective threat intelligence program. Being flooded with false positives will prevent you from keying in on important threat data—and may even help create data inaccuracies by starving a system of its resources.

 EXAM TIP Being able to corroborate threat data via multiple intelligence sources will go a long way in determining its accuracy.

Confidence Levels

Organizations often subscribe to multiple threat intelligence sources to enhance their threat knowledge, and, by extension, implement the cybersecurity prevention, detection, and mitigation capabilities that were recommended. Yet, collecting more data means organizations will have more false positives to weed through, which may increase the difficulty of distinguishing real threat indicators from normal data.

Once threat indicators have been analyzed, analysts will often assign them threat and confidence ratings to determine the threat's level of nastiness and the company's confidence in that determination.

 KEY TERMS **Threat rating** is a ranking of a threat's potential danger level. This is often measured on a scale of 0 to 5, with 5 representing the most critical type of threat.

Confidence rating (level) is a ranking of how confident we are that a threat rating is accurate. This is often measured on a scale of 0 to 100, with 100 representing the highest level of confidence. Note that confidence levels only apply to our trust in the source of threat information, not the likelihood that a threat will materialize.

Table 1.1-3 provides a generalized version of threat ratings that organizations may use.

In addition to the ratings, other threat characteristics may be described, including the threat's capabilities, whether it's an opportunistic or targeted threat, and the phase or phases of the kill chain the threat currently occupies. Most threats are opportunistic in that the attacker came upon a target by chance and was motivated simply by the target's weak security state alone. However, threats by themselves may not be enough to motivate decision-makers into spending time, resources, and dollars on countermeasures. We have to convince decision-makers that our confidence in potential and actual threats is well-founded. Table 1.1-4 shows a generalized version of confidence ratings that organizations may use.

TABLE 1.1-3   Threat Ratings

Level	Label
0	Baseline
1	Suspicious
2	Low
3	Medium
4	High
5	Critical

TABLE 1.1-4   Confidence Ratings

Type	Rating
Unknown	0
Discredited	1
Improbable	2–29
Doubtful	30–49
Possible	50–69
Probable	70–89
Confirmed	90–100

Our ability to classify threats into confidence levels is largely dependent on three things:

- Our ability to directly observe the threat
- The threat's feasibility
- Whether or not the threat can be corroborated with legitimate sources.

A higher confidence rating in a threat grants us reasonable assurance that our cybersecurity response to the threat will not be in vain.

Indicator Management

Organizations can't acquire sufficient threat data and intelligence in a vacuum. Maximizing cyber threat readiness requires our businesses, intelligence sharing communities, and security researchers to voluntarily share their threat intel with the global community. However, information sharing on a global scale will naturally raise some standardization concerns:

- What should the shared threat data look like?
- What's the best way to share threat data?
- What formatting should the threat data use to ensure efficient processing by recipients?

Fortunately, some cyber threat sharing protocols already exist to address these concerns. The three in particular we're going to look at are Structured Threat Information eXpression (STIX), Trusted Automated eXchange of Indicator Information (TAXII), and OpenIOC.

Structured Threat Information eXpression (STIX)

You need a universal way to *describe* threat intel, so what language should you use? Enter STIX. STIX is a standardized language for describing the "what" of threat data. Like TAXII, it was developed by MITRE and is now maintained by the OASIS Cyber Threat Intelligence (CTI) Technical Committee. STIX is maintained in an ad-hoc fashion by various intelligence-sharing communities and organizations across the globe. Due to STIX's structure, intelligence sharers are able to convey multiple characteristics about each threat:

- Threat motivations
- Threat capabilities
- Threat response

Table 1.1-5 shows the various components of the updated STIX 2.0 architecture in terms of all the threat information that can be conveyed to others.

So, if STIX describes the "what" of threat data, what do you suppose describes *how* to transfer that threat data to others? That is where TAXII comes in, which we're going to look at next.

TABLE 1.1-5 STIX Architecture

Domain Object	Description
Attack Pattern	The tactics, techniques, and procedures (TTPs) used by a threat actor to compromise targets.
Campaign	The sequence of attack behaviors exhibited by threat actors against targets over a period of time.
Course of Action	A target's security response to an attack.
Identity	Represents entities that may be targeted or are doing the targeting. It may also identify a source of information.
Indicator	Indicates a pattern of malicious or potentially malicious activities.
Intrusion Set	A group of malicious behaviors and resources caused by one threat actor.
Malware	Malicious software designed to compromise systems or data.
Observed Data	Describes data observed on a network or system.
Report	Collection of threat intel, including the attacker, method, and target details.
Threat Actor	Individual, group, or organization operating maliciously.
Tool	Software used by a threat actor to perform attacks.
Vulnerability	Weakness in hardware or software subject to exploitation by threat actors.

Trusted Automated eXchange of Indicator Intelligence (TAXII)

TAXII is a free cyber threat standard that describes how threat data can be shared. Designed to work directly with STIX, it uses a flexible communications API to make it compatible with the following multiple cyber threat sharing models:

- **Hub-and-spoke**   A two-way sharing model where a central organization (hub) manages threat data synchronization between itself and partner organizations (spokes). The hub and spokes can synchronize threat data in either direction only if the hub approves. This model is depicted in Figure 1.1-1.

- **Source/subscriber**   A one-way sharing model where a central organization serves as the single source of threat data for other organizations. This is illustrated in Figure 1.1-2.

- **Peer-to-peer**   A two-way sharing model where all participating organizations can send/receive threat data with each other without centralized approval requirements. Take a look at Figure 1.1-3 for a visual.

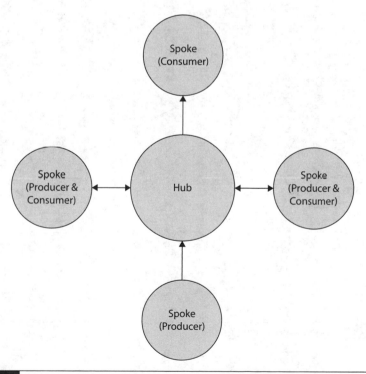

FIGURE 1.1-1   Hub-and-spoke sharing model

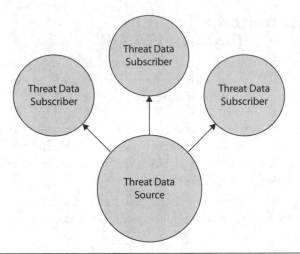

FIGURE 1.1-2 Source/subscriber sharing model

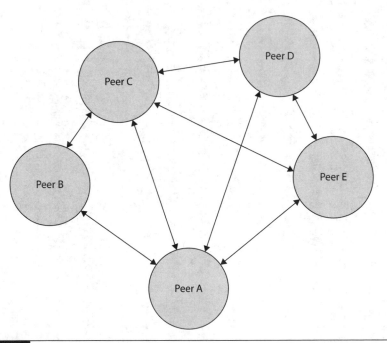

FIGURE 1.1-3 Peer-to-peer sharing model

OpenIOC

Although not as well-known as the aforementioned frameworks, OpenIOC is an open cyber threat sharing framework designed for exchanging threat data with other parties in a machine-readable format. It was developed by the American cybersecurity company Mandiant in November 2011 (later acquired by FireEye in 2013). OpenIOC is written in XML and is adaptable enough to permit incident responders easy translation of threat knowledge into a standard format. Businesses use OpenIOC to share IOCs with other businesses that serve the threat intelligence communities worldwide.

Threat Classification

Threats can be classified in many ways, depending on the methodology and the organizations that produce it. One of the most widely accepted classifications of threats comes from the National Institute of Standards and Technology (NIST) Special Publication (SP) 800-30 (revision 1), "Guide for Conducting Risk Assessments." In addition to providing an excellent methodology for conducting risk assessments, SP 800-30 provides a solid taxonomy of classifying threats and vulnerabilities and determining risk in general. Appendix D to this publication states that there are four different types of threat sources (also known as threat agents) that can cause or generate a threat event:

- **Adversarial** Includes malicious persons, groups, organizations, and nation-states
- **Accidental** Users or administrators
- **Structural** Equipment or software failure
- **Environmental** Natural or man-made disasters and outages

Appendix E describes a plethora of potential threat events caused by these sources and categorizes them based on adversarial or non-adversarial threat events, as well as presents their confidence levels.

Threats can be categorized in multiple different ways, depending on several factors. This can include the obvious, such as whether it's environmental or man-made, adversarial or non-adversarial, but we can also classify threats according to the type of attack they represent, through which avenue of attack (called a threat vector), and whether they are known or unknown.

Known Threats vs. Unknown Threats

Now let's turn our attention to known threats and unknown threats. The idea of a threat being "known" is subject to interpretation, as you can see in Table 1.1-6.

Predictably, "known knowns" are the most common threats we deal with. An example would be antimalware software detecting and eradicating a virus based on that virus's known signature. Most of the malware that we acquire will be detected and remediated in this manner.

 KEY TERM   **Signature-based detection** involves the detection of attacks by looking for specific known types of information unique to a threat, such as network traffic characteristics or malware code, and comparing its "signature" with a well-known database of malicious signatures.

Just as predictably, our antimalware tools won't have advance knowledge about all malware. For example, if a known polymorphic virus (one that can mutate) changes into an unknown variety, the new malware form will become unknown for some time. Since signature-based detection engines won't yet be able to detect this malware, another method will be needed.

What if we use a technique that focuses on what a threat is *doing* as opposed to what the threat *looks* like? Heuristic-based detection can detect previously unknown malware by identifying unusual or suspicious properties within the code. As malware continues to automatically mutate, heuristic-based detection is becoming increasingly important. You may need to "tune" the heuristic engine's detection level to a comfortable middle point. If the engine is too aggressive, more false positives will result. Predictably, if the engine is too passive, more false negatives will result.

TABLE 1.1-6   Known vs. Unknown Threats

Category	Description
Known knowns	Threats we're aware of and understand
Known unknowns	Threats we're aware of but don't understand
Unknown knowns	Threats we understand but are not aware of
Unknown unknowns	Threats we are neither aware of nor understand

EXAM TIP   Heuristic analysis can work *statically,* where suspected code is decompiled into source code for analysis, or *dynamically,* where the suspected code is isolated into a virtual environment where it can run in real time and be analyzed with less risk.

Zero-Day Threats

Microsoft has been warning us for years that after January 14, 2020, the Windows 7 "Extended Support" period will finally come to an end. To minimize any looming security exploitations, they've spent the past few years warning businesses and residential customers to upgrade to Windows 10 ASAP. Why? Zero-day threats. *Zero-day threats* are attacks against vulnerabilities that the hardware/software vendors don't know about or haven't created a security update for. A zero-day vulnerability refers to the time between when the existence of a vulnerability is known (to an attacker or even the vendor) and an exploit is produced for the vulnerability. In bad cases, this is zero days, meaning that when a vulnerability is discovered, an exploit for it is also discovered or known immediately as well.

However, when a vendor stops supporting a product—as in Microsoft's case with Windows 7—any vulnerabilities discovered thereafter will remain *indefinitely.* That's a major problem because a lot of businesses don't want to, or cannot, move on from Windows 7 for the foreseeable future.

NOTE   Organizations that elect to pay Microsoft for "Extended Security Updates" will be able to get patches—although the costs will be prohibitive, and will steadily rise, as an incentive for businesses to upgrade to newer Microsoft products.

Advanced Persistent Threats

Advanced persistent threats (APTs) are essentially today's digital spies. APTs are covert threat actors, typically at a military or government-sponsored level, who gain unauthorized access to systems with the goal of long-term data extraction and invisibility.

Here is the lifecycle for APTs:

1. Define target.
2. Find and organize accomplices.
3. Build or acquire tools.
4. Research target infrastructure/employees.

5. Test for detection.

6. Deployment.

7. Initial intrusion.

8. Outbound connection initiated.

9. Expand access and obtain credentials.

10. Strengthen foothold.

11. Exfiltrate data.

12. Cover tracks and remain undetected.

Threat Actors

Although the general public typically generalizes them as just "hackers," threat actors are *any* entity that causes a threat to materialize. Although many people immediately think of threat actors as malicious, they are not always so. Of course, there are malicious threat actors, but there are accidental threat actors and environmental threat actors. Earlier in the module, we discussed how NIST SP 800-30 defines threat sources (synonymous with actors or agents) as adversarial, accidental, structural, and environmental. Also, as mentioned before, threats, along with the threat actors, can be classified in different ways. Some of these include nation-state threats, hacktivists, organized crime, and malicious insiders.

Nation-States

Nation-states conduct all types of electronic warfare, intelligence, counterintelligence, and even cyber attacks on enemies, and even sometimes allies, to gain tactical or strategic advantages. Nation-states typically have entire divisions of cybersecurity professionals who are acting as state-sponsored hackers. Earlier we mentioned the advanced persistent threat, which is almost always a nation-state–sponsored threat. The goal of nation-states is typically to get any information that can give them an advantage over another country, whether it is militarily or economically. Examples would be any information regarding national defense, trade secrets or proprietary data, economic data, and even data used to blackmail individuals in other countries.

Hacktivists

Creativity notwithstanding, if you put the words "hacker" and "activist" together, you'll arrive at the term "hacktivist." Hacktivists are individuals who use hacking as a vehicle to bring about political or social change. The causes they typically fight for include human rights, free speech, information, and societal change. Regardless of the means that hacktivists choose to achieve their goals, they tend to view themselves as the "good guys."

History has seen many notable hacktivist individuals and groups, but perhaps two of the more "mainstream" variety deserve some mention:

- **Edward Snowden**   Formerly a CIA employee, Snowden became notorious for leaking highly classified NSA information due to his allegation that the NSA performed abusive surveillance practices domestically and abroad.
- **WikiLeaks**   This whistleblowing organization, created by Julian Assange, maintains a website that publishes secret or classified materials in an effort to "fight societal corruption."

CAUTION   Although not an exam topic, if you're a U.S. person possessing a U.S. federal government security clearance, including both federal workers and contractors, be advised that you might be banned by the U.S. government from viewing WikiLeaks due to it potentially possessing classified materials. This rule does not apply to any U.S. citizen who does not possess a security clearance.

Organized Crime

The stereotypical, lone-wolf, hacker-in-a-hoodie guy isn't the norm anymore. Hoodies are being replaced with suits, and lone wolves are increasingly working for cybercriminal organizations. With historic sums of money to be made today, huge global crime rings, hacker corporations, and state-sponsored groups have been built around this new cybercriminal business model. Cybercrime is definitely the next generation of organized crime.

With organized crime organizations spear-heading much of the hacking, we must prepare our defenses *for* such organizations. Groups like Anonymous, Syrian Electronic Army, Lizard Squad, and many others have the intelligence, capital resources, business plans, and operational efficiencies similar to large enterprises. It puts a whole new spin on cybersecurity to realize that we're not guarding our organization against mere hackers, but against organized crime hacker organizations!

Many of these hacker groups have large social media followings, and they're not above threatening or announcing their plans on social media as a way to taunt their targets. Do your homework as you would with any other threat vector.

NOTE   Organized crime groups are known for conducting widespread ransomware operations, cryptojacking, bribery, and blackmail, and they have a particular affinity for hustling millions of dollars out of duped CEOs. Collect whatever organized crime intel you can find and start raising awareness within your organization before it's too late.

Insider Threats

There's a reason why physical security is still the most important kind—because insider threats are still, on average, the most dangerous adversary to an organization. Insider threats are typically people who work for an organization and have privileged access and knowledge about that organization's operation and assets. Skilled or unskilled, malicious or not, the fact that insiders have keys, ID badges, and user accounts makes it easy for them to cause harm. However, not all insider threats are created equal, as we'll explore in the next section.

Intentional

Many insider threats fully intend on causing harm to the organization. Such staff are typically disgruntled and perhaps are about to resign or get fired. *Malicious insiders* are known for either sabotaging company assets or stealing confidential data.

In other cases, *professional insiders* were installed by, perhaps, a state-sponsor, competitor, or organized crime group for espionage purposes. They're looking to collect sensitive information to sell it to competitors or the black market for financial gain.

Although not the most common, *compromised insiders* are compelled against their will by an external threat actor. These individuals are manipulated by the external threat into performing various theft and sabotage exercises on their behalf.

Unintentional

Although research shows that most security incidents occur from insiders, what often surprises people is that the majority of those insider threats are *unintentional*. A significant risk to organizational data is accidents, which are caused by a negligent or complacent employee. Their lack of education on cybersecurity best practices and negligence on following company policies are the most common root causes of unintentional insider threats. Unfortunately, many organizations suffer both data and financial losses caused by the "innocent" mistakes of their staff.

Negligent employees bear watching and can be characterized by their poor password management habits, oversharing on social media sites, storing confidential materials on network drives or flash drives, and sending such data through conventional e-mail and IM messaging channels.

Intelligence Cycle

We've discussed various topics throughout this module, but let's recall that this exam objective focuses on the importance of threat data and intelligence. Getting such data, making it useful, and then basing cybersecurity decisions from it is what cybersecurity analysis is all about. To that end, let's talk about the methodical way cybersecurity teams make this happen through what we call the *intelligence cycle*.

The intelligence cycle is the never-ending process of collecting raw information, generating actionable intelligence from it, and sending it to stakeholders to make decisions that help the organization meet particular cybersecurity objectives. These stakeholders can range from security operations center (SOC) analysts to senior-level management. Through successful intelligence cycles, organizations stand to gain several advantages:

- Quick detection and remediation of threats
- Better regulatory compliance
- Reduction of confidentiality, integrity, and availability breaches
- Increased efficiencies of cybersecurity implementations

Although you'll see many variations of the intelligence cycle out there, we can safely anchor them to five essential phases, which we'll cover next.

Requirements

All cycles have beginnings, and, in the case of intelligence cycles, it starts with requirements. Defining requirements simply means that we're getting all our ducks in a row to conduct an efficient and sustainable intelligence cycle. It starts with the company stakeholders determining the cybersecurity goals of the intelligence cycle—chiefly the identification of cybersecurity issues and proposed resolutions. The following requirements will need to be defined to achieve the goals:

- Team roles and responsibilities
- Resources allocated to team members
- Timelines for meeting objectives
- Prioritization of assets, risks, and threats
- Sources for threat intelligence
- Determination of threat intelligence types
- Tools/techniques needed to collect, analyze, and report cybersecurity intelligence

Collection

Guided by aforementioned requirements, we start collecting raw data from a variety of open- and closed-source locations to help identify the current and most likely threats facing the organization. We'll use a range of tools to collect threat data, including the following:

- Security information event management (SIEM)
- Threat intelligence platforms
- Threat intelligence providers
- User behavior analytics (UBA)
- Network traffic analysis tool
- Cybersecurity communities

Once all relevant raw data has been collected, it'll need to be normalized and formatted into contextually useful information for analysis in the next phase.

Analysis

With threat data now in an intelligible format, analysis will help us turn that data into threat *intelligence*—which is when the data becomes contextually useful—and we can truly understand what it says. Analysis helps us to determine the significance and implications of the data, such as the following:

- Does the data show indicators of compromise?
- Does the data show that we're being targeted?
- What threat predictions can we draw from the data?
- What threat solutions should we consider implementing to quell the threats?

The last thing you should do in this phase is to make a report of all your analyzed findings. Stakeholders have no patience for data that is unwieldy, incomplete, inconsistent, or unreadable.

Dissemination

With the data carefully analyzed, we must disseminate that information to the stakeholders. This will come in the form of a concise and actionable report that someone can use to make effective and expedient decisions based on its contents.

Recall earlier that anyone, from cybersecurity personnel to senior management, can be a stakeholder. Make sure you know who they are and that you give careful consideration to how you disseminate intelligence to them. Take a look at the following for some guidance:

- Ensure the right stakeholder is given the data most relevant to their needs.
- Ensure data is formatted in the most understandable and useful manner.
- Ensure stakeholders are given updated information as it becomes available.

Feedback

The final phase of the intelligence cycle is feedback. As you can imagine, the producers of the intelligence (us) and the consumers of the intelligence (stakeholders) should discuss how well the intelligence efforts have met stakeholder requirements. Whether the requirements are sufficiently met or not, you can make some changes for subsequent threat collection and mitigation cycles. New requirements may arise, threat data collected may change, and new analysis and dissemination techniques may be needed to ensure requirements are better met going forward.

Commodity Malware

Recall from earlier in the text that attackers often handpick a specific organization, research its security defenses and people, and then carefully exploit its vulnerabilities, whether through phishing e-mails or malware. In these targeted instances, attackers are known for using malware specifically crafted for that organization. Although more likely to succeed in such targeted attacks, the malware's custom design, scarcity, and high cost don't make it a desirable fit for more generalized and opportunistic types of attacks.

Most malware encountered by organizations will be of the more prevalent sort—nowadays called *commodity malware*. Commodity malware is widely available—either for free or purchase on the dark web—for use in opportunistic and common attacks. Think of it as "off-the-shelf" malware akin to buying general-purpose products from the local store. Granted, it has a relative lack of precision, but that is mostly nullified by organizations softened up by poor patch management as well as antimalware and antiphishing countermeasures. Since most organizations fall under that banner, commodity malware is more common than advanced malware.

 EXAM TIP   Ransomware like WannaCry is a good example of commodity malware due to its use all over the world across all major sectors and industries.

Information Sharing and Analysis Communities

The final section of this chapter covers formal information sharing communities that serve federal and local governments. This is in contrast to the threat intelligence sources discussed earlier, which are more likely consumed by enterprises. As its more commonly known, an Information Sharing and Analysis Center (ISAC) is a non-profit organization that collects, analyzes, and distributes threat intelligence to public and private sector organizations with critical infrastructures. Its goal is to help these organizations protect themselves from all security threats, including cyber and physical threats.

Organizations with critical infrastructures are those that have systems, networks, or assets that are crucial to federal and local governments, plus society in general. These organizations may include the following:

- Chemical and nuclear
- Energy
- Financial
- Food and agriculture
- Health
- Public and legal order and safety
- Space and research
- Transport
- Water

ISACs serve a vital role for their respective industries, which is evident by having 24/7 threat warning and incident notification capabilities and may even set threat levels for their respective industries. And many ISACs have a track record of responding to incidents

TABLE 1.1-7   Healthcare Key Terms

Key Terms	Description
Electronic medical record (EMR)	Digital version of traditional paper records; individual records with a narrower focus
Electronic health record (EHR)	A broader digital record containing all patient data across all clinicians involved in a patient's care
Electronic personal health record (ePHR)	Same as EHRs but designed to be set up, accessed, and managed by patients
Health Information Portability and Accountability Act (HIPAA)	A 1996 U.S. law that provides data privacy and security requirements for safeguarding medical information
Health Information Technology for Economic and Clinical Health (HITECH)	A 2009 U.S. law that expands the enforcement of HIPAA by encouraging further adoption of electronic health technology, in addition to strengthening the Security and Privacy Rules of HIPAA

and sharing pertinent threat information more quickly than government partners. In the next several sections, we'll go over ISACs that are specific to certain sectors or industries.

Healthcare

You probably wouldn't think it, but healthcare data is one of the most sought-after information categories by cybercriminals and other threat sources worldwide. When money talks, data walks. Healthcare information fetches a great deal more black-market dollars than credit cards and Social Security numbers. Malware attacks, particularly ransomware and bots, are very common in this industry. There has also been a significant increase in socially engineered attacks in recent years, since healthcare users are an easy target for confidentiality breaches. Table 1.1-7 provides a few key terms that you should be aware of.

Health Information Sharing and Analysis Center (H-ISAC)

With so many cyber attacks against healthcare organizations today, proactivity is key. Healthcare organizations would be well-served to make frequent use of the Health Information Sharing and Analysis Center (H-ISAC) to obtain updated health-related threat intelligence. According to H-ISAC's official website, it is a "global, non-profit, member-driven organization offering healthcare stakeholders a trusted community and forum for coordinating, collaborating and sharing vital physical and cyber threat intelligence and best practices with each other."

H-ISAC's community is focused on sharing timely and useful threat intelligence, including incidents, vulnerabilities, tactics, techniques, mitigations, and cybersecurity best practices.

Financial

The financial industry is also one of the more targeted industries due to the tremendous value of informational and monetary assets up for grabs. These organizations have been seeing a lot of DDoS, phishing, man-in-the-middle, and credential-stuffing attacks (an attack where credentials stolen from one organization are used to compromise accounts in a second organization).

 EXAM TIP   The Gramm–Leach–Bliley Act (GLBA) of 1999 plays an important role in the financial industry. It requires financial organizations to disclose how they share and protect their customers' private information.

Financial Services Information Sharing and Analysis Center (FS-ISAC)

Like it's H-ISAC counterpart, the FS-ISAC is the global financial industry's go-to resource for all physical and cyber threat intelligence sharing. In the past 20 years, it has expanded its influence to include several industry initiatives to increase protection and services for the global financial services industry.

Aviation

For a very different reason, cyber attacks against the aviation industry should concern us all. As airplanes become more computerized, and Internet and Wi-Fi capable, hackers will be looking to disrupt airline systems to create flight delays, cancellations, and security alerts. Worse, airplanes can get hacked, which could prevent takeoff or landing, or the plane might be remotely controlled by attackers. An attacker may ask for millions of dollars in ransom, or worse, to halt an attack on an airborne craft and spare the lives of its passengers and crew, not to mention potentially thousands of innocent victims on the ground.

Aviation Information Sharing and Analysis Center (A-ISAC)

Aviation cybersecurity concerns are significant enough that multiple ISACs have sprouted around the globe. Of particular note is the A-ISAC, which, like most other ISACs, seeks to exchange threats, vulnerabilities, incidents, and best practices with its worldwide constituents. Europe has its own aviation-focused ISAC as well, called the European Centre for Cyber Security in Aviation (ECCSA). However, there is some concern that having multiple aviation ISACs might cause standardization challenges.

Government

By most accounts, governments are both the most cyber-targeted "industry" and, arguably, the least prepared to deal with it. Various reports reveal that U.S. government infrastructure often contains unpatched systems, outdated Windows XP and Windows Server 2003 systems, and even several-decades-old COBOL-based systems for which very few experts remain today.

This is a big problem considering people's reliance on government for obtaining passports, student loans, Social Security numbers, and drivers' licenses.

National Defense Information Sharing and Analysis Center (ND-ISAC)

Although government ISACs are more plentiful and may have specific focuses, the ND-ISAC is the U.S. national defense sector's ISAC to enhance our national cybersecurity. Like other ISACs, the ND-ISAC provides national defense sector groups, such as the Defense Industrial Base (DIB) ISAC, for example, with a community for sharing cyber and physical security threat intelligence, best practices, and mitigations.

Critical Infrastructure

The healthcare, financial, aviation, government, and many more industries all contain critical infrastructure. However, the CySA+ exam also considers critical infrastructure in terms of utility and public organizations such as electricity, nuclear, oil and gas, public transit, and water. Shown here are the ISACs for those respective industries:

- Electricity ISAC (E-ISAC)
- Nuclear ISAC (NEI)
- Oil and gas (ONG-ISAC)
- Public transit (PT-ISAC)
- Water ISAC (Water-ISAC)

 NOTE The National Council of ISACs (NCI) was formed in 2003 and is the ISAC "hub" for a few dozen different ISACs globally.

REVIEW

Objective 1.1: Explain the importance of threat data and intelligence   Intelligence sources are where much of our external threat data and, ultimately, threat intelligence originates. Threat data must be acquired in a timely manner, relevant to the organization's needs, and accurate to bring value to the collecting organization.

Once the threat data is analyzed, threat ratings are assigned to it to determine its potential danger level, with confidence ratings assigned afterward to indicate the organization's assurance that the threat rating is accurate.

Indicator management involves organizations packaging and distributing threat data in a manner acceptable to other collecting parties. The STIX language describes the "what" of threat data, and TAXII describes "how" to transfer that data. OpenIOC is a lesser-known but open framework for exchanging threat data with other parties in a machine-readable format.

Threat classification identifies different threat types, including known threats versus unknown threats, zero-day attacks, and advanced persistent threats.

Threat actors include the attackers that attempt to compromise our systems, applications, and data. They come in many forms, including nation-state hackers, hacktivists, organized crime, plus intentional and unintentional insider threats.

An intelligence cycle is a continual process of collecting information, refining it, and reporting it to stakeholders for making key cybersecurity decisions. An intelligence cycle includes five stages: requirements, collection, analysis, dissemination, and feedback on reported intelligence. If this process is done properly, organizations will continue to improve their ability to not only collect threat data but also improve their cybersecurity defenses against cybercriminals.

Commodity malware was discussed as an "off-the-shelf" and generalized form of malware used to attack systems with well-known vulnerabilities. This is in contrast to the more advanced forms of malware that are crafted specifically for handpicked targets.

Information Sharing and Analysis Communities, better known as Information Sharing and Analysis Centers (ISACs), are non-profit organizations that collect, analyze, and distribute threat intelligence to public and private sector organizations with critical infrastructures. They exist all over the world and serve many industries and sectors with cybersecurity intelligence sharing, including healthcare, financial, aviation, government, and critical infrastructure.

1.1 QUESTIONS

1. You're a cybersecurity analyst who works for a large financial organization based in the U.S. Your manager asks you how cybercriminals collect information about their targets during the early stages of an attack. Which of the following methods would you discuss with your manager? (Choose all that apply.)

    A. Footprinting

    B. OpenIOC

    C. Enumeration

    D. Escalation

2. Barbara is a security operations center (SOC) analyst who works in an SOC at a large international airport. Her threat intelligence sources include both open- and closed-source intelligence. Which of the following terms describes her trust in the information she receives through these intelligence feeds?

    A. Timeliness

    B. Relevance

    C. Confidence

    D. Fidelity

3. You are an IT security analyst working as a consultant for another company. You have almost completed upgrades from Windows 7 to the latest Windows 10 operating system (OS). You know that the Windows 7 "Extended Support" period ended on January 14, 2020. After that date, Microsoft no longer creates and distributes OS patches for Windows 7. Which of the following threats is Windows 7 now increasingly subjected to?

   A. Advanced persistent threat (APT)

   B. Zero-day threat

   C. Nation-state threat

   D. Insider threat

4. Bob is a threat intelligence analyst who works at Goss Industries. He has been tasked by Tom, the threat intelligence team lead, to document the phases of the intelligence cycle to prepare a course outline for training a group of recently hired threat intelligence analysts. What is the correct order of phases for the intelligence cycle?

   A. Collection, Requirements, Analysis, Dissemination, Feedback

   B. Requirements, Collection, Analysis, Dissemination, Feedback

   C. Collection, Requirements, Analysis, Feedback, Dissemination

   D. Requirements, Collection, Analysis, Feedback, Dissemination

5. Sarah is a cybersecurity specialist who works at Stark Industries. Recent threat intelligence, corroborated from multiple open-source intelligence resources, suggests that a new wave of "mutating" malware has been reported by other organizations in the industry. Sarah is concerned that this malware will escape traditional antimalware detection techniques. Which of the following techniques should she implement to best mitigate the concern?

   A. Update the antimalware tool with the latest signatures and then run a scan utilizing signature-based detection.

   B. Update the operating system and business applications with the latest patches.

   C. Update the firmware on the perimeter firewall and ensure all necessary ports are closed both inbound and outbound.

   D. Run an antimalware scan utilizing heuristic-based detection.

1.1 ANSWERS

1. **A**   Attackers begin many hacking attacks with footprinting, which seeks to collect all available information about the target. These attackers will look to collect information utilizing passive (non-interactive) and active (interactive) footprinting techniques.

2. **C**   Confidence levels describe the trust an analyst can have in their threat intelligence sources.

3. **B**   Zero-day threats involve attacks against vulnerabilities for which the hardware/software vendors haven't created a security update.

4. **B**   The correct order of steps is Requirements, Collection, Analysis, Dissemination, Feedback.

5. **D**   Running heuristic-based scans is the best choice since these scans can potentially detect and mitigate malware that hasn't been discovered yet, such as mutating (polymorphic) malware.

Objective 1.2 Given a scenario, utilize threat intelligence to support organizational security

Attack Frameworks

It's often said that to beat a hacker, you need to think like one. Helping us to do just that are *attack frameworks*. Frameworks are industry-proven methodologies and overarching processes, and attack frameworks specifically detail how adversaries behave before, during, and after cybersecurity breaches based on various circumstances. They help cybersecurity professionals acquire as much knowledge as possible regarding a specific adversary's tactics, techniques, and procedures (TTPs), which are defined as follows:

- **Tactics**   The highest-level description of an adversary's behavior. For example, an attacker's tactic may be the persistence of a connection to a target or privilege escalation.
- **Techniques**   Describe in more detail the behaviors used in a tactic. For example, creating a new service is a technique that will help achieve the tactic of persistence.
- **Procedures**   Describe in detail the tools and steps taken to create the new service to achieve persistence.

The CySA+ CS0-002 exam expects you to be familiar with three attack frameworks in particular—MITRE ATT&CK, the Diamond Model of Analysis, and the Cyber Kill Chain. Without further ado, let's dig in.

MITRE ATT&CK

The MITRE Corporation is a nonprofit organization funded by the U.S. government for multiple national research initiatives, including cybersecurity. Best known for developing and maintaining the Common Vulnerabilities and Exposures (CVE) database, it also created the

MITRE ATT&CK framework in 2013. ATT&CK is a public knowledgebase of threat tactics and techniques based on real-world observations of cyber attacks. It describes the many ways threat actors penetrate networks, move laterally across the network, escalate privileges, and evade target defenses.

Once a breach has been detected, organizations can use the framework to help determine certain specific information about the breach:

- How did threat actors penetrate the network?
- How are they moving around?
- What are they doing?

This framework also aids organizations in the development of their own threat models. If an organization wants to build a threat model for advanced persistent threats (APTs), it can easily reference the tactic and technique information found in ATT&CK.

 NOTE The ATT&CK "tactics" describe the *why* of an adversary's attack, and the "techniques" describe the *how* for achieving the tactic's goal. For example, the adversary's tactic might be Execution, and the technique could be PowerShell.

For more examples of tactics and techniques, take a look at Figure 1.2-1 for a partial view of the MITRE ATT&CK framework.

Scenario: Exfiltration

To follow this scenario correctly, have the MITRE ATT&CK framework handy to reference the tactics and techniques. Let's say an adversary wants to steal classified or sensitive files from a CEO. The adversary performs the Initial Access tactic to acquire the credentials of the CEO's

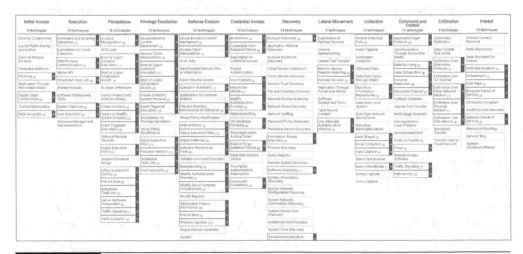

FIGURE 1.2-1 MITRE ATT&CK framework

secretary using a spear-phishing link delivered in an e-mail. Once they have the secretary's credentials, the adversary will look for a remote system in the Discovery tactic.

- **Tactics**   Initial Access and Discovery
- **Techniques**   Spearphishing Link and Remote System Discovery

Although various details are left out for brevity, analyzing attack scenarios using ATT&CK would help us to flag the various attacker and system behaviors as suspicious, and, ultimately, enable us to remediate the attempted breach.

The Diamond Model of Intrusion Analysis

Finalized in 2013, the Diamond Model of Intrusion Analysis serves as a practical analytical methodology for cybersecurity analysts to utilize before, during, and after cybersecurity intrusions. Aimed at strengthening our intrusion analysis, it's the first model of its kind that scientifically incorporates *both* the fundamentals of threat actors/activities (offense) and the analytical techniques needed to discover, understand, and counteract these threat actors/ activities (defense).

The Diamond Model underscores the relationships and characteristics of an attack's four main components:

- Adversary
- Capabilities
- Infrastructure
- Victim

Figure 1.2-2 shows a basic depiction of the Diamond Model mapping out an attacking *adversary* moving toward an intended goal by exercising a *capability* over *infrastructure*

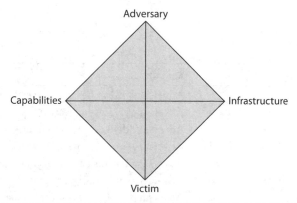

FIGURE 1.2-2   The Diamond Model of Intrusion Analysis

against a *victim*. Although the finer aspects of the Diamond Model are beyond the scope of the exam, cybersecurity analysts can use it to create a repeatable way to do the following:

- Characterizing organized threats
- Consistently tracking events as they progress
- Identifying and prioritizing one threat from another
- Identifying and implementing the most effective preventative, detective, and corrective countermeasures against such adversaries

Cyber Kill Chain

Militaries originally used the term "kill chain" to describe the stages of their attacks against enemies. It began with *finding* the enemy's general location, *fixing* a more precise enemy location, *tracking* enemy movements, *targeting* the enemy with a weapon, *engaging* the enemy with the weapon, and *assessing* the weapon's effect on the enemy.

Adapted into a cybersecurity context by the Lockheed Martin security and aerospace organization, the Cyber Kill Chain framework identifies the various stages of a cyberattack. Table 1.2-1 provides a summary.

That's a little disconcerting so, perhaps, a list of countermeasures would do nicely? Have a look at the "opposite" series of steps recommended to counter the phases of the Cyber Kill Chain:

- **Detect** Identify indicators of compromise.
- **Deny** Prevent or halt imminent data breach.
- **Disrupt** Minimize or redirect an attack away from key assets.
- **Degrade** Counter-attack threat actor's C2 server.
- **Deceive** Confuse C2 server with misleading traffic.
- **Contain** Isolate threat actor or threat to separate segment.

TABLE 1.2-1   The Cyber Kill Chain

Attack Phases	Description
1. Reconnaissance	Adversary researches target's security.
2. Weaponization	Adversary creates malware weapon.
3. Delivery	Adversary delivers weapon to target.
4. Exploitation	Adversary executes malware against target.
5. Installation	Adversary installs backdoor on target.
6. Command and Control (C2)	Adversary's malware permits remote access to target.
7. Actions on Objective	Adversary compromises target data or pivots to another target.

NOTE   The Cyber Kill Chain is sometimes criticized for emphasizing perimeter security countermeasures at the expense of internal security. Accordingly, a stronger Unified Kill Chain—which is an extended hybrid of the Cyber Kill Chain and MITRE's ATT&CK framework—was created to enhance and balance the perimeter/internal security zones.

Threat Research

The early-20th-century pioneering criminologist Dr. Edmond Locard famously stated that every contact leaves a trace. A century later, cybercriminals are inundating the world with countless millions of threat traces each year. Awash in threat data, organizations face the unending challenge of researching the latest threats to continuously figure out what security solutions are needed, how they should be used, and how to respond to threats.

Regardless of the type of threat intelligence you acquire through research, you can categorize the information in three general ways:

- **Strategic**   Intelligence that identifies the long-term and "big picture" viewpoint about adversaries and threat trends, likely targets, plus adversarial motivations.
- **Operational**   Intelligence that identifies threat methodologies, attacker tools of the trade, and tactics, techniques, and procedures.
- **Tactical**   Intelligence that leads to the identification of current or imminent IOCs, including malicious domain names, URLs, e-mail addresses, IP addresses, and hash values.

Threat research is an important topic, so let's dig into how it makes threat data visible and knowable to us. We'll explore threat reputations, behavioral characteristics of threats, IOCs, and the hugely helpful Common Vulnerability Scoring System (CVSS).

Reputational

One of the many things proffered through threat intelligence sources is threat reputation. Like people, threats acquire reputations through direct observations or interactions shared by other parties. These threat intelligence sources—which may include researchers, security vendors, and governments—are painstakingly sharing reputation data regarding the malicious activities of threats and their origins. Using a combination of direct threat assessments and information acquired through other intelligence sources, experts are determining which of these Internet objects have good, bad, or unknown reputations.

EXAM TIP Reputation data tends to describe suspicious DNS names, e-mail addresses, file hashes, IP addresses, URLs, and websites. Then, because it's now easier for us to determine "friend" or "foe," threats are formally assigned reputational *scores*. Higher scores indicate generally positive reputations, whereas lower scores indicate generally negative reputations. This information can then be automatically or manually distributed globally as part of threat intelligence sharing platforms.

Greatly aiding us in the distribution of threat reputation scores are services often provided by cybersecurity vendors called Threat Reputation Services (TRS). A TRS can automate the aggregation of threat data from other threat intelligence platforms, contextualize and score the data based on observed behaviors and shared intelligence, and notify subscribed members and devices immediately.

Behavioral

According to MITRE, an adversary dwells on an organization's network for an average of 146 days before being detected. This is partly due to organizations relying too much on tools and techniques that specialize in detecting *known* threats. Discovering unknown threats is where behavioral methods come in. Despite being unknown, threats are still exhibiting observable behaviors in the environment. Behavioral threat detection involves first understanding how our environment normally behaves over a period of time and then identifying patterns of behavior that deviate from the norm. Although behavioral differences can be a false positive, they may also signify a threat indicator. Such threat behaviors may include the following:

- DDOS/C2 traffic
- Phishing
- Unknown or unapproved devices
- MAC/IP spoofing
- MITM/hijacking
- Malware
- Autostart apps
- Sandbox evasion

In a module about threat intelligence—which focuses on what we, or someone else, knows—you may be wondering how the detection of *unknown* threat behaviors is related. User behavior analytics (UBA), sometimes known as user and entity behavior analytics (UEBA), bridges the gap. UBA focuses on *user* behaviors, and how such behaviors may correlate with unusual behavior events in the environment in order to discover an insider threat. Unfortunately, UBA isn't great at assigning *context* to the discovered behaviors. So, what entity is needed to provide context to threats? Threat intelligence. A threat intelligence platform could generate an alert that a suspicious user's IP address has been previously flagged as malicious or of poor repute.

Cross-Reference

UBA will be covered in more detail in Objective 3.1.

Indicators of Compromise (IOCs)

As the name implies, IOCs refer to events or data that identify potential or actual malicious activities on a network or system. Examples of IOCs are shown in Table 1.2-2.

As IOCs become known to your organization or others, they can be centrally shared with intelligence communities or shared peer-to-peer with organizations to enhance our global threat intelligence capabilities.

Common Vulnerability Scoring System (CVSS)

We know that threats are given reputation scores, but that can also apply to vulnerabilities. Enter the Common Vulnerabilities and Exposures (CVE) and the Common Vulnerability Scoring System (CVSS), which are discussed next.

TABLE 1.2-2   IOCs

IOC Possible Outcome	IOC Possible Cause
Excessive bandwidth usage	DDoS attack
Rogue hardware	Hacker laptop, wireless access point
Service outage	DDoS attack
Suspicious activity in administrator or privileged accounts	Compromised account from malicious insider or hacker
Suspicious e-mails	Phishing
Suspicious Registry and Startup entries	Malware
Unknown files, applications, and processes	Malware
Unknown port and protocol usage such as pings and port scans	Hacker port scanner (Nmap, hping)
Unusual activities such as traffic flow with countries the organization isn't involved with	Hacker proxy server, C2/botnet connection
Unusual increases in requests for certain files	Compromised account from malicious insider or hacker
Unusual logins, requests, access, or any activities that indicate probing	Malicious insider or hacker attempting to gain access to the system
Website defacement	System fully compromised by hacker

Operated by MITRE, the CVE is a dictionary of publicly known cybersecurity vulnerabilities that afflict widely used software. Each vulnerability is given its own CVE entry, which includes a CVE ID, a brief vulnerability description, and references.

Scenario: CVE-2019-1136

On July 9, 2019, a Microsoft Exchange Server vulnerability was assigned a CVE ID of CVE-2019-1136. The CVE ID structure is simple: CVE is a constant, 2019 is the year of release, and 1136 is an ID number assigned uniquely to the vulnerability in question.

 NOTE The CVE ID is widely used by cybersecurity experts, vendors, and researchers as a standard method for identifying vulnerabilities, even across their own security tools, databases, and services.

For more information about the vulnerabilities documented in CVEs, take a look at the National Vulnerability Database (NVD), which is separately maintained by the National Institute of Standards and Technology (NIST). The NVD stores a copy of all CVEs while adding analytical details:

- Vulnerability's severity scores
- Impact ratings
- Fix/patch information

In addition to CVEs, we also have the CVSS at our disposal. Since 2005, CVSS has been owned and managed by the Forum of Incident Response and Security Teams (FIRST). The CVSS is an open framework for scoring the severity of vulnerabilities. Unlike the distributed nature of threat reputation scoring, the CVSS scoring framework is centrally managed and standardized so that organizations worldwide have a single reference for assessing the risk presented by the vulnerability and, ultimately, determine the best course of action to address the risk.

Although more severity details exist, CVSS simplifies the scoring process of a CVE by assigning it a single Base Score. This score can range from None (0.0) to Critical (10.0). See Table 1.2-3 for a list of the CVSS ratings and scores used in CVSS Version 3.0 and 3.1.

TABLE 1.2-3   CVSS Version 3.x

Rating	CVSS Score
None	0.0
Low	0.1–3.9
Medium	4.0–6.9
High	7.0–8.9
Critical	9.0–10.0

CVSS v3.0 Severity and Metrics:

Base Score: 8.1 HIGH

Vector: AV:N/AC:H/PR:N/UI:N/S:U/C:H/I:H/A:H

Impact Score: 5.9

Exploitability Score: 2.2

Attack Vector (AV): Network

Attack Complexity (AC): High

Privileges Required (PR): None

User Interaction (UI): None

Scope (S): Unchanged

Confidentiality (C): High

Integrity (I): High

Availability (A): High

FIGURE 1.2-3   CVSS for CVE-2019-1136

Scenario: CVSS Base Score

Referencing our previous CVE-2019-1136 scenario mentioned earlier, it has a CVSS Base Score of 8.1 out of a possible 10—which is considered "High Severity." See Figure 1.2-3 for a fuller look at the CVE-2019-1136 as it appears in the NVD.

Threat Modeling Methodologies

Threat modeling is something people do every day: generals preparing against military foes, and cybersecurity analysts designing "attack trees" to identify threats and mitigations against cybercriminals. From an organizational context, threat modeling is most often applied whenever businesses are developing or acquiring new products, markets, and technologies, as well as the systems to support them, such as the introduction of new software, systems, networks, distributed systems, and even business processes. These are all qualifying conditions for threat modeling.

In its most common usage, threat modeling is the practice of identifying, prioritizing, and mitigating threats across all phases of a system's lifecycle. Unlike more reactive security practices, threat modeling seeks to address potential threat events early in the process before they become realized.

Viewed from the "attacker's point of view," threat modeling aids us in developing a deeper understanding of our organizational attack surface because we're simulating all possible threat causes and effects before actual attacks take place.

When designing a new system or application, we might consider asking and answering the following questions:

- What are the most likely threats to attack us?
- How will the threats attack us?

- Where are we most vulnerable to attacks?
- What assets are more likely to be targeted?
- Why would a threat attack us?
- What should we do to improve our security against the threats?

Common Threat Modeling Methodologies

Although there are several threat modeling methodologies out there, we'll focus on the most common ones here:

- **OCTAVE (Operationally Critical Threat, Asset, and Vulnerability Evaluation)** A threat model methodology that focuses on organizational risk, particularly operational risk, security practices, and technology.
- **Trike** An open-source threat modeling methodology that focuses on the security auditing process of risk management.
- **STRIDE (Spoofing Tampering Repudiation Information Message Disclosure Denial of Service and Elevation of Privilege)** A threat model methodology created by Microsoft to ensure Microsoft Windows developers incorporate security into the design phase of application development.
- **VAST (Visual, Agile, and Simple Threat Modeling)** A threat model methodology designed for scaling across both the organizational infrastructure and the entire Software Development Lifecycle (SDLC). It's designed for integration with Agile projects and provides actionable outputs for various stakeholders, including developers, cybersecurity pros, and senior leadership. VAST also utilizes an application and infrastructure visualization scheme to encourage participation from non-SMEs (subject matter experts).
- **PASTA (Process for Attack Simulation and Threat Analysis)** A threat model methodology designed to merge technical requirements with business objectives. It uses an attacker's perspective on potential threats and produces an asset-centric output.

Adversary Capability

Organizations implement threat models in large part to understand threats and how they might harm the organization. Our adversaries' capabilities are characterized in terms of their resources, methods, and attack vectors.

- **Resources** How much expertise do they have? How well funded are they? What technical resources can they employ? Adversarial resources can range from severely limited to national-level sophistication and strength.
- **Methods** Are their methods simplistic or very sophisticated? Will our adversaries use someone else's tools and malware, or will they develop their own specifically designed to attack us?

- **Attack vectors** Will they use cyber-based attacks, human-based attacks, or both? Will they attack us directly or go after our supply chain, which can include our vendors, suppliers, partners, ISP, and customers? Will they exploit our physical security? Wi-Fi? E-mail?

Total Attack Surface

Threat modeling provides an opportunity for us to analyze our attack surface from the threat actor's perspective. What are the total number of unlocked "doors" and "windows" in our business for the bad guys to gain unauthorized entry? Total attack surfaces are the sum of all areas of our network, systems, or software that contain vulnerabilities accessible to threat actors for exploitation. With cloud computing, mobile, and IoT permeating our business and personal spaces, our attack surfaces have increased tremendously. The more surface area exposed to attackers, the greater the likelihood that we'll experience a disastrous cyber attack.

Attack Vector

If total attack surfaces are the sum, attack vectors make up its parts. Attack vectors are individual pathways or methods by which threat actors can gain unauthorized access to systems. The threat intelligence collected from threat modeling will yield multiple cyber-based and human-based entrance points into our organization, a few of which you'll find summarized here:

- **Brute force** A trial-and-error process of guessing usernames, passwords, encryption keys, session ID numbers, and so on, in order to gain unauthorized access to a system.
- **Buffer overflow** Occurs when more data is written to a memory buffer than it was designed to hold. This can lead to a cascading overflow effect that crashes a program or permits privilege escalation attacks against it.
- **Cross-site scripting (XSS)** Involves the injection of malicious scripts into a vulnerable website, which are then run by a victim who visits the website.
- **Distributed denial of service (DDoS)** Malicious attempt to disrupt or disable an application or hardware system from being able to provide its services. Typically achieved by overwhelming the target with traffic from hundreds or thousands of senders.
- **Malicious insiders** Individuals inside an organization who may be current or former employees, contractors, vendors, or suppliers that intentionally breach organizational systems and data.
- **Malware** Making up the majority of attack vectors used, malware is any kind of malicious software designed to compromise systems or data.
- **Man in the middle** Attacks where adversaries secretly intercept and possibly alter the communications between two endpoints that believe they are directly communicating with each other.
- **Misconfiguration** Poor hardware or software configurations that make it susceptible to compromise.

- **Phishing**   Malicious practice of sending legitimate-looking e-mails to individuals in order to solicit confidential info.
- **Poor or missing encryption**   Lack of cryptography or continuing to use an older cryptographic algorithm like DES, Blowfish, or MD5 increases the success rates of brute force attacks against data at rest, in use, and in transit.
- **Ransomware**   A malicious program that either restricts victims from accessing data, systems, or networks or threatens to publish confidential information unless the attacker is paid a "ransom."
- **Session hijacking**   Practice of taking control of another user's session to gain unauthorized access to the user's account and data.
- **SQL injection**   A code injection attack in which the attacker inputs SQL code into a website form input box to gain access to unauthorized resources or make changes to sensitive data.
- **Supply chain attack**   A breach against any of your organization's producers, vendors, warehouses, transportation companies, distribution centers, or retailers that leads to the compromise of your organization's data.
- **Vulnerabilities**   Weaknesses in hardware, software, people, or processes that can be exploited by a threat actor.
- **Weak credentials**   A username, password, PIN, or other value used for identification that is easy to detect both by humans and computers.

Impact

With potential threats and attack vectors identified, threat modeling shifts toward the potential impacts such threat events can bring to the company. Impact describes the degree of damage or costs to the organization resulting from breaches. Organizations must carefully evaluate the degree of impact brought by threats in order to align security controls in the most urgent directions first. Here are some examples of organizational impacts:

- Breaches of legal, regulatory, or contractual requirements
- Classification level of impacted information (Confidential, Secret, Top Secret)
- Confidentiality, integrity, and availability requirements of breached assets
- Damage of organizational reputation
- Disruption of organizational plans and deadlines
- Loss of business and financial value

In Table 1.2-4, which originates from Federal Information Processing Standards (FIPS) Publication 199, you can see how these threat impacts are typically categorized as High, Moderate, or Low in terms of their effect on security objectives such as confidentiality, integrity, and availability.

TABLE 1.2-4 FIPS 199 Potential Impact Definitions for Security Objectives

Security Objective	Potential Impact		
	Low	Moderate	High
Confidentiality	The unauthorized disclosure of information could be expected to have a limited adverse effect on organizational operations, organizational assets, or individuals.	The unauthorized disclosure of information could be expected to have a serious adverse effect on organizational operations, organizational assets, or individuals.	The unauthorized disclosure of information could be expected to have a severe or catastrophic adverse effect on organizational operations, organizational assets, or individuals.
Integrity	The unauthorized modification or destruction of information could be expected to have a limited adverse effect on organizational operations, organizational assets, or individuals.	The unauthorized modification or destruction of information could be expected to have a serious adverse effect on organizational operations, organizational assets, or individuals.	The unauthorized modification or destruction of information could be expected to have a severe or catastrophic adverse effect on organizational operations, organizational assets, or individuals.
Availability	The disruption of access to or use of information or an information system could be expected to have a limited adverse effect on organizational operations, organizational assets, or individuals.	The disruption of access to or use of information or an information system could be expected to have a serious adverse effect on organizational operations, organizational assets, or individuals	The disruption of access to or use of information or an information system could be expected to have a severe or catastrophic adverse effect on organizational operations, organizational assets, or individuals.

Likelihood

Potential impacts must be balanced by the likelihood of occurring in the first place. Although asteroids careening into our building would generate severe impact, that's very unlikely to happen. Malicious port scanning is highly likely to occur, yet its immediate impact is minor or negligible at best. Impact or likelihood by themselves don't mean much, but, taken together, they help clarify the degree of risk we should ascribe to threats.

Cross-Reference

Impact and likelihood are the two key components used when determining risk to an organization, a system, or even a business process. These two components, as well as risk, are covered much more in depth in Objective 5.2.

To better understand the likelihood of human threat actors, we must also determine their motivation. Malicious hackers always have one or more motivations for conducting their nefarious acts. These things don't happen in a vacuum; therefore, you should consider the following motivations:

- Financial gain through information theft
- Espionage (competitor/nation-states)
- Egotistical or fun (challenge)
- Ideological (religious/political)
- Grudge (former employee/customer/partner)

Also important to plan for, threat sources may include natural disasters such as tornados, hurricanes, earthquakes, volcanos, floods, tsunamis, blizzards, and wildfires. An organization's region, proximity to a threat source, emergency procedures, awareness training, facility structure, as well as the time of year will play key roles in exposures caused by natural disasters.

Threat Intelligence Sharing with Supported Functions

Threat intelligence sharing involves organizations sharing their threat data with other businesses and groups in the global cybersecurity community. The latest threat data empowers businesses to make better decisions regarding defensive requirements, threat detection techniques, and remediation strategies. Plus, through the correlation and analysis of threat data from multiple sources, organizations can enhance existing threat information and make it more actionable.

 NOTE   Organizations that receive threat data, use it to mitigate a threat, and share that data with others are helping to prevent the spread of that threat. Locally, it may not seem like much, but this process will allow organizations to better detect campaigns that target specific industry sectors, industries, or organizations.

For various reasons, including lack of awareness, resources, and know-how, most organizations shy away from threat intelligence sharing. Fortunately, the government and other non-profit groups are helping to create a more receptive threat intelligence sharing ecosystem through laws and alliances, as detailed here:

- **Cybersecurity Information Sharing Act of 2015 (CISA)**   A federal law that seeks to "improve cybersecurity in the United States through enhanced sharing of information about cybersecurity threats, and for other purposes." It authorizes businesses to monitor and implement security defenses on their systems to counter cyber threats and provides certain protections to encourage companies to share IOCs and mitigations with the federal government, state and local governments, and other companies.
- **Cyber Threat Alliance (CTA)**   A non-profit organization working to improve the cybersecurity of our global digital ecosystem by enabling near-real-time, high-quality cyber threat information sharing among companies and organizations in the cybersecurity field.

Threat intelligence sharing is accessible to all organizations, big and small, and generally occurs in two different ways:

- **Unidirectional**   Instance where intelligence sharing occurs in one direction only. For example, open-source and closed-source sharing groups generate and share intelligence, while other groups and individuals merely consume it. Many entities elect not to share any intelligence due to lack of resources, privacy and liability concerns, lack of expertise, belief of having nothing valuable to share, or not wanting to disclose or give the impression that they've been compromised.
- **Bidirectional**   Instance where intelligence sharing occurs in two directions. The best examples of this are the Information Sharing and Analysis Centers (ISACs) and other Information Sharing and Analysis Organizations (ISAOs). These industry and government-based sharing organizations both share intelligence *and* receive it from other partner organizations.

Incident Response

Incident response focuses on detecting and responding to cybersecurity incidents. Its reliance on cutting-edge threat data makes it a perfect candidate for the information received through threat intelligence sharing mechanisms. As updated threat data is fed into an organization's security information event management (SIEM) tool, such as Splunk Enterprise or LogRhythm, the organization can accelerate its incident response and recovery actions much earlier into an adversary's attack cycle.

Vulnerability Management

Vulnerability management is the ongoing process of identifying, classifying, prioritizing, and remediating software vulnerabilities. Threat intelligence sharing is crucial to this effort through the acquisition of timely information on real-time threats, which helps improve detection and

| | TABLE 1.2-5 | Risks to Government, Business, and Home Users | |

Entity	Scale	Risk
Government	Large and medium government entities	High
Government	Small government entitles	Medium
Businesses	Large and medium business entities	High
Businesses	Small business entities	Medium
Home users	N/A	Low

mitigation response times. The correlation of vulnerabilities found on your systems with real-time threats, known exploits, malware, and available software patches can save your organization considerable time with vulnerability remediation.

Scenario: Google Chrome Vulnerabilities

The Multi-State Information Sharing & Analysis Center (MS-ISAC) shared threat intelligence on February 25, 2020, about multiple vulnerabilities in Google chrome possibly allowing for arbitrary code execution. It reported that CVE-2020-6418 (Google vulnerability) is being exploited in the wild. The risks to government, businesses, and home users are outlined in Table 1.2-5.

Recommended remediations are as follows (source: https://www.cisecurity.org/advisory/multiple-vulnerabilities-in-google-chrome-could-allow-for-arbitrary-code-execution_2020-025/):

- Apply the *stable channel update* provided by Google to vulnerable systems immediately after appropriate testing.
- Run all software as a non-privileged user (one without administrative privileges) to reduce the effects of a successful attack.
- Remind users not to visit untrusted websites or follow links provided by unknown or untrusted sources.
- Educate users regarding the threats posed by hypertext links contained in e-mails or attachments, especially from untrusted sources.
- Apply the principle of least privilege to all systems and services.

Risk Management

Threat intelligence plays an important role in an organization's overall risk management strategy. The information gleaned from threat intelligence sharing can help inform the security controls selected by an organization during its risk management processes.

According to NIST SP 800-37 Rev. 2, risk management is the management of security and privacy risks to organizational operations, assets, individuals, and other affiliated organizations. It focuses on information security categorization; control selection, implementation, and assessment; system and common control authorizations; and continuous monitoring. In other words, risk management seeks to reduce *all* security risks to the organization to an "acceptable level." Risk management processes can be broken down into seven unique phases:

- **Prepare**   Get the organization ready for risk management by identifying risk management roles and risk management strategy, conducting a risk assessment, establishing baselines, identifying security controls, prioritizing organization systems, and developing continuous monitoring strategy.
- **Categorize**   Key organizational systems are identified and described, plus the organization's security and privacy requirements are defined.
- **Select**   Security controls are selected, adapted, and documented for the protection of organizational systems.
- **Implement**   Selected security controls are implemented.
- **Assess**   Determine if selected security controls are implemented correctly and provide desired security.
- **Authorize**   Executive leadership determines if the organization's current security posture, resulting from the applied security controls, is acceptable and formally authorizes systems to operate if it is.
- **Monitor**   Continuous monitoring of organizational security posture and risk to determine if changes have or need to take place to ensure residual risks remain at an accepted level.

Security Engineering

Whereas cybersecurity analysis focuses more on the "offensive" side of security—identifying security issues, threat hunting, performing vulnerability assessments, and penetration tests—security engineering emphasizes the "defensive" aspects by constructing security solutions. Informed through the exchange of real-time threat information, organizations will respond by either enriching their existing security controls or implementing more "targeted defenses," which include the following:

- Harden platforms or systems targeted by the latest threats by strengthening their configurations or installing patches.
- Install new security tools designed to counteract the attacks detailed in the latest threat reports.

Detection and Monitoring

Threat intelligence sharing enhances an organization's detection and monitoring capabilities by allowing an organization to anticipate potential or real threats before they strike. Using shared threat information from reliable sources of threat intelligence, organizations can perform the following tasks proactively:

- Create custom IDS and firewall rules linked to real-time threat data
- Install more sensor equipment
- Utilize file integrity monitoring (FIM)
- Implement honeypots and honeynets
- Monitor access to specific files/URLs
- Implement log management technology/SIEMs
- Implement vulnerability scanners

REVIEW

Objective 1.2: Given a scenario, utilize threat intelligence to support organizational security   Attack frameworks are an important form of threat intelligence because they are well-known methodologies created by the cybersecurity industry to help us understand adversarial behaviors before, during, and after cybersecurity breaches. The MITRE ATT&CK, Diamond Model of Intrusion Analysis, and Cyber Kill Chain are some of the most popular attack frameworks that help cybersecurity professionals around the world analyze the tactics, techniques, and procedures of adversaries based on specific attack scenarios.

For more up-to-date information about potential and real threats, organizations conduct threat research to determine the reputations of threats, their behavioral characteristics, and known IOCs in order to strategize an effective cybersecurity response. Also, cybersecurity professionals research the vulnerabilities targeted by such threats by first determining the CVE ID number of the vulnerability and then determining the severity scores of the vulnerability through the NIST NVD.

Threat modeling allows you to examine your organization's security from the hacker's perspective. Various threat modeling methodologies exist, including OCTAVE, VAST, STRIDE, Trike, VAST, and PASTA. By employing these methodologies, you can better identify an adversary's capabilities, your total attack surface, attack vectors utilized by attackers, the impact that breaches could have on your organization, and the likelihood that the breach will occur in the first place.

Threat intelligence sharing, whether unidirectional or bidirectional, permits an organization to either share its threat knowledge with others or acquire others' knowledge for itself. The information obtained from the collaborative efforts of threat intelligence sharing will help enhance your incident response procedures, vulnerability management, risk management, security engineering, and detection and monitoring capabilities.

1.2 QUESTIONS

1. Sam is a cybersecurity analyst who works in a security operations center (SOC) at Rogers Enterprises. Part of his duties involves implementing attack frameworks to better understand how adversarial behaviors operate before, during, and after cyber attacks. Which of the following is the correct order of attack phases in the Lockheed Martin Cyber Kill Chain he should use when analyzing a threat?
   A. Reconnaissance, Weaponization, Delivery, Exploitation, Installation, Command and Control (C2), Actions on Objective
   B. Reconnaissance, Actions on Objective, Delivery, Exploitation, Installation, Command, and Control (C2), Weaponization
   C. Reconnaissance, Weaponization, Installation, Delivery, Exploitation, Command and Control (C2), Actions on Objective
   D. Reconnaissance, Actions on Objective, Installation, Delivery, Exploitation, Command, and Control (C2), Weaponization

2. Dawn is a cybersecurity analyst who works for a large corporation. Through her vulnerability research, she's discovered a "High" risk vulnerability with Microsoft Exchange Server. Which of the following resources should she access to discover the CVSS Base Score for this vulnerability?
   A. MITRE
   B. CVE
   C. NVD
   D. STIX

3. Ben is a threat intelligence analyst. The DevOps team is developing an application designed to remotely control unmanned aircraft. Ben wants the application development team to incorporate a threat model to ensure security objectives are integrated into the application development lifecycle from the start. Which of the following threat models was created by Microsoft to ensure developers incorporate security into application development?
   A. OCTAVE
   B. Trike
   C. STRIDE
   D. VAST

4. Adam is a risk manager for a major financial services company. Having recently collected a set of high-risk threat data from the threat intelligence sharing community, Adam responded by implementing a new intrusion prevention system (IPS) device. In which of the following NIST Risk Management Framework phases does his executive leadership determine that the IPS has provided adequate security protections to the organization?

   A. Prepare

   B. Authorize

   C. Assess

   D. Monitor

1.2 ANSWERS

1. **A** The correct order of phases for the Lockheed Martin Cyber Kill Chain is Reconnaissance, Weaponization, Delivery, Exploitation, Installation, Command and Control (C2), Actions on Objective.

2. **C** The CVSS Base Score is found on the National Vulnerability Database (NVD), which is stored on the NIST website.

3. **C** STRIDE is a threat model methodology created by Microsoft to ensure Microsoft Windows developers incorporate security into the design phase of application development.

4. **B** The Authorize phase is when executive leadership determines if the organization's current security posture, resulting from the applied security controls, is acceptable.

 **Objective 1.3** **Given a scenario, perform vulnerability management activities**

Vulnerability Identification

As cybersecurity analysts, we're tasked with performing vulnerability identification to determine how exploitable our organization is as well as with remediating discovered vulnerabilities before attackers find them first.

So, what is a vulnerability? As it relates to information security, vulnerabilities are weaknesses in an information system's design, implementation, operation, or management that, when exploited, can lead to the compromise of the confidentiality, integrity, or availability of that system. Countless vulnerabilities exist, so we will need to define a broader selection of vulnerabilities to get things started. Following are some examples of common potential vulnerabilities:

- **Hardware**   Susceptibility to humidity, dust, moisture, electrostatic discharge (ESD), and inadequate physical protection
- **Software**   Lack of testing and auditing, design flaws, missing patches, legacy, and misconfiguration
- **Network**   Unprotected cables, insecure network architecture, poor or missing encryption, poor segmentation, and poorly positioned network appliances
- **Personnel**   Poor recruiting practices, lack of security policy adherence, and poor cybersecurity awareness
- **Physical site**   Susceptibility to floods, fires, power outages, unauthorized entry, lack of surveillance, and lack of security guards
- **Organizational**   Lack of business continuity plans and disaster recovery plans

Vulnerability identification is a big undertaking that involves consistent internal vulnerability assessments, in addition to the acquisition of vulnerability intelligence from numerous vulnerability identification sources, as listed here:

- CVE
- Exploit Database
- IT system audit reports
- National Vulnerability Database (NVD)
- Open Web Application Security Project (OWASP)
- Previous risk assessments
- SANS Internet Storm Center
- Security advisories
- Security requirements checklist
- System security testing
- US-CERT
- Vendor advisories (Cisco, IBM, Google, Microsoft)
- Vulnerability listings

This module is about performing a variety of vulnerability management activities. We'll start by fleshing out some important vulnerability identification considerations, including asset criticality, active and passing scanning, and mapping and enumeration techniques.

Asset Criticality

Determining the criticality of organizational assets helps us prioritize our vulnerability management efforts. Assets are anything of value to the organization, including its people, facilities, networks, systems, information, processes, and reputation. Asset values are usually described in quantitative or qualitative terms:

- **Quantitative**   Measure of asset value expressed numerically. For example, an organization values a firewall asset at $1,000 for its replacement cost.
- **Qualitative**   Measure of asset value expressed in a more scenario-driven or generalized way. For instance, the organization values that same firewall asset as "critical" to its business processes.
- **Semi-quantitative**   Measure of asset value expressed in both quantitative and qualitative terms.

Organizations often perform "asset valuations" as part of broader cybersecurity initiatives like risk management and business continuity planning. Central to these initiatives is the determination of which assets are *most* critical to the organization. Being able to answer the following questions will help with this effort:

- **Criticality**   Which assets are most critical for the organization to continue its normal operations?
- **Probability**   Which assets have the highest probability of being compromised (lost, stolen, made obsolete, or experiencing a failure)?
- **Impact**   Which assets would cause the highest financial impact to the organization if compromised? What would be the non-financial impacts to the organization, such as loss of reputation?

 NOTE   Remember, the identification of critical assets helps anchor the organization's vulnerability remediation efforts to the most critical assets first.

Active vs. Passive Scanning

The most direct way to identify system vulnerabilities is through vulnerability scanning. Vulnerability scanning is the process of scanning hardware and software systems to identify weaknesses. These weaknesses can include the following:

- Application flaws
- Buffer overflow
- Default installations
- Default passwords
- Design flaws

- Misconfigurations
- Missing patches
- Open services
- Operating system flaws

In addition to being knowledgeable about the different types of vulnerabilities, you should also be aware of the active and passive ways in which scanning tools collect vulnerability data:

- **Active scanning**   Occurs when a scanning tool identifies system vulnerabilities by communicating directly with the system. For example, the OpenVAS vulnerability scanner scans a system and identifies dozens of well-known Windows 10 vulnerabilities officially tagged with CVE IDs.
- **Passive scanning**   Occurs when a scanning tool *indirectly* identifies system vulnerabilities but does *not* communicate with the system. Instead, the scanner looks for any unusual behaviors or known issues by observing the system's network traffic. As an example, the Wireshark packet sniffer captures packets coming from an Internet-facing web server sending out NetBIOS or SMB traffic—which will invite all kinds of trouble if not immediately resolved.

 EXAM TIP   Active scanning will result in more detailed vulnerability information but at the expense of the increased system and network resources. Conversely, passive scanning generates little to no load on the system and network resources but generally yields fewer vulnerability insights. It is helpful to the analyst to have a mixture of passive and active scans.

Mapping/Enumeration

Vulnerability scanning focuses on telling us what vulnerabilities we have, yet this is just a single step on the vulnerability assessment ladder. Sometimes referred to as vulnerability mapping or enumeration, vulnerability assessments are the broader process of identifying, quantifying, and prioritizing vulnerabilities with our devices and software. Mapping all the network assets and enumerating potentially vulnerable services through scans is important, but our cyber-security posture will not be enhanced until we complete the *full* set of steps of vulnerability assessments, as outlined here:

- **Discover**   Perform a complete inventory of hardware and software assets.
- **Assign criticality**   Label assets according to organizational criticality.
- **Identify vulnerabilities**   Scan assets to identify vulnerabilities (vulnerability scanning occurs here).
- **Assess risk**   Determine the likelihood of threats exploiting vulnerabilities.
- **Mitigate risk**   Remediate vulnerabilities based on priority and cost-effectiveness.

Validation

After identifying potential vulnerabilities, the next step is to make sure they are real. Vulnerability validation is the process of reconciling the potential vulnerabilities with other information sources inside and outside the organization. Validation attempts to answer the following questions:

- Are the reported vulnerabilities real or false positives?
- Did this scan cover all assets, including mobile devices, cloud services, and even the Internet of Things (IoT)?
- How exploitable are the vulnerabilities?
- Can we correlate the vulnerabilities with other data points in our environment?
- How much risk do the vulnerabilities pose to the organization?

The key is to correlate vulnerability scan results with other data points, such as network, operating system, or application logs. As with witnesses in a trial, if multiple sources say something is true, it's more likely to be the case.

Vulnerability validation can yield many results, which can include true positives, false positives, true negatives, and false negatives. Let's take a look at each of these in the following sections.

True Positive

A true positive occurs when an assessment tool correctly indicates the presence of a specific vulnerability that we do in fact have. In other words, our tool cried "wolf" when there was indeed a wolf present.

Scenario: True Positive

Tenable's Nessus vulnerability scanner correctly detected a "critical" Linux vulnerability with Bash Remote Code Execution (Shellshock). The CVE ID is CVE-2014-6271.

False Positive

A false positive occurs when an assessment tool falsely indicates the presence of a specific vulnerability that we do *not* have. In other words, our tool cried "wolf" when there wasn't a wolf present. Another name for a false positive is a Type I error.

Scenario: False Positive

A web application scanner indicates the presence of a specific SQL injection vulnerability when in reality there it isn't present.

 NOTE   Although the web application scanner may have been wrong with *this* particular indication, it doesn't mean that there aren't any SQL injection vulnerabilities lurking about on the web server.

True Negative

A true negative occurs when an assessment tool correctly does not indicate the presence of a specific vulnerability because there isn't one. In other words, our tool does not cry "wolf" because there isn't a wolf present.

Scenario: True Negative

You use an Nmap script to scan a system for the Heartbleed bug but were unable to locate the vulnerability because the system already had implemented Heartbleed bug patches.

False Negative

A false negative occurs when an assessment tool neglects to indicate a specific vulnerability that is present. In other words, our tool docs not cry "wolf" even though a wolf is present. A false negative is also known as a Type II error.

Scenario: False Negative

Microsoft recently publicized new vulnerabilities with Windows 10. Using Nessus, you scan systems and were unable to detect the vulnerabilities. You then realize that Nessus hasn't been updated in a week. After updating Nessus, you re-run the scans and successfully discover the recently publicized vulnerabilities. To be clear, this scenario has now changed from false negative to true positive.

 NOTE   Whereas a false positive can take up time and other resources in the effort to identify it or validate a finding, a false negative is the worst possible scenario because there is a vulnerability that goes unidentified and therefore unmitigated.

Remediation/Mitigation

After we've finished scanning, identifying, and validating vulnerabilities, we finally arrive at remediation. What qualifies as remediation? Let's take a look:

- Patch vulnerabilities, upgrade, or change configurations for hardware, operating systems, and applications.
- Perform larger-scale refresh on organizational infrastructure.
- Make changes to governing policies, processes, procedures, and configuration standards.

 NOTE   Despite the temptation, don't rush remediation unless you're willing to risk adding new vulnerabilities or losing functionality to one or more systems. Mitigations are more like surgery than applying a band-aid; therefore, care must be taken.

We're also not rushing through remediation because several prerequisite steps need to be taken in advance:

- **Organizational budget**   Ensure mitigations are funded.
- **Staff and infrastructure resources**   Ensure remediations can be facilitated.
- **Prioritization**   Ensure we focus on the most important remediations first. These priorities might be based on vulnerabilities with the highest critical CVSS scores or the criticality of the assets themselves.
- **Quality assurance testing**   Ensure remediations are tested in a sandboxed environment to ensure they don't break anything.
- **Change control**   Ensure proposed remediations conform to organizational change control policy. Remember, sometimes remediations can break functionality.
- **Timelines**   Ensure remediation predictability while minimizing disruption to other business units.

Although rushing is risky, moving *too* slowly is even riskier. Severe organizational losses can result from the exploitation of a single vulnerability. Navigating between the two fires of "caution" and "urgency" requires mastery of supporting processes such as configuration baselines, patching, hardening, compensation controls, risk acceptance, and verification of mitigation—all of which we're covering in the next several sections.

Configuration Baseline

Although most vulnerabilities are mitigated with patches, others are resolved by changing configurations to a device, operating system, or application. Yet, a potential roadblock to configuration changes is the existence of configuration baselines. Configuration baselines are a documented set of technical specifications for devices, operating systems, or applications that have been formally reviewed and agreed on at a given point in time. Proposing a change to a system's configuration means we're looking to create a *new* configuration baseline. Such a change can only proceed through an established change control process that ensures such proposals are properly vetted for considerations of costs, benefits, and compliance with organizational policies.

Assuming the change control committee approves the configuration change request, the prescribed remediation will be scheduled for deployment to resolve a particular vulnerability. Assuming this goes well, the current configuration state will be adopted as the newest configuration baseline.

 NOTE   What if a new configuration results in no change in vulnerability status, introduces a new vulnerability, or causes a system functionality loss? If remediation goes wrong, we can always return a system's configuration to the most recent configuration baseline that worked.

Patching

No matter how great an individual or team of software developers are, *all* software has flaws. These flaws can affect anything from the software's functionality, security, to its reliability. Most flaws discovered by vendors and attackers alike will be security-related. As vulnerabilities are discovered, developers create and distribute software "patches" to fix the flaws. Patching is the process of applying a software fix to an operating system, application, or hardware devices such as the firmware for firewalls, intrusion detection systems (IDSs), and intrusion prevention systems (IPSs).

Remediation through patching sometimes feels like you're picking your poison. If you patch systems too quickly, you risk breaking your systems. If you patch systems too slowly through initial quality assurance testing, you risk security flaws being exploited. Many organizations deploy a centralized patch management system to ensure that patches are deployed in a not-too-fast, not-too-slow manner. With this system, administrators can test and review all patches before deploying them to the systems they affect. Administrators can also schedule updates to occur during non-peak hours to minimize business impact. This is a good time to mention patch criticality—those patches that are deemed critical have priority over those that simply fix functionality. The criticality of systems or patches plays a role in scheduling and managing patches.

Types of Patches

Patches come in all sorts of varieties; the following list details the types of patches you can see in a Microsoft environment. Although other operating systems (such as macOS and Linux) have different names for their updates, they are similar in functionality.

- **Security patch**   Software updates that fix operating system and application vulnerabilities. Typically scheduled for release on a predictable cycle (like Microsoft's original Patch Tuesday).

- **Hotfix** Critical updates for various software issues that, unlike patches, should not be delayed.
- **Service packs** Large collection of updates for a particular operating system or application released as one installable package. A service pack usually includes new features, patches, and hotfixes. This is now frowned upon due to the turbulence experienced by combining new features *and* patches.
- **Rollups** Cumulative updates that contain a group of patches or hotfixes for a particular piece of software.
- **Feature updates (bi-annually)** New versions of Windows 10 that come out roughly every six months during the spring and fall. They are focused on providing new OS features only.
- **Quality updates (monthly)** Monthly cumulative updates to Windows 10 patches that fix bugs and errors, patch security vulnerabilities, and improve the reliability with the OS. They do not include new features.

Hardening

As discussed previously, vulnerability remediations also stem from changed configurations. Earlier you learned how configuration baselines help lock in a standard set of system configurations. However, what security benefits do we gain from security baselines? Simply, our systems get "hardened." Hardening is the general process of securing a system by reducing its attack surface. In other words, we're reducing the number of ways adversaries can attack our systems by removing unnecessary system components and services, securing configuration settings, and patching security flaws. The following are some examples of hardening techniques:

- Remove or disable unnecessary or built-in accounts.
- Change default passwords.
- Remove unnecessary applications.
- Disable unnecessary services.
- Apply patches.
- Restrict USB, Bluetooth, FireWire, Wi-Fi, and NFC access on host devices, as appropriate.

 EXAM TIP Hardening techniques must only be implemented to the extent that they meet security objectives, which must, in turn, align with organizational objectives. Security must always be balanced with both functionality and available resources.

Compensating Controls

For a variety of reasons, our preferred cybersecurity controls aren't always effective, don't always work the way we plan, or can't be fully implemented. Rather than doing nothing, as a result, we come up with a "Plan B," which is called *compensating controls*. A compensating control is an alternative security control put into place to compensate for any technical or business constraints placed upon a primary security control. Constraints can mean technology failures as well as lack of budget, personnel, or even expertise. Regardless of the cause, it's important to choose compensating controls that help fill in any security gaps left behind to ensure the organization maintains compliance with security requirements.

According to Payment Card Industry Data Security Standard (PCI DSS) v3.2.1, organizations must ensure that compensating controls satisfy the following criteria:

- Meet the intent and rigor of the originally stated requirement.
- Provide a similar level of defense as the original PCI DSS requirement, such that the compensating control sufficiently offsets the risk that the original PCI DSS requirement was designed to defend against.
- Be "above and beyond" other PCI DSS requirements.
- Be commensurate with the additional risk imposed by not adhering to the PCI DSS requirement.

Curious to see some examples of primary and compensating controls? Let's take a look at Table 1.3-1.

Risk Acceptance

So, we've completed the trifecta of identifying, validating, and remediating vulnerabilities to all our valued hardware, operating systems, and applications. What does this ultimately mean? It means that the original risks presented by the vulnerabilities have been reduced to a level that we must determine if it is enough. That level is what we call *risk acceptance,* which means

TABLE 1.3-1   Compensating Controls

Primary Control	Primary Control Failure	Secondary
Log management tool automatic alert generation	Automatic alerts fail to generate.	Manually audit the log files.
Physical segmentation of networks	Segmentation too costly.	Implement logical segmentation within Ethernet switch (VLAN).
Security guards	Security guards too costly.	Implement a fence.
Separation of roles and duties	Not enough staff to implement.	Maintain and review logs and audit trails.

that we will accept any residual risk that remains after all mitigations have been applied. We acknowledge that bad stuff can still happen, but we're willing to "risk it." At this tipping point, spending *more* dollars to reduce the risk further would be counterproductive.

 CAUTION Never forget that the goal is to reduce risk to an *acceptable* level. Go any further, and you might harm the organization's ability to perform crucial business tasks. If security negatively affects an organization's business processes, that, in itself, increases the organization's risk.

Verification of Mitigation

After we mitigate all known vulnerabilities, we should rerun our vulnerability scans to verify that previously identified vulnerabilities are gone and that no new vulnerabilities have been introduced. To be extra safe, verification may involve a separate auditing process to ensure remediated vulnerabilities are truly gone. This step not only helps you see that mitigations were successful but also ensures transparency and accountability across the company. It is through this verification process that we arrived at the point of risk acceptance.

Scanning Parameters and Criteria

Vulnerability scanning is relatively straightforward once all the key vulnerability scanning decisions, parameters, and other information are sorted out in advance. Although there's a lot to consider, here is a brief description of those questions that we're going to need answers to:

- **Risk** Are we prepared to mitigate the risks that scanning introduces, such as downtime?
- **Vulnerability feed** Are we getting the most up-to-date vulnerability information?
- **Scope** Which systems are we going to scan?
- **Credentialed vs. non-credentialed** Do we require authentication to scan systems?
- **Server-based vs. agent-based** Do the assets require locally installed scanning software or can it be done remotely?
- **Internal vs. external** Will scans be conducted on internal or external assets, and will they be conducted from within the organization or outside on the Internet?
- **Special considerations** Data types, technical constraints, workflows, sensitivity levels, and regulatory requirements.

Risks Associated with Scanning Activities

Ironically, vulnerability scans not only help reduce organizational risk, but also introduce some risk of their own. For example, if too many vulnerability scanner plug-ins are selected—particularly the DoS variety—a scan could crash certain systems. Vulnerability scans can also consume a lot of network bandwidth and system resources. The cybersecurity analyst would be wise to address any deterioration in the system and network performance of the target systems during scanning.

Malicious or improper use of scanning tools also presents a risk to the organization through the harm that may be caused to systems. A risk assessment might be to determine what risks are presented by vulnerability scanning, and how they should be mitigated beforehand. The organization would be well-served to establish policies and procedures that formalize vulnerability assessments.

Yet another risk, albeit a controlled one, is the risk that required downtime to scan introduces to critical business processes. We should consider standing up alternative processing systems that can take over while primary ones are being scanned or make the decision as to whether we can afford to halt critical processes while we are scanning.

Vulnerability Feed

Like threat intelligence feeds, vulnerability feeds are repositories of vulnerabilities made available to the public via commercial or community sources. Although your vulnerability scanning tool will likely be connected to its vendor-specific vulnerability feed, many scanners, like Nessus, have a connector to the NIST NVD via a standardized set of vulnerability best practices collectively called the Security Content Automation Protocol (SCAP). Regardless of your fed, you need to ensure that it is reliable and has the most up-to-date information on current vulnerabilities.

 NOTE   SCAP was created by NIST as a way of standardizing the way vulnerability scanning practices are expressed, including automation, reporting, scoring, and prioritization of scans.

Scenario: Nessus Vulnerability Feed

As part of a PCI DSS quarterly requirement, you initiate a vulnerability scan on your Windows workstations using Nessus. Once the scan is completed, the tool generates a report indicating dozens of vulnerabilities, including one in particular labeled CVE-2020-0796. This vulnerability affects the Server Message Block 3.1.1 protocol on Windows 10 and Windows Server 2016. It also achieves the rare distinction of a CVSS Base Score of 10.0 (Critical). Further research reveals this vulnerability can be patched via the KB4551762 update.

Scope

The scope of a scan defines which systems and networks will be scanned and how they will be scanned. You may wish to broaden the scope to see more potential issues or narrow it down to quickly identify problems you already suspect are present. Generally, the scope is all-encompassing in that scans will cover the entire organization. Yet, larger organizations tend to have network hierarchies divided up by firewalls, routers, and switches; therefore, more targeted scans on a segment-by-segment basis will be common. The risks and criticality of assets will often drive the scope of scans.

 EXAM TIP Scope might also include time-of-day requirements and frequency to ensure scans minimize impact to the business.

Credentialed vs. Non-Credentialed

Credentialed or non-credentialed scanning (also known as authenticated or unauthenticated scanning)? That is an important question. When a vulnerability scanner is using a domain or system account (typically a privileged account) to perform a vulnerability scan on a target, this is known as a credentialed scan. Not surprisingly, a non-credentialed scan involves a vulnerability scanner *not* using a domain or system account to perform the scan.

Credentialed scans are generally considered the superior of the two because, simply stated, more rights equal more vulnerability data acquired. Since the scan is conducted from the context of an authenticated user with elevated credentials, you'll see a view of the system's security posture from that account's perspective. You can expect to see more detailed reporting, less false positives, and more accurate reporting, too.

The best thing about non-credentialed scans is their "disconnected" nature makes such scans easier to execute and faster to complete. Plus, they don't require the provisioning of an account to conduct the scan, and they are less resource-intensive on both the network and the system being scanned. Another possible advantage to a non-credentialed scan is that by getting the same results an attacker would see if they do not have credentials, you can target vulnerabilities that are more visible and likely to be "low-hanging fruit" for an attacker.

 CAUTION Non-credentialed scans are *easier,* but easier doesn't equate to more discovery and remediation of vulnerabilities. Avoid non-credentialed scans unless your goal is to simulate the vulnerability scanning perspective of the attacker.

Server-Based vs. Agent-Based

Vulnerability scanning generally falls into one of two camps: server-based or agent-based. Server-based scans (agentless), which is sometimes known as network-based scanning, occur when a vulnerability scanner is installed on a single physical or virtual machine and scans a variety of other systems over the network. Here are the benefits of agentless-based scanning:

- Scans will work on devices that don't support agents.
- Scans can be performed immediately.
- Scans don't require the initial overhead of deploying agents to all devices.

CAUTION   Agentless scans are often frowned upon due to the number of network resources they consume. You'll be better off performing agentless scans during business off-hours.

The preferred of the two, agent-based scanning, involves the installation of software (agent) on assets that require vulnerability scans. Although agents may be installable on network devices, you'll more commonly find them on servers, workstations, or laptops. The benefits of agent-based scans are as follows:

- False positives are reduced.
- Reports contain greater accuracy and detail.
- Scans are generated within the system and then sent to the server; therefore, there is very little network overhead.
- Scans are more comprehensive when they run with privileges and are launched from within the target system.
- Scans can be scheduled to run during business hours on non-critical assets.
- Scans can be tailored to run on a frequency tailored to compliance requirements.
- Scans can run using credentials native to the system; therefore, no separate credentials are required.
- Scans can run on disconnected devices such as company laptops, smartphones, and tablets.

Internal vs. External

Internal vulnerability scans are conducted from within the internal network, which is the same as saying "behind the firewall." Internal scans are conducted on internal organizational assets such as desktops, laptops, servers, VoIP phones, scanners, and printers. It is commonly performed to verify proper patching has occurred while providing valuable insights into your patch management process. You may also be interested in simply generating a report of vulnerabilities in your environment.

 NOTE   Given the vantage point of being on the "inside," and the tendency to use credentials to authenticate the scans, you should expect to collect a lot more vulnerability details from internal scans.

External vulnerability scans are conducted from an Internet system, or "outside" the firewall, to identify holes in your organization's perimeter network and systems. Chief among them is the identification of firewall vulnerabilities and open ports. You'll also want to look at other perimeter systems such as your public-facing web server, e-mail server, DNS server,

VPN server, reverse proxy server, and more. You are more likely to encounter the use of external scans if you use a "scanning-as-a-service" cloud-based provider rather than setting up your scanning infrastructure.

 CAUTION   External scanning provides organizations with the "hacker viewpoint" of your network. Remediation of any vulnerable assets here should be a high priority.

Special Considerations

There are other considerations to vulnerability scanning that don't fit neatly into any of the previous categories. These are the topics we're going to expand upon throughout the next section:

- **Types of data**   What data types will we need to scan?
- **Technical constraints**   Will any technology, resource availability, or licensing constraints hinder our scans?
- **Workflow**   When and how should scans be performed to minimize the business impact?
- **Sensitivity levels**   What sensitivity should our scanning tools assign to vulnerabilities?
- **Regulatory requirements**   How frequently should scans be performed?
- **Segmentation**   How will segmentation help "compensate" for our vulnerability gaps?
- **Intrusion prevention system (IPS) and firewall settings**   How might the configurations of network appliances affect vulnerability scans?

Types of Data

Vulnerability scanners can usually scan more data types than anyone would need. As a result, you'll typically want to condense the scanning of data to what is needed for regulatory or compliance purposes. Compliance-based scans will often compel you to scan sensitive or classified data types since vulnerabilities in these areas would need to be prioritized. You'll also want to be mindful that scanning different data types, and the subsequent reporting, will be driven by different target audiences. When in doubt, get feedback from key stakeholders in the organization to determine what data types should be scanned. Also, limiting the types of files scanned improves the performance of the scan and our ability to enumerate the results.

Technical Constraints

Another valuable NIST publication, SP 800-115, "Technical Guide to Information Security Testing and Assessment," states that security assessments require resources such as time, staff, hardware, and software, and resource availability is often a limiting factor in the type of frequency of security assessments. In short, vulnerability scans can only be as effective as the technical resources afforded to them. Top-tier vulnerability scanners like Nessus and Open-VAS won't do much good if the network infrastructure, servers, desktops, laptops, and mobile devices aren't powerful enough to support the scans. Then, of course, there's the expertise (or lack thereof) of the technology professionals who are wielding the vulnerability scanning tools alongside those networks and systems. Finally, if you only have one scanning device, you are limited by the amount of scanning a single device can perform.

 NOTE   Licensing constraints with commercial vulnerability scanners may impair your scanning in terms of the number of IP addresses that can be scanned, bandwidth consumed, or the number of scans running concurrently.

Workflow

In quantum physics, the "observer effect" states that the mere observation of a phenomenon changes that phenomenon. Scanning systems is a form of observation, and one that could result in a system performing noticeably slower or, worse, becoming unavailable if we're not careful. We also want to be mindful of the experts conducting and analyzing the scan results. They, too, are not an unlimited resource.

Whether we're following the compliance requirements of PCI DSS or the requirements or guidelines of our internal security policies, what we want are standardized and repeatable vulnerability management processes. The impact of vulnerability scanning to organizational workflows should've already been figured out earlier when we were talking about risks associated with vulnerability scanning. Stemming from our requirements or guidelines is the need to maximize organizational workflow. This may involve constraining our scans to business off-hours, throttling the resource consumption of scans to minimize the impact of those systems during business hours, or reducing the frequency of the scans.

Sensitivity Levels

With seemingly endless systems to scan, cybersecurity analysts should take note of which systems contain sensitive data. Prioritization should guide every facet of vulnerability management. If any systems have the following sensitive data types, it should be prioritized for detection and remediation:

- Classified data (confidential, secret, top secret)
- Personally identifiable information (PII) such as Social Security numbers or addresses
- Financial information such as credit card numbers or bank account information
- Passwords
- Driver's license or passport numbers
- Medical information

NOTE These systems present a serious confidentiality risk to the organization if they were ever breached. They should be addressed before moving onto lesser critical systems.

Recall our previous discussion on how scanning introduces risks of its own to systems? If you think about it, this creates a double-edged sword. Scanning can sometimes create availability challenges for systems, and systems with sensitive data can't afford to be unavailable. Is the risk of making the sensitive data unavailable through the scan greater than the risk of not detecting and mitigating the system's vulnerabilities after being scanned? The good news is, as cybersecurity analysts, we're tasked with determining precisely which systems containing sensitive data should be scanned immediately versus deferred to a more opportune time to prevent potential availability issues.

Regulatory Requirements

Organizations are beholden to legal and regulatory requirements, which can vary based on country, state, or industry. Industry standards such as PCI DSS require vulnerability scans to be performed quarterly, after significant network changes take place, and by an approved vendor, for example, so we comply with the standard. Failing to abide by regulatory requirements can result in severe fines, business shutdown, and even the arrest of certain senior leadership members.

Here's a short list of examples of other compliance standards and their requirements regarding vulnerability scans:

- **ISO 27001** Requires scans to be performed in a timely fashion
- **HIPAA** Doesn't specifically require network vulnerability scans, but it does require the assimilation of vulnerability data that is best collected from network vulnerability scans
- **FISMA** Requires an annual report on selected controls that is typically satisfied through NIST's requirement for an organizationally defined scanning frequency

Cross-Reference
Compliance is covered in more detail in Domain 5.0.

Segmentation

Mitigating vulnerabilities with patches and configuration changes is great, but there's a small problem. They might be initially delayed by a few *weeks* to undergo the necessary change management and testing procedures. Although temporary, this gap in our security poses a significant risk to the organization. Fortunately, compensating controls can help here, particularly in the form of network segmentation.

Segmentation is the practice of dividing networks into smaller logically or physically separated subnetworks to enhance performance, manageability, and *security*. Without segmentation, attackers can take advantage of a single point of compromise to potentially breach all networked systems. With segmentation in place, we can perform vulnerability scans on very specific segments without affecting the performance of other systems. This might be a good idea when we must scan critical hosts but can't afford the downtime or delay in scanning the entire network. With segmentation, we can better manage and schedule scans to account for downtime and delays due to the configuration management process. Scanning specific segments incrementally can also help to identify and remediate any segmentation weaknesses in firewall rules, network switch configurations, or even with air-gapped systems.

 NOTE   Typically reserved for the most extreme scenarios, air gapping provides the most restrictive type of segmentation. Air-gapped devices have *zero* network connectivity with anything. The most common way to exchange data with an air-gapped device is through a USB flash drive.

Segmentation is also vital to the containment phase of incident response. To prevent malware from running amuck, a properly configured segment can help isolate malware from further spread.

Intrusion Prevention System (IPS), Intrusion Detection System (IDS), and Firewall Settings

Like anything else, network appliances like firewalls, IPSs, and IDSs have vulnerable default rules and configurations that an IT or security professional should change immediately. Failure to do so could lead to the following outcomes:

- **Vulnerable firewall**   Permits unauthorized access to networks and systems or unauthorized blocking of networks and systems.
- **Vulnerable IDS**   Increased false negatives of well-known malicious traffic.
- **Vulnerable IPS**   Increased false negatives of well-known malicious traffic. Also, compromised IPSs can lead to unauthorized traffic dropping.

Inhibitors to Remediation

It should be simple enough to solve problems once you have the solution, right? Not exactly. There are several possible remediation inhibitors, including the fear that remediation could temporarily disrupt or degrade business continuity, lack of approval from stakeholders, legacy or proprietary system challenges, and contractual restrictions. We're going to take a look at each of these considerations in the next several sections.

Memorandum of Understanding (MOU)

A memorandum of understanding (MOU) is usually a legally non-binding document used to describe an agreement between two or more parties. It is a written agreement documenting a set of intended actions between the parties concerning some common pursuit or goal. MOUs may contain specific security requirements or limitations on scanning scopes, frequency, schedule, and more. Because of their non-binding nature, MOUs are most often used between internal divisions of a larger single organization to delineate support responsibilities. For agreements between two different organizations, which are typically required to have legal enforcement, you likely will see contracts or service level agreements used.

Service Level Agreement (SLA)

A service level agreement (SLA) is an agreement between parties detailing the expectations of services to be provided to consumers by a service provider. SLAs are typically included as part of a service contract and set the level of technical expectations. As with MOUs, SLAs may contain specific requirements on scanning scopes, frequency, schedule, and more.

Organizational Governance

Organizational governance refers to the process of top-level management exerting strategic control over all organizational functions. The governance committee ensures that all managerial roles under it are following business processes to ensure the business vision, mission, and objectives are being met. With the focus on business objectives cemented into their minds, governance committees may not see the benefits of certain cybersecurity initiatives and may fail to approve certain remediation efforts. Organizational security governance is most often seen in the forms of an information security strategy and security policies that articulate rules and requirements. Policy, the primary instrument of internal organizational governance, can be a double-edged sword here. A policy may dictate particulars with vulnerability scanning that both constrain the cybersecurity analysts responsible for vulnerability while at the same time force different divisions within the organization to allow their assets to be scanned and remediated.

Business Process Interruption

As discussed earlier in the module, scanning should not be performed to the extent that it outright prevents the organization from conducting business. However, there must be a balance between vulnerability scanning and remediation and conducting business processes.

There are different ways to allow these two divergent processes to coexist, such as scanning primary systems while business processes are running on secondary systems, scheduling scans during off-peak business hours, and deferring scans until business processes can safely be interrupted. All of these involve accepting some level of risk.

Degrading Functionality

Largely just a smaller version of business interruption, we don't want vulnerability scans can occasionally disrupt or degrade systems and applications in the infrastructure. For less-crucial systems, this may be tolerated, but certainly not for critical systems. As previously mentioned, the organization should consider deferring the vulnerability assessments to a more opportune time to limit or prevent the degradation of functionality. If this proves not possible, the organization should research alternative solutions or consider accepting the risk as it is.

Legacy Systems

Legacy systems are any devices, operating systems, applications, or other technologies that are outdated but still in use at the organization. Although these products still work, they probably aren't supported by the vendor anymore, which usually means no more patches are being produced. However, some organizations aren't aware of which systems (and how many of them) constitute a legacy system and what risks they present to the business. A vulnerability scan may help us identify such systems and, hopefully, identify any present vulnerabilities afflicting them.

So, how does one remediate legacy system vulnerabilities if the vendor has abandoned the product? Although we can't mitigate the vulnerability directly, we can implement compensating controls such as system hardening, monitoring, and segmentation to minimize the inherent risk to the organization.

Proprietary Systems

Perhaps more difficult to mitigate than legacy systems are proprietary systems. Whereas legacy systems are largely outdated but otherwise well-known entities, proprietary systems are more likely to be fringe, and, by extension, obscure to us.

A good example of a proprietary system is a supervisory control and data acquisition (SCADA) system, which you'll encounter in industrial environments like power, water, sewage, and nuclear organizations. Whereas traditional computing systems usually have a better balance of confidentiality, integrity, and availability capabilities, SCADA equipment is designed to be available, period. Such a design can make certain security efforts almost impossible. Although patching is often made available, it can take months of testing before approval due to the critical nature of the systems.

Cross-Reference

SCADA systems are discussed in more depth within Objective 1.5.

Scenario: SCADA

A large power company has merged much of its SCADA systems with its IP-based network. Despite the company gaining enhanced control and monitoring benefits, the merger also exposes the SCADA systems to a new frontier of IP-based attacks that they weren't designed to deal with. Given the proprietary nature of the SCADA equipment, vulnerability scans are run with surgical precision to offset the risk of knocking a SCADA system offline (for many of these organizations, this is would be a serious incident). After coordinating with the SCADA vendor, the company decides to chance installing a patch during its annual maintenance period.

 NOTE   Some oil companies are known to wait a couple of years before installing a patch to ensure all the kinks have been ironed out. There are few organizations in the world more risk-averse than the industrial variety.

REVIEW

Objective 1.3: Given a scenario, perform vulnerability management activities   Vulnerability identification is an important part of the vulnerability management process. The key to this effort is the identification and prioritization of the most critical organizational assets to ensure their vulnerabilities are addressed first. Given the variety of system and network types under your purview, you'll likely employ a combination of active and scanning techniques to ensure all required systems can be scanned.

After identifying potential vulnerabilities, the next step is ensuring they are valid. Vulnerability validation helps us separate real vulnerabilities from false positives, determine their exploitability, correlate them with other data points in our environment, and evaluate their overall risk to the organization.

Once we validate the existence and severity of our organization's vulnerabilities, we create a plan to remediate the vulnerabilities. Remediation will typically involve installing software patches or implementing configuration changes. Planning mitigations is crucial because cybersecurity analysts must navigate the potential minefield of change management procedures, revisions to configuration baselines, hardening requirements, and compensating controls in case mitigations fail. The success of mitigations must be independently verified to determine that our vulnerability risk is at an acceptable level.

Many factors influence vulnerability scanning in terms of when, how, and where they should be performed. The risk of the scans themselves will need to be ironed out. Tempering the scanning risks requires a balanced approach of keeping abreast of the latest vulnerability feed data, scoping scans to only required internal or external systems and networks, knowing when to use credentials (or not), and knowing when agents are a viable option (or not). In addition, we need to know what data type should be scanned, any constraints placed upon our scans, and any potential interruptions of workflows (particularly to systems with sensitive data), as well as ensure all regular requirements on vulnerability scans are met.

Despite the complexities inherent in the preceding criteria, there are also several potential remediation inhibitors, including the fear that remediation could temporarily disrupt or degrade business continuity, lack of approval from stakeholders, legacy or proprietary system challenges, and contractual restrictions contained in MOUs or SLAs.

1.3 QUESTIONS

1. You run vulnerability scans of several critical hosts. You expected many vulnerabilities to show up from the scans, but the scan results show very little data, and the data that is produced is generic and is not very detailed. Which of the following is the most likely reason for these results?

   A. The scans were unauthenticated and ran with no credentials.

   B. The hosts are already hardened and up to date with all patches, so there are no vulnerabilities.

   C. The scans were authenticated and ran with administrative-level credentials.

   D. The vulnerability feeds on your scanning tool have not been updated with the latest information.

2. Working as a vulnerability analyst for your organization, you've completed a vulnerability scan of all Windows 10 desktop and laptop computers. Although your scan did not discover any new Windows 10 vulnerabilities, you recall reading about a brand-new Windows 10 vulnerability that was posted on a vulnerability feed just yesterday. Working backward, you determined that both your vulnerability scanner and Windows 10 received all available updates today. Which of the following vulnerability validations has occurred?

   A. False positive

   B. False negative

   C. True positive

   D. True negative

3. You're a cybersecurity analyst working for a large financial organization. You've implemented a log management tool designed to automatically generate alerts when indicators of compromise have been detected. After a recent crash of the log management system, you notice that the automatic alerts are no longer being generated. Which of the following solutions best represents a compensating control?

   A. Replace the log management tool with a comparable product.

   B. Manually audit the log files.

   C. Temporarily accept the reduced functionality of the tool and research alternative solutions.

   D. Remove the malware that caused the log management tool to crash.

4. You are a vulnerability analyst for a large hospital chain. You wish to perform a vulnerability scan on all the laptops used by doctors to conform to HIPAA's risk analysis requirements. However, certain doctors are off-site with their laptops and therefore disconnected from the hospital network. Which of the following is the best solution for scanning disconnected physician laptops?

   A. Perform a credentialed scan against the laptops.

   B. Perform a non-credentialed scan against the laptops.

   C. Install an agent on the laptops that runs on a frequent schedule.

   D. Remotely connect into the laptops and run a credentialed scan.

5. You're a cybersecurity analyst working for a chain store that specializes in selling eyewear. The organization still uses a DOS-based application for all data entry, purchases, billing, and appointments. Since the software vendor completely stopped supporting this application many years ago, which of the following is the best compensating control to protect this system?

   A. Segmentation

   B. Hardening

   C. Monitoring

   D. Patching

1.3 ANSWERS

1. **A**   The scans were unauthenticated and ran with no credentials.

2. **D**   This is an example of a true negative because the vulnerability scan correctly determined that this particular Windows 10 vulnerability does not exist on these systems because they received the patch already.

3. **B**   Manually auditing the log files is a compensating control because, although useful, manually auditing the log files is a secondary choice as a result of the primary choice becoming unavailable.

4. **C** Installing an agent on the laptops and running scans automatically on a schedule is the best answer because the agent can run regardless of the whereabouts of the laptops.

5. **A** Segmentation is the best choice because it helps prevent attackers from getting close enough to attack the system.

Objective 1.4 Given a scenario, analyze the output from common vulnerability assessment tools

Vulnerability Assessment Tools

To discover the weaknesses in our systems, we have a wide variety of vulnerability assessment tools at our disposal. Finding vulnerabilities in systems isn't a process strictly confined to using technical tools, however. During a full vulnerability assessment, we should use a variety of methods that will expose weaknesses in all aspects of the system. Analysts should be reviewing system documentation, such as log files, architectural diagrams, and so forth, to determine how the system is designed and constructed, and to confirm that it has been built and performs securely. Assessors should also be interviewing and asking questions of systems personnel, such as system administrators and security technicians. And finally, another method for determining vulnerabilities is to *observe* the system in operation. Watching someone perform a security function on the system, to confirm that it works as it should, is a viable method for determining if a system has any weaknesses. However, the focus of this objective is the technical tools we use to determine technical configuration vulnerabilities in the system. There are so many technical tools available for us to use, and we will classify them, as the exam does, according to their function and use. Keep in mind that these are not necessarily all the tools available to you, but these are key tools you will need to have some familiarity with for the exam. Also, there's no way we could cover every function of every tool, and the exam will not specifically ask you for that either, but it's a good idea to study them, understand them, and even install and use them in a lab environment to prepare for the test.

EXAM TIP You will not be expected to know the details of every single tool, but you should be familiar with their basic use and know a scenario in which you might employ them.

Application Tools

Application tools can be broken up into web application scanners and more generic software code tools. These are classified according to the type of application or service that is provided, such as web-based applications and client/server applications. Obviously, in today's world, you're going to see a mix that can't easily be defined by a distinct boundary. However, web application tools focus more on vulnerabilities associated with web-based infrastructures, and the software application tools we're going to discuss focus more on the application code itself.

Web Application Scanners

Our first category of application vulnerability assessment tools is web application scanners. These give us insight as to technical vulnerabilities, such as configuration issues, on web-based applications and the underlying servers that host them. Web application scanners can give us detailed information on weaknesses that might lead to web-based attacks, including cross-site scripting, cross-site forgery requests, buffer overflow attacks, and several others.

OWASP Zed Attack Proxy (ZAP)

The Open Web Application Security Project (OWASP) operates as a non-profit focused on software security. It has developed several open-source software projects, including the most popular one, the Zed Attack Proxy (ZAP). ZAP, and some of the other web application vulnerability scanners we will discuss coming up, falls into a category of typically browser-based proxies that will allow the analyst to send and receive highly customizable traffic from a web application and analyze that traffic to determine vulnerabilities in the web application itself. As with other web application vulnerability scanners, ZAP will scan a web application and determine if it has common vulnerabilities, such as cross-site scripting, injection vulnerabilities, input validation issues, and so on. It can also determine if the web application server has nonsecure files and directories, insecure permissions, and other configuration problems. Figure 1.4-1 shows ZAP in action, identifying serious vulnerabilities within the target web application.

Burp Suite

Burp Suite is another highly popular web application vulnerability scanner whose free community edition comes with popular Linux-based penetration testing distributions, such as Kali Linux. It allows the user to construct highly customizable and complex scan options. Burp has several modes, including a proxy mode that allows a user to inspect every request and response sent to and from a web application server. Burp also allows the analyst to customize traffic sent to the web application to elicit specific responses and take advantage of any discovered vulnerabilities. Burp has an intruder mode, which can execute customizable attacks against the server. Burp's interface can be daunting at first, as it is complex and requires a significant level of web application and penetration testing knowledge. The paid professional version offers a significant number of additional features.

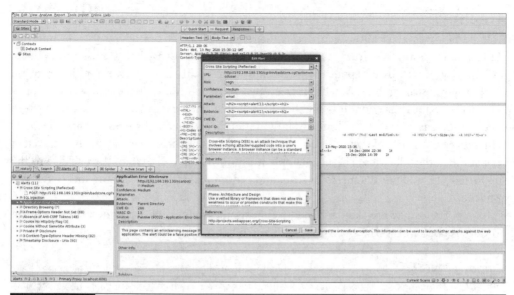

FIGURE 1.4-1   Zed Attack Proxy in action

Nikto

Nikto is an older web application vulnerability testing tool and is usually seen as a command-line tool. Like ZAP and Burp Suite, it is also included with the penetration testing Linux distribution, Kali Linux. While lacking the finesse and complexity of some of its more modern, GUI-based brethren, Nikto is lightweight and very quick with simple scans that can determine several key vulnerabilities in a web application. Figure 1.4-2 shows sample output from a Nikto scan.

```
root@kali:/home/bobby# nikto -host 192.168.189.130
- Nikto v2.1.6
---------------------------------------------------------------------------
+ Target IP:          192.168.189.130
+ Target Hostname:    192.168.189.130
+ Target Port:        80
+ Start Time:         2020-05-14 11:39:41 (GMT-5)
---------------------------------------------------------------------------
+ Server: Apache/1.3.28 (Unix) mod_ssl/2.8.15 OpenSSL/0.9.7c
+ Server may leak inodes via ETags, header found with file /, inode: 331, size: 3583, mt:
y 14 16:16:23 2006
+ The anti-clickjacking X-Frame-Options header is not present.
+ The X-XSS-Protection header is not defined. This header can hint to the user agent to p
inst some forms of XSS
+ The X-Content-Type-Options header is not set. This could allow the user agent to render
nt of the site in a different fashion to the MIME type
+ OSVDB-3268: /backup/: Directory indexing found.
+ Entry '/backup/' in robots.txt returned a non-forbidden or redirect HTTP code (200)
```

FIGURE 1.4-2   Nikto scan output

Arachni

Arachni is a web application security scanner framework that can operate across multiple platforms, including Windows, macOS, and Linux. It is Ruby-based and is used to evaluate the security of web-based applications. Its multiuser, multiscan intuitive interface can use preconfigured scan profiles. Arachni is free, open-source software whose source code is publicly available for inspection. It is highly customizable, allowing the user to develop custom checks, plug-ins, reporters, and other configuration items. One of its many positive features is that it's easily installable, and there are no required dependencies, such as databases, system services, or other libraries. The user simply must download and extract the package to the supported OS, add an IP address to scan, and can immediately be scanning the target web application server.

Its reports formats are standardized, like most other vulnerability scanners, in that it can produce reports in HTML, XML, CSV, PDF, and other common formats.

 NOTE   Many of these web vulnerability application tools can perform the same functions, so it becomes a matter of preference as to which tool you might use in a given scenario. As a matter of thoroughness, many analysts use multiple tools at once to verify that a vulnerability is real and not a false positive. If more than one tool reports the same vulnerability, you can be more assured that it is a valid finding.

Software Assessment Tools and Techniques

Software provides many different threat vectors and avenues of attack for malicious entities. This is particularly true with software in a web-based application since it may be directly exposed to the Internet. Web servers and their underlying applications and databases are constantly attacked, so cybersecurity analysts must be vigilant in staying on top of any vulnerabilities found in these systems. Cybersecurity analysts can use several methods to detect vulnerabilities, including static and dynamic analysis, reverse engineering, and fuzzing. These methods should be used by an experienced cybersecurity analyst who has a background in software application programming. All these methods should be used in different ways to determine the whole vulnerability picture for a web server and application.

Static Analysis

One of the many ways in determining vulnerabilities in software is to get down into the weeds and look at its underlying code. There are different ways to perform what we call *code reviews*, and one of them is static analysis. Static analysis is when we use an automated method, usually a specific type of vulnerability or security tool, to analyze the application's code. These vulnerability tools typically look for a wide variety of known software or security flaws, such as embedded passwords, for example. They can also be configured to look for more unusual issues, depending upon the specific application they are looking at. Manual code review can also be performed on software applications, but typically a manual review involves a human being looking for specific flaws that an automated tool may not catch. Both are preferred methods of reviewing code and looking for vulnerabilities.

Dynamic Analysis

While static analysis and manual code review are excellent in looking for specific flaws that are typically known to cybersecurity analysts, they're not always good at predicting how a piece of software will behave once it is running. That's what dynamic analysis can do. Dynamic analysis is characterized by actually executing the binaries of the application in a controlled environment, typically a sandbox, so we can see how the application behaves. We can use this type of analysis to record and analyze software actions to determine if it's behaving in a way that would violate security policies.

 EXAM TIP   Remember that static analysis involves reviewing code through automated or manual means without executing the code. Dynamic analysis means that you actually execute the code and run the software program in a controlled environment such as a sandbox.

Reverse Engineering

While we should use both static and dynamic analysis to help discover vulnerabilities such as security flaws and unstable behavior in applications, this is typically only useful if we have the source code available to us, such as in the case of in-house application development. Sometimes, however, we may acquire a piece of software that is suspected to be malware or otherwise could cause harm or damage to our systems. In this case, it is useful to reverse engineer the software. While we can reverse engineer both hardware and software, in the case of applications, what we are doing is disassembling the components of the program into its component parts. This means decompiling the executables down into their lower-level languages, such as assembly or even machine language. This allows us to see how the program is constructed, what its executables are capable of, and their characteristics. This could help us determine if a piece of application code is, in fact, malicious or not.

Fuzzing

Fuzzing is a unique way of determining vulnerabilities in an application. Both security analysts and hackers use fuzzing to elicit results from an application by sending it unusual or malformed data requests, typically through user interfaces such as web forms, for example. If the application has not been designed properly from a security perspective, it may react unusually or unexpectedly to non-standard input. In some cases, it could allow memory contents to be overwritten, causing the system to be unstable, force the system to give up data that an attacker should not be able to access, or even result in an attacker escaping outside the confines of the application into the underlying operating system, where they could conceivably run arbitrary code at their discretion.

Infrastructure Tools

Included in our analyst's toolbox are vulnerability scanners for networks and hosts. These don't focus on application code, but rather on how network hosts connect and how secure configurations and protocols transport data over the network. First, we'll discuss network enumeration tools, which provide us with a wealth of information about the network and can give us insight into potential vulnerabilities involving ports, protocols, and services. Then, we'll look at more specific vulnerability scanners that can get into the operating system and application level to tell us what system patches and configuration changes may be needed.

Network Enumeration

When we discuss enumerating the network, what we're talking about is discovering information about what operating systems may be on the network, ports that these operating systems have open, protocols they use, and services they provide to the network. Network enumeration can tell us if any non-secure elements could be exploited for vulnerabilities. It can also generate a useful map that tells us what type of hosts are on the network and how network traffic might flow between them.

Active vs. Passive Enumeration

Two types of network vulnerability scans you will see are active and passive scans. An active scan attempts a connection with the network host during the scanning process and is generally considered better in terms of the accuracy and volume of information it generates. A passive scan does not attempt a connection with a host. However, a passive scan does not generally yield as much or as accurate information as an active scan. An active scan is considered "noisy" in that the connection attempts are easily detected and recorded by intrusion detection systems and audit mechanisms. This isn't necessarily important if you're a system administrator performing an authorized scan on your network, but for a malicious actor, an active scan is generally avoided unless they believe there is little chance of detection by the target network. A passive scan may not be detected, depending on the type of scan you use and the types of intrusion detection systems present.

 EXAM TIP Keep in mind that an active scan attempts to make a connection to a host, which can be easily detected by either a network- or host-based intrusion detection system. A passive scan does not attempt a connection, but it does try to elicit a response from the host that may look like routine traffic to an IDS. A passive scan is meant to be stealthy and reduce the risk of the attacker getting caught.

Nmap

Nmap (for Network Mapper) is a tried-and-true tool that network administrators have been using for decades to scan their networks to discover what hosts are present and what services they are running. Nmap is extremely useful in that it can be configured to use a wide variety of specialized scanning techniques, including the use of various protocols to elicit information from network hosts. For example, Nmap can attempt a full TCP connection to a host, or it can use Internet Control Message Protocol (ICMP) packets to get a response. Nmap essentially sends specially crafted network traffic to a host, and depending on the port or protocol used, it can get a predictable response from the host that will tell you if a TCP or UDP port is open or closed, which protocol is being used, if a particular service is running, and which operating system is in use.

Nmap is widely used as a command-line tool, making it highly customizable and extremely easy to script, but there have also been several GUI front-end programs developed for Nmap, such as Zenmap and NmapFE, that provide an easy-to-use interface. Figure 1.4-3 shows the results of a scan using Zenmap, and Figure 1.4-4 shows the output of the Nmap command-line interface.

Nmap can scan a particular host or even an entire logical network segment if given the proper network address and subnet mask. Nmap can also output to a wide variety of formats,

FIGURE 1.4-3 The results of a network scan using Zenmap

```
root@kali:/home/bobby# nmap -sT -O -T4 192.168.189.0/24
Starting Nmap 7.80 ( https://nmap.org ) at 2020-05-13 13:46 CDT
Nmap scan report for 192.168.189.1
Host is up (0.00064s latency).
Not shown: 997 filtered ports
PORT    STATE SERVICE
135/tcp open  msrpc
139/tcp open  netbios-ssn
445/tcp open  microsoft-ds
MAC Address: 00:50:56:C0:00:08 (VMware)
Warning: OSScan results may be unreliable because we could not find at least 1 open and 1
rt
Device type: general purpose
Running (JUST GUESSING): Microsoft Windows 2008 (85%)
OS CPE: cpe:/o:microsoft:windows_server_2008::sp1 cpe:/o:microsoft:windows_server_2008:r2
Aggressive OS guesses: Microsoft Windows Server 2008 SP1 or Windows Server 2008 R2 (85%)
No exact OS matches for host (test conditions non-ideal).
Network Distance: 1 hop
```

FIGURE 1.4-4 Output of the Nmap command

TABLE 1.4-1 Nmap Command-Line Switches for Various Scanning Techniques

Switch	Type of Scan
-sT	Full TCP connect scan
-sn	Ping scan
-sU	UDP scan
-sA	Ack scan
-sN/sF/sX	TCP Null, FIN, and Xmas scans

including the ubiquitous CSV format. Table 1.4-1 lists some of the more commonly used command-line options for various scanning techniques.

hping

hping has also been used for many years, and although it can also be used for simple port and service scanning, its value lies in the fact that it can manipulate packets to spoof IP addresses, use customized flags, and insert arbitrary data payloads in a packet. Hping3 (the current version of the tool) is the tool of choice to send specifically crafted packets to a host to not only elicit a response that can send useful information back to the attacker but also to initiate an attack. Although more often than not used by attackers, hping can be used by cybersecurity analysts to determine how the network host will react to certain traffic sent to them, thereby revealing potential vulnerabilities that should be mitigated.

responder

responder, developed by Trustwave SpiderLabs, is a tool used in different Linux penetration testing distributions, such as Kali Linux. It is used to poison name resolution services in Windows operating systems. If a Windows host is unable to resolve a name to an IP address using DNS, two protocols can be used to send name resolution requests out to the local network:

the Link-Local Multicast Name Resolution (LLMNR) protocol and NetBIOS Name Service (NBT-NS). responder can be used to gain credentials and password hashes from systems by responding to these requests when they occur. Like hping and other attack tools, responder can be used to discover previously unknown vulnerabilities on hosts.

Network Vulnerability Scanners

Network vulnerability scanners are probably the most useful tools you can have in your cyber-security analyst's toolbox. This tool is used to scan a wide variety of network hosts and report back patching and misconfiguration issues for both operating systems and some applications. Remember that server-based scanners send specific traffic to an entire network segment, without the need for any specialized software installed on the host. Agent-based scanners rely on a small piece of software installed on the host that can scan the host periodically and simply report the results to a centralized scanner. The advantage of an agent-based network scanner is that it does not generate as much network traffic, thus saving on bandwidth and reporting scan results more efficiently.

Another aspect of network vulnerability scanners you need to be aware of is the question of whether to run credentialed or non-credentialed scans. Remember that credentialed scans are more accurate but require some level of privileges on the host, so it's necessary to configure the scan with those privileges. Non-credentialed scans do not return as much detailed information about network hosts but have the advantage of reporting results back as a potential attacker might see them. Typically, credentialed scans are more useful and most often used.

Nessus

Nessus is one of the more widely used network vulnerability scanners, originally starting as an open-source product and then gaining in popularity enough to become an enterprise-level, scalable commercial product from Tenable. Nessus is available as both cloud-based and server-based solutions. Nessus is highly configurable and can allow you to use a wide range of plug-ins (scanning signatures based on vulnerability or operating system). It can scan a wide variety of operating systems and applications, including all flavors of Windows, macOS, and most Linux distributions. It can also scan the odd embedded OS devices as well. It can produce vulnerability results on a variety of popular applications as well, including Microsoft Office, Java, Adobe products, and so on. You can create preconfigured scans, target lists, and several other options when configuring a scan. You can also exclude certain checks in the scan that might be considered "dangerous," meaning that they may cause a device to shut down, hang, or reboot.

Nessus reports provide information on missing patches and updates, configuration issues, and so on. It can break those down into OS, network segment, vulnerability severity, and many other categories. Nessus can output its results in a variety of report formats, including its native Nessus (XML) format, PDF reports, and CSV format. An example of a critical vulnerability in a Nessus report is shown in Figure 1.4-5.

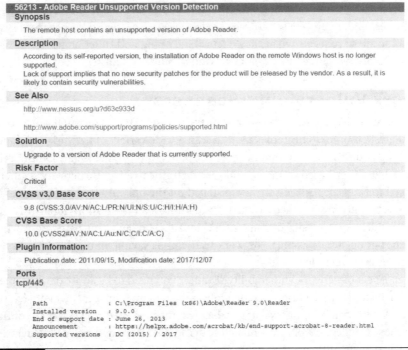

56213 - Adobe Reader Unsupported Version Detection

Synopsis

The remote host contains an unsupported version of Adobe Reader.

Description

According to its self-reported version, the installation of Adobe Reader on the remote Windows host is no longer supported.
Lack of support implies that no new security patches for the product will be released by the vendor. As a result, it is likely to contain security vulnerabilities.

See Also

http://www.nessus.org/u?d63c933d

http://www.adobe.com/support/programs/policies/supported.html

Solution

Upgrade to a version of Adobe Reader that is currently supported.

Risk Factor

Critical

CVSS v3.0 Base Score

9.8 (CVSS:3.0/AV:N/AC:L/PR:N/UI:N/S:U/C:H/I:H/A:H)

CVSS Base Score

10.0 (CVSS2#AV:N/AC:L/Au:N/C:C/I:C/A:C)

Plugin Information:

Publication date: 2011/09/15, Modification date: 2017/12/07

Ports
tcp/445

```
Path              : C:\Program Files (x86)\Adobe\Reader 9.0\Reader
Installed version : 9.0.0
End of support date : June 26, 2013
Announcement      : https://helpx.adobe.com/acrobat/kb/end-support-acrobat-8-reader.html
Supported versions : DC (2015) / 2017
```

FIGURE 1.4-5   A critical Adobe vulnerability detailed in a Nessus report

OpenVAS

OpenVAS is a widely used open-source network vulnerability scanner, a fork of the earlier Nessus open-source code. It has been maintained since 2009 by Greenbone Networks, which has included the open-source vulnerability scanner into its commercial Greenbone Security Manager products. You can also use the community open-source version on the Kali Linux penetration testing tool distribution, although it is more limited in both function and signatures. OpenVAS uses Network Vulnerability Tests, or NVTs (similar in concept to Nessus plug-ins or vulnerability signatures), to scan for over 50,000 potential vulnerabilities and configuration issues. Like Nessus, it also has a web-based interface and can be configured as a client/server setup. Figure 1.4-6 demonstrates the results of an OpenVAS vulnerability scan.

NOTE   Most reputable network vulnerability scanners perform the same functions, so which one you use is a matter of choice, based on quality of vulnerability feeds, economic model, and standards set by the organization. However, sometimes it's a good idea to run more than one scanner so you can verify their results with each other. A finding from one scanner confirmed by a different scanner can give you confidence that the finding is not a false positive.

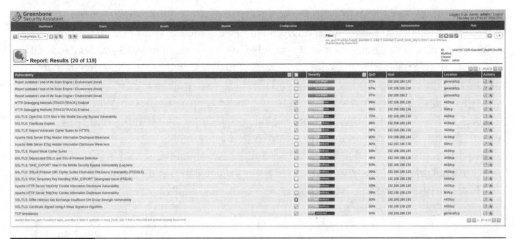

FIGURE 1.4-6   Results of an OpenVAS scan

Qualys

Qualys has been a leading vulnerability scanner for years and can compete head-to-head with Nessus. It is frequently used to conduct scans satisfying compliance requirements, such as PCI DSS requirements. Qualys is usually seen as a collection of cloud applications, using a subscription-based model to perform targeted scans on your network periodically. In addition to its vulnerability scanners, Qualys consolidates its cloud vulnerability scanning application with its inventory application, as well as vulnerability management, detection, and response applications.

 NOTE   Depending on the size and complexity of the network segment you are scanning, vulnerability scanners can sometimes take long periods of time without showing any results, due to "hanging" on a particular host. One good way to make sure that the vulnerability scanner is still doing its job is to run a network sniffer, such as Wireshark, in the background so that you can see active traffic passing between the scanner and the hosts. If you see that there is no active traffic for long periods, it may indicate a problem with the scan. This can usually be resolved by restarting the scanner; in rare cases, you may need to reconfigure the scan.

Wireless Assessment

Traditional wired networks have the advantage of all being physically connected. Wireless networks, on the other hand, are connected only by radio waves. This can actually present some challenges with vulnerability assessments. A variety of tools, both hardware and software, are used to assess wireless vulnerabilities. To assess vulnerabilities over wireless media, specialized wireless network cards may be required so that they may be able to intercept traffic not designated for a particular host. This is often called placing the card into *monitor* or *promiscuous* mode. Not every wireless network card is capable of being placed in those modes of operation, and Windows, in particular, does not have wireless network card drivers built into it natively to take advantage of those modes. Usually, you would have to purchase third-party drivers along with specialized wireless network cards to use those capture modes in Windows operating systems. Linux distributions usually are capable of placing wireless cards into either of those modes, provided you have a card with a chipset that supports it.

As with traditional wired network vulnerability assessment tools, a wide variety of wireless tools are available. Obviously, we can't cover every available tool in this book, but the three specific tools mentioned on the CySA+ objectives—Aircrack-ng, Reaver, and oclHashcat—will be discussed in the next few paragraphs.

Aircrack-ng

Aircrack-ng is an open-source suite of wireless assessment tools typically found on Linux distributions, although it has also been ported to Windows operating systems. Aircrack-ng can be used to monitor wireless networks, intercept traffic, disrupt wireless communication between hosts, and even crack wireless keys, such as those used in WEP and both WPA2 and WPA3. Aircrack-ng consists of several separate tools, each with a specific purpose. Table 1.4-2 lists some of the more commonly used tools found in the Aircrack-ng suite, as well as some of their more useful functions.

Reaver

Reaver is a wireless vulnerability assessment tool that has a specific purpose. Reaver is used to launch attacks against wireless access points that use the Wi-Fi Protected Setup (WPS) feature. When this feature/protocol was included in wireless access points, it was designed as a way for users to connect to a wireless access point without having to remember the wireless access key or any configuration information. WPS unfortunately has a major flaw in how it validates the WPS password, or PIN, required for connection. Reaver takes advantage of the fact that

TABLE 1.4-2   Aircrack-ng Tools and Their Functions

Tool	Function	Usage
Airmon-ng	Enables monitor mode on wireless interfaces	# airmon-ng <start|stop> <interface> [channel] or airmon-ng <check|check kill>
Aircrack-ng	Used to crack 802.11 WEP and WPA/WPA2-PSK keys	# aircrack-ng [options] <capture file(s)>
Airodump-ng	Used to capture raw 802.11 frames on a particular channel	# airodump-ng <options> <interface>
Aireplay-ng	Used to inject frames during a wireless attack	# aireplay-ng <options> <replay interface>

the PIN is divided up into two halves, and each half is validated by the access point separately. This has the effect of limiting the key space available for the key, which allows Reaver to quickly crack that portion of the key. It's worth noting that Reaver must use a wireless interface that has been put into monitor mode already. Reaver is typically used as a command-line interface tool and is included with the penetration testing distribution Kali Linux. The tool is straightforward to use; you simply include the -i and-b switches, which specify the interface and the MAC address of the wireless access point, respectively, as indicated in the following example:

```
#reaver -i wlan0mon -b 00:90:4C:C1:BC:21
```

The best way to prevent this type of attack is to simply disable WPS on the access point.

oclHashcat

oclHashcat (sometimes referred to simply as Hashcat, from its previous versions) is a modern password-cracking tool that takes advantage of the high-end graphics processors found on newer computers. Because these high-end graphics cards (typically used by gamers or others who require high-performance video graphics) have dedicated CPU cores and memory, they can be used to perform complex mathematical operations quickly and separately from the primary CPU in the computer. This can speed up password-cracking operations by several orders of magnitude faster than what normally might be performed on a typical computer, which must share its CPU with the operating system and other applications.

oclHashcat supports a wide variety of password-hashing algorithms, including MD4, MD5, and the secure hashing algorithm (SHA) family. It also supports the secure network protocols that use many of these hashing algorithms, including Kerberos, NTLM, TACACS+, DNSSEC, and others. Additionally, it can crack passwords that are specific to particular applications, including those created in 7-Zip and VeraCrypt.

Hashcat can use a variety of common password attack methods, including brute force attacks, dictionary attacks, hybrid attacks, and many others. It comes standard with Kali Linux as well, although you can download versions of it for Windows and macOS.

Cloud Infrastructure Assessment

While cloud solutions are becoming more common in day-to-day business, managing a cloud infrastructure can be more complex than it seems at first. One of the key issues for cybersecurity analysts is the issue of monitoring parts of their infrastructure that are either connected to the cloud or actually a part of the cloud and hosted by another organization. There are challenges to securing a cloud infrastructure, and those include assessing risk and scanning for vulnerabilities within the infrastructure. This is an issue that must be addressed in the contract your organization may have with the cloud service provider. There are likely security responsibilities that are shared between your organization and the provider. Vulnerability scanning may be one of those shared responsibilities, in that your provider may have a responsibility and exclusive power over scanning off-premises parts of the infrastructure. This is something that needs to be determined in the contract negotiations with the provider.

Having said that, there are several tools available to security analysts to assess the security of cloud infrastructure services that an organization may employ. The three key ones you'll need to know for the exam are Scout Suite, Prowler, and Pacu, which we will discuss next.

Scout Suite

Scout Suite is an open-source security auditing tool developed by the NCC Group. It uses application programming interfaces (APIs) exposed by cloud service providers. Scout Suite can gather configuration data and show potential attack surfaces for cloud infrastructures.

Scout Suite can support a variety of cloud providers, including Amazon Web Services, Microsoft Azure, Google Cloud Platform, Alibaba Cloud, and Oracle Cloud Infrastructure. Scout Suite is a series of Python scripts, and its rules for each type of cloud service are created and stored in a customized JSON file. Its results can be viewed and imported into a wide variety of formats. Scout Suite should be used only when you have appropriate contracts and/or service agreements that allow you to use it in your provider's cloud environment.

Prowler

Prowler is a cloud security tool specifically developed for analyzing best security practices of Amazon Web Services (AWS) cloud infrastructures. Prowler uses the Center for Internet Security (CIS) AWS Foundations Benchmark and other security checks that focus on privacy, particularly the General Data Protection Regulation (GDPR) and Health Insurance Portability and Accountability Act (HIPAA) privacy requirements. It is a command-line tool and can currently run over 140 separate checks against the organization's AWS implementation. It is also useful for auditing best security practices, forensics, and system hardening. As with many other assessment tools, it can output its reports in a multitude of formats, including comma-separated values (CSV). It runs primarily on Linux and macOS.

Pacu

Pacu is a cloud security tool that goes one step further and is an effective penetration testing tool for AWS cloud services. Pacu is written in Python and provides many automated attack scripts. It consists of over 35 Python modules that enable a plethora of penetration testing tasks, including infrastructure reconnaissance, persistence, privilege escalation, system enumeration, sensitive data exfiltration, and even manipulation of logs. Like Prowler, Pacu is supported on Linux and macOS.

 CAUTION Before you use any cloud-based security tools, make sure you are within your right to do so, as specified in your service agreement with your cloud service provider. Failure to do so may result in legal issues between your organization and the cloud service provider, since you may be considered an attacker and not as an analyst performing a legitimate, authorized security test.

REVIEW

Objective 1.4: Given a scenario, analyze the output from common vulnerability assessment tools   In this module, we reviewed several vulnerability assessment tools, including application and infrastructure tools. Popular application tools, specifically web application scanners, include OWASP ZAP, Burp Suite, Nikto, and Arachni. Each of these tools searches out and identifies common web application vulnerabilities, which include cross-site scripting, input validation issues, and injection weaknesses. We also looked at software assessment tools and techniques, including static analysis, dynamic analysis, reverse engineering, and fuzzing. Static analysis involves analyzing the code using either automated or manual techniques. Dynamic analysis requires us to run the code in a protected environment, such as a sandbox, to determine how it executes. Reverse engineering allows us to disassemble unknown binaries to determine their characteristics and function. Finally, fuzzing allows us to send a wide variety of unorthodox input into an application to determine how it will react, thus identifying any unusual behaviors or unexpected vulnerabilities.

The infrastructure tools we examined include those designed to enumerate networks, scan for vulnerabilities, assess wireless networks, and audit cloud infrastructures. We discussed network enumeration techniques using both active and passive enumeration, as well as tools we would use to perform enumeration, including the ubiquitous Nmap. We also discussed specialized attack tools, including hping and responder. You also learned about network vulnerability scanners, including the ever-popular Nessus, OpenVAS, and Qualys. Aircrack-ng is a suite of tools used to intercept and disrupt wireless network traffic. Reaver is used to defeat the WPS protections on an access point, and oclHashcat is used to crack passwords that can be intercepted from wireless or wired networks as well as applications. Finally, we discussed the issues involved with auditing cloud infrastructures, and we reviewed three critical tools that can be used to assess an organization's cloud presence: Scout Suite, Prowler, and Pacu.

1.4 QUESTIONS

1. Dawn is a cybersecurity analyst who works in a security operations center. Part of her duties involve routinely scanning for vulnerabilities in the organization's infrastructure. She was recently tasked with analyzing code for a web application that will be implemented soon on the organization's web servers. Dawn needs to review the code using a variety of methods, but more importantly, she needs to know about the security issues that might occur while the code is executing. Which of the following would be the best method for achieving this?

   A. Static analysis

   B. Dynamic analysis

   C. Fuzzing

   D. Reverse engineering

2. Bobby is a cybersecurity analyst who works at a major university. He routinely must assess the university's wireless network for vulnerabilities. He has been tasked with determining if there are easy-to-guess passwords for the wireless network. Which of the following tools might he use to intercept wireless passwords and attempt to crack them?

   A. Nessus

   B. OpenVAS

   C. Reaver

   D. Aircrack-ng

3. Barbara has been authorized to conduct a security assessment on her organization's AWS cloud infrastructure. In addition to ordinary vulnerability scanning, she has been authorized to perform penetration tests on the infrastructure. Which of the following tools would be best suited for this task?

   A. Pacu

   B. Scout Suite

   C. OpenVAS

   D. oclHashcat

4. Tom is performing a routine vulnerability scan on the company network. He just updated the organization's subscription to Nessus and altered several preconfigured scan options. Once he completed the scan, he noticed that the scan results yielded little information back from most of the hosts on the network. Tom knows that he should have gotten back a great deal more information from the scan. Which of the following could have contributed to this issue?

   A. Credentialed scan

   B. Non-credentialed scan

   C. Incorrect subnet mask

   D. Out-of-date scan plug-ins

1.4 ANSWERS

1. **B**   Dynamic analysis allows an analyst to observe the characteristics, function, and behavior of executing code in a controlled environment, such as a sandbox.

2. **D**   Aircrack-ng is a suite of tools that can be used to monitor and intercept wireless traffic, disrupt wireless traffic, and collect and decrypt password hashes.

3. **A**   Pacu is not only a vulnerability assessment tool but also a Python-based penetration test tool suite.

4. **B**   A non-credentialed scan typically does not have the privileges necessary to gather data from a host, so it will return limited data. Tom should have performed a credentialed scan and used administrative-level privileges in the scan configuration.

Objective 1.5   # Explain the threats and vulnerabilities associated with specialized technology

Many IT specialists, and even new cybersecurity analysts, have worked with the basic technologies that we see in a corporate environment, including Windows and Linux hosts, possibly switches and routers, and maybe even firewalls or intrusion detection systems. These are all very standard systems in a corporate network infrastructure. However, there are also specialized technologies that many cybersecurity analysts don't get exposed to during their entire professional career; when they finally do, very often they may not know how to interact with those technologies. In this module, we're going to discuss several of these non-standard technologies, including mobile devices, system-on-chip, embedded operating systems, real-time operating systems, building automation systems, and several others. Although we're not going to go in depth on the particular technologies we discuss, we are going to discuss the threats and vulnerabilities inherent to these technologies. An in-depth discussion of the technical aspects of each of these technologies is beyond the scope of this book, and there are better books written to describe them. However, by the end of this module, you'll be familiar with some of these technologies at a basic foundational level, and more importantly, their inherent threats and vulnerabilities, to be better prepared for the exam.

Mobile Devices

As mentioned earlier, we're not going to go in depth on the wide range of mobile technologies, devices, operating systems, protocols, and so forth. We are going to discuss, however, the threats and vulnerabilities associated with the general class of mobile devices. Mobile devices, of course, include smartphones, laptops, tablets, PDAs, and a variety of other smart devices that may include even watches, cameras, and other specialized devices. All of these devices process data in some form or fashion that someone might like to obtain, whether it is personal data or business-related data. Most of these devices have some type of storage capacity where data is permanently stored and may be accessible simply by plugging the device into a computer.

By their very nature, mobile devices are, well, mobile. This means that they are small and can be easily removed from corporate areas. While the advantages of mobile computing power and instant information access far outweigh any disadvantages, some considerations must be discussed.

Mobile Device Threats and Vulnerabilities

The first and most obvious threat to mobile devices is theft. Mobile devices are stolen every day. Most of them are likely stolen by people who just want to take advantage of an opportunity to grab a cool-looking device. Typically, those threats are easily mitigated by the fact that most mobile devices are also password or PIN protected. There are enterprising thieves, though, who may be able to take advantage of lax security on a device and access a user's personal data, including photographs, e-mails, and other information. Many ordinary users don't bother to secure their mobile devices as well as they should. The same is true for the loss of mobile devices. Even if a device is simply lost, it can be found by someone who might unscrupulously try to access data on the device.

In addition to physical issues, there's also a wide variety of other inherent threats and vulnerabilities. These include network vulnerabilities, software or app vulnerabilities, and device vulnerabilities. Network vulnerabilities can manifest by using insecure protocols, such as older versions of SSL, but can also take the form of mobile device–specific protocols, such as those used in cellular communications.

Application vulnerabilities are similar to software vulnerabilities also found in traditional systems, such as workstations and servers, for example. Non-secure programming methods can result in issues associated with a lack of input validation, buffer overflows, and even web-based attacks. Like their larger system counterparts, mobile apps must be developed in a secure environment and tested for a variety of security issues. This also includes the operating systems that run mobile devices.

Cross-Reference

Software assurance best practices are discussed at length in Objective 2.2.

Device vulnerabilities can present themselves as issues with how the device is constructed and what hardware is used. Just as it is in larger systems, hardware can be counterfeit or subverted if there is a compromised supply chain in the manufacturing and distribution process. It is incumbent on device vendors to track hardware components throughout the entire device lifecycle, from manufacture through testing, and finally assembly. Potentially compromised hardware could include wireless transmitting components, the CPU, RAM, and other sensitive pieces of hardware.

Cross-Reference

Hardware assurance best practices are discussed at length in Objective 2.3.

Corporate Device Considerations

Corporate devices, whether owned by the organization or shared with a user in a bring-your-own-device (BYOD) infrastructure, may offer a few more protections for the device and its data, but it is still subject to theft, loss, and the other vulnerabilities we discussed. In the case of a corporate device, the user may be targeted specifically, rather than randomly, to obtain sensitive business information about the organization. This would imply that the theft may be premeditated if the thief knows that the device is used in a corporate environment. Motivations might include industrial espionage, to gain a competitive advantage, to steal sensitive or proprietary information, or even blackmail.

Mobile Device Protections

In a corporate environment, mobile devices should be managed centrally. There are a plethora of mobile device management (MDM) enterprise applications that can easily inventory, update remotely, and secure mobile devices. To counter theft or loss, the device can also be remotely wiped to erase any corporate data. Some of the protections that a corporate environment can offer or impose on a mobile device include the following:

- Geofencing (alerting or causing the device to not function if it leaves a specific physical area)
- Remote wipe or erasure
- Remote patching and updating
- Network access control to prevent an unsecured device from joining the network
- Remote messaging to someone who might find a lost device
- Containerization of data to separate personal from business data on the device
- GPS tracking, since most mobile devices these days are GPS enabled

All of these protections, when used in combination, can be very effective encountering any threats and inherent vulnerabilities that introduce risk into the mobile device infrastructure.

 EXAM TIP   The number-one threat affecting mobile devices is theft.

Internet of Things (IoT)

The term *Internet of Things* (IoT) describes a wide variety of non-traditional devices connected to the Internet. These include devices that are not necessarily considered computers, servers, traditional network devices, and so on. You'll see these devices in homes, such as refrigerators and smart televisions, and these days they may be connected to the home network or even the Internet. You might even see home temperature controls that can be connected to the Internet so that a homeowner can monitor them and change them remotely, usually over a smartphone app. IoT devices aren't just used in the home for consumer convenience, however. They are also used in industry, and some examples include power and utility company monitoring devices, which may be little more than reduced footprint computers connected to the Internet. In any case, IoT devices have caused an explosion in the number of devices connected to the Internet to make life more efficient for all of us. However, there's also a massive explosion in system and device vulnerability, since many devices that were previously considered secure because they were isolated and protected are now connected to a network where they may be accessed remotely. In this module, we're going to discuss the vulnerabilities and threats, as well as some mitigations for some of these devices. We're going to talk about embedded devices, physical access control devices, building automation systems, vehicles, and industrial control systems. These are but a sampling of the wide variety of devices available that are not considered traditional computing devices but are still connected to the Internet, accessible from a network, and vulnerable to attack.

All IoT devices and technologies we will discuss during this module suffer from some of the same threats and vulnerabilities, including the following:

- Insecure network connectivity using older protocols
- Weak or no encryption mechanisms
- Low computing or process power
- Limited facility for patching or configuration changes
- Weak or no authentication
- Limited signal range
- Proprietary parts and systems that are not always interoperable with others
- Physical access control vulnerabilities
- Difficulty in performing vulnerability scans on the system

Embedded Devices

An embedded system is unique in that it may appear like a traditional computer, such as a workstation, but it runs a specialized operating system that is usually embedded on a device's firmware, such as a computer chip. Embedded systems are difficult to update, which means they can become vulnerable if weaknesses are found in their underlying operating system configuration, since they can't be easily patched. Embedded systems are used in a wide variety of technical applications, such as flight control computers, industrial control systems, utilities, medical devices, and so on. We will discuss the threats and vulnerabilities involved with some of these embedded systems, including real-time operating systems, system-on-chip, and field programmable gate arrays.

Real-Time Operating System (RTOS)

A real-time operating system is a specialized operating system, sometimes developed from an existing operating system such as Windows or Linux, that is run on electronic devices, usually system control type devices. An RTOS is installed on an electronic chip, rather than on a hard drive, and is static. That is to say, it is not easily updatable, patchable, or configurable once it is embedded into the electronic chip. The advantage of using an RTOS is that it's extremely fast and requires very little processor or memory overhead. The disadvantage is that it's hard to update in the event vulnerabilities are discovered in it. Many RTOSs are either Linux- or Windows-based, or something altogether different. There are even embedded RTOSs based on old Windows XP, which obviously presents issues in that any version of Windows XP is no longer supported by Microsoft, and as such there are no new security patches or updates provided for it. Another example of a popular RTOS is VxWorks. VxWorks is used in devices such as medical equipment, industrial controllers, and so on. Organizations must take extreme mitigations when one of these RTOSs is used and discovered as vulnerable. If the RTOS cannot be replaced, updated, or reconfigured, as is very often the case with medical devices, there are a few other mitigations the organization may take. These include segmentation and isolation from other network hosts, the use of encryption and strong authentication across network connections that may connect to the device, and even increased physical protection to prevent the device from being compromised.

 EXAM TIP   The biggest vulnerability with a real-time operating system is the fact that it is not easily patched or reconfigured when a vulnerability is discovered, due to its static nature.

System-on-Chip (SoC)

A system-on-chip is an embedded system in which software and hardware are integrated into a single computer chip. This computer chip is self-contained and consists of a processor, system RAM, and other critical components miniaturized on a single integrated circuit. The advantage of having a system-on-chip implemented into a piece of hardware is that it's extremely fast, self-contained, and self-reliant. Also, it uses much less power and is more efficient. However, one of the downsides of using this configuration is that it is a single point of failure in hardware. If a system-on-chip becomes unstable or otherwise breaks, the entire electronic assembly or piece of hardware will fail. System or hardware redundancy would be a mitigating factor for this particular vulnerability. System-on-chip also suffers from the same vulnerability that an RTOS and other embedded systems endure, in the sense that they are embedded, and their configuration is static in nature, so it is sometimes difficult to update and patch them.

Field Programmable Gate Array (FPGA)

A *field programmable gate array* (FPGA) is an improved version of a system-on-chip configuration. FPGAs are used in a wide variety of electronic devices, including medical devices, automotive electronics, industrial control systems, and even consumer electronics. The advantage of using an FPGA is that it is more flexible and allows programmers, and even users, to install firmware updates to reconfigure the hardware so that new software functionality, as well as security mitigations, can be implemented on it. If you've ever used an entertainment device that connects to wireless networking, such as a smart Blu-ray player or Smart TV, then you've seen an FPGA in action when it prompts you to go online and perform system updates to its firmware.

Vulnerabilities with FPGAs include those traditionally found on embedded systems, but since they are more accessible for change and reprogramming, they are also vulnerable to attackers who may be able to access the hardware description language and update processes to introduce malicious configuration or even malware into the system. Mitigations would include tight control over the reprogramming and update process and other system-level security mitigations such as manufacturer-enforced integrity checks on firmware updates, strong access controls and authentication, enhanced security protocols, and, of course, physical security.

 EXAM TIP Remember that field programmable gate arrays are somewhat more flexible than system-on-chip configurations. FPGAs can be found in a wide variety of modern IoT devices because their firmware, software, patches, and configurations are more easily updatable.

Physical Access Controls

Physical access controls are greatly facilitated by automated control systems. Examples of physical controls that are enhanced by using embedded or automated specialized devices include the following:

- Badge readers
- Secure electronic door systems
- Closed-circuit television systems
- Physical intrusion detection systems
- Alarm systems
- Biometric authentication systems

Very often, embedded or automated devices are seen as sensors, so they can read an RFID badge or scan a fingerprint or accept whatever identification mechanism a person is required to use to gain physical entry to a facility or controlled area. These physical controls are typically connected to an overarching identification and authentication database and an integrated security system. This database uses stored user data to authenticate based on the identification method presented. It can also record and audit where the user has been at various points in the facility, at various times.

Physical access control vulnerabilities include some that are complex and require a concentrated technical effort to exploit, as well as those that take advantage of human vulnerability. These include, from least to most sophisticated, the following:

- Tailgating
- Social engineering
- Badge duplication or cloning
- Signal replay

Physical access control vulnerabilities and threats can be mitigated by layered defenses, including the human variety. Human beings are an integral part of physical access controls.

Alarms and camera systems must be monitored; guards should be employed in sensitive areas along with automated controls. Employees and other personnel must be vigilant to potential physical threats. The electronic automated systems that connect to physical sensors must also be secured using traditional methods, including secure authentication, encryption, strict access controls, and so on.

EXAM TIP   Traditional physical access controls, such as doors, gates, and so on, benefit from automated control systems that can centralize physical access control.

Building Automation Systems

As an extension of the discussion on physical access controls, many automated electronic specialized devices are used in automation systems used in buildings and other facilities. In addition to controlling physical access, building automation systems, as these are commonly referred to, can help control other aspects of physical security, including the environment and safety.

Environmental controls, often automated through sensors and computerized systems, come in the form of automated temperature and humidity controls, moisture controls, and so on. These controls are usually observed by humans but typically controlled through sensors that detect variations from established baselines. Again, these are usually in areas such as temperature or humidity. If the temperature exceeds a certain predetermined level, the sensor will alert the automation system, which will take steps to turn on the HVAC system and attempt to cool the area and lower the temperature. The same would occur if the temperature is too low, or if the humidity is too low or too high. Sensors can also detect a variety of other undesirable conditions, such as floods, for example, if water levels get to be too high in sensitive areas. Again, humans must also monitor the systems to ensure they are functioning properly.

Safety is another critical function automated controls can assist with. Sensors located throughout a facility can be used to detect smoke as well as variations in light and heat that can indicate a fire. The sensors can then trigger automatic controls to turn on fire suppression systems, set off fire alarms, and automatically unlock doors along a fire escape route. Sensors can also detect oxygen and gas variations, which might indicate unsafe conditions, such as a gas leak. All of these different types of sensors and automated systems are part of an overarching building automation system and can be integrated with computerized systems that also provide for physical access, intrusion detection, logging, and other functions.

EXAM TIP   Building automation systems include not only those allowing physical access control but also environmental and safety control. Examples of environmental and safety controls that are enhanced with automation include fire detection and suppression, gas leaks, and flood control.

Vehicles and Drones

Automated systems are also used in various modes of transportation. The flight and ground systems of all types of aircraft depend on automated systems for a wide variety of tasks and processes. This includes flight control, location, navigation, radar, and communications. Even ground vehicles, such as modern cars and trucks, use automated systems for everything from temperature sensing to diagnosing engine issues. Drones are also a modern marvel used by everyone from hobbyists to research scientists, soldiers, and surveyors, for all manner of useful tests. In the next couple sections, we discuss the use of automated systems in vehicles and drones.

Vehicles and the Controller Area Network (CAN) Bus

More and more modern vehicles are manufactured with automated systems integrated into them. These automated systems can perform a wide variety of functions, including managing and monitoring environmental controls, safety controls, and system performance. If you've ever seen your automobile console display engine statistics, such as RPMs, temperature, and so on, then you have witnessed vehicle automation systems in use. Another more sophisticated use of this technology is through the standard vehicle OBD (onboard diagnostics) port, which can provide data to a specialized device that can read engine failure codes and determine other automobile performance issues. The standard, known as OBD-II, is essentially an onboard embedded computer that monitors various automobile factors such as emissions, speed, mileage, temperature, and so on. This embedded system notifies you through your check engine and other console monitor lights if there is an issue. Since this is a vehicle standard used throughout the industry, this embedded computer uses a standardized 16-pin port, usually located under the driver's dashboard, where a reader can be plugged in to download diagnostics codes. Increasingly, these automated systems have been integrated with communication technologies, such as cellular and wireless networking. This is useful so that a repair shop or car dealership can communicate with your vehicle at various points (while it's on the road or in the parking lot, for example) and figure out potential trouble issues with it before it even rolls into the repair bay. Vehicle health and performance data, as well as location, is often reported automatically through these systems to the dealership or even the user via a smartphone app. This is all made possible by automated systems.

One of the core underlying technologies of vehicle automation is called the *controller area network* (CAN) bus. This is a commonly used vehicle standard that defines how independent vehicle control system components are connected and communicate with each other. These components communicate independently with each other in each vehicle and do not require a centralized controller located at a dealership for this to take place.

Threats and vulnerabilities associated with this system include a lack of communications signal encryption between individual internal vehicle components as well as the entities who might receive this data over wireless communications networks. There's also no standard mechanism built in for authentication in the event an over-the-air update to the vehicle's control system firmware is initiated. This makes it possible for someone with the right technology and knowledge of the vehicle's systems to transmit potentially malicious updates to the vehicle. This is not only theoretical; it has been physically shown to be possible through proof-of-concept demonstrations by various security researchers. This directly affects the performance and safety of the vehicle, since a flawed update or intentional communication to the vehicle could cause it to turn off a safety feature and possibly crash, at worst, or at least seriously inconvenience the driver. Consider what would happen if a malicious actor turned off the airbag system or even caused your fuel gauge to read as full on a very long trip between gas stations. Neither of these scenarios would be desirable, and could even possibly be dangerous.

> **EXAM TIP**   The CAN bus is a standardized architecture protocol used in vehicles to facilitate communications between internal components.

Drones and Other Unmanned Aerial Vehicles (UAVs)

It has been said that a drone is nothing more than a flying robot; at first, when these new types of vehicles were invented, they were primarily used by the military. These are the large-scale vehicles that more resemble aircraft than simple flying toys. They have been used in armed conflicts to deliver munitions, launch missiles, perform surveillance activities, interdict supply lines, and provide secure communications on the battlefield. These larger-scale vehicles are typically called *unmanned aerial vehicles,* or UAVs. While most UAVs use highly complex automated electronic systems, they can also be controlled using state-of-the-art, hardened tactical ground stations that are mounted in vans, trucks, or Humvees. They are controlled using a wide variety of secure communications, including radio, line-of-sight microwave, and so on.

The little brothers of UAVs are typically called *drones*. Drones evolved initially as small flying toys but then gained the interest of hobbyists and working professionals. The simplest of drones can fly a few hundred feet and take high-quality photographs or high-definition movies for families on vacation. However, the more upscale models contain higher-quality cameras that are used by professional photographers, land surveyors, and even law enforcement. Law enforcement and the intelligence community use drones for crime investigation and antiterrorism activities, such as communications jamming, eavesdropping, and high-resolution, long-distance photography.

UAVs and drones both suffer from some common threats and vulnerabilities, although not always of the same caliber. The larger military-grade drones can suffer from communications jamming as well as from directed missiles or other heavy munitions being fired at them. There have also been rumored instances of drones suffering from communications takeover by hostile forces, which can then direct them to land in enemy territory for further examination or send them off course and force them to crash. And even systems in these sophisticated pieces of machinery can suffer from software flaws that can be exploited by a malicious actor if the conditions are right and they have access to the systems either through faulty supply chain management or physical access.

Commercial and recreational drones, on the other hand, can also suffer from some of the same vulnerabilities, albeit on a smaller scale. These can be unintentionally jammed by a stronger signal, can be knocked out of the sky by small arms fire, and can also suffer from firmware or software flaws (via the apps that sometimes control them) that can be exploited.

In addition to the vulnerabilities and threats drones can experience, drones also can present their own threats. For example, it's not uncommon for hobbyists and other individuals to violate the airspace of commercial aircraft, either accidentally or intentionally, or to fly within areas that are restricted for safety or security reasons. Drones also can infringe on the privacy of individuals, particularly if they have powerful enough eavesdropping equipment, such as microphones or cameras that can invade privacy.

Mitigations to counter typical threats that drones can suffer from include being aware of the power and range restrictions for the model drone you have, making sure its software is kept up to date through vendor firmware updates, ensuring the apps you use to control the drone are updated, and having general situational awareness.

Industrial Control Systems

Industrial control systems (ICSs), also sometimes called *cyber-physical systems,* are systems used to integrate specialized software with physical devices. Also sometimes referred to as "operational technology," these systems use specialized software that can be written in a multitude of programming languages and run various operating systems, from the centralized computer on the network. However, this technology communicates with specific automated devices that control systems and processes. Think of factory automation systems, for example. We'll discuss a few examples of these types of systems, such as workflow and process automation systems, as well as the systems that might control utilities such as power grids, for example.

Workflow and Process Automation Systems

Yet another example of the use of automated systems is in professional and industrial settings. These can be simple activities where automated systems are used as timers, simple sensors, and single-function devices, all the way through complex systems that are used to run factories and assembly lines. These automation systems can be used to control the timing on the assembly line, ensure the exact amount of a chemical is poured or used in a process, or ensure that two critical pieces of an assembly are put together and sealed correctly. There are far more actual and possible uses for automation systems in factories and other workflow processes than we can mention here, but suffice it to say that a huge majority of any modern manufacturing or assembly process is controlled by automated systems. These systems, again, also suffer from the same threats and vulnerabilities the other automated technologies suffer from.

Supervisory Control and Data Acquisition (SCADA)

Supervisory control and data acquisition (SCADA) systems control a wide variety of geographically separated systems, including utilities such as power grids, water treatment plants, and even nuclear power plants. What distinguishes SCADA implementations from other types of ICS or consumer-grade automation systems are their sheer scale and geographical scope. Most SCADA systems are geographically dispersed and may have no permanent human presence, or are minimally crewed or only periodically maintained by people, and rely on wide-area communications systems for monitoring between sites. SCADA systems use highly specialized software, as well as specialized hardware control systems. Most SCADA systems have built-in redundancies and for the most part are fairly resilient, except where it concerns the cybersecurity aspect. This is where many of these systems are vulnerable.

The same vulnerabilities inherent in other automated types of systems are also the ones found in SCADA systems. Network weaknesses include non-secure communications systems and protocols, lack of encryption, and poor authentication between devices and systems. Some of the highly specialized software used in the systems is dated and not often patched or updated. This software is also proprietary and uses proprietary protocols, such as MODBUS (discussed next), which doesn't easily lend itself to traditional security controls. Many of these systems have never had a vulnerability scan on them, or it is difficult to conduct scans on them because of their proprietary nature, geographical dispersion, and isolation. Physical vulnerabilities are also more prominent with SCADA systems, as they often exist in uncrewed facilities that may or may not have adequate physical security controls in place.

MODBUS

MODBUS is a communications protocol developed in 1979 by Schneider Electric (then called Modicon) for use in industrial electronic automation systems. For those of you familiar with the popular Open Systems Interconnect (OSI) networking model, this protocol takes place at layers 1 and 2 of the OSI model, as it is a physical and signaling protocol. It is primarily used in programmable logic controllers (PLCs) and is often considered the de facto communications protocol for industrial control systems. MODBUS is both open-source and royalty-free, making its use more widespread in the industrial automation industry. Management and ownership of the protocol was transferred from Schneider Electric to the Modbus Organization in 2004, which is a consortium of industry partners and manufacturers that build MODBUS-compliant devices.

 EXAM TIP   MODBUS is an older industry-standard communications protocol used in a large majority of industrial control systems and SCADA networks.

REVIEW

Objective 1.5: Explain the threats and vulnerabilities associated with specialized technology   In this module, we discussed specialized devices and technologies—specifically non-traditional devices such as mobile devices, embedded devices, physical access controls, building automation systems, vehicles and drones, and industrial control systems. Mobile devices have unique threats and vulnerabilities, but the largest one is probably physical theft or loss. They also suffer from threats that affect network communications and applications, and they have inherent vulnerabilities resulting from poor device design and development. Mobile device protections include geo-fencing, corporate MDM implementations, remote wipe, and location tracking.

The Internet of Things is a term describing non-traditional devices with embedded operating systems that serve to control devices traditionally not connected or physically isolated. This could include consumer devices such as refrigerators and televisions, but also includes electronic systems that help to control aircraft, factories, utility grids, and so on. Embedded devices are usually found with real-time operating systems, which are implemented for speed, efficiency, and limited functionality. They also include integrated software and hardware in system-on-chip implementations, as well as the more flexible FPGA systems.

Physical access controls not only include automation systems that control physical entry into restricted areas, but also environmental systems. Examples of physical access controls include badge readers, electronic doors, and temperature and humidity monitoring systems. Building automation systems also include environmental and safety systems as well, including fire detection systems, fire suppression systems, and flood monitoring. Many of these systems use older or proprietary software applications, hardware, and communications protocols.

Vehicles are increasingly being manufactured with automated systems that help control their environmental and safety functions, as well as the engine and chassis systems' performance and function. You learned that the CAN bus is the primary technology used in vehicle automation systems. Drones include the military variety as well as the hobbyist and commercial versions. Both vehicles and drones are subject to the same vulnerabilities that other specialized devices are, including network protocol issues, application vulnerabilities, communications jamming, and the inability to easily update patches and configurations.

Industrial control systems include those that are implemented to manage workflow and automate different assembly processes, as well as SCADA systems. SCADA systems are characterized by larger systems, such as power utility grids, which may be geographically separated and not closely monitored by human beings. They rely heavily on proprietary software, specialized hardware, and special communications protocols. They are also vulnerable to the same vulnerabilities as other automation systems. The primary technology used in SCADA systems is MODBUS, which consists of lower-level communications protocols.

1.5 QUESTIONS

1. Alberto is a cybersecurity analyst who works for a major power company. He's trying to improve the security of some of the older SCADA systems the power company uses to monitor and control power fluctuations. Which of the following protocols will he most likely encounter in his system configuration upgrades?

   A. MODBUS

   B. CAN bus

   C. IPX/SPX

   D. AppleTalk

2. Rhonda is a cybersecurity analyst who works for an automotive manufacturer. She's helping to design a next-generation vehicle automation system and wants to ensure that security is designed throughout the system. Which of the following improvements should she make to existing vehicle automation system design?

   A. Implement MODBUS as the primary protocol for the vehicle automation system.

   B. Implement communications encryption throughout the entire system.

   C. Implement CAN bus as the primary protocol for the vehicle automation system.

   D. Require username and password authentication for each of the components of the system.

3. Taylor is part of the security team hardening automation systems in a military-grade UAV system. Which of the following is *not* a concern when designing cybersecurity for the drone's internal computer systems?

   A. Encrypted communications

   B. Strong authentication

   C. Security patching and configuration updates

   D. Shielding the systems against possible munitions attack

4. José is a cybersecurity analyst tasked with improving the physical access controls in an aging production facility. He would like to be able to automate building entry, review audit logs of who entered restricted areas, and be able to grant specific access to restricted areas for certain individuals. Currently, there is no system in place to accomplish those objectives, and individuals must each have an old-fashioned brass key to unlock a heavy, manual steel door to enter a restricted area. Which of the following would be an ideal solution for José to implement?

   A. Implement automated physical access controls tied to a security database that can track individual users' entry as well as assign access permissions to individuals.

   B. Implement automated physical access controls such as badge sensors and proximity readers.

   C. Replace antiquated brass key locks with an entry control guard who can visually allow access to certain individuals and log that information in manual logs.

   D. Keep existing locking mechanisms in place, but implement a security database that records which individuals are allowed entry into restricted areas.

1.5 ANSWERS

1. **A**   Alberto will likely encounter the older MODBUS protocol in his SCADA systems.

2. **B**   Rhonda should implement communications encryption throughout the system. MODBUS is not the best solution, because it is used in ICS automation. CAN bus is already an older protocol used in vehicle automation systems that do not natively support encryption. Using username and password authentication would seriously interfere with the quick and efficient operation of a vehicle control system and could affect safety.

3. **D** Shielding the system against a potential munitions attack is not a concern for including cybersecurity into the design of the internal computer automated systems of the drone. All the other choices are design considerations for securing drone automation systems.

4. **A** José should implement automated physical access controls tied to a security database that can track individual users' entry as well as assign access permissions to individuals. None of the other choices meet all of the desired objectives.

Objective 1.6 Explain the threats and vulnerabilities associated with operating in the cloud

Traditional network and application architectures have given way to the trend of moving infrastructures to the *cloud*. As you probably already know, using the cloud is nothing more than using the resources of someone else's computing power, whether it be storage, CPU, network infrastructure, or even applications. *Cloud computing* simply means that you are using the resources of a *cloud service provider*. Typically, cloud infrastructures reside in large data centers, full of robust, resilient, high-powered computing networks. These large infrastructures are used to provide services to customers through various subscription models. The key thing to remember in terms of security is that your data and your processing is not confined to your enclosed, protected network. No matter how complex a cloud infrastructure is, the bottom line is that your data resides on someone else's computers. Therefore, you don't have complete control over who accesses the data as well as how it is used, stored, and protected. On the surface that sounds very scary, but as you'll see in this module, there are solid mitigations that can be put in place to protect your organization's information.

In this module, we're going to talk about cloud computing models and how they work, with specific emphasis on cloud threats and vulnerabilities. We will also discuss how to mitigate some of these threats and vulnerabilities.

Cloud Service Models

As mentioned, cloud computing is usually provided to customers through some sort of subscription-based model. Customers, whether they are individuals, small businesses, or even large multinational corporations, contract with cloud service providers for various services. This includes applications, infrastructures, data storage, security, and a multitude of other services. The reason the cloud service models exist is that, from an economic point of view, it makes sense to reduce operating costs by reducing the amount of infrastructure the organization has to manage. This includes physical servers, data center space, and, of course, the people who would be required to run the infrastructure. In a cloud service model, all of this is outsourced to a cloud service provider. The issues with using a cloud service model include data accessibility, service availability, performance, and shared responsibility. All of these different aspects of cloud computing should be detailed and resolved in the agreement between the organization and the cloud service provider.

The agreement or contract between the organization and the provider should include guaranteed service levels, responsibilities between both organizations, data protection requirements, legal liability, and so on. Most larger providers, such as Google, Microsoft, and Amazon, have standard agreements that effectively cover these items since they have the power of money, infrastructure, and reputation to ensure that data is kept secure. Smaller cloud providers may require a little bit more scrutiny and negotiation with their contracts. In any case, there should be guaranteed service levels, as well as details regarding the responsibilities of both parties.

In the next few sections, we discuss the different models that organizations can employ when using a cloud service provider. Organizations can use any one or combination of these models to get the services they need, based on their unique requirements. These are the most common models found in cloud computing offerings, but sometimes there is no defining line between them. We will discuss different cloud service models, including software, platform, infrastructure, and function as different services offerings.

Software as a Service (SaaS)

Software as a Service (SaaS) is probably the cloud service that most non-technical people, including individuals, small businesses, and large businesses, have heard of. If you're using a version of Microsoft 365, for example, as even many home users are, then you are using the SaaS cloud service. SaaS was probably the first major offering of cloud services. Essentially, the model involves you subscribing to general commercial off-the-shelf software, or even custom software, for a fee. The software resides "in the cloud" at the provider, and the software is accessible either through a web interface, a mobile device app, or, in some cases, even as a download. Although Microsoft 365 might be one of the most common examples of SaaS, you can get subscriptions to graphics suites, complex accounting software packages, and customer relationship packages. You can also get teleconference solutions and other remote productivity applications.

The advantages of SaaS are that you don't have to maintain custom software, and the software is almost always kept up to date because there's only one place to update it—and that's the cloud provider. Usually, new features or improvements are automatically included in the subscription. Security is also an advantage because any issues that are discovered are quickly updated centrally in the cloud provider's space. The organization doesn't have to worry about patching; the cloud vendor provides all of the service and support for the software. You also don't have the long-running problem of software piracy that you may have if individual copies of licensed software on CDs are kept at your business site. Collaboration is another advantage, in that multiple users can access the same software packages and share data between them seamlessly.

There are a few disadvantages of this model, but they likely don't outweigh the advantages. One disadvantage is that you're paying a monthly or yearly fee, versus buying the software license outright. Another disadvantage is that the organization, for the most part, cannot manage the software on its premises. Although it may manage the licensing to access cloud-based software, the cloud providers are pretty much in charge of updating the software, ensuring its availability, providing for its security, and so on. Although the cloud providers typically perform security patching updates as soon as vulnerabilities are discovered, there is a remote possibility that a zero-day vulnerability will be discovered and exploited before the vendor or the cloud provider is aware of it, which can affect millions of licensed users of the product.

Security vulnerabilities involved with SaaS are typically focused on identity and access management (IAM). This also includes data access by unauthorized persons. The organization has a responsibility to allow only those personnel authorized to access the software and the underlying data, but this is often not managed very well. Typically, there are more users from the organization who have access to the software and data than the cloud provider has on record, simply because the organization has given that access to more people than they have concurrent licenses for. While collaboration is a true advantage, it also can result in security vulnerabilities in that unauthorized persons may access data they are not intended to, because of the ease at which collaboration takes place. This makes it incumbent on the organization to manage authorization to access the cloud apps, as well as the data that supports them. Lack of the use of encryption by the organization can sometimes be an issue as well.

Platform as a Service (PaaS)

Platform as a Service (PaaS) is a step beyond SaaS. Rather than providing software for an organization to use, the cloud provider provisions a development environment so that the organization can develop its unique line-of-business applications. The organization can build its cloud-based applications for its use or to market to other businesses. Normally, an organization that would use the service cannot find a more specialized solution available as SaaS. They may have very unique data requirements, access control requirements, or interoperability requirements with other systems. In any event, PaaS gives them the advantages that a cloud service provider offers, while at the same time giving them more control over their development environment.

Since applications developed in a PaaS environment are more under the control of the organization, rather than the provider, it is incumbent upon the organization to build proper security into the cloud app, in the form of identification and authentication mechanisms, secure configuration, patching, encryption, and so on. Therefore, it makes sense that some of the chief vulnerabilities in a PaaS environment aren't necessarily the cloud service provider's environment but the security of the application developed in it by the organization. This makes it similar to typical in-house development models because the organization still must use a secure coding methodology and take into account vulnerabilities such as input validation, injection attacks, buffer overflow and other memory attacks, and so on.

Infrastructure as a Service (IaaS)

Infrastructure as a Service (IaaS) is also a widely used cloud service model. In this model, the cloud provider offers the organization the opportunity to manage its network without large overhead costs associated with acquiring, care, storage, and disposal of hardware assets. Cloud service vendors provide the hardware, network, and storage assets so that the organizational user can install and use any operating system, applications, and so on. The organization can move most, if not all, of its server services up to the cloud—on its Windows or Linux servers, for example. The cloud service provider can offer scalable solutions in the form of increased RAM, enterprise-level storage, multiple CPUs, and even GPUs that can be employed in a virtual server setting. The organization can then build its customized servers and network them together virtually using the cloud provider's assets. Another advantage of this model is that hosts can be easily backed up and re-created from copies of the virtual machines if there are issues with malware or service loss.

As with the PaaS model, the more control over cloud assets you give to the organization, the more vulnerabilities that are traditionally seen in on-premises infrastructures appear. The IaaS model is no exception to that; organizations incur most of the same vulnerabilities they would have if they maintained their on-premises infrastructure. Additionally, other vulnerabilities can affect bare-metal hypervisors that could compromise the cloud provider's customers. For the most part, however, vulnerabilities that result in attacks on IaaS infrastructures are more often the result of customer configuration and patching issues.

Serverless Architecture and Function as a Service (FaaS)

A recent addition to the cloud services that many providers offer is the *serverless architecture*, which means that the customer does not have to set up a server, real or virtual, but instead is provided various functions, which are abstracted from a particular server installation. In other words, the services the client requests are what is provided, regardless of the underlying server architecture. The customer isn't paying for a Windows or Linux server, just the services that those servers could offer. This leads to a new offering called *Function as a Service* (FaaS). The customer may want services that include messaging, storage, compute, or even network services such as DNS or DHCP, for example. The customer doesn't care what server offers the services, so long as they are functional, accessible, robust, and secure. The advantage of this model is that most of the management of these functions is controlled by the cloud service provider; the customer does not have to provide the overhead associated with maintaining and managing the services. The different functions the customer wants are also dynamic; functions can be executed on the fly via code when the client requires them. An example of this service is Amazon Lambda.

Infrastructure as Code (IaC)

Infrastructure as Code (IaC) is another new, dynamic functionality offered by cloud service providers. It allows developers to dynamically change the infrastructure based on changes in their code. This functionality doesn't rely on static servers or hosts but instead allows infrastructure to be created as it is needed and changed as necessary. For example, an application might require that the server is changed to a different VLAN or network; IaC can accomplish this. This is just a simple example, however. IaC services can change entire portions of a customer's infrastructure based on how an organization needs to function, changes in architecture, and quick reaction to some environmental event, such as a natural disaster or malicious attack. A popular example of IaC is Amazon's AWS CloudFormation services, which can provide templates for developers to use to rapidly change an organization's infrastructure.

 NOTE   Be familiar with the different services offered by cloud providers as well as their definitions.

Cloud Deployment Models

In addition to the various subscription models offered by cloud service providers, there are different physical and virtual models that an organization can use not only to get the services it needs but to ensure the security of its data and infrastructure. These models define the separation of infrastructure as well as data accessibility from other organizations and entities. In some cases, shared infrastructure works best for an organization, such as for a university. In other cases, such as a cleared defense contractor, strict separation from other organizations' infrastructures is required. In the following sections, we discuss the different models that make this possible, which include public, private, community, and hybrid cloud deployments.

Public

A public deployment model is one in which the cloud provider owns all of the resources used to provide services to your organization, including hosts, network infrastructure, applications, and so on. Any organization can subscribe to resources in a public provider setup, but each organization has its unique piece of the public cloud infrastructure, so they are logically separate from your organization's part of the infrastructure. Organizations may have their piece of the cloud infrastructure located on the same physical servers as your organization; however, public doesn't necessarily mean that anyone can access your infrastructure. There is still separation and security provisions for organizations that buy a piece of a public cloud, such as the services offered by Microsoft, Google, and Amazon. The vulnerabilities for a public cloud are commonly found in the cloud provider's infrastructure and policies since they are more likely to control more of the maintenance and management portions of the infrastructure. Any weakness suffered by the cloud service provider in this model is suffered by all of the organizations that subscribe to its services.

Private

In a private cloud model, the organization typically owns all the resources used to provide cloud services. Normally, larger organizations may elect to do this so they can keep control over the entire cloud infrastructure—and they have the money and resources to do just that. Organizations may choose to operate in a private cloud infrastructure for several reasons. This may include government or regulatory requirements because of the data they process (healthcare or sensitive financial data, for example). The organization is responsible for the maintenance and management of all the resources used in the private cloud, including servers, network infrastructure, applications, data storage, and, most importantly, the data itself. Because of this nuance, the threats and vulnerabilities for the private model include those that you might have for any privately owned or on-premises infrastructure, such as insufficient perimeter security, lack of access controls, weak authentication, excessive permissions, and so on. Additional threats inherent to cloud infrastructures in general may also be seen, including some level of lack of visibility by organizational infrastructure security personnel, vulnerabilities in cloud-reliant applications, and so on.

Community

A community cloud model is used when you have multiple organizations that have similar infrastructure requirements and may need to share data at some level (for example, multiple universities engaged together in various academic pursuits or research projects). It could include any group of organizations that need to share data and must have consistency in data types, formats, security requirements, and so on. Each organization can still maintain its security requirements for its data; the community cloud model is there to provide a common infrastructure for all the organizations. Vulnerabilities in this model typically are found in the implementation of the security and sharing policies for the different organizations that share the community cloud.

Hybrid

Hybrid models, which are becoming more common, are different combinations of the three preceding cloud deployment models. An organization could have a private cloud for some aspects of its operations as well as subscribe to public cloud services for other portions of the operations; as long as they are kept logically and physically separated, there is no issue. There can also be different combinations of both community and private clouds or community and public clouds. Organizations can also use these different cloud models as alternate processing capabilities or failover for their internal infrastructures. The point is, there's no one-size-fits-all solution for all organizations, so the ability to be flexible and take advantage of a hybrid deployment model is often an advantage for an organization.

EXAM TIP   Be familiar with the different cloud deployment models and how they are advantageous to the organization.

Cloud Vulnerabilities

Now that we've discussed the basics of cloud services, including subscription models and deployment models, it's time to discuss the issues organizations can face when using the cloud. These include threats to cloud computing as well as the inherent vulnerabilities found in these models. You'll find that a great majority of these issues come from the shared responsibility model of a cloud deployment, in terms of who has responsibility for which part of security, privacy, and risk management. Many of these issues also come from the interaction of the cloud infrastructure with external components, such as programming and data interfaces, encryption services, and storage. Although we can't cover every possible vulnerability you may encounter in a cloud deployment, we will discuss the more common ones you will most likely see on the exam. These include insecure application programming interfaces, improper key management, unprotected storage, logging and monitoring issues, and data accessibility by both authorized and unauthorized personnel.

NOTE   Many of these vulnerabilities are shared by either the cloud service provider or the customer organization, or combination of both, but it depends on what responsibilities each party has in providing infrastructure, maintenance, management, and security for the different cloud services and deployment models.

Insecure Application Programming Interface (API)

Cloud service providers allow interfacing with their services through application programming interfaces (APIs). These APIs allow the organization to connect different applications and services to those provided by the cloud and can also enable the organization to develop applications within the context of the cloud provider's services. Unfortunately, APIs are not always secure, for various reasons.

One common reason is that access to the APIs is often uncontrolled; insufficient permissions or authentication may be involved in accessing the API by unauthorized personnel. Here's a list of some of the other issues involved with insecure APIs:

- **Broken object-level authorization**   Failure to authorize access on an object basis
- **Broken user authentication**   Failure to account for all the different ways a user could authenticate to the API, such as through other applications
- **Excessive data exposure**   Failure to limit the amount of data exposed to a user to only the data they require

- **Lack of resources**   Failure to control resources, such as memory, that are used when a user is accessing applications or data
- **Lack of rate limiting**   Failure to implement throttling to conserve resources
- **Broken function-level authorization**   Failure to restrict unauthorized functions
- **Mass assignment**   Failure to properly authenticate users and limit data access
- **Security configuration issues**   Failure to change default security settings
- **Injection attacks**   Failure to validate user input
- **Asset mismanagement**   Failure to manage the different data assets that an API has access to
- **Insufficient logging and monitoring**   Failure to monitor and log API actions with potential security consequences

 NOTE   Any of these vulnerabilities could result in unauthorized or improper access to cloud-based services and applications from internal or external entities.

Improper Key Management

Managing cryptographic keys used to access encrypted data and systems is extremely important. If an organization fails to manage its encryption keys, it could result in unauthorized access to systems and data, or, almost as bad, prevent unauthorized users from accessing that same data. Encryption keys should be centrally managed, usually by the organization, since that's not often a function of the cloud service provider. Although the cloud provider may provide encryption services, normally the service provider leaves it to the organization to determine who has access to applications, systems, and data. Data should be managed for encryption during storage and transit. Encryption and decryption keys should be:

- Centrally issued and tracked
- Tied to the user's credentials for non-repudiation purposes
- Created for only a limited duration
- Suspended or revoked if there is a suspected key compromise

Unprotected Storage

It goes without saying that the organization should securely manage its storage, even if that storage is located in the cloud. The security measures that an organization takes to protect its data in the cloud are not much different from those it must take if the storage is located on its premises. Even in a cloud model, if the organization doesn't protect data storage, the data can be accessed by unauthorized personnel, modified, destroyed, or even stolen. The cloud service provider will usually have an interface or facility for the organization to use to protect data storage. At a minimum, the organization should ensure the following:

- It has assigned the correct rights and permissions to the data.
- Sensitive data is encrypted while in storage.
- Cloud-provided or organizational Data Loss Prevention (DLP) solutions are implemented.
- Data backups take place to secure backup storage.

Insufficient Logging and Monitoring

Very often, user actions are monitored and logged by a combination of the cloud provider and the using organization. They may monitor and log different actions, but together the service provider and the organization should be logging all access to applications and data that may have critical security ramifications. The shared responsibilities for monitoring and logging data access and use should be spelled out in the cloud service provider's agreement. If there is a failure to monitor application, system, or data access, as well as audit this access and log it, then of course the possibility exists that unauthorized access, data compromise, and misuse of applications and systems will be undetected. The cloud service provider and the organization should jointly determine what should be monitored, how much detail should be in the audit logs, and whether certain events will trigger alerts for administrators on either side. However, at a minimum, the organization should monitor and log the following:

- All access to sensitive data
- All privileged account use
- All configuration changes to the cloud and organizational infrastructures
- Denied actions, such as failed logins and denied data access or modification

Inability to Access

Yet another threat to cloud subscribers is the inability to access their applications and data. This could be for various technical reasons, including communication line failures and data center issues, but it could also be because of malicious acts, such as those from a compromised insider or external hacker. In any case, the wide gamut of security controls available to both the organization and the cloud service provider should be used to ensure that authorized personnel have access to systems and data whenever they need them. Availability levels should be guaranteed in the service level agreement (SLA) between the cloud service provider and the organization, but they must be implemented as strong security controls to ensure availability.

 EXAM TIP   You should be familiar with these vulnerabilities and their potential mitigations, as they are specifically stated in the exam objectives.

REVIEW

Objective 1.6: Explain the threats and vulnerabilities associated with operating in the cloud   In this module, we've discussed the threats and vulnerabilities associated with cloud computing. We discussed the various cloud service models, which essentially describe the types of "something as a service" that an organization can obtain from cloud service providers. These include simple application services (SaaS), computing and development platforms (PaaS), and network services (IaaS). These also include specific computing functions, such as perimeter security. They come in the form of functions as a service that are abstracted from a particular server platform. There is also Infrastructure as Code (IaC), which allows an organization to dynamically create and change its infrastructure based on its needs.

We also discussed the various deployment models commonly in use, including private, public, community, and hybrid models. Private models are contained internally to the organization for its exclusive use, and all assets used to create the private cloud are owned and controlled by the organization. Public models are used when an organization subscribes to a public cloud service provider, along with other organizations whose services may use some of the same physical infrastructure. Community models involve sharing infrastructure and possibly data between like organizations that have similar requirements, such as several different universities collaborating on a research project. Hybrid models can take the form of any combination of the previously mentioned models.

Different cloud service and deployment models suffer from some of the same threats and vulnerabilities that traditional on-premises models suffer from, but to varying degrees. These include access control, authentication, encryption, and other potential issues. However, the focus is on whether the provider may endure these threats and vulnerabilities to some degree more than the customer will, and this depends on the chosen services and deployment model.

Specific cloud vulnerabilities discussed in this module include insecure application programming interface services; poorly managed cryptographic key management; unprotected storage, which may have improper access permissions; mismanaged logging and monitoring functions by the organization; and availability issues, which may result in the organization not having effective access to its resources and data.

1.6 QUESTIONS

1. Ash has been put in charge of migrating the organization's application infrastructure to the cloud. The organization is contemplating a subscription model where lines of business and desktop applications are accessible over a web-based interface. The organization wants to move the responsibility of keeping the applications updated to the cloud provider. Which of the following service models should Ash consider?

   A. IaC

   B. IaaS

   C. PaaS

   D. SaaS

2. Robin is a cybersecurity analyst who works at a major research facility. The researchers there are collaborating with several other large think tanks and universities on a significant economic research study and must share data and resources, including computing power and storage. The research facility manager has directed Robin to move the researchers' work into a cloud configuration so they can collaborate more easily with their counterparts in other organizations. Which of the following would be an appropriate cloud deployment model for this project?

   A. Public

   B. Private

   C. Community

   D. Hybrid

3. You are in charge of managing your company's cloud service provider contract. Lately, there have been reports that sensitive data has been exfiltrated from the organization and published on the open Internet. This seems strange to you because no sensitive data is stored on company servers; it is all stored in the cloud provider's secure data center. Collaborating with the cloud service provider's security team, you should look at which of the following first to determine if there any security issues that may have resulted in unauthorized data access?

   A. Lack of key management

   B. Unprotected storage

   C. Weak authentication

   D. Lack of audit logs

4. You are a cybersecurity analyst who keeps receiving phone calls from internal customers stating that they can only access sensitive data files on an intermittent basis. Upon further examination, you determine that all of the inaccessible data stores are cloud-based. You begin to troubleshoot the issue and look for potential causes, including faulty permissions and authentication issues. Regardless of what's causing the data to be inaccessible, what is the key issue here?

   A. Data availability

   B. Data confidentiality

   C. Unprotected storage

   D. Insecure API

1.6 ANSWERS

1. **D**   Software as a Service (SaaS) is the model Ash should choose because it allows the organization to use applications remotely without the need to worry about security patches or updates.

2. **C**   Robin should contract with a cloud service provider for a community cloud deployment model so that the researchers within the organization can collaborate with other organizations and share data and resources.

3. **B**   The first thing you should examine is the data storage within the cloud provider's infrastructure. Data storage areas may not have the appropriate permissions assigned to personnel or may have some other weakness, such as a lack of encryption for data in storage. Even if one of the other issues—weak authentication, lack of encryption, or a lack of audit trails—is the core problem, you should first look at the storage to see if any of these other three weaknesses are inherent to the storage area. In any event, even these weaknesses indicate unprotected storage.

4. **A**   Data availability is the key issue here. Regardless of what is causing it, the data is inaccessible to authorized users, and this may violate the service level agreement between the cloud service provider and the organization.

Objective 1.7 Given a scenario, implement controls to mitigate attacks and software vulnerabilities

Both software and hardware have many inherent vulnerabilities that open them up to a multitude of attack vectors. In this module, we're going to discuss different software vulnerabilities and the corresponding attacks that exploit those vulnerabilities. We're also going to talk about the different controls that can be implemented to mitigate these attacks. The vulnerabilities we discuss include improper error handling, dereferencing, insecure objects, race conditions, authentication issues, exposure of sensitive data, and several other vulnerabilities inherent to software. We also discuss the various attacks that could take advantage of these vulnerabilities, including XML attacks, SQL injection, various overflow attacks, remote code execution, privilege escalation, man-in-the-middle attacks, session hijacking, cross-site scripting, and many others. By the end of this module, you should be able to identify popular and commonly seen vulnerabilities as well as the different attack vectors that can take advantage of these vulnerabilities.

Vulnerabilities

In Objective 1.3, we stated that a vulnerability could be a weakness in a system, but it also could be the absence or ineffectiveness of a security control. An example of a system weakness could be software that was not developed under secure programming conditions and contains flaws that might allow an attacker to gain access to data they should not be able to access. A control weakness example might be the absence of encryption over a network or using a weak encryption algorithm that can be easily broken by an attacker. Either of these conditions constitutes a vulnerability. Remember also that vulnerabilities are taken advantage of, or exploited, by threat events, which are in turn caused by threat actors. Vulnerabilities exist on assets or even in an organization through its management programs. No matter where the vulnerabilities reside, cybersecurity analysts must actively work every day to find and eliminate them. The vulnerabilities we discuss in this module are more specific to software or code and serve to give you a primer on modules we will discuss in Domain 2, which is focused on software security. Keep in mind that we won't cover every single known vulnerability in software, but we will go over the ones you are likely to see on the exam as well as the ones you are likely to see in the real world. This CySA+ exam objective closely mirrors the vulnerabilities found in the OWASP Top 10 Application Security Risks. We discuss these vulnerabilities and then the attack scenarios that could take advantage of them, resulting in system compromise. We also discuss the different potential mitigations for each of these attacks.

Improper Error Handling

No software is built perfectly. Even software that has been stable over a few versions can be prone to errors. Errors involving functionality or performance aside, what is important is how the software handles errors. If coded incorrectly, the software could deal with an error unpredictably, causing the program or even the underlying system to hang or crash. Even worse, if the afflicted program does not properly handle errors, this could give a potential attacker a way to exploit the system, because a serious error condition might leave the system unstable and vulnerable to attack. An attacker could take advantage of improper error handling through input validation issues, buffer overflows, or escaping outside the software's processing bounds.

An additional issue with error handling is that the system will often throw error messages that are at best cryptic, but at worse may give an attacker too much information about the system that they can use to exploit any discovered vulnerabilities in the software. Error messages should give enough information for a user or a technician to solve problems but at the same time should not give away information about the underlying architecture. Critical error information that a programmer or technician should have should be sent to a log file that has restricted access. An attacker trying to exploit a piece of software over the Internet should not be able to gain any information from improper error handling.

Dereferencing

Dereferencing occurs when a program attempts to access a stored value that doesn't exist. A null pointer dereference is the most common instance of this vulnerability. The application dereference is the pointer that the application expects to be valid but, in fact, is empty, or null. Most often, the application crashes when it experiences this condition. Several different software flaws can cause a null pointer dereference. These include flaws that we have already discussed, such as complex race conditions, but could also include simple programming errors. Attackers use dereferencing to cause system instability, which may allow them to bypass security mechanisms and gain privileged access to the system, or to access underlying data that they might not otherwise be able to.

Most null pointer dereferencing cases occur in common languages, such as C, C++, and Java. Paying particular attention to error and exception handling can allow unexpected null pointer dereference occurrences to be resolved without allowing attackers to take advantage of them.

Insecure Object Reference

Sometimes applications need to access underlying data and must use different methods of referencing that data. If a malicious person can infer a pattern or mechanism for accessing that underlying data, they can use that to further access data they should not be able to see. For example, suppose a URL accesses a database record using an identifier such as a Social Security number (SSN). An attacker can modify the HTTP request and substitute a different SSN to access a different record out of the database. Another example might be if there is a file or directory reference in that URL that can easily be derived or predicted. While these are rather simplistic examples, they show that programmers should use random values or values that have no meaning to reference internal pieces of data. The solution to this is that programmers should avoid directly exposing internal references by creating what is called an *indirect reference map*. This map, or table, can translate the arbitrary values used in the request to a reference that has meaning in the underlying internal database or application and then access the correct data. Substituting another value in the request would not do anything for the attacker, as that value would not have any translation in the application's reference map, so attempting to access a different record or file location using this method would be ineffective.

 EXAM TIP   Insecure object references are most often seen in the referencing URL in a web application.

Race Condition

The sheer volume of threads and processes that occur in a single second of processing in a modern computer system is staggering. The effort that goes into managing all those threads and processes is equally as staggering; however, because of this complexity, sometimes conditions known as *race conditions* can occur. A race condition is one of many issues that fall under the category of timing or sequencing issues in the system. A race condition is a software flaw that happens when different threads or processes need to access an object or resource that affects other threads or processes. If one thread, for example, relies on a value produced by calculation from another thread, and that value is in the process of being computed, then the first thread cannot use or access that value until the second thread has computed it. If the second thread or process does not produce that value or produces it out of sequence, then it creates a condition where the first thread cannot complete its task. Essentially you have a condition where the sequence of calculations or events is disrupted and out of order.

Race conditions can be difficult to predict and fix and are dependent on *race windows*—a period when concurrent threads or processes compete to alter the same object at the same time. The goal in avoiding race conditions is to identify the race windows where they exist and to design systems so they are not attempting to concurrently access an object. This is known as *mutual exclusion*.

Yet another timing issue is created between the time a program checks for a value and the time it uses that value; during this time, the value could change if manipulated by a malicious process between those two events. This is also known as a *time of check/time of use* (TOC/TOU) attack. Using this attack, a malicious person could substitute values, such as tokens or session IDs, and essentially hijack processes or threads. Secure coding standards, as well as careful attention to thread and process timing, can help avoid these vulnerable conditions.

 EXAM TIP Remember that race conditions are a vulnerability in the timing or sequence of application threads and processes, which may result in a timing attack against an application.

Broken Authentication

Broken authentication refers to a myriad of attacks on weak authentication systems. Most authentication attacks are targeted against username/password authentication methods, as well as ineffective session management. During most of these attacks, attackers try one or more of several methods to gain access to credentials and take advantage of weak authentication mechanisms. This could include a lack of limiting failed login attempts, account lockouts not implemented, and easy-to-guess passwords. Other attacks can be slightly more complex and involve taking advantage of improperly validated session IDs. This is when a user session or authentication token is not properly validated during a logout from the session or a period of inactivity during the session. In many cases, an attacker can take advantage of these vulnerabilities and interrupt or hijack an existing session.

 EXAM TIP Broken authentication vulnerabilities result in attacks on an application's authentication mechanism, including weak password requirements, no limit on failed login attempts, failure to implement account lockouts, and vulnerabilities associated with the way that authentication credentials are passed to the application and validated.

Sensitive Data Exposure

Software applications and their underlying architectures, including their APIs, do not always protect critical data such as passwords, session IDs, and so on. This allows attackers to access sensitive data processed by the applications. This may include healthcare data, personal data, and proprietary or financial data. Exposure could result from any number of conditions, including lack of input validation, overly permissive access to underlying data, unpatched vulnerabilities, lack of encryption, weak authentication, and so on. Examples of how attackers could take advantage of these conditions include stealing credential information, initiating man-in-the-middle-attacks, and performing injection attacks.

Insecure Components

Software is built on so many different components in a complex architecture. These components include cryptographic modules, libraries, APIs, runtime modules, and objects. Any one of these can have vulnerabilities that can be taken advantage of through a variety of attacks. In addition to having inherent vulnerabilities, such as lack of input validation, memory mismanagement, and logic issues, these components can also have issues with authentication and authorization, such as faulty permissions or lack of authentication mechanisms. Components can also suffer from inefficient resource allocation and access, which may cause issues with memory, hard disk space, and CPU processing time. Any of these vulnerabilities can allow an attacker to interrupt system processing and potentially hijack a piece of software functionality, exposing its underlying data.

Insufficient Logging and Monitoring

Most software applications have some logging facility, either producing their own log files or sending events to the operating system's log facility, such as Windows Event Viewer or syslog. Some of the better applications allow you to pick and choose which events and to what level of detail the application can log. However, this doesn't always mean that individual cybersecurity analysts take advantage of those logging facilities, have them set properly, or even pay attention to the logs when they are produced. Given this deficiency, a serious and often subtle attack on a software application could go unnoticed by a security administrator. Therefore, it is incumbent upon all cybersecurity administrators to ensure that they are not only monitoring the application for functional and performance issues but also auditing for security issues as well. When combined with operating system and other security logs, adding application logs to the mix can construct a clear picture of a series of events for security administrators when they're trying to determine the origin, cause, scope, and eventual resolution of an attack. It's also, of course, helpful to send application logs to a security information and event management (SIEM) system for aggregation and more detailed analysis.

Weak or Default Configurations

Right of the box, most applications, and indeed some operating systems, are not secure. Their default configuration is typically set to allow a user of the least technical ability to install and configure the software application. There may be default settings that are not secure, such as vendor default passwords or no encryption. While there are security hardening guides available for many of these applications, security administrators don't always take the time to go through the steps to secure the application itself, and many times these default settings are left in place, just waiting for an attacker to take advantage of them. Cybersecurity analysts should use industry best practices when securely configuring an application after it has been installed. This includes tightening down security settings, implementing encryption wherever possible, changing default vendor passwords, placing users in restricted groups, and assigning those groups limited permissions to only perform the actions they need to do their jobs.

Use of Insecure Functions

Insecure functions are those that can have unexpected results when used in programs and be taken advantage of by attackers. Most of these insecure functions result in buffer overflow conditions, where memory is corrupted and overwritten. This can cause a system to become unstable and crash, or even allow an attacker to arbitrarily execute code of their choosing and gain privileged access to the core of the application or even the underlying operating systems. Many examples of insecure functions are found in the C/C++ programming language, but most programming languages have examples of insecure functions that should be avoided if at all possible, or at minimum use function parsers to determine when an attempt is made to exploit them.

One popular function, strcpy(), can be used to copy a large number of characters into a smaller memory area, which can result in unstable conditions and allow an attacker to overwrite buffers. The strcpy() function can copy a source string (src) of characters to a destination (dest) string. If the memory buffer size of the destination string is sufficient, then a terminating null character is the result. Note that this function does not specify the required size of the destination buffer. Therefore, if the destination buffer area is less than the source string length, it will overwrite the destination buffer and potentially corrupt other memory areas, with no terminating null character to discern the input from existing memory contents. Similar to this is the strncpy() function.

 NOTE   Sometimes it is difficult to distinguish the various vulnerabilities that may result in different attacks; often the attacker will take advantage of several vulnerabilities concurrently to stage a comprehensive attack against an application.

Attack Types

As mentioned earlier, vulnerabilities are exploited by threats. A threat event can manifest itself as an attack upon the system. The method that is used for the attack is called the *attack vector*. This is sometimes used interchangeably with the term *threat vector*, but they are not the same thing, as a threat vector indicates just one potential avenue for an attack that a threat event may use, versus the actual attack. The threat event can make use of any one or combination of different threat vectors, but only the ones used are called attack vectors. The attack types or vectors that we will discuss in this module specifically target software vulnerabilities, which we discussed earlier as well. In this section, we talk about the type of attack, the vulnerability it can target, and potential mitigations that may lessen the impact of an attack or stop it altogether. While we won't cover every potential attack from which a software vulnerability could suffer, we will discuss the more commonly seen attacks as well as those you must know as part of the learning objectives for the CySA+ exam.

Injection Attacks

The injection attack is one of the most common forms of attack seen in the modern Internet era. Injection attacks occur because programmers don't adequately validate user input, typically from web forms or web-based applications. An injection attack is when a malicious user inputs something that the web application cannot properly parse or validate. Typically, the user will enter code as their input into a common field such as a name field. The web application doesn't know how to interpret this input, so it may respond in one of several ways. It may return an error, it may return data that the user does not have access to, or it may result in the user getting privileged access to the underlying application or even the operating system. Injection attacks can be used with Structured Query Language (SQL), operating system (OS) commands, Extensible Markup Language (XML), the Lightweight Directory Access Protocol (LDAP), and other common methods. Examples of attacks also include directory transversal, cross-site scripting (XSS), and cross-site request forgery (CSRF). In the next few sections, we discuss these particular injection attacks and how they work.

 EXAM TIP   Remember that injection attacks take advantage of a lack of input validation, making it possible to enter or inject code and other malicious input into an application.

Extensible Markup Language (XML) Attack

Extensible Markup Language (XML) is a programming language, referred to as a *metalanguage,* that allows users to create their own markup languages. XML is used to format and display information from documents to databases on the Web and can be used to exchange data between different platforms. It can be used to assist in querying and presenting data from database-driven website applications. An XML injection attack is one in which the attacker manipulates XML application or service logic. This involves injecting XML content or structures into a web application to bypass the program logic of the application.

Structured Query Language (SQL) Injection

Structured Query Language (SQL) is a language, usually seen in the form of SQL statements, that is used to access, query, and update databases. Typically, SQL is used for relational databases. Many web applications today are *multitiered* applications; that is to say, their programming logic may reside on one server, the user interface or web page on another server, and possibly even a back-end database on yet another server. In this type of setup, a user may require information from the back-end database, but for security reasons is not allowed to access the database directly. The web interface typically provides forms and fields that allow a user to interact with a limited set of data from the database. Programmers don't always do a good job of validating input for these forms and fields, and as a result, ordinary users, and sometimes even malicious entities, can input anything from pure garbage to specially crafted data into these forms. In the case of the latter, an attacker could formulate SQL statements that can, if they are not validated, access the underlying database and return data that the user should not be able to see—or worse yet, update the underlying database with data of the attacker's choosing. This entire attack, based on invalid input, is known as SQL injection.

To execute an SQL injection attack, an attacker must do the following:

- Input a few test values to see if the database is accessible and can be manipulated through injection attacks.
- Use different SQL inputs that may generate error messages to enumerate and map out the database.
- Input a specially crafted SQL statement to get the desired results.

As an example of an SQL injection attack, let's say a user accesses a web application that has an input form. This input form has a login field to access the web application. The user must input their username and password. The web application passes this information on to access a database. In this scenario, the attacker intends to set up an injection attack using the following SQL statement:

```
SELECT * FROM UsersTable WHERE username = '<user_name_input_field>' AND
 password = '<password_input_field>'
```

For this statement, assume that UsersTable is the table in the database that stores usernames and passwords used to access the database, <user_name_input_field> is the form field where a user would input their authorized username, and <password_input_field> is a form field where a user would input their password. These last two values would normally be found in the UsersTable of the database for an authorized user. However, a normal user would not input this SQL statement; they would simply enter their information in the appropriate fields.

An attacker could enter this entire SQL statement in one of the fields, using the following information:

```
SELECT * FROM UsersTable WHERE username = 'administrator' AND ' password =
 'whatever'
```

Note the use of the ' character before the password. This actually tells the field that the remainder of the statement is a comment and can safely be ignored. Essentially, this makes the entire statement look like this to the database:

```
SELECT * FROM UsersTable WHERE username = 'administrator'
```

This has the effect of confusing the web application if input validation has not been properly programmed and will cause the application to potentially allow access to the database as an administrator. Note that this is a simplistic example, and depending on how the web application has been programmed and the type of underlying database that supports the application, variations in this statement may be necessary. The key point here is that if user input validation is not conducted by the web application, a carefully crafted SQL statement could result in getting administrative access to the database. Also, other statements could be constructed that would return a list of usernames and valid passwords, or even complete records on individuals. As with all other types of injection attacks, simply validating user input could help prevent these attacks.

 EXAM TIP   Attacks on the back-end database of applications are usually conducted via an SQL injection attack.

Cross-Site Scripting (XSS) Attacks

Cross-site scripting (XSS) attacks cause a user's browser to execute malicious code stored on a website the browser trusts. The attack primarily targets sensitive information, such as user passwords or session information that can be used to impersonate the user. In a *persistent* XSS attack, a user visits the site and unknowingly executes malicious code hidden there, typically through content that is posted to the site (for example, through user comments, scripts, or files) by a malicious person. There are also a couple of other different variations of an XSS attack; in addition to persistent attacks, there are reflected and Document Object Model (DOM) attacks.

In a reflected (non-persistent) attack, the malicious attacker takes advantage of a server software flaw. Typically, the attacker will craft a special link with the hope that the link will be clicked by unsuspecting users. If they click the link, the browser goes to the site and reflects the attack back to the hapless user. Again, since this type of attack targets sensitive user information and session details, this information can be used to intercept user passwords, session information that could be used for impersonation attacks, and so on. In the reflected attack, a malicious entity could send links to this compromised site through e-mail, text messages, or even documents.

Document Object Model (DOM) is a standard dictating how client browsers interact with HTML presented from the server. In the DOM version of the XSS attack, an attacker injects malicious script into the client-side HTML, which the browser parses. If for some reason the web app does not practice input validation, an attacker could modify code between the browser and the application to set up an XSS attack.

Remote Code Execution

Remote code execution typically isn't a mode of attack but rather what the attacker is after in terms of a goal. Injection attacks, as well as overflow attacks, can give the attacker the ability to execute arbitrary code of their choosing (meaning scripts or whatever code they choose to input into a web form) remotely from their connection. This arbitrary code could be malicious in nature and used to carry out a denial-of-service attack on the web server, or it could be more sinister and be used to laterally move across a network or elevate privilege levels on different hosts. The key point here is that the code is whatever the attacker chooses if they can achieve this goal. Remote code execution comes from vulnerabilities that are a result of sloppy programming, including lack of input validation and bounds checking, and causes the application to not be able to distinguish between code that should be executed and data that is input.

Directory Traversal

Directory traversal—also known as directory climbing, "dot-dot-slash" attacks, and path traversal—is the ability of an attacker to access folders and directories outside of the web application's web root folder. The web root folder is typically used by the application to service web requests. Users should not be able to read the contents of this directory through a directory listing; however, they must be able to execute certain code in it to get the services from the web application. A directory traversal attack allows an attacker to navigate outside of that directory system into other directories, including potentially sensitive directories such as the operating system file directories and other directories that contain sensitive data.

 EXAM TIP   Directory traversal attacks simply involve the ability to view folders and files outside of an application's root directory and may include the ability to view operating system directories as well as other directories that contain sensitive data.

Authentication Attacks

Authentication attacks are a class of attack that attempts to authenticate an attacker as a valid user. The attacker's goal is to enter into a communications session or access resources as the targeted user. Authentication attacks use a variety of methods, including credential stealing, password cracking, password spraying, credential stuffing, impersonation, and man-the-middle and session hijacking attacks. These attack methods are discussed in the following sections.

Password Spraying

Password spraying is a simplistic attack; traditional brute force attacks attempt to break into a single account by repeatedly trying many variations of the password in a short period. In a password spraying attack, however, the attacker uses one or only a few passwords across many different accounts in an organization. The theory is that some commonly used passwords may be valid for an account somewhere in the system, even if it's not the user account the attacker is interested in brute forcing.

Most often, the attacker will use easily guessed passwords that most organizations warn their users against using. They will also use social engineering tactics to profile the organization and its users to derive a shortlist of potential passwords. Password spraying can also be attempted against a single user, but across many different accounts, such as e-mail, banking, and other services.

Password spraying can be prevented if the organization or individual uses multifactor authentication instead of simple username/password combinations. If passwords must be used as authentication, then the organization should enforce the use of strong passwords, with large keyspace, complexity, and length requirements. Passwords should also expire regularly, and a minimum length of time restriction for password changes should be required.

Credential Stuffing

Credential stuffing is an attack technique that allows the attacker to make use of previous data breaches. Instead of going through all of the trouble to obtain usernames and passwords through brute force or stealing password hashes, an attacker will use usernames and passwords obtained through a previous data breach. For example, an attacker may purchase a list of usernames and passwords from the breach of a major e-mail provider. The attacker would then target a user or organization and use those same usernames and passwords to attempt to compromise additional accounts.

The defense against credential stuffing is to ensure that, when a breach is discovered, users immediately change their passwords with the breached organization or service, as well as ensure that the same passwords are not used for other personal or organizational accounts. To see if your users' passwords show up in popular hacking databases as having been compromised, you can check online databases such as "Have I Been Pwned" (https://haveibeenpwned .com). An even more effective defense against credential stuffing is to use multifactor authentication, as well as additional authentication methods such as tokens or one-time passwords.

 EXAM TIP   Understand the difference between password spraying and credential stuffing. Remember that password spraying simply involves using a few passwords to attempt to compromise many user accounts across an organization. Credential stuffing is the use of usernames and passwords already obtained from a previous data breach in another organization to see if the same usernames and passwords are valid in the target organization.

Impersonation

In an impersonation attack, the attacker will attempt to steal credentials or forge them to impersonate a person or other entity, including a trusted server. Impersonation can be accomplished in a variety of means, including man-in-the-middle attacks and session hijacking (both discussed in the next two sections). Impersonation can even be used to a fool a client into thinking the attacker is a trusted Certificate Authority (CA).

Man-in-the-Middle Attack

A man-in-the-middle (MITM) attack is characterized by an attacker attempting to impersonate multiple entities in the communications session. The attacker may try to impersonate two individuals by intercepting and interrupting the communications session, or even impersonate a client and server. In this manner, the attacker acts as a proxy and inserts their own host in the middle of the conversation between the two parties. Both parties will believe that the attacker is the other party, enabling the attacker to send and receive all information to and from both parties at their discretion, modifying it as they see fit. Within an unencrypted connection, a man-in-the-middle attack is quite simple, but even with encrypted sessions, the attacker could potentially interrupt a secure session if they have compromised the client or server certificate or otherwise broken the SSL/TLS connection and inserted themselves in the middle. This often happens in the case of HTTPS connections, where the client browser establishes a secure connection with the attacker instead of the server. The attacker then establishes a secure connection with the target server. Sometimes either the client or server may get an error message about the validity of the other party's certificate, but most people ignore those error messages and click right through them, allowing the communications session to happen. It should be noted that many organizations have instituted HTTPS or SSL proxying on their outbound connections to prevent users from using encryption to exfiltrate data or otherwise engage in activities that are against company policy. While the legality or ethics of this practice are questionable, this is an example of a sanctioned man-in-the-middle attack.

Session Hijacking

Session hijacking is a type of attack used to take over a communications session or conduct a man-in-the-middle attack. In a session hijacking attack, the attacker can intercept and use valid communications session information. This includes authentication information, such as username and passwords, cookies, TCP sequence numbers and timestamps, and so on. A replay attack is one method of session hijacking; this may take advantage of stateless HTTP traffic, for example, and communications sessions that use multiple TCP connections to maintain state information.

Session hijacking can be prevented through a variety of means—strong authentication, including multifactor authentication versus the use of usernames and passwords, strong session encryption, TCP sequence unpredictability, and other measures.

NOTE   Session hijacking and man-the-middle attacks are similar but can use different means and have different goals. A man-in-the-middle attack is designed to break into a communications session and authenticate as both parties of the session to each other. A session hijacking attack is also designed to break into a user session but typically involves only masquerading as one of the parties involved. Instead of breaking into the middle of the conversation and assuming both roles of the endpoints of the communication, it assumes only one of the endpoints of the communications session.

Overflow Attacks

Overflow attacks all have one simple goal in common: writing more data to a memory buffer than is allocated for that input. These types of attacks can take several forms, including buffer, integer, and heap overflows. Most overflow attacks, if successful, can result in the ability of the attacker to cause system instability or gain privileged access. Overflow attacks occur because programmers don't include bounds checking in their program logic. This allows invalid input to escape the bounds set by the program allocated for the input. Famous examples of buffer overflow attacks include the very first worm, the Morris worm, which was released in 1988, and more recent malware such as Code Red and Slammer. We discuss the major types of overflow attacks in the following sections.

Buffer

A buffer overflow attack is probably the most common type of attack that most cybersecurity analysts are familiar with. This type of attack can be carried out using a wide range of methods, but the central goal is to overflow the buffer size of the memory space allocated to the input. The goal is to overflow that memory space and overwrite other memory locations. Again, this can cause system instability or allow the attacker to get into restricted areas of the application or operating system.

Buffer overflows are caused by programmers being inattentive to bounds checking as well as by inherent weaknesses in some programming languages such as C. Many different functions in C permit overflows because they were originally designed with performance and memory space in mind instead of security. Examples of some of these unsafe functions include the strcpy() function, mentioned earlier in the module, and the gets() function.

Integer

Integer attacks are based on how numbers are stored in variables and memory locations. Normally, software applications store numbers based on a defined size. Integers are stored in 8-, 16-, 32-, and 64-bit locations and either as signed or unsigned numbers (absolute values or negative/positive, respectively). For example, a 32-bit integer unsigned number is a number whose value is in the range of 0 to 4,294,967,295. A 32-bit signed integer can be in the range of –2,147,483,648 to +2,147,483,647. Integer overflow attacks take advantage of a numerical value that is larger than the space assigned for it. An attacker can create a mathematical operation and inject it through invalid input into a field that expects a number of a specific range. When the number exceeds that range, it can overflow the memory location specified for the range and then result in different responses, including system instability, error messages, privileged access, or the ability to run arbitrary code at the attacker's discretion.

Like other overflow attacks, integer overflows can be mitigated using secure coding methods, sometimes specific to the particular programming language used. Exception handling is one good method; this means that programmers build in exception handling code anticipating an integer overflow, which can deal with the out-of-range numerical values. The application can then display a customized error message while keeping the system stable and secure. Another sound method is input validation, where mathematical operations resulting in these large numbers are not allowed as input.

Heap

Heap-based attacks are closely related to buffer overflow attacks. System memory is broken into two parts: the *stack,* which is a data structure that allows data in on a last-in, first-out basis, and the *heap,* which is unstructured and used on a space-available basis. In a stack-based buffer overflow attack, the attacker attempts to overwrite key areas of the stack so that the attacker's arbitrary code can be executed instead of legitimate application code.

Conversely, in a heap-based attack, the attacker attempts to exhaust the memory dynamically available for the application in the heap. Normally, a heap-based attack is more difficult to execute since data in the heap can't only be overwritten, it must also be corrupted.

 EXAM TIP All overflow attacks target memory usage in an application, to overwrite contents of adjacent memory locations in the hopes of creating an unstable condition that may result in the ability to execute arbitrary code or gain elevated privileges in an application or operating system.

Privilege Escalation

Privilege escalation is not an attack, per se—it's more the goal of an attack. Many of the attacks described in this module can result in privilege escalation. The goal of a privilege escalation attack is to gain the additional privileges that a higher-level user, such as an administrator, may have. This is called *vertical privilege escalation.* An attacker may, if they cannot successfully gain higher-level privileges, seek to get privileges of other users at the same level. This is called *horizontal privilege escalation.* An attacker may use horizontal privilege escalation if they don't necessarily desire the privileges of an administrator but need access to areas that an equivalent user may already have access to, such as sensitive files and databases.

Rootkits

A rootkit is a highly specialized form of malware that can be extremely difficult to both detect and eradicate. Rootkits don't typically take advantage of applications; they directly target operating system core files. This could include restricted binaries, device drivers, dynamic link libraries, kernel modules, and so on. These core files typically operate and run on a highly privileged level, either as an administrator or as the operating system itself. Rootkits can be installed through infected boot media or other more sophisticated means. Unfortunately, because rootkits often replace sensitive core operating system files, they may easily fool antimalware software, making them difficult to detect. Evidence of rootkits can span a variety of indicators, including system instability, strange or unusual operations, performance issues, unauthorized access to files or data by processes that don't normally have that access, unusual network traffic, and so on.

Rootkits are often only detected by booting to known-good clean media with specialized antimalware software that is designed to test system file integrity and notify the user of system files that don't conform to verification checks. Rootkits are also extremely difficult to eradicate. More often than not, the entire operating system has to be wiped and reinstalled, running the risk of losing user data on the system.

 CAUTION   Rootkits are extremely dangerous to an operating system; they are difficult to detect and eradicate. Because the only sure way to eliminate a rootkit is a complete rebuild of the system, you must have known-good backups so you can restore data after a rebuild.

REVIEW

Objective 1.7: Given a scenario, implement controls to mitigate attacks and software vulnerabilities   In this module, we discussed various software vulnerabilities and the attacks that can take advantage of those vulnerabilities. Vulnerabilities include those that can be corrected through secure programming techniques and involve flaws in the application. These include improper error handling, dereferencing, insecure object reference, and various timing attacks, including race conditions. We also discussed other vulnerabilities such as broken authentication, exposing sensitive data, and using insecure software components such as APIs. You also learned that insufficient logging and security monitoring are issues, as are using default software configurations. Using insecure functions that allow attackers to take advantage of software flaws, such as the strcpy() function, is also something programmers should pay attention to.

There are several different types of attacks that take advantage of these vulnerabilities. Three of the major types of attacks are injection attacks, authentication attacks, and overflow attacks. Injection attacks are made possible through a lack of input validation on the part of the program when the application code is written. Injection attacks can use many different methods, including XML attacks, SQL injection, and cross-site scripting. Injection attacks can result in the ability to access restricted areas of the application or even the operating system, as well as the ability to arbitrarily run remote code at the attacker's discretion and the ability to break outside of the directory structure of the application into more sensitive areas.

Authentication attacks include those that target authentication systems and breaking into communications sessions. These types of attacks can be non-technical, such as password spraying and credential stuffing. They can also be manifested as more sophisticated attacks, such as man-the-middle and session hijacking attacks. Usually with these last two types of attacks, impersonating an authorized user is the goal.

Overflow attacks take advantage of software flaws associated with the use of memory in an application. Also, overflow attack generally will attempt to break out of reserved memory for a function and overwrite the contents of other memory locations. These types of attacks include buffer, integer, stack, and heap attacks.

Finally, we discussed the use of rootkits by an attacker to substitute critical system files for the application or operating system. These types of attacks are extremely difficult to detect and eradicate and may necessitate a complete rebuild of the system to eliminate the rootkit. We also discussed various goals of the attacker, such as the ability to run arbitrary code remotely as part of an attack, as well as the goal of privilege escalation to gain administrative-level rights in the application or host.

1.7 QUESTIONS

1. Emilia is a cybersecurity analyst with an application programming background. She has been tasked to work with some of the company's web application programmers to ensure that they are considering security in their programming logic. During application security tests, Emilia discovers that she can input statements into a username field that will return a list of users from the application's back-end database. Emilia has discovered that the web application is vulnerable to which of the following types of attack?

   A. Command injection attack

   B. SQL injection attack

   C. XML injection attack

   D. Heap overflow attack

2. Evie is a cybersecurity analyst who works at a major research facility. While performing a routine audit of user access, she discovers that someone has been repeatedly trying the same set of ten passwords across various usernames and accounts within the organization. Which of the following types of attack has she discovered?

   A. Password spraying attack

   B. Credential stuffing attack

   C. Man-in-the-middle attack

   D. Session hijacking attack

3. Ben is a penetration tester hired to test a new web application for his client. After testing some of the input fields on a web-based form, he discovers that the application does not adequately protect against overwriting memory contents. He tries various attacks and is finally successful when he can corrupt and overwrite memory contents by exhausting all available memory for the application. Which of the following types of attacks has Ben been able to successfully execute?

   A. Cross-site scripting attack

   B. Integer overflow attack

   C. XML injection attack

   D. Heap overflow attack

4. Sam is a programmer who is writing a web-based application for his company. One of the cybersecurity analysts in his organization has just tested the prototype for the application and discovered several security flaws that must be corrected. One flaw, in particular, is associated with thread and process timing and causes issues because two processes are trying to concurrently access the same object, and the resulting conflict allows an attacker to execute arbitrary code. Which of the following software flaws has the analyst discovered?

   A. Broken authentication

   B. Race condition

   C. Use of insecure functions

   D. Improper error handling

1.7 ANSWERS

1. **B**   Emilia has discovered that the underlying web application logic has not been tested for input validation and is thus vulnerable to an SQL injection attack since it directly affects a database and allows an attacker to potentially access database records that they should not be able to see.

2. **A**   Evie has discovered that someone is attempting a password spraying attack on the organization. They are trying only a few passwords but across multiple accounts.

3. **D**   Ben has successfully executed a heap overflow attack, which is a difficult attack to achieve. It can completely corrupt and overwrite memory contents by attempting to exhaust all of the dynamic memory available to an application.

4. **B**   The particular flaw that the cybersecurity analyst has discovered is called a race condition. This condition affects process and thread timing and proper sequencing. Race conditions can allow several attacks, including remote code execution and injection.

Software and Systems Security

DOMAIN 2.0

Domain Objectives

- **2.1** Given a scenario, apply security solutions for infrastructure management.
- **2.2** Explain software assurance best practices.
- **2.3** Explain hardware assurance best practices.

Objective 2.1 # Given a scenario, apply security solutions for infrastructure management

Infrastructure Management

Managing an organization's infrastructure can be a nightmare at worst, and a lot of hard work and attention to detail at best. This is especially true when you consider what is involved with infrastructure management. First, let's define what *infrastructure* is. At first glance, the infrastructure may seem to be just the network devices, cabling, servers, and so on. But an organization's infrastructure includes all those things and so much more. A complete picture of an infrastructure includes not only servers, network devices, and the physical cabling that connects them, but also hosts and applications. It contains data flows and interfaces. It also includes storage locations. It even consists of the policies and procedures that impose the requirements on the infrastructure for how it will protect, transport, and store information.

Often the infrastructure is broken up and managed by function; that is, there may be a group of people in the organization that manages only applications or only the network devices. However, these different groups have to work hand-in-hand across organizational boundaries because all of these pieces of infrastructure are still connected and require a unified approach. All these different levels and segments of the infrastructure are responsible for creating, processing, transmitting, receiving, storing, and protecting data, which transits across management and organizational functions.

In this objective, we're going to look at different aspects of managing an organization's infrastructure. We'll talk about managing infrastructure within a cloud service offering versus on-premises infrastructure management. We will discuss managing assets, and segmenting those assets, both physical and virtual. We'll also discuss the network architecture itself and different aspects of how modern networks are designed and managed. We'll discuss change management practices and their importance. We'll also talk about specific techniques to manage an infrastructure, such as virtualization and containerization. We'll also discuss the importance of identity and access management in the organization. Finally, we will discuss a hodgepodge of other essential aspects of managing the infrastructure, including cloud access security brokers, honeypots, infrastructure monitoring and logging, encryption, and certificate management. We will also emphasize active defense as a critical part of infrastructure security.

Cloud vs. On-Premises

In Objective 1.6, we discussed the different threats and vulnerabilities associated with cloud service models. You are already aware, then, that some of the advantages of using cloud models are a reduction in costs, less of a need to maintain in-house expertise, and less infrastructure to manage. The disadvantages, however, include a lack of management visibility on organizational data and the assets that process that data. The same advantages and disadvantages apply to managing an organization's infrastructure.

In a cloud-based infrastructure, your service level agreement (SLA) allows you to depend on the service provider to maintain an up-to-date infrastructure, to include patching, secure configuration, and state-of-the-art equipment. You also rely on them for guaranteed reliability and availability. These are issues you don't have to concern yourself with as much as assets located on your organization's premises. However, you are forced to transfer some of the control you might generally have to the service providers. You don't always get to determine or dictate how assets are employed in support of the organization's mission. The following table summarizes the advantages and disadvantages of cloud-based infrastructure versus on-premises infrastructure:

Infrastructure	Advantages	Disadvantages
Cloud-based	Efficiency; cost savings; less required personnel and expertise; less required equipment, facilities, resources; infrastructure is kept up-to-date, secure, and modern; some risk can be transferred to the cloud service provider.	Lack of control over asset and infrastructure; contract or SLA must be comprehensive and written to cover all possible issues; some liability, responsibility, and accountability cannot be transferred; the customer also sustains a vulnerability or attack suffered by the cloud service provider.
On-premises	Control over infrastructure and assets; visibility over how infrastructure is employed.	Cost; requires trained personnel; requires extensive equipment and facilities; incurs greater inherent risk that is not transferred.

Asset Management

Asset management is a broad term used to describe managing any asset that is a part of the organization's infrastructure. Many inexperienced cybersecurity analysts believe that asset management is simply computer hardware inventory; it's so much more than that. Remember the definition of an asset: an asset is anything of value, tangible or intangible. Assets directly contribute to business operations and successful missions. An asset could be computer equipment, to be sure, but it also includes software, other specialized equipment, facilities, and people. Assets can also include knowledge or information or data. These are all tangible assets, or assets you can physically touch, see, read, and so on. Although there are intangible assets as well, such as customer or stockholder confidence, the focus of this module is on specific tangible assets used in the organization's computing infrastructure.

Asset management is also more than merely inventorying physical devices. Of course, you will maintain an accurate, up-to-date inventory of hardware and software, but it also means managing licenses, provisioning services and users, and supporting business operations. It may mean reallocating resources to critical processes from noncritical ones. Asset management is an ongoing, constant process.

Asset Tagging

Asset tagging refers to the practice of identifying assets, both hardware and software, through logical or physical means. Physically, computer hardware can be tagged using metal plates or other types of physical markings. A physical tag should include the name of the asset, make, model, and serial number. It also may indicate additional information, such as the organization that owns the equipment. A logical tag could apply to the underlying software or firmware that resides on the equipment. For example, modern firmware, such as a BIOS or UEFI implementation, may have that same information, such as make, model, and serial number embedded in it. Even software can have the same information embedded in it, from its licensing agreement when it is purchased and installed. Sometimes this information is changeable by administrators, but sometimes it is not.

Both physical and logical asset tagging doesn't end with merely applying a tag to a physical piece of equipment or embedding information in its firmware or software. By itself, tagging only serves to identify an asset visually. Where asset tagging is particularly useful is in having that information connected to a database or integrated asset management system. In this way, assets can be tracked according to their location, user, owner, and even the customer they support.

Wireless and mobile assets benefit from asset tagging because you can add much more information about the asset into your asset management system and track its location in real time, using its wireless or cellular capabilities. This can help you track where the asset, such as a smartphone or tablet, is currently located, where it has been, and where it is going. You can also set up advanced features such as geofencing, which enables you to set a physical boundary in which the asset cannot leave that area or at least notify you when it does. This is typically only used for highly valuable or sensitive assets that may contain sensitive data and should not leave company premises.

Segmentation

Large network infrastructures are typically not flat, or contiguous. Networks are usually broken up both logically and physically, by location, by connection to certain other network devices, and through IP address subnets. Segmentation is important because it can help network performance, make it easier to organize the different assets and systems in use, and give you an additional level of protection in terms of security. For example, from your earlier networking studies, you are probably already aware that smart switches are preferred over simple hubs to segment hosts because they can separate collision domains. Routers are also used to segment hosts, and indeed entire network segments, because they help eliminate broadcast domains. These logical and physical segmentations benefit the infrastructure's performance. However, security is also a benefit of segmentation. Segmentation can allow a user to access only specific hosts on the network, because sensitive hosts are segmented away either logically or physically from users. Only certain groups of users may be able to access those hosts. In this section, we will discuss several different categories of segmentation, all falling into the two types of physical or logical. These include physical, virtual, jump box, system isolation, and air gap.

Physical

Physical segmentation can involve a couple of different aspects. First of all, the physical location itself can segment critical assets. They can simply be in different parts of the building, or across the country in different geographic areas. This not only can help ensure redundancy in the case of duplicative equipment, but also ensure that if an adverse event occurs at one location, it spares another location where other critical assets are kept.

Second, physical segmentation can make use of network devices, such as switches and routers, to physically separate hosts from being on the same physical network segment or cable. This can be especially advantageous if a piece of fiber or Ethernet cable is cut, for example, or the organization suffers a power loss to parts of its infrastructure that may not affect other parts due to the physical device segmentation.

Virtual

Virtual segmentation is a type of logical segmentation. This can take many forms. First, at a basic level, hosts and entire networks can be logically separated through the use of different IP subnets. Even if they are all attached to the same physical media, the traffic between hosts is logically separated in that it doesn't have to be transmitted or received by all hosts on the network due to a logically separated addressing scheme.

Logical separation can also be employed using encryption methods. It's not uncommon to see sensitive information or even all traffic from specified hosts be encrypted and sent over unencrypted links that are shared with non-sensitive hosts. Each host that transmits or receives encrypted traffic must be specially configured to do so and can be set up to communicate only with other hosts that use the same encryption algorithms and keys.

Still another form of virtual segmentation is the use of virtual hosts. Virtualization will be covered a little bit later in this objective, but segmentation using virtualization involves running independent virtual machines on a physical host where hardware is abstracted from the virtual machines. The virtual machines could be configured to communicate with any, all, or none of the other virtual machines, even if they reside on the same physical hardware.

Jump Box

Sometimes sensitive systems on the network have to be given special consideration for segmentation or protection away from the general population of the organization. There are many different ways to do this, and one of them is to use a jump box. A jump box is a specially configured host whose sole purpose is to log on to or access a sensitive network segment or systems. For example, rather than using a desktop computer, which is typically employed for routine tasks such as e-mail and web surfing, an administrator might use a specially configured box to access sensitive servers to perform administration tasks on them remotely. These servers would not be accessible from any ordinary workstation due to physical or logical segmentation. In this case, the jump box serves as an access point from where the administrator can perform their administrative duties on those sensitive hosts.

While not a firewall or a bastion host, the jump box could be considered a chokepoint or a single-entry point into accessing sensitive systems. The jump box typically would be securely configured, stripped of unnecessary services and software, and hardened more than a regular workstation might. The jump box might also have more than one network card, enabling it to be logically on two or more different network segments, effectively allowing it to segment ordinary hosts from sensitive ones.

System Isolation

System isolation is used when you have a particularly sensitive host or system that needs to be separated from the general population of users and hosts on the network. Perhaps only certain users or hosts should be able to access this sensitive device due to the nature of the data it contains. There are several different ways you could isolate the system, and segmentation is one of them. For very sensitive systems, both physical and logical segmentation would be ideal. This might include dedicated subnets, switches, and routers. It also might mean the use of encryption for all traffic between that particular host and others. It obviously should require different authentication methods for access, including multifactor authentication, if possible. Sensitive hosts might reside on their own specific VLAN as well, and there might be intermediate network devices that use very strict access control lists to control who accesses the system, using only explicitly allowed ports and protocols. This would likely be a special-use box, not intended for anyone to access for e-mail or other general purposes. The key here is to isolate the system from the general-use network and other systems and ensure highly restrictive access to it.

Air Gap

An air gap is the ultimate in system isolation and segmentation. Essentially, there is no logical or physical connection to the host or network segment from the Internet or the general-use network. Any data transferred between an air-gapped system and another system would have to use physical media of some sort, such as a USB drive or CD. Even these might be highly restricted in their use; only specific external media devices might be allowed, and they might have to be part of a carefully controlled inventory. The system requiring an air gap segmentation would likely be for highly sensitive or specialized use and would require no connection to the outside world or the company network. An example of an air-gapped system might be one that you use to scan external media for malware. Anyone bringing any type of removable media into the organization, such as a USB stick or CD, would put that media in the air-gapped system and scan it for malware. Once it is determined to be safe, the media can be used on other systems connected to the network. Another example of an air-gapped system might be one that contains a specialized database. The database doesn't need to be connected to anyone, and only periodically someone might need to go to the system to retrieve specific data that must be manually input into a networked system. This ensures that the database itself is not connected to any network, so the risk of its loss or unauthorized access would be highly minimized.

 EXAM TIP Keep in mind that segmentation is used to separate sensitive hosts from the general population of users in the network, no matter which method—physical, virtual, jump box, system isolation, or even air gap—is used.

Network Architecture

The term *network architecture* refers to how a network is designed and constructed. Networks aren't merely a collection of hosts connected through cables or wireless networks to each other. There are both physical and logical aspects of network architecture you should be familiar with from your studies of basic networking, which we will discuss in the upcoming sections. Network architecture also describes data flows and interfaces, addressing, device placement, controlled entry points, and so on. We'll take a look at both physical and software-defined (logical) network architectures, as well as how network architectures can be virtualized, such as through virtual private clouds and virtual private networks.

 KEY TERM   **Network architecture** describes how a network is designed and constructed at various layers, including the physical and logical layers. It also illustrates how components of the network interface with each other, how data flows between those interfaces, the security mechanisms in place across the network, the ports and protocols used to communicate on the network, and even how applications communicate across the infrastructure.

Physical

Physical network architecture describes the way that hosts are physically connected through different types of cabling or media to different network devices. The physical network architecture also describes, to a degree, the different types of signaling or connections that are involved in the architecture (Ethernet, wireless, or token ring, for example).

From your basic network studies, you probably remember the different types of basic physical architectures:

- **Star**   Uses a centralized hub or switch from which hosts are connected individually through a network cable
- **Bus**   Describes hosts that are attached to the same physical media, usually by tapping into a centralized cable
- **Ring**   Uses a central hub with a cable connecting all stations in a logical circle or ring configuration
- **Mesh**   Employs multiple hosts that are all connected
- **Hybrid**   Could be a combination of any or all of these physical designs

Smaller networks use simplistic designs; however, larger and more complex networks use highly complicated versions of these same basic physical architectures.

 EXAM TIP   You are not expected to answer questions directly regarding physical architecture, but you should be aware of the different physical layouts, including star, bus, and ring architectures.

Software-Defined Networking

Logical network architecture refers to how network devices are named, assigned addressing information, and communicate with each other via different network protocols. More often than not, software or operating system utilities determine these design elements. These are all straightforward elements; however, there are more sophisticated logical network architectures that are completely built within the software and define not only protocols and addressing but also subnets, network segmentation, access control, and so on. *Software-defined networking (SDN)* is a term that describes a network architecture built entirely in software, wherein various applications are responsible for determining data routing and control within the network. This approach also defines dynamic network programmability; this means the network can change as the organization's requirements change.

Software-defined networking is defined in an Internet Engineering Task Force (IETF) Request for Comments (RFC) document, RFC 7426, and describes the structures used to create and manage these networks. It also defines standardization for how these programmable networks will use resources, network devices, interfaces, applications, and services.

 EXAM TIP Remember that logical architecture is separate from and can be different than the physical architecture. The logical architecture is almost always defined in software or network services.

Virtual Private Cloud (VPC)

A *virtual private cloud* (VPC) is a set of dedicated resources, set aside for one organization's use, either in its own data center or even in a cloud service provider. We've already looked at cloud models in Objective 1.6, so remember that this is one of the many models you can use to implement a cloud infrastructure with a cloud service provider.

If a virtual private cloud is set up in an organization's own data center, using organizationally owned resources and assets, there's much not much difference between it and an on-premises infrastructure; it simply emulates a cloud infrastructure and is suited for use across geographically dispersed locations within the same organization. If the virtual private cloud is part of a public cloud service provider's infrastructure, then it is segregated so that no other cloud service user outside the organization can access it. The organization dictates access controls, such as authorized users, authentication methods, and so on, subject to the provider's offerings.

Virtual private clouds are most commonly seen as an Infrastructure as a Service (IaaS) offering from a cloud service provider. The piece of the cloud that the service provider has segregated for the organization's use is isolated using a multitude of technologies, including virtual LANs (VLANs), and even dedicated physical and virtual servers in some cases, as well as other structures that ensure complete privacy and isolation from other customers also supported by the cloud service provider.

Major service providers that offer a virtual private cloud implementation include Amazon Web Services, Microsoft Azure, IBM Cloud, and Google Cloud Platform.

KEY TERM A **virtual private cloud** is a cloud infrastructure set up using an organization's own resources and data center, and for the exclusive use of the organization, no matter where it is geographically dispersed and located.

Virtual Private Network (VPN)

A *virtual private network* (VPN) is essentially two private networks separated by a larger public network, such as the Internet. In a virtual private networking setup, a single host or even another branch office (called a site-to-site VPN) can logically connect to a private network through the use of a secure tunnel. Tunneling protocols provide the ability to encapsulate sensitive traffic inside other traffic. Think of putting a confidential message inside an envelope and sending it through the public United States Postal Service (USPS) system. The envelope is sealed and addressed appropriately so that it can travel through the postal system network to its intended recipient. The envelope, usually being opaque, prevents anyone from seeing the private message inside.

VPNs work similarly. The client typically has to have specialized VPN software, which allows it to establish a connection through a public network, such as the Internet, using a tunneling protocol. The client is authenticated to the organizational network through a specified VPN gateway server at the organization's private network, typically using credentials especially provided for VPN connections. Sensitive data is sent through the Internet, usually encrypted, using the tunneling protocol until it arrives. The traffic is deconstructed, and the sensitive information decrypted, which is then forwarded on through to the organization network, just as if the client was part of that network.

The tunneling protocol generally used for modern VPNs is the Layer 2 Tunneling Protocol, or L2TP. L2TP is an updated version of a combination of two older VPN protocols: Point-To-Point Tunneling Protocol (PPTP) and Layer 2 Forwarding (L2F), developed by Microsoft and Cisco, respectively. Note that L2TP does not do anything except encapsulate the traffic that travels through a public network such as the Internet. It can't encrypt or otherwise protect sensitive traffic; therefore, it's usually used in conjunction with security protocols, such as IP Security (IPSec), which provides those encryption and authentication services. Note that there are also VPN connections that can take place over secure web browsers, using the HTTPS protocol, which uses Transport Layer Security (TLS) as its secure transport mechanism.

IPSec is a security protocol that's relatively new to the IP version 4 stack. It is native to IPv6, however, and mandated for use whenever IPv6 networks are used. IPSec has two modes of use: transport mode and tunnel mode. In transport mode, the IP address headers are not encrypted; this allows it to travel within a private network. When used in tunnel mode, however, it requires a tunneling protocol, such as L2TP. In tunnel mode, the IP address header information is encapsulated by L2TP, making it better suited for traveling across a public network. Tunnel mode is the mode associated with VPN connections. IPSec also uses two primary security protocols: Authentication Header (AH), which is used for data integrity and data origin authentication, and the Encapsulating Security Payload (ESP), which provides data encryption and other security services. IPSec uses security associations, where all parties of the communications session establish and share security attributes, such as algorithms and keys, so that all may communicate securely.

 EXAM TIP VPNs make use of tunneling protocols, such as L2TP, and must also use security protocols such as IPSec for encryption and authentication services.

Change Management

An essential part of infrastructure management is managing change. Change management is concerned with the organized processes of approval, testing, and implementation of infrastructure changes, whether it's adding new servers or subnets, updating enterprise applications, or adding new capabilities to the infrastructure. If the organization allowed random or unplanned changes to take place, the infrastructure would be severely impacted. There might be performance issues, interoperability issues, lack of standardization, and certainly security problems. Change management is the formal process that requires management involvement and approval for all infrastructure-related changes.

The organization should have a change management policy and procedure, as it should with most processes. The change management policy and procedure, directive in nature, should include the following items:

- Roles and responsibilities
- Formal change management processes
- A requirement for business cases for all significant infrastructure changes
- A requirement for security, functionality, and performance analysis for all proposed changes
- Procedures for introducing, testing, and implementing all changes
- Procedures for backing out changes that adversely affect the infrastructure
- An impact rating for changes
- A requirement for establishing a formal change control board (CCB)

For this last requirement, the policy should direct that a change control board be chartered. A CCB should include mid- to senior-level managers who are in charge of receiving recommendations for major infrastructure changes and deciding whether or not those changes should be allowed, based on risk to the organization. Even a change from a well-meaning system administrator might incur risk for the organization, such as causing the infrastructure to no longer be interoperable or secure. Because changes can impact the entire organization, it's only common sense that management can review the proposed changes and have the power to approve or veto them. The CCB serves that function.

For the change management process to work, a requester or initiator for the change must present a business case, often provided by a business unit, to the CCB, as well as documentation about the particulars of the change and how it will impact the organization. If the CCB initially approves the change, then ideally the next step would be to test the change on a development or test system before actually putting it into production. Based on the results of the test, the CCB may formally approve the change being placed into implementation. Once the change is final, the CCB is informed of any issues that have been caused by the change, or notified that the change has been implemented and is performing as expected. One item the CCB may require is a backup plan, in the event the change causes unexpected disruption or damage to the infrastructure. The backup plan would provide procedures for technicians to undo the change and restore the infrastructure to its original pre-change state.

Another crucial part of the change management program is to create a rating system that defines changes based on their impact to the organization; this impact could be the risk to the organization if the change is not implemented, such as a low-impact change, a high-impact change, or critical change. There should also be provisions for emergency changes, in the event an incident or other significant event happens that requires changes that should be approved by the CCB.

It's important to note that configuration management is a subset of change management. Where change management can be viewed as managing sweeping changes in architecture, design, services, interoperability, and security across the infrastructure, configuration management happens at the system level. Configuration management is the process of ensuring that baseline configurations for network hosts and devices are maintained, updated, and monitored. Although technically a configuration change to a server's baseline falls under change management, if the organization has set up a change rating structure, then routine changes to host configurations might not require full CCB approval. This might include regular patches, security configuration changes, and so on. Obviously, patches and updates should be tested and approved by someone before being implemented, especially critical patches, which may break the infrastructure. However, it may not require the full CCB for approval. The CCB should make policies and procedures for configuration changes across the infrastructure and how to deal with them.

 EXAM TIP   A change control board is usually created under the auspices of a charter, which details the board's makeup, decision-making authority, meeting schedule, and levels of infrastructure change that require its approval.

Virtualization

Virtualization is another recent technology that has made managing infrastructure easier and more efficient. Virtualization involves creating multiple dynamic instances of hosts through software, called *virtual machines,* on physical machines. In other words, it's possible to create a Windows 10 host, for example, through software known as a *hypervisor,* which resides on yet another Windows or even Linux host. Virtual machines behave as if they are actual physical machines; indeed, they share physical hardware with their host machine. The host, through the hypervisor, shares its physical hardware and manages access to memory, CPU, disk space, and networking, as well as other physical resources. If a physical host has enough memory, CPU power, and disk space, it could support many virtual machine instances on it. These virtual machines can be treated as regular hosts, running and providing a variety of services for users. They can also be backed up, replicated, and easily put into production, which makes managing them much easier, since when they are inactive, they are essentially files on disk.

As mentioned, the host machine is the physical hardware that we traditionally think of as a networked host. It can run multiple virtual (guest) machines simultaneously, including those that have different operating systems than the host. Virtual machines rely on the underlying hardware power and robustness of the host machine for their performance. The host machine uses a hypervisor to manage and maintain the virtual machines. You will typically see two types of hypervisors: Type I and Type II. A Type I hypervisor, also called a bare-metal hypervisor, is installed on a physical machine with a bare minimum of operating system files on it—essentially just enough to create and manage virtual machines. Also, it does not require an underlying operating system, as a Type I hypervisor actually *is* the operating system. Examples of a Type I hypervisor include VMWare's ESX server and Microsoft's Hyper-V. A Type II hypervisor, on the other hand, is simply an application that sits between the host operating system and the virtual machines. Examples of Type II hypervisors include VMware Workstation, Fusion, and VirtualBox. These all require a base operating system to be installed on the host before they are installed and can manage virtual machines.

Virtual Desktop Infrastructure (VDI)

A virtual desktop infrastructure (VDI) is yet another way of implementing virtualization. It provides a way for users to have a desktop that is able to access network resources without requiring intense computing power for the client. Users use VDI software to make remote connections to shared network resources, such as file shares, applications, printers, and storage. The user's client device is known as a *thin client,* since most of the processing takes place on a remote robust system, which delivers the visual and control experience to users' display and peripherals. If this sounds a bit familiar, it's because we may have come full circle with this paradigm, since way back in the early days of computing, using devices called *terminals,* this was almost exactly the architecture that existed because computing power and storage space was at a premium.

VDI has several advantages. First of all, it can help keep expense of resources to a minimum, as a user's client machine does not have to be a high-powered, resilient workstation, since all the data processing and storage take place on a more robust server. The only thing the client workstation is responsible for is rendering video, accepting input from a user to send to the VDI software, and delivering output to the user. If the user's workstation crashes, theoretically there's no data lost. Second, VDI is useful from a security perspective. Since the user, in a restricted environment, may not be able to use external media devices, this can help prevent data loss through accident or malicious intent. Most VDI solutions also offer advanced authentication mechanisms, where the user would have to log in to their thin client and then centrally authenticate through to the VDI solution. This also enables more efficient, centralized monitoring and auditing of protected resources that can only be accessed through the VDI. Finally, a third advantage for using VDI is that it is easily implemented in mobile or teleworking environments. VDIs are particularly useful for implementation in a VPN environment.

VDI implementations can be straightforward, such as using Microsoft's Remote Desktop Protocol (RDP), or very complex, using enterprise solutions such as Citrix, or even cloud-based solutions that might use Desktop as a Service (DaaS). Critical factors in implementing a VDI solution, particularly across the enterprise, are network speed and latency as well as infrastructure robustness and resiliency.

 NOTE Virtual desktop infrastructure is not the same type of technology as virtualization; it is referred to as "virtual desktop" because the user's desktop presentation is a function of the VDI software and represents what's taking place on the remote server.

Containerization

Just as operating systems can be virtualized within other operating systems, applications can be virtualized as well. On the surface, this may seem strange; an application is typically simply installed over an operating system, which provides it resources such as hardware, services such as authentication, and other software such as libraries. Additionally, you could conceivably create virtual machines for the sole purpose of installing applications in them to protect the host operating system from insecure applications. The virtual machine's hypervisor can provide a layer of protection against aberrant applications, since they only affect the virtual machine they are running within.

In the concept of containerization, all related files for the application are installed in a "container," which is insulated from the operating system by another layer of abstraction; this controls communications between the application and the operating system, as well as between the application and hardware, libraries, and other services, including networked services. The reason for this is that it provides an additional layer of security and protection for both the operating system and the application itself.

The container may be constructed from another management application, sometimes called the *container runtime*. This container application serves the same purpose as its hypervisor counterpart with virtualization. The container provides a space for the application and its libraries, files, and dependencies to run separately from those provided by the operating system; it translates all the application needs to and from the operating system to provide those resources. Whereas virtual machines are considered an abstraction of the hardware layer of the machine that supports them, containers are an abstraction of the software layer of the supporting operating system.

Containers can assist in providing security for the overall system because they can shield applications from vulnerabilities suffered by the operating system, and vice versa. A disadvantage is that any issues encountered by the operating system can affect the containerization application, and may even allow damage to all containerized applications if the operating systems itself has been compromised.

Popular containerization applications include Docker and Kubernetes. Applications that benefit from containerization include those that are created under Microsoft's .NET framework and applications that make extensive use of the Java programming language.

 NOTE Keep in mind the difference between virtualization and containerization: virtualization describes virtualized operating systems that are separated from the physical machine's operating systems by a hypervisor, whereas containerization involves separating applications from the operating system through a software runtime layer.

Identity and Access Management

Identity and access management are two critical processes in the world of cybersecurity, especially in larger organizations. As cybersecurity analysts, one part of our job is to ensure that users and other entities are authenticated so they can use network resources. This is accomplished by validating the identity that an entity presents and then further controlling whatever access they have to our internal resources. We achieve this through several different methods and processes. In this section we are going to cover some of those methods and processes as well as discuss the particulars associated with the exam objectives that focus on identity and access management. We'll talk about privilege and account management as well as discuss authentication methods, such as multifactor authentication, single sign-on, and federated authentication. We'll also discuss access control models, such as discretionary, mandatory, role-based, and attribute-based models. Finally, we'll talk about the necessity to monitor and review all of our different identity and access management processes.

Authentication Methods

While we can't discuss every single authentication method you might encounter in your career as cybersecurity analyst, there are some essential concepts you must understand regarding authentication. Of particular importance is the role of multifactor authentication, single sign-on, and federated authentication. You should also be familiar with the basics of account and privilege management, which we'll discuss next.

Privilege Management

Privilege and account management go hand in hand. They are two separate processes, but we can discuss them together. First of all, account management is the process associated with provisioning, maintaining, monitoring, and deprovisioning user accounts. This function may be delegated to a single entity, such as the help desk, or it may be dispersed across several different functions, such as within different departments. In any case, the account management function concerns itself with validating user accounts so that users can have approved and controlled access to the network and its resources. User accounts should normally be approved through several entities. First through human resources when someone is initially hired and then through the personnel security section so that their security clearance, if required, and suitability for access can be verified. They also need to be validated as requiring accounts by their supervisory chain. There are processes and procedures that go into account management to ensure that only authorized users have accounts, that these accounts can only access specific resources, and that actions these accounts can perform on those resources are controlled and monitored.

Privilege management involves the ongoing verification and validation that a user account has access to the correct resources and that they can perform the proper actions on those resources. Privilege management should be driven by the principle of least privilege, which means that a user should only have the minimum amount of privileges necessary to perform their job function, and no more. If a user's privileges are not adequately monitored, they can eventually increase over time. This can happen if people move around from department to department and accumulate different privileges along the way. It can also happen when someone is granted privileges for special occasions that should be temporary, but then these privileges are not taken away. Initial privileges should be granted by resource or data owners who should periodically validate that user accounts still require those privileges. Privileges, which can include rights and permissions to perform actions and access objects, should be validated periodically and removed when they are no longer needed. Whereas account management may be assigned to a particular function that controls accounts across the organization, privilege management could be a function of individual resource or data owners who must approve access to those particular resources. The account management function can also be assigned to grant or revoke those privileges as resource and data owners see fit.

EXAM TIP   Privilege management and account management are two different processes, although in the practical world they may be combined and serviced by the same administrative group in an organization. Account management involves the provisioning of user accounts, and privilege management is a function of resource owners granting access to those users.

Multifactor Authentication (MFA)

Remember that authentication is the process of validating that a person or entity is who they claim to be. Authentication has several requirements to it. In order to authenticate, obviously an individual or entity must present some sort of credentials as identification. Credentials could include a username and password combination, a smartcard or token, and a personal identification number (PIN). Other identifying characteristics can also be presented, such as biometric items like a fingerprint or retinal scan.

Authentication is often thought of in terms of single factor or multifactor. There are several *factors*, or requirements, that must be met for authentication. Factors include the following:

- Something you *know* (knowledge factor), such as a username and password combination
- Something you *have* (possession factor), such as a smartcard or token
- Something you *are* (inherent factor), such as a fingerprint or retinal pattern

In a single-factor authentication scheme, a user only needs one of those factors to identify themselves and authenticate. The most common example of a single-factor authentication system is the username/password combination, which uses the knowledge factor.

Multifactor authentication uses more than one of these factors. This is because individually, a single factor could be defeated, and someone can be impersonated. For example, someone could discover your username and password and use that to authenticate themselves. Multifactor authentication is more difficult to defeat because you must have at least two separate factors. For example, to withdraw money from a bank's ATM, you must have a debit card (something you possess) and also know its associated PIN (something you know). If you lost the debit card, it would be much harder for a malicious person to find it and use it, since they do not know the PIN that must be used with it. Multifactor authentication requires at least two factors, such as something you have, like a smart card, along with something you know, such the PIN. You can also see multifactor authentication in use with a fingerprint (something you are) and a PIN. Note that the use of the username and password combination is *not* multifactor authentication. It is single factor because it only uses one requirement—the knowledge factor.

In addition to these three factors, authentication systems can augment these factors with temporary characteristics, or *attributes,* that can modify the authentication requirement for a given instance. For example, location and time (temporal attribute) can be used to specify additional requirements for authentication. In addition to requiring multifactor authentication, the system may also require that authentication occur between certain hours of the day, or from a specific geographical location (either logical, such as from a particular IP address, or physical, such as from a specific host in the building).

 EXAM TIP Remember that multifactor authentication requires at least two *different* factors in use during the identification and authentication process. Username and password authentication is only single-factor authentication because it only uses one factor—the knowledge factor.

Single Sign-On (SSO)

Single sign-on (SSO) is an aspect of authentication that involves the use of a single credential to access multiple systems or resources. Most frequently, you will see single sign-on in a centralized authentication model, such as a Windows domain. In this type of model, you would authenticate once to the centralized authentication server, such as a domain controller in Windows, and not be required to authenticate to other resources on the network, such as shared folders, printers, and so on, as long as those resources are configured to use the same authentication credentials. This requires that those resources and the servers that house them trust the centralized authentication mechanism.

In environments that don't use single sign-on, you not only might be required to authenticate for every single resource you use, such as a shared folder or a website, but your authentication credentials might be different, and even have different requirements, such as password length and complexity. For single sign-on to work, resources have to trust a centralized authentication mechanism, and the appropriate protocols have to be in place. Examples of authentication protocols that enable single sign-on include both Kerberos and Sesame.

Federation

A federation is also another aspect of an authentication model in which you may have multiple organizations that either trust each other, so that authentication mechanisms and credentials are transitive across organizations, or use a centralized authentication provider. Trust is the key in a federated model; an organization must trust the authentication provider that is validating the user's credentials, and those credentials must be valid for use in that organization. An example of a federated authentication provider that you may have seen is Google. For example, given Google's wide range of products and services, you might use your Gmail username and password to authenticate to other Google services. Even non-Google services might accept your Google credentials. In the corporate world, an example might be where several companies trust each other and permit the use of one company's credentials to access resources in another company, or the credentials that are authenticated through a common third party. Federated identities are often also used in single sign-on environments.

Because there many third-party identity providers (IdPs) that maintain user credentials and enable users to employ the same credentials to log in to multiple sites across different organizations, standardization was needed to ensure that all these different authentication services could communicate with resources and the federated identity managers associated with the organizations. OpenID is one such standard. OpenID enables users to authenticate to different organizations and services using these third-party authentication providers. The standard defines three roles in this process: the end user, who desires to be authenticated to a resource; the relying party, which is the organization or infrastructure that owns the resource itself; and the OpenID provider, which is where the user account and credentials reside that will be used for access.

Access Control Models

Access control models dictate how users and other entities (such as hosts, processes, services, and daemons) are given the appropriate access to resources, based on functional need, role, and even level of trust. There are several different access control models, and we will cover the more commonly used ones—particularly the ones you will see on the exam. We'll discuss discretionary, role-based, attribute-based, and mandatory access control models. Each has its place, depending on the requirements of the organization, and in fact there can be different combinations of each in use in the same organization, depending on data sensitivity and other protection requirements.

Discretionary Access Control (DAC)

The discretionary access control (DAC) model dictates that the owner of a resource be able to grant privileges for that real resource at their discretion (hence the name). They alone have the power to determine who has different levels of access to their resources. They can use whatever criteria they wish, but more often than not it's based on their job role's functional need, what role they play in the data process, and other factors determined by the resource owner. This is the most common access control model seen in large environments. Rights, permissions, and privileges can be granted to individuals or to groups of individuals who have like access requirements.

Mandatory Access Control (MAC)

Unlike DAC, mandatory access control (MAC) is not a model where access is left up to the discretion of the creator or owner of the resource. Access is only granted by specific administrators. This model uses data sensitivity separation as one factor; for example, systems can be dedicated to a specific data sensitivity level, such as Top-Secret or Secret. All data is labeled with a specific data sensitivity level. Users can only access the level of data sensitivity that they are allowed by the administrator. They also must have the required security clearance level and the need to know. Data is highly compartmentalized in this model, and even if a user had the proper security clearance, they may not have access to data at the same level. The MAC model is only used in environments where the data is highly sensitive, such as a military organization.

Role-Based Access Control (RBAC)

In a role-based model, access is not granted to individuals, but to *roles*. An individual may serve in one or more roles, such as a database administrator, account manager, and so on. Roles normally have defined functions, so privileges are granted according to what functions they must perform. In most role-based models, privileges can be cumulative, as users can be a member of more than one role, such as a database administrator and supervisor, at the same time. Note that you should not confuse roles with Windows groups, although they can be similar. Windows groups are constructs that provide convenient administration for groups of similar users. If you include all administrative users into a group and then assign privileges to that group, you are in fact assigning privileges based on roles, but you are still using a discretionary access model, since the owner of a resource still has discretion over assigning privileges to whichever users they like inside or outside the group. In a strict role-based model, only specific administrators can assign privileges roles, whether or not they are the resource owner.

Attribute-Based Access Control (ABAC)

With attribute-based access control (ABAC), certain attributes or characteristics can be added to an authentication requirement. Most of these attributes are temporary in nature, such as location and time of day. In other words, the user must also meet these additional requirements to authenticate, but may not be in a position to do so if they are trying to authenticate from another location or during a different time of day. Attributes can be set for the authentication process, or even as part of the requirements to access a particular resource (a folder, for example). Resources such as printers may only be available during business hours and not available afterward (in order to prevent someone from printing large volumes of personal materials on corporate printers, for instance). Here are some of the more commonly used attributes:

- **Subject**   Attributes about the person requesting access, including role, location, and security clearance
- **Object**   Characteristics of the resourced accessed, including data sensitivity level, topic, and file location
- **Action**   Requested action, such as add, delete, or modify
- **Context**   Characteristics of the access session, including time of day, subject, and object status

ABAC offers the ability to finely tune access control, since theoretically you could grant access based on certain hours of the day, only to certain people with a specific clearance, only from a particular location, and only to files that have been changed in the past 24 hours, for example. The downside of ABAC is that it can be administratively prohibitive if it's not well organized and maintained.

 EXAM TIP   DAC is the least restrictive and most flexible access control model, and the most commonly used. MAC is the most restrictive model and is only used in highly secure environments.

Access Management Manual Review

Like most of the security processes, identity and access management can be monitored through the use of automated tools. Most often, these are auditing types of tools, which serve to audit actions on objects taken by individuals. However, automated auditing tools may not catch everything; manual review is often required to look for anomalies that may be connected but are outside the normal baseline for automated tools to catch.

When reviewing identity and access management, cybersecurity personnel should look for anomalous or strange patterns in behavior—a user employing privileges they have never used before, for example, and doing so without explanation. Audit logs can provide an event-by-event breakdown of which user accounts have been using which privileges, as long as auditing is properly configured. Object access must also be reviewed, which assumes that object auditing has been properly configured as well. This data can be combined with other sources, such as operating system or application logs, and fed into an aggregation engine, such as a SIEM system, to help with manual analysis and to determine if there are any disturbing patterns in access control management.

Cloud Access Security Broker (CASB)

In a modern organization that uses cloud services, it's not very often that you find your organization is exclusively tied to one cloud service, where the connection is simplistic and easy to manage. More often than not, organizations use multiple, different cloud service product providers for different services. Cloud service providers don't always have standardized methods of access control or monitoring, and every service that the organization uses may require different types of access control mechanisms, authentication protocols, and so on. One solution for this is to use a cloud access security broker (CASB), which sits between the organization and all of its different cloud services. A CASB can be configured to monitor all activity between users and cloud services, handle authentication, enforce access control policies, and audit for malicious action or policy violations.

 KEY TERM A **cloud access security broker** is an intermediate management mechanism that manages and negotiates authentication and security services between users or internal hosts and various external cloud service providers.

Honeypot

A *honeypot* is nothing more than a sophisticated decoy that's set up to attract malicious entities so they will focus on it instead of attacking your network. A honeypot is a special host, usually placed in an isolated segment away from critical or sensitive hosts, that has numerous vulnerabilities programmed into it. The idea of a honeypot is that if an attacker is looking to attack your network, they will be distracted by the decoy and focus their time and attention on it. This can give your intrusion detection and prevention systems time to alert your administrators so they can monitor the attack, learn about the attackers techniques, and attempt to detect details about the attacker that can be used to stop them, locate them, and prosecute them.

Larger organizations may deploy many such decoy hosts in a network configuration, called a *honeynet*, which may be very sophisticated in nature and appear to be a full-fledged segment with sensitive hosts, network devices, and so on. The idea is to offer enough potential attack surfaces to a malicious entity that they will be kept busy with the honeynet and not get around to attacking your real network.

NOTE   When setting up a honeypot or honeynet, it is critical that you make sure your organization is reasonably secure, since you are essentially inviting a malicious entity to attack your network. Ensure you have performed your due care and diligence in setting up intrusion detection systems, perimeter defenses, and other security controls to prevent those attackers from attacking your real network.

Monitoring and Logging

Two critical processes in the life of the cybersecurity analyst—monitoring and logging—have both been covered off and on throughout this book, where we have focused on various aspects of each. We discussed the importance of monitoring threat intelligence as well as insufficient monitoring and logging as a vulnerability. You might believe that there's not much more to say on either topic, but there is still plenty. We could devote an entire book to each subject and still not adequately cover all the different nuances of monitoring your network and logging its activities. These are both common themes throughout the major objectives of the CySA+ exam. In this section, we will cover yet another aspect of monitoring logging as it pertains to overall infrastructure management. We will also discuss monitoring and logging a bit more in depth during the different objectives of Domains 3, 4, and 5, as we discuss security monitoring, monitoring in the incident response context, and continuous risk monitoring.

In terms of infrastructure management, monitoring and logging are critical processes because you need to monitor several aspects of your network, its hosts, applications, and even your users. You need to understand what's going on in the network at any given moment. You will be monitoring for major events, of course, but you're also monitoring day-to-day smaller issues that could lead up to major events. Monitoring includes not only security monitoring, but performance monitoring, function monitoring, and user behavior monitoring. All this monitoring should be considered smaller pieces of a bigger puzzle that you're looking to put together, sometimes on a day-by-day basis, and sometimes over a longer period of time. You want to know not only what's happening at a point in time, but also to be able to perform historical and trend analysis so you can detect longer-term issues and problems. Here are some of the key elements of your infrastructure you will monitor:

- Network device, server host, and application performance
- Bandwidth utilization
- Routine network traffic
- User behavior (also called *real user monitoring,* or *RUM*)
- Endpoint security
- Infrastructure changes, through a formal change management program

This is definitely not an all-inclusive list, as you will get down into the weeds and monitor so many more things, including anomalous network behavior, ports, protocols, services, and so much more. The point of all this monitoring is that you need to know what's going on across your network at all times. However, monitoring does you no good at all if you are not doing something with the data that you get. Remember that information is data given context, and unless you give it context, it's all just a lot of meaningless trivia. Aggregating all this data, developing context, and analyzing it is where the payoff comes in. Monitoring serves not only to point out all the small little things going on your network, but how all infrastructure events, no matter how small or large, are connected and show how your network is performing and how secure it is. This is where automated monitoring comes in.

No single person or even a group of people can effectively monitor all of the events going on in your infrastructure. In a large network infrastructure, data will be generated at a massive rate—sometimes at a rate of thousands of events per hour, faster than human beings can sort and review them. Automated systems are needed to consume that data, aggregate it into useful information, give it context, and provide it for analysis to human beings. Security information and event monitoring (SIEM) systems have been mentioned already in this book, and they are the key to successful infrastructure monitoring. A good SIEM system can take thousands of data points from a wide variety of disparate sources and put them together so that an analyst can see multiple data points at a time, how they are related, the patterns they may generate, and how they are affecting the overall infrastructure. This gives the human analyst the ability to see the overall big picture, as well as to drill down to the weeds if they need to without being inundated with so many data points that they can't see the forest for the trees.

Cross-Reference

SIEM systems are covered more in depth in Objective 3.2.

Logging goes hand in hand with monitoring. While monitoring can be in real time, as events are happening, it also occurs over time. For monitoring to be effective, data has to be captured in some manner. That's where logging comes in. Logging captures data that is of importance to a cybersecurity analyst so that it can be monitored after the fact, and over longer periods. There are two key considerations with logging: logging the right data and actually reviewing the logs. If these are done properly, there's no point in logging at all, and by extension no point in monitoring the network's security and performance.

Logging, also closely related to auditing, involves determining what data points are useful and configuring your systems to collect and store events related to those data points. Logging can occur on a system basis, on an application basis, or on a network-wide basis. You can log performance information for your systems, security event information, and error information. All this information could be related, as security issues sometimes cause performance problems and generate errors that might be misunderstood until aggregated and put into context with other data sources.

Most modern operating systems and applications can be configured to log specific data; however, the out-of-the-box configuration that most operating systems and programs use for logging is usually not sufficient. Knowledgeable cybersecurity analysts have to determine which specific data they need logged, and how they will use it. Logging is a balancing act, since logging everything requires a great deal of storage space and increases the amount of data, both useful and otherwise, that you must go through to discern important, relevant information. On the other hand, insufficient logging means that you won't get any data of consequence that you can use to make informed decisions.

Cross-Reference

Logging is also discussed in greater detail in Objective 3.2.

The key takeaway from this discussion is that you cannot adequately manage your infrastructure, including its performance and security aspects, without adequately logging the events and activities that occur in your network, and monitoring them for a potentially negative impact.

Encryption

Although a technical discussion of encryption is a different focus from the CySA+ exam and this particular objective, encryption in the context of infrastructure management is critical. You should remember the essential concepts of encryption from your Security+ studies and other experiences, but we'll go over the key concepts here in a brief refresher. If you feel you're weak in the area of cryptography, you should take the time to review a more detailed explanation of its foundational concepts.

Cryptography Concepts

Remember that cryptography encompasses a variety of processes, including encryption, decryption, and hashing. Encryption is the process of turning ordinary human or machine-readable data, or *plaintext*, into data that is scrambled or otherwise obfuscated, rendering it unreadable. The result of encrypting plaintext is called *ciphertext*. Decryption reverses that process and returns ciphertext back to its readable form. Cryptography supports many security goals—particularly confidentiality and data integrity—because it prevents unauthorized access to data by entities who cannot decrypt the data as well as ensures integrity by generating cryptographic fingerprints of data that, when changed, indicate the data has been disturbed in some way. Cryptography uses various techniques to encrypt data—some of them very simplistic, such a simple substitution and transposition ciphers, and some of them quite complex, using techniques that make them almost mathematically impossible to decrypt. Encryption depends on strong algorithms and keys, discussed in the upcoming section, in order to be effective.

Algorithms and Keys

A cryptographic algorithm is a mathematical method or process used to transform data from plaintext into ciphertext. Most modern cryptographic algorithms are extremely complex and rely on advanced mathematical constructs or formulas. Algorithms are usually subject to scrutiny by experts in order to ensure their validity and discover any weaknesses that may expose the encryption method to compromise. It is outside of this scope of the CySA+ exam objectives to know the various algorithms properly used in cryptography, but some of the more common ones are the Advanced Encryption Standard (AES), Blowfish, Twofish, and the Rivest–Shamir–Adleman (RSA) algorithm.

Encryption requires an algorithm and a key. The key portion of this process, since the algorithm is publicly known and tested, is what is kept confidential. Whereas the algorithm is a mathematical formula, the key is the unique piece of information the algorithm uses to encrypt and decrypt data. Keys can be created or generated by users or applications or other cryptographic mechanisms and may come in the form of passwords, PINs, or other unique sets of data. Except for public keys, keys are normally kept confidential. In simplistic cryptography, a key is used to encrypt data, in conjunction with the algorithm. When data is decrypted, the same or related key must be used. Without keys, encrypted data cannot be decrypted.

 NOTE Robust encryption requires both strong algorithms and keys. Make sure you're using cryptographically proven algorithms that have not shown any weaknesses, as well as a large key space. Remember that keys are strengthened by length and number of possible characters.

Symmetric Cryptography

You should be familiar with two general types of cryptography: symmetric and asymmetric. Symmetric cryptography is fairly simple to understand. It typically uses a single key to encrypt data, and the same key must be used to decrypt that data. Symmetric cryptography is sometimes also known as *secret key* or *session key* cryptography. It is most often used to encrypt a large amount of data, since it is very efficient. The problem with symmetric cryptography is that key exchange can be an issue. For a simple exchange of information, two individuals only need to ensure that each one has the correct key. However, think of using symmetric cryptography on a large-scale basis, where you have multiple users or entities. If you're sharing the same data that everyone can access, you still need a single key. However, if certain individuals can have access to the data, but other individuals can't, then you start getting into having many more keys that are only used between particular individuals. Additionally, key distribution is an issue because sending the key to decrypt confidential information over an unsecure means, such as e-mail, means that the key could be easily compromised, and someone who obtains the key can access the encrypted data.

Symmetric algorithms are normally classified in two ways: as blocks or streams. A block algorithm encrypts chunks of plaintext in predefined blocks consisting of a number of bits. For example, you could encrypt a block of plaintext in a 64-bit block. Streaming cipher, on the other hand, encrypts data one bit at a time. There are many different block algorithms, such as 3DES, AES, Twofish, and Blowfish. The most popular streaming algorithm, used in both SSL and TLS as well as in wireless security protocols such as WEP, is the RC4 algorithm.

EXAM TIP   You are not expected to recite or identify various encryption algorithms on the CySA+ exam, but you should be familiar with them from your earlier studies or experience in security, as they are a fundamental part of security knowledge.

Asymmetric Cryptography

Whereas symmetric cryptography uses a single key in its most simple form, asymmetric cryptography uses two keys. These keys are always generated in a pair; they are not the same key, but are closely related mathematically. These keys are normally referred to as a public/private key pair. One key is kept secure and confidential, and the other key is released for public knowledge. You know these keys are not identical; they are mathematically related. Therefore, what one key encrypts, the other key is able to decrypt. Using this key pair method, the paradigm for encryption and decryption changes somewhat. Anyone possessing the public key can encrypt a message to the owner of the key pair, and only that person who possesses the private key can decrypt it. This process makes it so one-way encryption to a particular individual is possible without worrying about key compromise, since anyone can have the public key but only the intended recipient of the message possesses the private key. When multiple people have key pairs, and all public keys are in possession of each party, anyone can encrypt a message to anyone else without having to worry about key exchange. Only authorized recipients can then decrypt messages.

Using the public key to encrypt data for an intended recipient ensures confidentiality, since only the private key can decrypt it. However, if the opposite process were to occur, where a message was encrypted using the private key from an individual, this would not ensure confidentiality, since anyone holding the public key could decrypt it. In this scenario, confidentiality is not the goal. Nonrepudiation is a benefit of this process—only the person holding the private key could have encrypted the data since the private key is kept confidential. Anyone holding a copy of the public key can decrypt this data; therefore, authenticity, versus confidentiality, is the goal here. This is the basis of digital signatures.

A disadvantage of *public key cryptography,* as asymmetric cryptography is often called, is that it's not efficient at encrypting and decrypting a large amount data, because of the computational power required for encryption and decryption using public and private key pairs (since asymmetric algorithms require a great deal of computational power due to their complexity). However, key exchange is not an issue as it is with symmetric cryptography, since the public key can be freely given away to anyone who wants it without compromising confidentiality.

The process of generating and issuing public/private key pairs, while ensuring that the identity of the individual or entity receiving these keys is authentic, as well as managing those keys throughout their lifecycle, is called a *public key infrastructure* (PKI). These keys are often issued to individuals by a trusted authority in the form of an electronic file called a *digital certificate,* which we'll discuss in the upcoming section.

As you'll see later on when we discuss cryptographic applications, we can use the advantages of both symmetric and asymmetric cryptography to cancel out the disadvantages of each and create a system where key exchange is not an issue, confidentiality is maintained, the ability to encrypt large pieces of data is easy, and both integrity and authenticity can be ensured.

 KEY TERMS **Symmetric keys** are the ones more often used to send and receive encrypted data back and forth between two entities. **Asymmetric keys** are primarily used for identification, authentication, secure key exchange, and nonrepudiation.

Hashing

Hashing is a cryptographic process, but it is not the same thing as encryption. Hashing is the process of running a hashing algorithm, such as MD5 or SHA, on a piece of plaintext and generating a finite-length piece of data, called a *hash* or *message digest*. This hash does not represent encrypted data that can be decrypted. Just like a fingerprint on a human being does not represent the entire human being, but it does, however, uniquely identify that person. A hash serves to uniquely identify the piece of data in the state it was in when the hash function was performed. The data can be variable length in nature; a Word document or a JPEG file or any other piece of data can be hashed. However, the hash itself that is produced is of finite length, meaning that it will only be a certain number of digits, depending on the hashing algorithm used. For example, an MD5 hash is a 32-bit hexadecimal number, regardless of the length of plaintext used in its generation.

Hashing is used to support the security goal of integrity. When the same hash function is performed against a piece of plaintext, it always produces the same hash value, as long as that document never changes. Since a hash is the resulting fingerprint uniquely identifying a piece of data, if that data changes at all, even by one bit, then the hash will change. Even changing a single letter or adding a space to a 50,000-page document would change the hash produced the next time the same hashing function is run against that document. Based on two different hashes produced by running the same algorithm against this document, you would know that that document has been altered in some way. Either intentionally by someone or accidentally in some way, possibly by disk or file corruption, faulty data transmission, and so on. In this way, the hashing process guarantees data integrity.

Note that no cryptographic system is perfect; algorithms are often discovered to have flaws in them that could enable a malicious person to compromise them and be able to access or change data they are not otherwise authorized access. This is true with both symmetric and asymmetric algorithms, and it is also true with hashing algorithms. There have been both theoretical and demonstrable attacks on weak hashing algorithms where a *collision* (the instance of two different pieces of plaintext producing identical hash values, which should be theoretically impossible) could occur.

EXAM TIP Hashing is not the same thing as encryption, because it does not transform data into an unreadable form; it merely produces a fingerprint of the data in its current state. Hashing cannot be "decrypted" or reversed since there is no key to decrypt or reverse it.

Cryptography Applications

Although the details of cryptography applications are not within the scope of this book, it's helpful to discuss these topics as a refresher before you take the exam. Now that we've talked about the different forms of cryptography, such as symmetric, asymmetric, and hashing, we can briefly discuss how all of these work together and are applied to create secure solutions.

Remember in its basic form, cryptography involves encrypting a piece of data with a key. Whoever is the intended recipient for that data, whether it's over e-mail, using data at rest, or sending/receiving data in transit, must have the same key to decrypt it. One of the problems involved here is secure key exchange. As mentioned, symmetric key encryption is not particularly good with key exchange, and it doesn't scale very well to large numbers of people or entities. This is where you can use a combination of symmetric, asymmetric, and hashing cryptography to ensure secure data transmission.

Let's look at the following scenario to illustrate this point. You need to encrypt data to send to a particular recipient. You also need to get them the key that will be used to decrypt this particular piece of data. Obviously, you should not use the same symmetric key over and over, because just like passwords, they can be compromised since an unauthorized person could conceivably intercept the key and be able to access all the encrypted data you ever send. So, you should use different keys every time you send encrypted data to an individual. Because you're only using the key once, this is called a *session key*, and it's used only for that particular communications session.

Now take a look at key exchange. How do you get the other authorized individual the session key, especially when it may change? You can't very well send it over unsecure means, such as e-mail or chat or even snail mail, since all those can be easily intercepted and read. This is where you can use public/private key cryptography to ensure secure data exchange. If both parties had a public/private key pair, you could try to use this to send data back and forth with the other party, but because asymmetric key cryptography does not handle bulk data very well, this might be inefficient. However, you could combine symmetric and asymmetric cryptography methods and encrypt the session or symmetric key with the other party's public key and send it to them. Then, they can use their private key to decrypt the message containing the secret session key. Both parties could then use the session key to encrypt data throughout the remainder of the communications session.

The scenario works very well to ensure confidentiality in secure key exchange. We can also add data integrity, sender authenticity, and nonrepudiation to the mix by adding hashing cryptography into this process. In addition to sending encrypted data back and forth between the two parties after they have encrypted and decrypted the session key with their public/private key pair, the user generating the session key could also create a hash of that key. That user could then encrypt that hash using their private key. They would then send that to the recipient. The recipient could decrypt that part of the message using the sender's public key, so this would ensure sender authenticity. It would also ensure nonrepudiation since no one else could have sent that message because no one else has the private key. Once the receiver decrypts the hash, they could run the hashing function against the session key they received in a separate message to ensure that those hashes match. When they do match, this ensures data integrity. If they do not match, then there's a possibility that the message was altered during transmission or otherwise compromised.

Note that this sounds like an overly complicated process, but with most modern cryptography applications, all of this is completely transparent to the user, assuming they have been issued public and private keys. Most cryptography applications generate the session key without user intervention, so the user doesn't even have to know what the session key actually was. The cryptography application will take care of all hashing, encryption, decryption, and digital signature processes. For the most part, this all happens so quickly during the initial parts of the communications session that the users never even realize it has occurred. The method we've just described using a combination of symmetric, asymmetric, and hashing cryptography has a wide variety of applications. This is how users communicate with secure banking sites, for example, or use secure e-mail.

Managing Encryption in the Infrastructure

How do you manage encryption in your organization? As with all other things, it starts with policy. The organization must develop a policy that covers the use of cryptography throughout the infrastructure. The policy should address the following:

- Instances where encryption is both required and not allowed (for example, for e-mailing sensitive information and off-site backups)
- Requirements for encryption of data at rest and in transit
- Required encryption strength and algorithms
- Use of organizational-approved encryption products versus personal encryption
- Key management

Note that your encryption policy should go hand in hand with your data sensitivity policy. The data sensitivity policy should detail, based on stated sensitivity levels, which data should be encrypted, and under which circumstances. Once the policy is developed and approved, supporting procedures for encrypting data can be developed. The procedures should detail which cryptography applications users are allowed to use, how they use them, and what configuration settings (algorithms, key strength, and so on) must be used.

One important aspect of managing encryption in the organization is key management. Keys must be centrally managed, balancing the requirements for nonrepudiation and ensuring that encrypted data is recoverable. Nonrepudiation, as a reminder, ensures that a user cannot deny that they took an action. If keys are centrally managed (meaning that administrators need to and should control access to them), it could be argued that a user did not act if it can be shown that a rogue administrator used a private key belonging to someone else for nefarious purposes. On the other hand, if a disgruntled user were to encrypt the only copy of highly sensitive or critical data, and then that user leaves, the data cannot be recovered. Key management must balance between these two requirements by carefully controlling access to keys, while at the same time ensuring the organization has a back door that can be used to decrypt critical data if absolutely necessary.

To balance those two requirements, an effective key management policy provides for secure private key provisioning (key generation, issue, storage, and controlled access to the same), strict usage policies, and auditing key usage.

 EXAM TIP Managing encryption in the infrastructure is critical; unmanaged encryption can lead to more security issues than it prevents. Ensure you have a solid policy regarding the use of encryption within the organization, and actively spell out the use of encryption for sensitive data as well as key management practices.

Certificate Management

As part of your overall key management strategy and supporting policies and procedures, managing digital certificates is a critical process. Digital certificates are issued to individuals for signing and encrypting e-mail as well as for accessing systems, so they are an important part of an organization's identity and authentication management process. Since digital certificates contain cryptographic keys, protecting them and preventing their compromise is of utmost importance.

Certificate Management Concepts

From our earlier discussion on symmetric and asymmetric cryptography, you know that asymmetric cryptography involves two different keys: a public key and a private key. A trusted authority issues these public/private key pairs after validating the ID of the individual or entity requesting the keys. Digital certificates are electronic files that essentially contain not only the keys issued to an individual, but also the trusted path from the issuer. Certificates contain information about the issuer, the purpose for which the certificates are issued, and the expiration information for the certificate. Digital certificates can be issued for a variety of purposes, but the most common are for digital signatures and encryption purposes.

Certificate Infrastructure

An organization can maintain its own public key infrastructure, or it can use the PKI of an external organization, such as a commercial trusted entity that issues certificates. The requester of a digital certificate can be an individual user or another entity such as a corporation.

The basic organization of a PKI consists of an entity called a *Certificate Authority* (CA). The CA generates a public/private key pair and issues a digital certificate to the requesting entity based on a positive identification of the entity requesting the certificate, as well as any other criteria they determine as critical. In the case of large organizations that may handle a large volume of requests, the portion of the process related to identity verification may be performed by another entity known as a *Registration Authority* (RA). The CA infrastructure is hierarchical, with a *root* CA server at the top. This is usually the first CA server created in the hierarchy, and it holds the root certificate. The root certificate may be self-generated, or it may be issued from yet another trusted CA, further extending the trusted path. In small organizations, the root CA may be the server that issues the actual digital certificates, but usually in larger organizations the root CA generates certificates for subordinate CA servers and is then taken offline to prevent its potential compromise. The root CA should be the most trusted certificate in the organization, and it generates a path of trust for any certificate it generates, including the subordinate CA servers. Therefore, if the root CA is compromised, it jeopardizes the trust path of all certificates it has ever generated. Subordinate CAs (also sometimes called *intermediate CAs*) handle the daily tasks of issuing certificates to individuals, entities, and even subordinate CA servers further downstream.

Occasionally, organizations must trust other organizations' certificates. This happens in the event of a business partnership, for example, where users from one organization must authenticate to resources in the other organization, so the certificates used to identify those users must be trusted. In that event, a cross-certificate trust is set up between the infrastructure of both organizations.

Certificates are normally not valid for long periods of time; their life span is usually set to expire after a specified period, in accordance with the certificate policy of an organization. Certificates expire and become invalid after the specified period (typically two to three years) to prevent their eventual compromise or misuse. The certificate must then be renewed and reissued by the CA.

Certificates can also be suspended or even revoked. A suspension occurs when the organization temporarily invalidates the certificate, due to some event (an investigation, for example). The certificate can be reinstated for use pending the outcome of the investigation. A certificate is revoked if it has been determined to have been misused or compromised in any way. In the event of a certificate revocation, a new certificate must be issued to the user or entity, if determined to be appropriate by the CA. The old certificate can no longer be used for authentication or digital signature purposes. The organization periodically publishes a certificate revocation list (CRL), which lists all certificates that have been suspended or revoked. Through a process that is fairly transparent to the user, certificates are checked through online means to ensure they are still valid. For example, when a user accesses a secure site and their browser checks the site's certificate validity, it is compared against a CRL published online by the issuing CA. If the certificate is expired, suspended, or revoked, or if there is any other issue with the certificate, the user will likely get a warning informing them of this and asking if they still wish to trust the certificate and its authenticity. Unfortunately, many users click through this warning and expose themselves to a serious security vulnerability in the process by trusting an invalid certificate.

As mentioned earlier, certificate management is a critical process in the overall key management and security infrastructure management program. Keys, root certificates, and the servers that generate them must be protected at all times.

 EXAM TIP Be familiar with the basic certificate management infrastructure, including CAs, RAs, and subordinate CA servers.

Active Defense

For years, traditional cybersecurity theory taught that we should focus on perimeter defense only, and this would keep malicious entities out of our network. In the current threat landscape, we know this is no longer the case. For our defensive measures to be effective, we must be more proactive and adopt a defense-in-depth (also known as a *layered* defense) mentality. We must actively monitor for threats and constantly strive to strengthen our security posture. Active defense is a critical part of infrastructure management.

Layered defense means we cannot just rely on perimeter defense; firewalls and border routers that filter solely on ports and protocols are not effective against malware, phishing attempts, compromised applications, malicious scripts hiding in allowed traffic, or, the most critical vulnerability of all, human beings.

Active defense means constantly monitoring each layer of our infrastructure and determining new threats and vulnerabilities. At a minimum, the following are key areas that must be constantly monitored and strengthened:

- Perimeter devices
- Inbound and outbound traffic
- Allowed applications and programs
- Rogue devices
- Privileges
- Humans

To actively monitor and strengthen our defenses, we must look at each of these areas, determine what vulnerabilities we have, what threats they may be exposed to, what impact the organization would face if those threats exercise those vulnerabilities, and what the likelihood of this happening is. In other words, we need to determine what our risk is. To minimize this risk, active defense requires us to do the following:

- Harden all network devices, servers, and hosts.
- Ensure that we have a proactive patch management strategy.
- Maintain up-to-date antimalware software and signatures.

- Filter and examine inbound and outbound network traffic.
- Ensure users understand their role in securing the organization's assets.
- Train users on how to deal with social engineering attacks.
- Require the use of encryption for sensitive data.
- Implement strict access controls based on the principle of least privilege.
- Implement allowed/denied lists for applications, network traffic, websites, e-mail, and user privileges.
- Actively monitor and log relevant events that occur on our infrastructure.
- Perform threat modeling and vulnerability assessments.
- Take steps to reduce risk whenever possible.

Remember that active defense is more than just configuring security devices or mechanisms and leaving them to do their job. You must always be vigilant to verify that your security controls are working, as well as validate that those controls are the ones that are most effective for reducing risk and securing your infrastructure.

 KEY TERMS   **Active defense**, **defense in depth**, and **layered defense** are all terms that essentially mean the same thing—a focus on proactive defensive measures at various layers of the infrastructure.

REVIEW

Objective 2.1: Given a scenario, apply security solutions for infrastructure management   In this objective, we focused on managing the organizational infrastructure, and we discussed several technical and managerial solutions enabling us to do so. We discussed the pros and cons of cloud-based versus on-premises infrastructure, as well as the importance of managing assets such as data, servers, hosts, network devices, and other equipment. You learned about the importance of segmentation, including how you can use physical and logical segmentation to protect highly sensitive assets. We pointed out the differences between system isolation and air-gapped separation and the scenarios in which you might use each. We also discussed the use of virtualization and the importance of a jump box in accessing sensitive segments and hosts.

Network architecture describes how the infrastructure is designed and constructed; we looked at different aspects of physical and logical architecture, including physical layout, software-defined networking, virtual private cloud, and the use of a secure virtual private network implementation.

Change management is an important part of managing your infrastructure, as unintended and potentially malicious changes in infrastructure can cause performance, function, interoperability, and security issues. We talked about the importance of the change control board and how changes are initiated, tested, approved, and implemented. Configuration management is a subset of change management, and while it does not involve major changes across infrastructure, it is critical to maintain a known-good baseline across all network devices and hosts. Any changes to those baselines should be carefully considered for incurring more risk to the network.

Virtualization enables you to run discrete operating systems on top of physically abstracted hosts, through the use of hypervisors. Type I hypervisors serve as the physical machine operating system, and Type II hypervisors are merely applications that run on top of an existing server operating system. Hypervisors manage the interaction between the physical machine and the virtual machines, communicating with physical hardware, providing resources, and adding a layer of security to the overall virtual machine infrastructure. We discussed the virtual desktop infrastructure paradigm, which is essentially thin clients that access resources located on other more powerful machines, enabling you to save on costs of robust desktops and further secure your network by minimizing the amount of data that users run on their workstations.

Containerization is similar to virtualization, except that software containers are abstracted from operating systems and use a containerization manager or runtime environment to communicate back and forth with the operating systems about the use of resources as well as security. Containerization protects both the application and operating system from each other's inherent weaknesses. Containerization is an important part of locking down your hosts and infrastructure and preventing potentially compromised applications from enabling an attacker to do further damage to your network.

We covered a great deal about the critical processes of identity and access management. We looked at the importance of privilege and account management. We also talked about authentication technologies such as multifactor authentication, single sign-on, and federated identities. We discussed access control models such as DAC, MAC, RBAC, and ABAC, and how each of them grants a different degree of privileges and access to resource owners, roles, and individuals.

Organizations that use many different cloud services can benefit from a cloud access security broker (CASB) to serve the secure management layer between users and cloud services of all types.

We also discussed the benefits of using a honeypot and honeynet to delay an attacker's entry into the network while giving us time to analyze the attack, trace the attacker back to their point of origin, and alert the authorities. Honeypots and honeynets emulate vulnerable hosts and may distract an attacker long enough for administrators to engage in detective and preventative measures. They also increase our incident response capability.

Monitoring and logging are two critical pieces of infrastructure management, and they cover a wide variety of topics throughout security. We discussed the importance of determining what the organization must monitor, at different levels, including applications, network devices, hosts, and users. You know that you must be very particular about what you log because logging generates a lot of data that takes up storage, and it can be difficult to sift through if it's more than the analysts can handle. We looked at the importance of using automated tools, such as a SIEM system, to collect, aggregate, and assist in analysis with large volumes of log data.

Additionally, we discussed the importance of managing cryptography in the organization. We discussed various cryptography fundamentals, including algorithms and keys, symmetric cryptography, asymmetric cryptography, and hashing. We also discussed how to use these different cryptography methods in our daily applications, such as secure e-mail and digital signatures. We also talked about the importance of managing digital certificates in the organization, including their expiration time and the certificate revocation list.

Finally, we discussed the importance of active defense in the organization, beyond merely monitoring the perimeter. We talked about the different layers of defense that we should be paying attention to, including network devices, traffic, hosts, applications, and users. Each one of these presents different vulnerabilities that we must constantly assess and monitor for risk. We also discussed some of the various ways we can proactively strengthen each of these areas.

2.1 QUESTIONS

1. Evan is studying cybersecurity at his local community college. His professor asks him to write a short paper describing network segmentation. How should Evan explain virtual segmentation?

   A. Virtual segmentation describes how network hosts are connected via cabling to switches and routers.

   B. Virtual segmentation describes how virtualized operating systems are run over a hypervisor.

   C. Virtual segmentation uses logical means, such as IP addressing and logical subnets, as well as encryption, to separate network segments and hosts.

   D. Virtual segmentation uses a specially dedicated host security as a single-entry point into sensitive networks and hosts.

2. Charisse is an experienced cybersecurity analyst whose company must now suddenly provision large numbers of remote access accounts for teleworkers due to the COVID-19 pandemic. Her company is largely unprepared for the numbers of talkers who will require remote access. She has set up three VPN concentrators that use L2TP and IPSec as their protocols, but they will not support the large numbers of users who require VPN access. Which of the following is a temporary solution Charisse can use to enable VPN access for her users, with minimal resources or client configuration?

   A. SSH VPN

   B. PPTP VPN

   C. Transport mode VPN

   D. HTTPS VPN

3. Peter is a cybersecurity analyst who was just tasked by his management to figure out how to consolidate authentication and other security services for the many different cloud offerings to which his company subscribes. The company uses multiple cloud service providers and various services, including Software as a Service (SaaS) and Infrastructure as a Service (IaaS). Which of the following is the best solution for Peter to explore?

   A. Cloud access security broker

   B. Virtual private cloud

   C. Virtual private network

   D. Public key infrastructure

4. Charles is a cybersecurity analyst in a small company that was recently acquired by a much larger corporation. In their efforts to consolidate services and incorporate the smaller organization's network into the larger corporate network, the larger company has directed that users in Charles' company use a new authentication method. This authentication method uses a third party to authenticate all corporate users to not only internal resources and sites, but also to those of its business partners and subsidiaries. This type of identity and authentication management technology can best be described as which of the following?

   A. Discretionary access control

   B. Single sign-on

   C. Federated identity management

   D. Mandatory access control

5. Tia is developing an encryption policy for her organization. Company management wants to use encryption for sensitive data when in storage and when transmitted outside of the organization. Tia's managers also want to implement the use of secure e-mail as well as digital signatures to sign sensitive documents. In addition to the appropriate policies and procedures, Tia must also set up a PKI in the organization. Which of the following should Tia include in the policy to enforce the use of only organizationally approved encryption methods and keys?

   A. She should restrict the use of personal encryption tools and mandate the use of the organizationally issued digital certificates.

   B. She should require that only symmetric cryptography be used within the organization.

   C. The policy should ban the use of asymmetric cryptography for official organizational use.

   D. The encryption policy should require only block algorithms.

2.1 ANSWERS

1. **C**   Virtual, or logical, segmentation relies on nonphysical means to separate sensitive network segments and hosts, including logical IP addressing and submitting, encryption, virtualized hosts, and virtual LANs (VLANs).

2. **D**   In lieu of a more robust VPN solution using a concentrator, users can also access the corporate VPN through a secure web browser, using HTTPS and the TLS protocol.

3. **A**   A cloud access security broker (CASB) is an intermediate management layer technology that consolidates and manages authentication and other types of security processes between the organization and its cloud service providers.

4. **C**   In a federated identity management infrastructure, the users in Charles' company will be able to use a central third-party authentication provider to authenticate not only to internal resources but also to external sites that trust the authentication provider.

5. **A**   Tia's encryption policy should restrict the use of any personal encryption applications or tools, regardless of algorithm or key strength. The policy should mandate the use of organizationally issued digital certificates for secure e-mail, authentication, and digital signatures.

Objective 2.2   # Explain software assurance best practices

Computing devices have two major components: software and hardware. We will discuss hardware assurance later in the next module, but software assurance is extraordinarily important. This is where most users, and indeed security professionals, have their issues with security. The environment within which software, hardware, data, and the user interact with each other is complex.

In this module, we will discuss several aspects of software assurance, from many different angles. First, we'll discuss software platforms, such as mobile, web, and client/server, among others. We'll also discuss the software development lifecycle, and a relatively new paradigm, DevSecOps. You'll also learn about software assessment methods as well as analysis tools. We will talk about service-oriented architecture, as well as software security best practices such as secure coding. All these ingredients are critical for assurance that software performs as expected, is functional, and secure.

Platforms

The platform that software runs on is a function of different things, including hardware (for example, processor type and architecture), operating system (for example, Windows versus macOS or Linux), and implementation paradigm (web-based versus client/server versus mobile device). The platform describes the entire environment that the software runs on; in this module, we will discuss the various popular platforms, including mobile devices, web-based applications, and traditional client/server architecture. We will also discuss specialized platforms such as embedded systems, system-on-chip, and firmware implementations. While there are many software assurance practices and processes that are common across all platforms, each different platform implementation also has unique characteristics that we will discuss.

 EXAM TIP Remember that the platform an application runs on consists of its hardware, operating system, and entire operating environment.

Mobile

Mobile platforms are ubiquitous throughout the world. With the advent of smartphones, tablets, laptops, and other personal mobile devices, software design and deployment methods changed. There are many different manufacturers of mobile devices as well as different operating systems and mobile applications, or apps, that present different issues. You may find a certain mobile app, for example, that you can download and run on any type of mobile operating system, but under the surface, the app is different for different hardware types and mobile OSs.

Some mobile apps are designed for individual use, and you can download them from the respective app store for the mobile device platform you are using, such as iOS or Android. Some apps are developed for business use and may be deployed even from an organization's own app store. The development model for each of these types of apps is different. For example, Apple severely restricts its developers and applications with stringent requirements, including security. Android, on the other hand, allows developers to have a freer hand in developing apps that are deployed in the Google Play Store and other online app stores.

Another issue with mobile apps is the services and data they are allowed access to on a mobile device. Some apps tend to embrace an all-or-nothing paradigm in that you must allow all the data and services that it wishes to access, or simply not use the app, whereas other types of apps may allow you to be more granular and pick and choose the services and data on your mobile device that they are allowed to access. This goes back to one of the most fundamental principles of security: the principle of least privilege. An application should only be allowed to access the data and services it needs to perform its functions, and no more. Some applications seem to require more access than they truly need, and this can probably be traced back to collecting user data for the application developer to use for marketing purposes, or maybe even for some nefarious reason. For example, does the latest photo-editing app that you want to download *really* need the ability to make phone calls, as well as access your contacts, location, and other sensitive data?

Web Application

Web applications represent a significant portion of the applications that are developed today, due to the wide availability of high-speed Internet, tiered architectures, and the rich content available for these applications. Web applications can be created for almost anything—from personal banking applications to cloud-based office productivity suites, social media, and much more. These applications represent the future for many users, and they are popular due to their modularity and portability across different platforms.

The simplest of web applications can be deployed using a web server, with either static or dynamic content, serving as the front-end user interface, with a back-end application engine on the same server. When you add more layers of complexity, such as an application server on a different host, load-balancing capability through clustering, authentication mechanisms, and possibly a separate database server connected into the application, you have the most common architecture of all—the *n-tier* architecture, where *n* can represent any number of layers of components.

Web applications are built with many different components, with HTML as one of the fundamental building blocks, but also consisting of other programming languages, such as Java, Microsoft's .NET framework, XML, and many other components. When you also include an enterprise database application, as well as the supporting infrastructure, this causes the application to become overly complex. Not only does it expand the attack surface for a malicious entity, but it also expands the application and user space you must secure.

Client/Server

The client/server architecture is the traditional one that we have seen in computing for many years. There are two pieces to this architecture. In this architecture, a client (for our purposes here, a piece of software that presents a user interface and interacts on the user's host machine) accesses a server, which can be a physical machine running server-based software, and exchanges data with that software. An example of this paradigm would be an application residing on the user's host machine, which accesses a database on a remote server.

This is a simplistic architecture, and the primary concerns here are the security of the client application and how it interfaces with the operating system on the host machine as well as how it interfaces with the server software. Considerations here include the protocols that it uses to exchange data, as well as authentication mechanisms that it uses to authenticate the user to the server-side software. Note that both the client application and the server component it communicates with can also exist on a single machine; although typically not seen this way, the client/server paradigm is not only limited to separate hosts.

Embedded Platforms

Embedded systems are typically not standalone computing devices; they are part of a larger device, and they serve to control those devices, which traditionally may not be connected or simply physically isolated. This could include consumer devices such as refrigerators and televisions, but it also includes electronic systems that help to control aircraft, factories, utility grids, and so on. Embedded devices are usually found with real-time operating systems, which are implemented for speed, efficiency, and limited functionality. Embedded platforms usually have software implemented as specific code that is very utilitarian in nature. The code that goes with embedded systems is usually not easily upgradable, except through specialized hardware and software, since it is imprinted on the chip and is not erased when power is removed from the device.

 KEY TERM **Embedded platforms** are typically specialized devices (as opposed to general computing devices) that have their operating systems implemented as firmware on a chip. They perform highly specialized functions and can be seen in industrial control systems, consumer electronics products, and other Internet of Things (IoT) devices.

Firmware

Firmware is the software embedded on a chip or other hardware device. It is static in nature and can be difficult to update or change its configuration. Firmware is software used for a specific purpose; it is not general-use software. It is used to store and load initial configuration information for hardware on a computing device, for example.

System-on-Chip (SoC)

As described in Objective 1.5, a system-on-chip (SoC) is an embedded system in which software and hardware are integrated into a single computer chip. The chip is self-contained and consists of a processor, system RAM, and other critical components miniaturized into a single integrated circuit. A system-on-chip implemented into a piece of hardware is extremely fast, self-contained, and reliant; it uses much less power and is more efficient. A software consideration for a system-on-chip, implemented as firmware, is that it is embedded; the software configuration is static in nature, making it difficult to update and patch without specialized equipment. This means that if there are any discovered vulnerabilities in the firmware, they are difficult to mitigate.

Service-Oriented Architecture

Examining software from a platform perspective is especially useful since it looks at the entire operating environment the software must work in. Another way, however, of looking at software is by the functionality or service it provides. This is called *service-oriented architecture* (SOA), which describes software components that interface and interact with each other to provide services via standardized components. These components include an *application programming interface*, or API, which allows developers to create code to interact with various components and pass data and services between each other. SOA makes heavy use of markup languages, such as XML, for communications between components.

There are several basic requirements of a service-oriented architecture:

- Self-contained components
- Platform neutrality

- Modularity
- Component reusability
- Standardized APIs and other protocols to service requests from and provide responses to other components
- Business function-oriented services

In this section, we're going to discuss various components that a SOA can use to provide services between and make use of. A few of these are, but certainly not limited to, the Security Assertions Markup Language, the Simple Object Access Protocol, Representational State Transfer, and microservices. We will briefly describe each of these in the upcoming sections.

 EXAM TIP   Service-oriented architecture is concerned about the services that the components of an application can provide to other components of other applications, as well as how they communicate and interact with each other.

Security Assertions Markup Language (SAML)

Security Assertions Markup Language (SAML) is a markup language much like HTML and XML. Markup languages, as you will recall, essentially format, or mark up, different elements of a text-based file. They simply tag these elements for use by an application. SAML has specific tags in its structure that allow applications to use formatted information about the user, including their identity and other authentication and authorization information. The current standard is SAML 2.0. There are generally three components to SAML:

- The user (called the "principal")
- The identity provider (the entity authenticating the user's identity)
- The service provider (the entity who controls the service or application the user is authenticating to)

SAML is a common standard used across identity and service providers. When a user requests a service or access to a website, for example, the service provider requests identification information from the user, who submits it through an application such as a web browser. The service provider then takes that information and requests authentication from the identity provider. The identity provider replies to the service provider with authentication information as well as a token containing assertions, which are essentially authentication and authorization information for the user. Based on this information, the service provider can then allow or deny access to the service, application, or resource.

Simple Object Access Protocol (SOAP)

Simple Object Access Protocol (SOAP) is used in the enterprise service bus, which is where all communications and interactions take place between different services and applications. SOAP is a messaging protocol used to facilitate these communications and allows clients to access services over HTTP, regardless of the application server platform. SOAP has three major components:

- Message envelope (determines which messages are allowed and how the recipient processes them)
- Encoding rules used to define data types
- Standards on which remote procedures and services can be accessed

SOAP uses XML as the basis of its communications since this is an open, common standard. However, SOAP sometimes has difficulty with complex communications, which can be a detriment to its performance and functionality.

Representational State Transfer (REST)

Representational State Transfer (REST) is an architectural method used to overcome some of the limitations with the older Simple Object Access Protocol. It is designed to allow stateless communications between services, applications, and web-based resources. REST has the following characteristics:

- Uses standardized URLs to identify resources.
- Uses a client/server architecture.
- All transactions are stateless, meaning that each request and response contains enough information to be complete and understood by both systems, regardless of previous transactions.
- Responses dictate whether they are cacheable or not by a web proxy.
- Has a uniform, modular interface.

Microservices

Microservices are also a popular service-oriented architectural method, like REST. Microservices are individualized deployable application services that are focused on business transactions. They are very decentralized and do not have a lot of dependencies on other services; they are designed to perform very individualized tasks independently of other services. Because of their size and independence, they are easily developed. However, security can be an issue in that they all interact with each other and other services independently, with little security overhead. This is where log collection aggregation is useful, in that you can determine the activities and interactions between microservices when aggregating and analyzing log data.

Software Development Lifecycle (SDLC) Integration

The Software Development Lifecycle (SDLC) is a process that describes how software is planned, designed, created, tested, implemented, and maintained throughout its useable life. It is a formalized framework consisting of steps, tasks, and processes that drive all activities associated with software development and use. There are several models used for SDLCs, including the older Waterfall development model, spiral or iterative models, as well as newer models such as Rapid Application Development (RAD), Agile, and other prototyping or rapid deployment models.

All of these models impose, to various degrees of structure and rigidity, a formal process for setting software functionality, performance, and security requirements; designing the software; building or acquiring it; testing and integration; as well as implementing it in the organization and maintaining it. For the most part, performance and functionality requirements have been traditionally the focus of development models, with little emphasis on security requirements. This is changing, however, and security is increasingly a part of software development, with the advent of secure coding practices (discussed later in the module), as well as newer development models, such as DevSecOps, discussed next.

 EXAM TIP   You are not required to know the various SDLC models for the exam, but they are useful to understand.

DevSecOps

In a traditional development model, programmers did not always interact effectively with the people who would be the end users of the software they were producing. This often led to issues including unmet functional requirements, performance issues, and general unsuitability of the software for its intended purpose. As time passed, these issues were addressed by a more integrated community of developers and users. This paradigm became known as DevOps since it combined the development and operations worlds. However, security was still left out for the most part, causing a longer-term problem of few or ineffective security measures integrated into the software. The end result was that, quite often, security was considered after the fact. In other words, it was "bolted on" rather than being "baked in," or integrated into, the software.

This was the case until fairly recently, when a new paradigm, consisting of development personnel, operators and users, and security personnel, was invented. This, of course, is called DevSecOps and allows those three segments of stakeholders to integrate requirements while the software is being developed. The result of this new way of doing business is that software is developed with continual input from both users and security personnel, as well as quality assurance folks, thus significantly reducing errors and security issues as well as functionality and performance problems. This saves significant time that would have previously been spent on rework or fixing software bugs. This allows a more rapid development cycle while still maintaining quality software, which in turn allows faster integration and implementation.

Secure Coding Best Practices

As previously mentioned, software developers have not always integrated security considerations into their development processes or code. Security functions were often left out in favor of creating software that was useful, functional, and performed well. Functionality has always been the antithesis of security; generally, the more functional a piece of software or system is, the less secure it is since security tends to restrict functionality. People who are not security-minded generally accept this, because the thought is that functionality also equals convenience, speed, and efficiency. The problem with this thought process is that software can be extremely functional and fast right up until the point when a security issue occurs, and it creates a denial-of-service condition or allows data to be accessed by an unauthorized person. Then, the organization tends to pay for that speed and efficiency with data loss and, potentially, liability. Functionality and security must be in a delicate balance, and once this was realized by the development community, there was a concerted effort to create secure software. In order to accomplish this goal, development practices had to be changed, with a focus geared more toward the security side while maintaining functionality.

From this great realization came secure coding best practices. These practices form a framework that drives how programmers must develop software to be as functional as required, yet maintain integrated security functions that prevent data leakage, ensure data integrity, and be robust enough to be available when the user needs it. In the next few sections, we are going to discuss a few of these key practices, although there are many more. These key practices include input validation, output encoding, session management, authentication, data protection, and parameterized queries.

Input Validation

Input validation is one of the most important secure coding practices that programmers should implement to cover a wide variety of potential security issues. Many different security vulnerabilities, particularly injection attacks, could be solved if input validation were performed within the application itself. This includes validating textual and numerical data as well as preventing program escaping by unauthorized input.

Input validation can occur on the client side, such as through the client application or even web browser, or on the server side, where the application code resides. Client-side validation is often implemented using scripts and can be more efficient because it eliminates potential input problems early in the process. However, client-side validation can be easily circumvented using a variety of tools. Server-side validation may be less efficient, but it ensures that the validation process is sound.

Output Encoding

Attackers can use a wide variety of techniques to inject malicious code into an application. One of them is to use scripts (for example, with the <script> HTML tag) as part of their input. Input validation, if it is properly implemented, should intercept this before the application has a chance to execute it, but this does not always happen. Another technique to prevent this type of attack is called *output encoding*, which converts any user input, including potentially malicious embedded scripts, to inert data that a web browser cannot interpret as HTML. This technique is widely used to help in preventing cross-site scripting attacks.

Session Management

A typical web browsing session consists of, in its basic form, a series of requests and responses between the client browsers and web servers. Sometimes these transactions depend on each other or a previous transaction to process completely. However, HTTP is a stateless protocol; in other words, it does not track the state of requests and responses in relation to each other. Each request and response is completely independent of the transaction that happened before it and retains no "memory" of the previous request or response. To get around this, every time there is a session between the client browser and a web server, a small text file is generated and stored on the client to retain information necessary for future requests and responses. These text files are called *cookies*. An issue with cookies is that they may sometimes contain sensitive information, such as authentication information. Cookies are sometimes created, stored, and sent back and forth in plaintext, which enables an attacker to intercept the information stored in the cookie.

Securing a session is the process of ensuring that sensitive information sent back and forth during a web session cannot be easily sniffed or intercepted by a malicious entity. Using the HTTPS protocol is one way to do this. HTTPS, remember, encrypts the session using Transport Layer Security (TLS). Additionally, secure coding techniques can go far in securing the session between the user and a web server. These techniques include the following:

- Use encryption, such as HTTPS, whenever possible.
- Use strong authentication methods.
- Encrypt and expire cookies after each session.
- Disallow third-party cookies.
- Use session IDs that are difficult to predict (using complex pseudorandom numbers whenever possible).

Authentication

Authentication has been mentioned repeatedly in this book, and this is yet one other area where programmers need to be mindful of how they write code to accept authentication into an application. Many applications rely on external secure authentication methods, such as pass-through authentication from Active Directory. However, some applications use their own authentication mechanisms, which are not always secure or robust. Programmers can cause authentication issues for their applications by using simple username and password combinations, for example, that don't require complex passwords or encryption. They could also hardcode passwords into application code, which is a bad idea since an attacker could gain access to that code and determine any embedded passwords.

Programmers who need to create their own authentication mechanisms in applications should attempt to use multifactor authentication whenever possible and avoid username/password combinations. However, if username/password combinations are required, they should enforce standard password rules, such as complexity, minimum length, and password expiration. Passwords should never be stored or transmitted in cleartext; there should be encryption modules built in to the application to handle encrypting credentials whenever possible. Additionally, mechanisms that prevent brute force attack, such as account lockout, should be implemented. And, finally, all access to the application, especially privileged access, should be logged and audited.

Cross-Reference

Authentication security is also discussed in Objective1.7.

Data Protection

Software applications, in addition to protecting authentication information, must protect all sensitive data that is processed or generated by the application, as well as data that is stored, transmitted, or received through the application. Data typically exists in three states: at rest, meaning while it is stored on media; in transit, meaning it has been transmitted over a networking medium; and in process. *In process* means that it is currently residing in memory and being used by the CPU.

Data at rest can be protected using various methods. In conjunction with the operating system and its security mechanisms, such as rights, permissions, and so on, an application can also protect data in storage by allowing access to it from only authorized users. Both the operating system and application can also encrypt or otherwise obfuscate data while it is stored. Some applications may store data in a format other than simple files; large relational databases are an example of this. Database records are stored in multiple database files, of course, but not as a single file entity that can be accessed by means other than through the database application itself.

Data in transit can also be protected by both the operating system and application. Even if the operating system or network does not encrypt the application's data, the application can be responsible for encrypting any data that is sent between it and the receiving application on the remote host. Applications can also be configured to send and receive data only to and from particular hosts or domains, as well as use stronger authentication mechanisms. Applications can also have built-in integrity mechanisms to ensure that data has not been altered during transit between applications on remote hosts.

In Objective 2.3, we will discuss secure enclaves and the Trusted Execution Environment, which provide for data security while it is in use by the CPU. However, this is primarily a function of hardware, although some software/firmware extensions are involved. In terms of secure application programming, developers can do their part to ensure data protection by using secure techniques to ensure memory protection so that both the application and data can execute in secure memory areas that are not easily overwritten or corrupted by buffer overflow attacks, for example. Programmers must ensure that only secure functions are used during program execution so that data being processed will not be compromised or altered in any way.

Parameterized Queries

Another form of input validation, specifically designed to thwart SQL injection attacks, is *parameterized queries*. This type of input validation treats all user input as parameters to a function rather than a literal query, so anyone attempting to input an SQL statement into an input dialog box on a web form, for example, will be disappointed. Programmers can specify exactly what type of parameters they wish for their functions, such as date, number, or even a username and password combination. This way, the attacker cannot put SQL statements into the input field of a web form, for instance, and generate a structured SQL statement.

 NOTE All these secure coding best practices should be used in conjunction with each other, especially input validation, output encoding, and parameterized queries, since this is a multilayered approach to preventing some of the more common attacks.

Software Assessment Methods

Secure coding is just one part of software assurance. After the code has been developed in as secure a manner as possible, we must examine it to make sure that it fulfills its functional and performance requirements, but also is secure. There are several things we look for in software security—data leakage, strong authentication, and so forth. These things are determined by assessing the software through various types of tests and reviews. In the next few sections, we're going to discuss some of these assessment methods. We will look at user acceptance testing, stress testing, security regression testing, code review, and look at some of the analysis tools we can use to assess software security. We'll also quickly discuss the formal methods that organizations can use to verify that software meets its critical functional, performance, and security requirements.

User Acceptance Testing

While there are many kinds of application tests, including unit testing, regression testing, and so on, user acceptance testing is critical in that this is where the user tests the application and checks for performance and functionality. The user has the responsibility to make sure that the software works as advertised and meets the requirements originally levied on the programmers.

User acceptance testing also presents the opportunity to closely look at the different interactions a user may have with software, to make sure it performs as expected and to uncover any issues that may have been missed by programmers. For example, one security consideration in user testing is how the user interacts with the login and authentication facility. If the user can cause errors during the process or if the login process is not built correctly, it could actually present a security issue if it allows an attacker to take advantage of a programming mistake.

Stress Testing

Stress testing is a type of test designed to put an application under a load from a large amount of network traffic, processes, or data. It is designed to work an application hard to uncover any performance or security issues that may result from an application not being able to handle its designed workload. There are several manual and automated methods for performing stress testing, including sending large amounts of network traffic or data to an application, throttling its bandwidth during heavy processing times, connecting large numbers of users at one time, and so on. The goal is to push an application to its limits to see how it reacts and to make sure it can handle its projected workload.

Many applications react badly to heavy processing loads, which may cause them to crash, perform very slowly, or even throw errors. In turn, this could allow an attacker to gain insight as to how the application is built. In a worst-case scenario, an excessive performance load could cause an application to default to a nonsecure state or allow an attacker to take advantage of it and run arbitrary code. Stress testing is a vitally important part of security testing.

EXAM TIP   Application stress testing involves sending high volumes of data, including network traffic, into an application to see how it reacts to an excessive workload. The goal here is to cause the application to max out its RAM, processor, and other resource usages, so you can observe how it reacts to those conditions. Some applications will crash or cause a security issue if they are overtaxed.

Security Regression Testing

Regression testing involves introducing a new system or application into an environment where there are already existing systems and applications. The goal is to see how the new application interacts with the other ones; this can uncover any interoperability issues, but also security issues as well. For example, if older applications are designed with legacy security controls, such as older encryption algorithms, the newer application may not communicate with them at all or may default to a less secure state to maintain interoperability. Security regression testing tells you if your security methods and mechanisms built into a new application are compatible with your older ones. This is where design tradeoffs may have to occur in that you may have to force your new application to default to less secure communications and authentications methods if you must maintain compatibility with legacy applications. This also may cause you to determine that you must replace those older applications or at least upgrade their security mechanisms.

Code Review

Code review is an assessment process that involves an in-depth check on software application code, to make sure it has been written properly, is well structured, meets its functional and performance requirements, and is, of course, secure. Different review methods are available as part of a secure development methodology, including both manual and automated review processes.

A manual review involves an individual, typically another programmer familiar with the programming language and software requirements, going line by line over the code to look for structural issues, common mistakes, and so on. Automated code review involves the use of software applications that can take code apart and look for predetermined issues, particularly security vulnerabilities. An automated review is typically very quick and efficient for looking for a set of known programming mistakes or security issues and confirming that structure, syntax, and so on, are sound. However, a manual review can look for items not included in an automated code review application's vulnerability library. An experienced programmer will often use their intuition and knowledge of programming, as well as security, to look for issues that an automated program may not find.

Code reviews typically take place iteratively during various stages of the Software Development Lifecycle. Along with code review, several tools can be used for code analysis, including static analysis and dynamic analysis, discussed next.

Static Analysis Tools

When using automated tools, there are primarily two different types of analysis we can perform on application code to test its security. Static analysis tools are those that use predetermined libraries of issues to check for in code. These tools examine code line by line, looking at different objects, checking their properties, references, and so on. Static analysis tools can check for a wide variety of issues automatically, such as input validation weaknesses, code injection, and so on. Again, these are predetermined and already programmed into the static analysis tool. Checking for these common vulnerabilities can save considerable time and effort on the part of programmers since the entire process of checking for common vulnerabilities can be pretty much automated and checked quickly and efficiently. There are many different static analysis code tools in the marketplace, but a few popular examples are Fortify, Coverity, and SonarQube.

Dynamic Analysis Tools

Even with manual code review, which uses programmer knowledge, insight, and experience, as well as static code analysis, there's no way to accurately predict how software will behave until it is actually executing. Dynamic code analysis uses automated tools to examine code during execution. Dynamic analysis tools employ many different options, allowing you to stop code execution automatically upon discovery of certain error or security conditions, as well as halt execution at predefined checkpoints. Some dynamic analysis tools allow a wide variety of input to be used during code execution so that the tool can follow different execution paths based on different test conditions. The more complex the code, the more difficult and time-consuming it is for a dynamic analysis tool to adequately cover the range of all possibilities of execution; *code coverage* is the measure of how much of a program can be examined by the tool. Dynamic tools only can only give results about code that has been examined during execution; if there are parts of the software that have not been executed, the dynamic analysis tool can provide no information.

Formal Methods for Verification of Critical Software

In addition to the methods we have discussed already, there are also some highly structured testing methods used for critical software (software that could control medical infusion pumps, aircraft in flight, or missile defense systems, for example). These software applications must be immediately responsive, resilient, and secure. Formal methods use statistical and other mathematical models to clearly define every single parameter of a piece of software and predict its behavior under a variety of circumstances. These formal methods are used throughout the entire Software Development Lifecycle—from requirements, design and architecture, development, testing, and even beyond, through the implementation and maintenance phases of the software's life.

Formal methods can be very time-consuming, tedious, and expensive to perform. Typically, only large organizations developing and running some of the aforementioned types of critical software may use them because of this. This is in addition to all the other methods we have discussed thus far.

EXAM TIP   Understand the differences between manual code review, static analysis, and dynamic analysis. Manual code review is performed by an experienced programmer. Static analysis is an automated method that looks for predetermined vulnerabilities, such as SQL injection. Dynamic analysis is an automated method that requires the code to be running so it can observe any unpredictable behaviors.

REVIEW

Objective 2.2: Explain software assurance best practices   In this module, we discussed various methods and processes for ensuring that software is developed in as secure a manner as possible, as well as assurance that it secures the data it uses. First, we talked about different platforms that software can run on, including on mobile devices, web applications, client/server architecture, and embedded devices, as well as their software assurance challenges.

We also discussed service-oriented architecture, which looks at software in terms of the services it provides to other applications. We talked about three service-oriented architecture methods in particular: SAML, which is used to exchange secure authentication information about a user to different applications; SOAP, an XML-based protocol used to exchange messages between applications; and REST, an architecture method used to exchange data between applications, considering the stateless nature of the Web. Microservices are individual, deployable services that are focused on performing specialized transactions.

We also discussed the overall Software Development Lifecycle (SDLC), which is a formal methodology of managing software from its inception all the way to its retirement. Various SDLC models include Waterfall, Agile, and RAD. DevSecOps is the synthesis of the development, operations, and security communities, working together to ensure that software performs as required, meets its functional requirements, and is secure.

To ensure that software is both functional and secure, we discussed secure coding best practices, which can be used to help prevent many of the common security issues seen in modern applications (injection attacks, for instance). We discussed the importance of input validation, which can prevent many of these attacks simply by ensuring that any user input is checked and rendered ineffective as executable code. We also discussed output encoding, which effectively does the same thing to any user input so that it cannot be executed by the application. Session management is the process of securing sessions between the client and a server, through encryption as well as strong authentication methods. Authentication methods should be left to the underlying operating system or, absent that practice, implemented as secure authentication mechanisms in applications that do not store or pass credentials in cleartext, that enforce password complexity requirements, and that use strong authentication methods whenever possible. Applications should also protect any data that they use, either in storage, in transit, or residing in memory. Various methods include encryption, of course, as well as rights and permissions and strong authentication. Developers can use multiple secure coding techniques to protect data, including bounds checking and memory protection. Parameterized queries are a method of preventing injection attacks, particularly SQL injection, by rendering any user input as a parameter of a function rather than as executable code.

To have faith in our software as secure, we must test it. Software assessment methods include user acceptance testing, application stress testing, and security regression testing. All three of these methods are designed to ensure that users can interact securely with applications, that the applications can handle the maximum required workload without failing a nonsecure state, and that the applications interact with other components in a secure manner. Code review is a method of examining the application software code to ensure that it is functional, secure, and does not have any inherent vulnerabilities in it. Manual code review requires an experienced programmer who understands both programming and security. This is typically a line-by-line code review. We can also use automated tools to analyze code. Static analysis refers to looking at code for predefined vulnerabilities, such as injection attacks and buffer overflows. Dynamic analysis refers to looking for issues while the code is actually executing, to see if it behaves in an unpredictable manner. In addition to static and dynamic methods, there are also formal methods used primarily on critical software, where security failures could have dire consequences. These methods are expensive, tedious, and primarily involve deep mathematical analysis throughout the entire SDLC.

2.2 QUESTIONS

1. On which of the following platforms are you more likely to see software implemented as firmware on a component that includes a processor, system RAM, and other critical components miniaturized into a single integrated circuit?

   A. Web application

   B. Database server

   C. System-on-chip

   D. Service-oriented architecture

2. Taylor is learning about software assurance in her cybersecurity college course. She is trying to explain service-oriented architecture to a fellow student. Which of the following best describes service-oriented architecture?

   A. It focuses on the services that applications provide to each other.

   B. It is dependent on operating system services that support the software.

   C. It focuses on the types of platforms the software is running on.

   D. It is dependent on the processor architecture.

3. During security testing for a new application, cybersecurity analysts have been able to create SQL injection attacks against the web-based application and its underlying database. You need to recommend secure coding practices for the developers to implement to prevent this type of attack. Which of the following two secure coding practices should you recommend? (Choose two.)

   A. Secure authentication

   B. Parameterized queries

   C. Input validation

   D. Session management

4. The development team at your company is ready to test a new application. It has been user-tested and subjected to stringent code review, static analysis, and dynamic analysis. It passes all tests and has been approved to be implemented. However, when the software is implemented, other applications cannot communicate securely with it, and sometimes it fails to negotiate a secure encryption method, instead falling back to an older insecure method. Which of the following types of tests would have discovered this issue?

   A. Stress testing

   B. Interoperability testing

   C. Penetration testing

   D. Security regression testing

2.2 ANSWERS

1. **C** Software is implemented on system-on-chip implementations as firmware.

2. **A** Service-oriented architecture focuses on the services that the application can provide to other applications or services.

3. **B C** Two secure coding practices that can help prevent SQL injection attacks are input validation and parameterized queries.

4. **D** A security regression test involves testing new applications and security mechanisms with existing applications and systems, to ensure that all can communicate securely among each other. A security regression test would have discovered any issues with secure communications across the network among the new and existing applications.

Objective 2.3 # Explain hardware assurance best practices

In the previous objective, we discussed software assurance. This particular topic gets a lot of attention because most of the vulnerabilities that are obvious to users, as well as security practitioners, involve software. However, software vulnerabilities are not the only thing we should be noticing. The other half of the computing device, the hardware, also has numerous vulnerabilities and concerns that we need to address. Hardware vulnerabilities may not be as obvious to ordinary users or cybersecurity analysts, but they're just as important because they can cause just as much damage and may be more challenging to address in some cases.

In this objective, we're going to discuss the different aspects of hardware assurance, including the hardware root of trust, firmware, trusted manufacturing processes, secure processing, anti-tamper methods, and methods to protect hardware, such as self-encrypting drives, firmware updates, and trusted boot.

Hardware Root of Trust

To begin the discussion, let's talk about what the hardware trust chain looks like. Software is ever-changing, and we must constantly be alert to the environment in which software executes. This environment is the hardware itself—the CPU, memory, and permanent storage. This environment, regardless of what software is running, must always be trusted, stable, and secure. This is where the hardware root of trust comes in. Hardware root of trust is a term given to a trusted execution environment. As part of this environment, there are tamper-resistant hardware, cryptographic functions that encrypt data and ensure its integrity, and processes that ensure that the data is secure, from generation to processing, storage, and transit. Different components contribute to this hardware root of trust, including the manufacturer using authentic, trusted components, the logistics and supply chain, and the end-user environment. Two important components of the hardware root of trust are Trusted Platform Modules and hardware security modules. These provide cryptographic functions at a minimum, but also provide the trusted environment needed to run the software.

EXAM TIP   The hardware root of trust is the collection of secure supply chain management, the trusted hardware itself, and the secure processes that create a trusted environment for the operating system (OS), applications, and data to process within.

Trusted Platform Module (TPM)

Previously we discussed the concept of system-on-chip (SoC). As a reminder, this is almost a complete computer system that operates using firmware on a secure chip that is part of the motherboard in a piece of hardware. The Trusted Platform Module, or TPM, is such a system. It resides on the motherboard and is responsible for security functions, including storage and generation of cryptographic keys and digital certificates, both symmetric and asymmetric cryptography, and hashing. The TPM was developed by the Trusted Computing Group, which is an organization involved with creating and maintaining open standards of security for computing platforms.

TPMs perform several functions, including the following:

- Binding the hard drive computer to the system, encrypting it, and requiring that it remain with the system it is bound to in order to be decrypted
- Sealing a system state, which means that the system's specific hardware and software configurations are recorded and locked so that attempts to modify the system configuration will be thwarted
- Cryptographic key generation and storage

The TPM uses several different types of keys and components for different services. The TPM has two different types of memory: *persistent* memory, which holds its values even when power is turned off, and a volatile type of memory called *versatile* memory. These components/keys perform different functions and are stored in different sections of memory. A summary of these components is given in the following table:

Key Type	Function
Endorsement Key (EK)	Public/private key pair installed in the TPM when it is manufactured; stored in persistent memory
Storage Root Key (SRK)	Master key used to secure all other keys stored in the TPM; stored in persistent memory
Attestation Identity Key (AIK)	Used to attest to the identity of the TPM; stored in volatile or versatile memory
Platform Configuration Registers (PCR)	Storage space for cryptographic hashes used in sealing a hard drive; stored in versatile memory
Storage Keys	Keys used to encrypt storage media; stored in versatile memory

Hardware Security Module (HSM)

A *hardware security module* (HSM) is similar to a TPM; however, whereas a TPM is installed as a system-on-chip on the motherboard of the computing device, an HSM is an external piece of hardware plugged in to the device, either as an add-on board or as an external device that can plug into a system port. HSMs can perform the same cryptographic functions as TPMs, including key generation, storage, and processing. For devices that do not contain a TPM, an HSM can be used to perform the same functions. Cryptographic functions can be processor-intensive, so the HSM offloads those intensive functions from the system itself.

 EXAM TIP TPMs and HSMs perform essentially the same functions; keep in mind that the real difference is that TPMs are embedded on the motherboard, whereas HSMs are a plug-in card or peripheral device.

eFuse

An eFuse is a technology invented by IBM in 2004. It is intended to be a form of one-time programmable memory. It is a single bit of memory, constructed as a simple circuit, that is physically and electronically set to indicate the value of a binary "1" and is by default open and allows current to pass through it. It can be electronically changed, via inducing power to its chemical makeup, to block current, making it a resistor instead. This has the effect of changing it to a physical and electronic binary "0" value when the current is applied. Once this change takes place, it can never be reprogrammed again. This type of technology is used to create circuits made of eFuses, which can be changed once to a permanent value that remains with the device during its lifetime. Examples of practical uses of this technology are disabling functionality on a chip, including test and development features used during the manufacturing process, as well as permanently loading a value, such as a key, into the device. Since it cannot be reprogrammed after its initial programming, this makes the value permanent.

 EXAM TIP Remember that eFuses are set to a default value of binary 1 and, once programmed as a binary 0, cannot be programmed again since the circuit has been physically dissolved into the "open" state.

Unified Extensible Firmware Interface (UEFI)

Computing devices rely on startup instructions in order to boot up, locate their operating systems, and execute programs. The startup instructions, since they are required before the main operating system is even loaded, must be permanently stored on the device. These instructions, as well as sometimes a basic rudimentary operating system used for configuration and troubleshooting purposes, are stored as firmware on the device. Firmware means that, unlike software, it is reasonably permanent and cannot be erased, even when power is taken away from the device.

For many years, the firmware used to load the startup instructions for a device was called the Basic Input/Output System, or BIOS, originally developed by IBM. The BIOS was stored in read-only memory and could not be altered. It contained information about the system's hardware, including its CPU, RAM, and permanently attached storage. It also contained values that could be set, such as the time and date. These volatile values were maintained by an onboard battery, which, when removed, would revert these values to their default settings. Later, manufacturers developed a technology to update the system BIOS periodically, using different utilities that could be loaded at boot time.

System BIOS was very limited in the functions it could perform, particularly security functions. It could be easily bypassed and changed by unauthorized processes or persons. A better system was required, especially to address performance, function, and security issues that came as part of newer operating systems. Enter the Unified Extensible Firmware Interface (UEFI).

UEFI is a vast improvement to the original BIOS in terms of functionality and security. Its functionality improvements include recognizing drive partitions over 2 TB in size and allowing more flexible boot options, such as from a variety of removal media, via a local network, and even using the HTTP protocol. From a security perspective, it provides the following improvements over the original BIOS:

- Establishes a hardware and software root of trust
- Assists in loading cryptographic keys for decryption of hard disks and other media
- Initializes hardware in the trusted chain, thereby preventing booting from unauthorized devices
- Uses onboard digital certificates belonging to trusted hardware and software vendors
- Provides an enhanced, configurable, and secure user interface prior to boot

UEFI has been installed on computing devices manufactured in the last decade, and its most obvious feature for most users is the ability to securely boot from trusted media. When configured for secure boot, it prevents an unauthorized person from inserting boot media and accessing sensitive files through an insecure boot process. For better or for worse, secure boot can be disabled in specific circumstances, such as in testing and development environments.

Trusted Foundry

The term *trusted foundry* comes from the U.S. Department of Defense and is used to describe a program for vetting and approving vendors of trusted hardware. This program was developed in 2004 and is used to ensure a secure supply chain for critical military and government systems. These vendors have been put through a rigorous process of vetting, including process audits, verification of component procurement, and secure manufacturing, and then approved to provide components in systems to the government. These components are trusted because they come from known manufacturers, using a validated supply chain. These components and systems can be validated as being authentic, and without any unintended or malicious modification to their subassemblies, lower-level components, or firmware. One prominent disadvantage in the trusted foundry process is its cost. The increased measures needed to provide assurance of secure manufacturing, production, and supply chain cost vendors significantly, which drives up the cost of trusted components versus their counterparts that are not part of a trusted foundry program.

Secure Processing

Data typically resides in one of three states: at rest (while it is in storage and not in use), in transit (while it is being transmitted or received across a network connection between hosts), and in use (while it is being processed). You already know how data is protected in the first two states. Encryption can protect data both at rest and in transit, so it cannot be accessed by unauthorized entities. It can also be protected using permissions associated with a user's account. But how is data protected while it is being processed, or in use? For normal applications, encrypting data while it is in use is not feasible since it must be continually decrypted and encrypted—something that is beyond the capability of most applications to deal with. This is where hardware can come into play. Trusted hardware can create an environment where data can be processed securely, using a combination of hardware, a trusted execution space, and applications that are specifically designed for this process. There are different combinations of methods used to create a trusted space for data to be processed within. These include a trusted execution environment, or secure enclave, as well as the use of processor security extensions. This also involves the use of atomic execution. All three of these will be discussed in the upcoming sections.

Trusted Execution and Secure Enclave

We have already discussed the use of sandboxing and containerization as initial environments in which we can run applications. These environments prevent outside applications or processes from interfering with their execution and protect the underlying operating system (OS) from vulnerabilities that may be inherent in those applications, providing us with a sort of mutual protection layer. These trusted environments can also be created using a variety of different methods. One method is to create a protected part of the computer, such as memory, in which trusted data and applications execute without interference from outside influences, such as other applications or data. Another method is to use more secure processor designs that contain special extensions used to create protected environments for each application. Still another method is for applications to temporarily gain exclusive use of the processor and memory to protect themselves from outside influences until they have completed executing. Let's take a moment to discuss these in turn.

In a trusted execution environment (TEE), a software abstraction layer creates containers in which several applications can run, protected from the underlying OS and any potential vulnerabilities inherent to the OS (and vice versa). Note that a trusted execution environment is also referred to sometimes as a *secure enclave,* particularly when referring to Apple devices. As we previously discussed regarding containerization, this trusted execution environment is analogous to a virtualization environment, where a hypervisor abstracts hardware and processes to the virtualized operating system. Containerization works the same way, except that it abstracts the operating system from the software applications executing in the container. Note that a trusted execution environment or secure enclave can be used to run many applications within the trusted environment, or, as we will discuss with processor security extensions, used to create microenvironments for individual applications.

 NOTE   Trusted execution environment (TEE) and secure enclave are synonymous terms. Secure enclave is what Apple uses to refer to its TEE.

Processor Security Extensions

Processor security extensions are specialized components found in modern CPUs. These extensions work together to create a trusted execution environment. Applications must be written to take advantage of these security extensions, which may include setting up a reserved area of memory for an application's process to execute securely. This might even include encrypting and decrypting those areas of memory dynamically, protecting the application processes and data that resides in them. The main function of processor security extensions is to provide a protected area for data execution.

Atomic Execution

In Objective 1.7, we discussed race conditions and the time-of-check/time-of-use (TOC/TOU) attacks possible when conditions allow for certain processes to be executed out of sequence or when there is contention for the exclusive use of a resource, such as CPU time or memory, by multiple processes. A method for preventing these types of attacks is *atomic execution,* which is used for controlling a programming run so that processes must execute in a specific sequence and cannot be interrupted between the time when the process starts and when it ends. This prevents other applications or processes from interfering with resources used by a particular process. Essentially, it allows exclusive use of those resources during processing time. Atomic execution works as a combination of secure programming and the allowed use of hardware in this manner.

One word of caution regarding atomic execution: it should only be used sparingly. Overuse will incur serious system performance degradation, as it requires more processing power to dynamically lock and unlock resources as well as track and manage multiple processes that must be performed in sequence.

Bus Encryption

Bus encryption is yet another measure taken to prevent data from being compromised during the processing state. We've seen how data can be encrypted while in storage or while in transit, but it is theoretically possible for an attacker to implant malware on a system that can intercept data as it is being decrypted and transferred from the drive to the CPU or on its way to RAM. Even with self-encrypting drives, the data must be decrypted at some point for processing. Bus encryption simply moves the encryption point from the drive to the CPU. Data is transferred in encrypted form to the CPU and handled by a special chip, called a *cryptoprocessor*. This cryptoprocessor decrypts data upon arrival to the CPU and protects keys in memory. Cryptoprocessors are typically used in specialized machines, such as highly secure, real-time processing devices used in military weapon systems, banking systems (for example, ATMs), and so on. An example of where you might see a cryptoprocessor used in common household computing devices is a cable or satellite TV box that descrambles encrypted signals only for channel subscribers.

Anti-Tamper

In widespread efforts to combat counterfeit and compromised hardware in the supply chain, component manufacturers, vendors, industry partners, and cybersecurity professionals have created an overarching program known as *anti-tamper*. The goals of an anti-tamper program are to ensure that authentic, trusted hardware is manufactured, sold, transported, received, and used by organizations such as companies, governments, and even individuals. Anti-tamper looks at all stages of the supply chain—from architecture and design to manufacturing, logistics, and assurance. Vulnerabilities are assessed and mitigated at every stage in this chain. These efforts are intended to thwart counterfeit or compromised hardware and software, but also to ensure that legitimate hardware cannot be reverse engineered so that it can later be compromised or duplicated. For example, some attackers engage in reverse engineering components by applying voltages to chips and observing how they react. This makes it possible to map the functions of the chip and gain information on how they work. Attackers also engage in visual inspection of components by cutting them apart with precision tools, such as lasers, or with chemicals. Visually observing chips with a high-powered microscope enables a potential attacker to expose chip architecture, design, and function, and may yield information on how to circumvent security measures or even counterfeit those chips. Anti-tamper is concerned with preventing these instances by developing countermeasures against them. This includes random signal generation, which may thwart electronic probing, as well as automatic destruction of chip circuitry in the event a chip is physically compromised.

Cross-Reference

A related subject to anti-tamper is the subject of supply chain assessment, discussed in Objective 5.2.

Self-Encrypting Drive (SED)

The self-encrypting drive (SED) does exactly what its name suggests. However, rather than using software such as Windows BitLocker, for example, it is a hardware-based solution. A cryptographic module is part of the drive hardware, typically built into the disk controller itself. Like TPMs, self-encrypting drives meet the standards promulgated by the Trusted Computing Group in Opal Storage Specification (OSS) 2.0. For the most part, an SED does not natively use the TPM because its hardware is built in. However, it performs some of the same functions in that it is bound to the machine it resides in and cannot be used outside of that machine once the binding occurs.

SEDs typically use an Advanced Encryption Standard (AES) 128- or 256-bit key, which is stored permanently in the cryptographic module attached to the drive. The user creates a password, which is used to then encrypt the drive's key. In the event the user changes the password, the drive key is simply re-encrypted with the new password. When the drive is wiped (effectively by simply encrypting the entire drive's contents), a new drive key is created.

 EXAM TIP   A self-encrypting drive has its own cryptographic module attached to its drive controller and does not normally require a TPM for its encryption and decryption operations.

Trusted Firmware Updates

Traditional firmware updates for older BIOS implementations involved a user downloading a firmware image from a vendor site, running a specialized program that updated the firmware, and rebooting the device while the firmware update process takes place. Unfortunately, firmware, particularly when downloaded arbitrarily from an untrusted site, could be used to compromise the machine at the BIOS or operating system kernel level. This is one effective way a rootkit can be installed on a machine.

Trusted firmware updates, however, eliminate this issue. A trusted firmware update process eliminates the need for user intervention or downloading from an untrusted site. In this model, the ability to update firmware securely is part of the function of the computer's firmware itself. Of course, in order to perform this function, the firmware update must be digitally signed and able to be verified by the firmware. This is an additional function that can be fulfilled by a TPM.

Cross-Reference

Firmware is also discussed in Objective 2.2.

Measured Boot and Attestation

Earlier we discussed the process of a secure boot, which requires that the computing device boot into a trusted operating system, using strict security measures to prevent booting from untrusted media. There may be times, however, when the machine is required to boot into an alternate system, particularly in test or development environments. Most UEFI implementations support a nonsecure boot mode, sometimes referred to as a "legacy" boot option in its menu. However, this would seem to negate the entire reason for having a secure boot process in the first place. Not to worry: the boot process, even when used from an alternate operating system standpoint, can be controlled as well as audited. This is done by performing what is known as a *measured boot*. In a measured boot scenario, the system automatically hashes the alternative boot code and securely stores the hashes. These hashes can later be verified during the *attestation* process, which is the process of examining the hashes at a different station and confirming that they match known hashes of the alternate boot code. This way, when the system is booted from alternate code, it can be compared against known-good hashes to ensure that it is still booting to a known-good source.

 KEY TERMS   **Measured boot** is the process of collecting hashes of startup or boot files when booting in a mode other than secure boot. **Attestation** is the process of comparing those same hashes to known-good ones to validate the startup or boot files.

REVIEW

Objective 2.3: Explain hardware assurance best practices   In this objective, we discussed hardware assurance. You learned that the hardware root of trust is simply the ability to trust hardware all the way from its manufacturer through the logistics supply chain, including the fact that it is authentic and has not been compromised. Two components that help develop this root of trust are the Trusted Platform Module (TPM), which is a system-on-chip embedded on the motherboard, and the hardware security module (HSM). The TPM handles cryptographic functions, including key storage, as well as binding an encrypted hard drive to its computing device. An HSM essentially performs the same functions, except that it is an add-in card or external device.

An eFuse is a special circuit that can only be programmed once. It defaults to a binary 1, and once it is programmed, it changes to a binary 0. When many of these circuits are combined in their various 1 and 0 binary states, they represent data permanently embedded in the computer system. Once an eFuse circuit has been programmed, it cannot be reversed.

Replacing the older BIOS firmware is the new UEFI firmware, which provides additional functionality and security for modern computing devices. This firmware makes it possible to recognize larger hard drives as well as ensure a secure boot option.

Trusted foundry is the name given to vetted and approved vendors who can provide assurances of hardware from manufacture all through the logistics supply chain. This ensures that hardware is authentic and has not been compromised by an unauthorized third party. This is essential in maintaining a secure supply chain as well as a hardware root of trust. The trusted foundry program was developed by the Department of Defense in 2004 but is also used by industry.

Secure processing is the method of securely executing applications and data in a trusted environment, while data is in use. A trusted execution environment, or secure enclave, is one way to ensure secure processing by giving an application and its data an area where it cannot be altered by other applications or data. Containerization is one form of a trusted execution environment. Processor security extensions are built into newer CPUs and provide dynamic encryption and decryption of data for the CPU to use so that it cannot be intercepted between its decryption in storage and its use by the CPU, or as it travels through the internal computer components. Bus encryption similarly prevents access to data by other applications and ensures that data stays encrypted right up until it is processed by the CPU. Atomic execution contributes to secure processing since applications can be designed to take advantage of secure hardware by exclusively using that hardware for specific processes and executing instructions in sequence without interruption.

Anti-tamper is a program and process developed by the industry to come up with solutions to prevent counterfeit hardware and compromise early in the supply chain, as well as, to a certain extent, reverse engineering by malicious entities. This may include physical protections on chips as well as destruction of data if these components are disturbed in any way.

A self-encrypting drive makes use of a cryptographic module attached to the drive controller itself. It is transparent to the user and does not rely on software from the operating system or on the computer's TPM.

Trusted firmware updates provide a process whereby the firmware itself can check for updates, request and receive those updates, and install them securely. It typically does not involve any user interaction, which may widen the attack surface (for example, downloading updates from a potentially untrusted site).

While UEFI provides for a secure boot process and other security functions, sometimes a legacy boot or a boot from an untrusted operating system in a development or test environment is required. Measured boot allows for hashing of boot and startup files for later review to ensure that those files can be verified. Attestation is the act of checking those hashes to ensure they are part of a trusted operating system and can confirm that the hashes from the boot files are valid.

2.3 QUESTIONS

1. You are attempting to secure legacy systems that cannot be replaced at the present time. External governance requires that you must implement a hardware-based system to generate and store cryptographic keys, but these older machines have no such built-in capability. Which of the following would satisfy these requirements?

   A. TPM

   B. HSM

   C. TEE

   D. SED

2. You are attempting to lock down a computer system as much as possible to prevent its compromise. You would like to ensure that it can only boot to trusted media, so a potentially malicious person with physical access to the machine will not be able to start the machine with compromised media. Which of the following options should you make sure is set in the machine's firmware?

   A. Secure boot option

   B. Legacy boot option

   C. BIOS boot

   D. UEFI boot

3. Juan is an experienced cybersecurity analyst who is trying to explain how secure processing works to another analyst. Which of the following statements regarding secure processing is true?

   A. Atomic execution executes only one instruction at a time.

   B. Processor security extensions are a software add-on option that can be installed from Windows.

   C. Trusted execution allows for hardware and specially written applications to create a secure processing space for applications and their data.

   D. A self-encrypting drive relies on the TPM for its encryption and decryption capabilities.

4. Juanita needs to test several functions of a specially developed operating system, so she turns off the secure boot option in her test machine's UEFI configuration. She wants to ensure, however, that when the system boots to the alternate OS, it boots using a known-good boot image. Which of the following processes validates that the hashes collected during boot time match the hashes she has already collected and stored from the known-good alternate boot image?

   A. Measured boot

   B. Attestation

   C. Trusted execution

   D. Atomic execution

2.3 ANSWERS

1. **B**   A hardware security module, or HSM, would fulfill these requirements, since it can be installed as an add-in card or external peripheral and does not require that the legacy machine have a built-in cryptographic capability.

2. **A**   The secure boot option of UEFI firmware must be set in order to ensure booting to trusted, secure media.

3. **C**   Trusted execution allows for hardware and specially written applications to create a secure processing space for applications and their data.

4. **B**   While measured boot is the process of collecting hashes from an alternate boot image, *attestation* is the process of verifying that those hashes compare favorably and match a stored set of hashes from a known-good boot image, thus validating that the boot files are trusted.

Security Operations and Monitoring

DOMAIN
3.0

Domain Objectives

- **3.1** Given a scenario, analyze data as part of security monitoring activities.
- **3.2** Given a scenario, implement configuration changes to existing controls to improve security.
- **3.3** Explain the importance of proactive threat hunting.
- **3.4** Compare and contrast automation concepts and technologies.

Objective 3.1 ## Given a scenario, analyze data as part of security monitoring activities

To understand what is going on in our network infrastructures, we must collect data. And it is not enough to simply collect this data and let it sit; we must analyze it. But data collection and analysis are not random efforts where we collect everything possible and are faced with analyzing terabytes of data, although sometimes it can seem that way. Data analysis should be a carefully planned process and involves collecting the right data from the right sources and using both automated and manual means for presenting and analyzing this data to look for specific patterns.

In this module, we will discuss the particulars of data collection and analysis, and how you can use that analysis to improve the security of your infrastructure. We will look at the various ways we collect data, from both hosts and the network, and how we can review logs and other sources of data to determine the security impact on the organization. We will also look at the particulars of security information and event management (SIEM) systems, as well as the basics of writing queries and rules for those systems. We will also discuss e-mail analysis and how it affects organizational security, since e-mail is a very commonly used avenue of attack for malicious entities.

Heuristics

We have different ways to analyze some of the data we get. Signature- or pattern-based analysis is used when we have a known pattern of behavior that can be judged against previously recorded patterns for comparison. One example of something we monitor using signature-based patterns is, of course, malware. Malware can have patterns, or signatures, and whenever a piece of malware is encountered, it is compared to previously recorded patterns to see if there is a match. Another example is network traffic patterns. A specific type of network attack, for example, can match a previously known pattern so that it can be conclusively stated that we are encountering that attack pattern again.

Another form of analysis is called *behavior analysis,* which is what we use when we encounter behaviors of systems, data, or even people that are outside the norm. To conduct behavior analysis, however, we must start with a baseline of what normal behavior consists of. Once we have established that baseline, usually by monitoring systems over time, we can easily detect when behavior does not follow the normal baseline.

Heuristic analysis is a form of behavior analysis, in that it looks for behaviors or characteristics that are not part of a normal behavior pattern. However, rather than simply flagging something as abnormal behavior and alerting on it (which most behavioral-based systems do), it attempts to match those unusual behaviors with characteristics that could indicate an attack, whether it is abnormal network traffic, potential malware, or other possible malicious attacks.

Heuristic analysis, however, only offers possible matches of characteristics with abnormal behaviors; it is not as accurate as signature-based analysis.

KEY TERMS The difference between ordinary behavior analysis and heuristic analysis is that **behavior analysis** simply alerts you when an event occurs that is outside the normal behavior baseline, whereas **heuristic analysis** attempts to match that abnormal behavior to known characteristics of an attack. Note that heuristic analysis does not use an attack signature to compare the behavior to; it simply looks at possible characteristics of an attack. This makes it less accurate than the signature-based analysis.

Trend Analysis

Trend analysis is looking at a broad range of data to determine causes, patterns, and behaviors. Two important types of analysis are *temporal analysis* and *spatial analysis*. In temporal analysis, we collect and examine data along a spectrum of time. It could be over a short or long period of time or from specific points in time. This type of analysis is often evident in *historical analysis,* which looks for patterns in events we have already encountered so we can derive information about those events and explain them. We can also use temporal analysis, combined with statistical analysis, to use data from past events to predict future behavior or trends. If we encounter a series of events, such as abnormal bandwidth spikes, we can look at the relevant data and attempt to explain what caused the bandwidth spikes. We can further take that data and extrapolate patterns that may take place in the future, thus predicting future bandwidth spikes.

Spatial analysis looks at data relevant to physical or logical spaces (locations), such as geographical locations (for example, a specific regional office), IP subnets, or even specific hosts. This analysis can tell us about events occurring in those spaces. Consider data that points toward a specific IP address or even country as the origination point of an attack, for instance, or a specific web server that has repeatedly received unusual traffic.

EXAM TIP The two types of trend analysis you will be expected to know are temporal (time-related) analysis and spatial (logical or physical location) analysis. Historical analysis is a form of temporal analysis and seeks to explain historical events using available data.

Endpoint Data

An *endpoint* is typically a host on the network. This is where user processing occurs. Keep in mind that an endpoint does not necessarily have to be a user device; it could be a workstation, server, a mobile device, network device, an Internet of Things (IoT) device, or even a sensor connected to a network. Regardless of what it is, endpoints generate data that lends itself to ready analysis, if collected, aggregated, and analyzed properly. In the next few sections, we'll discuss the different types of endpoint data and how to use specific data analysis techniques to determine the security posture of the endpoint, as well as how it aggregates with other data in the enterprise and affects the overall risk posture of the entire infrastructure.

Known-Good vs. Anomalous Behavior Analysis

In every infrastructure, there is a "known good." This means there are known, predictable patterns of behavior, such as network traffic, user behavior, file access, data transfer, and so on, that are considered normal and acceptable. Cybersecurity analysts know what these normal, acceptable patterns are because they have observed them over time. Even unusual events that only occur infrequently might also be known and predictable, if there is a valid explanation for them. Regular peaks in processing, such as during certain times of the year (for example, fiscal year closeout or tax season), as well as increased network usage, which might immediately precede a new product release, are both events that are easily predictable and explainable.

Cybersecurity analysts must baseline the behaviors of the network, hosts, and users in order to understand what exactly is "known good" and what is not. *Baselining* refers to the practice of observing behavior over time to understand which behaviors are normal, routine, expected, and predictable. Baselining can also tell analysts which behaviors are not normal or at least are unacceptable. Baselining is not a simple exercise that happens once and then is done; it constantly occurs over time in mature environments. Data is constantly being collected and fed into analysis tools, such as SIEM systems, and the baseline is always being updated, refined, analyzed, and adjusted as the operating environment changes. What the baseline was one day may change the next, but hopefully due to explainable circumstances, such as a new company acquisition or product line development. In these cases, the changes are predictable, and the change is accounted for and becomes part of the baseline.

It is the anomalous behaviors that can indicate a problem with security in the infrastructure—unexplained spikes in bandwidth, a larger volume of traffic exiting the network bound for an external host, or even an increase in account lockouts one day. These can all be indicators of compromise (IOCs) that may be the first alert you have to an attack or other malicious activity on the network. The key here is *unexplained* behaviors. If you know what behaviors should be exhibited on the network, then any unusual behaviors that can't be readily explained are the ones worth investigating.

There are both manual and automated means of detecting and analyzing unusual behaviors from a host, a user, or devices on the network, such as host-based intrusion detection and prevention systems, SIEMs, and so on. These should be used to fine-tune the detection of unusual behavior as well as analyze it to see if it is explainable and potentially malicious. Of course, if you lack data, you cannot easily analyze behaviors, so it is vitally important that endpoint data be collected and analyzed as you would with other data. Endpoints have logs, of course, that must be collected and analyzed, but they also contain other data that analysts should obtain. Examples of that data, which we will discuss shortly, include memory and file system data.

EXAM TIP To have a valid notion of known-good behavior, you must first establish a baseline over time.

Malware Analysis and Reverse Engineering

We discuss malware throughout this book, but for the purposes of this objective, you should know that malware analysis is more than simply detecting malware on a system and eradicating it. Malware analysis involves somehow obtaining a copy of the malware code, either through the executable located on the host or some other means, and recording its characteristics as much as possible. This includes the processes it spawns, memory locations it resides in, any registry entries it changes for a Windows host, files it accesses, actions it performs, and any network traffic it generates. Recording these characteristics can help you analyze the malware. Obviously, the best way to analyze it is to obtain a copy of its executable and execute it in a controlled environment, such as a sandbox environment.

Cross-Reference

Sandboxing malware for the purposes of reverse engineering is covered in more depth in Objective 3.2.

Memory Analysis

Memory analysis is one of those processes that can be extremely difficult to complete. Almost any analysis of data resident in memory runs the risk of changing that data in some way. Additionally, most often, if you are going to analyze memory contents, you are going to do it during a live forensic analysis of the host. We discuss forensics later in the book, but for now, you should understand that memory can be imaged just as a hard drive can be, although the process is somewhat different. In terms of data analysis, you are looking for processes in memory that shouldn't be there, processes that may match known malware, traces of processes connected to an executable that could be malicious in nature, and so on. Ideally, you would like to obtain an idea of what data was occupying all memory locations used at the time you took the snapshot of the memory. Again, memory (in addition to hard drive and file system analysis) is really a function of deep forensics analysis and likely not something you would do unless you have firm evidence that some sort of system-level compromise has taken place.

Cross-Reference

More details on memory analysis are given in Objectives 4.3 and 4.4.

File System Analysis

File system analysis can tell you a lot about a potentially compromised host. There are file system–related indicators of compromise that you should look for on an endpoint. First, you may have to do a complete forensics analysis of the hard drive or media involved. You should look for the following:

- Potentially altered files, by comparing their previously known hashes
- Time and date stamps to see when they were last accessed or modified
- Possible malicious files disguised as legitimate system files, indicating a possible rootkit

Obviously, you would want to check the media for malware, but you would also want to look for traces of deleted files that might indicate an attacker had tools on the box and attempted to hide or deleted them to avoid detection.

System and Application Behavior

In developing your baselines, you should also be developing a baseline of both individual systems as well as applications that run on them. You should determine what is considered a normal behavior and what is not. Operating systems exhibit behaviors that are easily identified, tracked, recorded, and analyzed. When any of these behaviors are outside the normal baseline, they should also be easy to detect. The same applies to the applications that run on these systems. Applications should follow a normal baseline behavior; there are certain files that they may access frequently, a certain amount of memory that they occupy, a certain percentage of CPU time that they use. If any of these or other factors fall outside the normal baseline, then you should shift your attention to the abnormal behavior to discover what is causing it. It could be a malicious event, but it could also be a malfunctioning application or system. It could also be a hardware problem or even an end-user issue. Any of these things are likely to cause operating systems and applications to behave abnormally, but once they are ruled out, you should start looking for potential security issues.

User and Entity Behavior Analytics (UEBA)

If you're sensing that analyzing unusual patterns of behavior is a key focus of this objective, you are correct. This is true with almost any data you can collect and analyze. It is also true with a technique called user and entity behavior analytics (UEBA). UEBA is not simply about looking at logs of user actions; it is about looking for patterns of unusual behavior. Understand that there may not be malicious intent involved, but sometimes user behavior can lead to security issues on the network and can also be malicious in nature. These are the things we are looking for with this technique.

As with other types of behavioral analysis, we must first collect data and baseline it as normal user behavior. You could collect data and aggregate it, with groups of users, and develop some very useful pattern analysis. For example, you could determine that during lunchtime hours, web traffic typically spikes because people may surf the Web a little bit while they are sitting at their desks eating their lunch. That is an obvious result of behavior analysis. You could also look at specific groups of users, such as administrators. If you see that one or two administrators are using their administrator accounts for more than performing privileged tasks, such as day-to-day e-mail use, that would be an indicator that you need to enforce policies for those accounts. More in-depth use of this process, however, is to look at normal user behavior and develop a baseline, so you can determine when there are unusual, unexplainable behaviors across the entire infrastructure. This is the key to much of the analysis discussion we have had so far; you must look for unusual and unexplainable behaviors that may indicate a security problem.

 NOTE The word "entity" is included in this technique because it isn't simply users that have accounts; remember that services or daemons can also possess accounts, so you must determine what their normal baseline behaviors are as well so you can detect any unusual behaviors exhibited by these accounts.

Analysis of Endpoint Exploitation Techniques

We are not going to discuss specific exploitation techniques in this module; what is important here is how you detect these exploitation techniques, collect the data on them, and analyze them. Even prior to a potential attack, you should be familiar with the various techniques that attackers use to exploit your network and systems. Based on the knowledge of these techniques, you should be employing this knowledge when threat hunting; this would lead you to look for and detect potential compromises. Some of the more advanced machine learning systems, as well as other data analysis tools, such as SIEM systems, also include exploitation and attack techniques in their libraries so these patterns can be looked for in data. These include network traffic attack signatures, malware signatures, and so on, but signature-based analysis can be used only so far. It is important that potential attacks be analyzed using behavior-based and heuristic techniques as well. Knowledge of various attack methodologies, such as the MITRE ATT&CK framework, would also help you identify and analyze potential attack and exploitation behaviors.

It takes a good amount of experience and analysis to recognize patterns of exploitation versus normal behavior, but as long as you have a good solid baseline of what known-good behavior is, anomalous behaviors that could indicate a system compromise will be more obvious to you.

Cross-Reference

You should review the various attack frameworks, including the MITRE ATT&CK framework, detailed in Objective 1.2, to have a better understanding of how to analyze exploit and attack techniques.

Network

Like endpoint-related data, network data is of critical importance in your analysis. In addition to point-in-time analysis of specific network traffic, you also must examine network traffic over a period of time, looking for aggregated traffic or specific traffic-related events that may tell you what happened during an incident or to predict possible future trends. There are several aspects of network data analysis to consider. The primary, and most obvious one, is network traffic, which is captured and examined. There are also, however, other aspects of network data you should examine. Uniform Resource Locators and DNS data analysis, as well as network-related malware analysis, are all important. We will briefly describe each of these in the following sections.

Uniform Resource Locator (URL) and Domain Name System (DNS) Analysis

The domain name system is critical to the operation of a network infrastructure. Unfortunately, it can also be the source of many different avenues of attack. These include false entries in DNS servers, false entries in a host's DNS cache, and diverting DNS queries to a false or malicious source. There are also attacks directly on a DNS server that take advantage of insufficient permissions, allowing zone transfers from an organization to an unauthorized server.

As with all infrastructure servers, DNS allows for advanced logging that can be fed into a centralized log server, or, preferably, a SIEM system. Combined with logs that come from a host, DNS logs can indicate if there is a potential problem with name resolution both on the internal network and to external domains. Sometimes troubleshooting a DNS security issue can be problematic, in that queries can be passed from one DNS server to another. If there is a false or inaccurate entry in a DNS server, it must be traced back to the source server that has a bad entry. Often, the trouble lies either in the host's resolver cache or through DNS redirection from a malicious or compromised website.

Uniform Resource Locators (URLs) can also be problematic, in that the issue may not be a DNS entry; it could be a misleading or obfuscated URL. Many end users may not recognize that the URL has been changed slightly from a legitimate one, particularly if the URL contains different characters or is many levels deep. Network security devices, including intrusion detection systems, next-generation firewalls, application-level firewalls, and so on, can analyze URLs to determine if they are legitimate or not, but they will not always catch everything.

Sometimes specific URLs must be configured to redirect traffic to a sinkhole on the network. This means that a user, or even an automated malicious bot, will not be able to communicate with the URL since its traffic will be diverted to the server on the internal network. This is to prevent users and hosts from attempting to communicate with malicious websites. URLs placed in a deny list can be logged for later analysis, and when combined with host logs regarding user actions as well as DNS server logs, this can be useful in determining exactly how false or malicious URLs are being used to target users and hosts on the network.

One technique of determining if the URL could be malicious or not is to use reputation-based services. Reputation-based services employ online databases where known malicious URLs have been reported and recorded. Many of these databases can be accessed through a subscription feed service and are compatible with different network security devices such as application proxies, WAFs, and next-generation firewalls.

Domain Generation Algorithm

It is useful to know about domain generation algorithms (DGAs) and how they fit into all of this. DGAs are used to dynamically generate domain names and URLs. Unfortunately, this technique is used to enable malware to communicate with external command-and-control servers. Once a security analyst determines a malicious domain that malware may be communicating with, they can, of course, block this domain or send it to a sinkhole. However, malware writers use a DGA to enable malware to dynamically switch to new domains, even after administrators have blocked other target domains. DGAs will generate what appear to be random or nonsensical-looking domain names, which are hard to develop rules for. This is one instance where an allow list of only permissible domains would be of more value than a deny list, which only denies specific domains but may allow others generated by a DGA to slip through.

Flow Analysis

Flow analysis is the name given to a technique of analyzing network traffic. An example of flow analysis is a technology originally developed by Cisco called *NetFlow*. NetFlow works by grouping traffic into *flows* based on common characteristics. This way, all traffic originating from or destined to a specific IP address, for example, and containing specific ports or protocols can be examined in aggregate to look for patterns. These patterns include all traffic entering your network from a particular source, or all traffic destined for a particular destination, or all traffic containing a specific protocol. The objective is to look for patterns, particularly when any element of that traffic is considered unusual. Flow analysis is not very useful for singular or one-time communications sessions, as it would be difficult to discern a pattern; it is far more useful when looking at aggregated traffic.

Packet and Protocol Analysis

Traffic analysis can take many different forms. In the previous section, we discussed the technique of NetFlow analysis, but there are also ways of analyzing traffic that focus specifically on protocol, TCP/UDP port, or network service. For example, you could analyze all network traffic inbound to various chat services on your network, or traffic using a specific source port. To analyze traffic, you should first capture it in a file that can be dissected and analyzed. There are different packet capture/traffic analysis tools available, with the most popular being the open-source Wireshark tool and the built-in Linux/UNIX utility tcpdump.

Captured (saved) traffic is much more useful for forensic analysis after the fact. Real-time analysis is possible but difficult; this type of analysis usually involves simply alerting an analyst that unusual or potentially malicious traffic has been detected. This can help you by alerting you to an attack so defensive measures can be activated and the attack stopped. Unfortunately, this type of analysis is not very useful for post-incident forensics.

Regardless of which traffic analyzer you use, you should develop filters that enable you to separate out the traffic of interest that you wish to view. There are capture filters and display filters; capture filters only capture and retain the specific traffic you build into the filter and do not store any other traffic. With a display filter, you are capturing and storing all traffic, but only displaying to the analyst the traffic of interest that you specify for the filter. You can, however, always change the display filter to show any or all traffic of interest to you. Here are some of the elements you may want to filter and analyze:

- Source address
- Destination address
- Source or destination port
- Protocol
- Network service
- Plaintext or encrypted traffic
- Volume of traffic (for example, the volume of traffic above a certain level in a certain amount of time)

When analyzing traffic, you are looking for patterns that could indicate potentially malicious network traffic, of course. This could be a specific communications session or an aggregate of all communications sessions over a period of time entering and exiting from your network. Traffic analysis is extraordinarily useful during incident response and for a forensics analysis after an incident. When combined with other infrastructure data sources in context, traffic analysis can give you an accurate picture of what has occurred on the network, enabling you to determine the root cause or even predict potential trends.

 NOTE You should carefully plan for capturing traffic on a routine basis. Traffic captures require a great deal of storage space; you should capture and retain only the traffic that could be of forensic value to you and set data retention policies for it.

Network-Based Malware Analysis

In addition to reverse engineering malware (that is, looking at it from a code perspective), it is also useful to look at malware from a network point of view. Many pieces of malware are designed to initiate network-based attacks. This includes automated bots that communicate with other hosts on the network to further spread the malware, as well as communicating with a central command-and-control server on the Internet. Part of your malware detection and eradication strategy should be to monitor your network traffic for unusual ports, protocols, services, external destination addresses, and volume of traffic. These are all telltale signs that malware could be on your network and attempting a network-based attack. Of course, there is also malware that can attempt to use allowed protocols, such as HTTP, to engage in an attack and send command-and-control messages to other hosts on the network as well as external addresses. This is where packet inspection and content filtering come into play. Using tools such as NetFlow, DNS analysis, and DGA inspection will assist you in detecting network-based malware.

Log Review

Almost all operating systems, applications, and devices, when properly configured, generate log data. This is essentially an audit trail of events that have happened on a system or in an application. Log data can tell you what happened, who caused it to happen, when it happened, and, when aggregated with other types of data, can sometimes tell you how the event of interest happened and even give you enough information to hypothesize as to *why* it happened. There are many different sources of log data, even from a single system. For example, on Windows devices, you can have system logs, which detail events related to the operating system and its hardware resources, the security log, which obviously gives you information on security events, and application logs. There are also service and application logs created that you could put in the proper context to determine what exactly is going on with those services or applications. In the next few sections, we will cover only a brief list of log sources you should examine that could be key to an investigation or an audit, as well as assist you in passing the exam. These include events logs, syslog, firewall, web application firewall, proxy, and IDS/IPS logs.

Event Logs

Event log is a generic term for logs that could cover a broad range of areas, including system events, security events, application or service events, user events, and so on. The keyword here is *event,* which is an occurrence of an activity or happening. An event is something that is considered on a singular basis and has defined characteristics. The basic information regarding an event in a log should include the following:

- Definition of the event
- System or resource affected by the event
- IP or MAC address
- Entity causing or associated with the event
- Start and end time and date of the event
- Action that caused the event (for example, account creation, file deletion, or privilege escalation or use)

A particular activity on a system may be broken down into smaller, individual activities; for example, the creation of a new user account likely isn't a singular event in itself; it is likely made up of several smaller events that can be decomposed into individual singular actions. Normally, events have codes associated with them that indicate the event type and identification. These are usually unique to the operating system or application logging the event. Most operating systems and applications have built-in facilities for reviewing events, but not all of them function equally well. Also, most of them do not look at aggregated events to see how they relate to each other.

Syslog

Syslog is a type of log typically found on a UNIX or Linux system. It is the core event log for those types of systems. *Syslogd* is the name of the service that runs the event-logging service on those operating systems. A syslog server is a dedicated server to which events from various hosts are collected and forwarded for further aggregation and analysis. There is also a considerable number of utilities that are useful for examining syslogs from different hosts to discern patterns and facilitate analysis.

 NOTE Although syslog is a specific type of logging service that runs on UNIX/ Linux hosts, it has become a more generic term in the cybersecurity community to indicate a centralized logging server that collects logs from all types of hosts and operating systems.

Firewall Logs

Firewall logs are useful in that they can give you information on all the traffic entering or leaving from a network interface. These logs can tell you basic details and characteristics about traffic that includes time/date, ports, protocols, services, and source and destination IP addresses. More advanced firewall logs can also give you detailed information about the application protocol content itself. This can help you analyze, for example, the characteristics of an Internet-based attack. Firewall logs, like most other types of logs, can be sent to a centralized syslog server or, preferably, fed into a SIEM system for better aggregation and analysis.

Web Application Firewall (WAF)

As mentioned elsewhere in this book, a web application firewall is dedicated to protecting the web application server. It serves as an intermediary between users who access the web application through their browsers and the server containing the web application and its data. It is useful in preventing attacks such as cross-site scripting, injection, and so on.

WAF logs can be helpful in determining what type of potentially malicious actions transpired in a particular user session that may have compromised the web application.

Normally these types of logs can give you the same types of information as other, more general firewall logs but can also include detailed information on the HTTP traffic that was passed back and forth between the client and the server.

Proxy

Proxy logs can tell you details about communications session between users or clients and Internet destinations and applications. You can view information from these logs concerning types of traffic that pass between the user and the web application, as well as what type of content was transferred, its characteristics, and what type of content or sites may have been attempted access but denied.

 EXAM TIP   Remember that a proxy intercepts Internet requests from clients and forwards them on to Internet hosts, and in turn passing their replies to the client. Proxies can be used to prevent malformed HTTP and other web-based protocol requests from compromising clients as well as to prevent internal unit users from attempting to violate policy by accessing prohibited websites.

Intrusion Detection System (IDS)/ Intrusion Prevention System (IPS)

Intrusion detection systems (IDSs) and intrusion prevention systems (IPSs) are among the most valuable types of network logs you can analyze to gain information on a potential malicious event. In addition to the data that other network device sources provide, such as network traffic information, content, and so on, you can also get information from these logs that may detail how an attacker attempted or succeeded in attacking the network. You may get information on what type of traffic was allowed, denied, or dropped. You should also be getting information on different attack techniques malicious entities may employ.

Impact Analysis

When examining all the data we discussed, one of the key pieces of information you need to develop out of all this analysis is the impact. This could be an impact on the organization, a specific system, or even a user. Sometimes you are looking at the impact of a single event for a single system. Other times you are looking at what is called aggregate impact, which is the combination of all the different measures of impact, throughout the organization or a system, that an event may cause. For example, a malicious attack from the Internet may impact individual systems differently than it does the entire organization. A system could be restored or replaced, but the impact to the organization could be far worse in terms of reputation, fines, or other liability. Remember that impact could come in several forms, including damage to a system or data, financial impact, legal liability, and impact that can be difficult to measure, such as reputation or loss of market share. In the next two sections, we will talk about organizational impact versus localized impact, which may be specific to a system. We will also discuss the difference between immediate and total impact caused by an event.

Organization Impact vs. Localized Impact

The organizational impact could be considered the aggregate impact. If an attack compromises several different systems, for example, or even results in a data breach, the organizational impact is likely at least equal to, but possibly even greater than, the measures of impact for individual systems. Individual systems can be restored, repaired, or replaced, based on their value and criticality to the organization. But the organization may suffer far greater than the sum of the total impact for each system; it can suffer severe legal liability, particularly in the event of a breach, when it may incur fines, loss of customer confidence, lawsuits, and so on. It can also suffer longer-term effects in that it may have to make major changes to its infrastructure to prevent future similar attacks. This can mean upgrading equipment, hiring additional personnel, and so on.

A localized impact is typically measured for an individual system or set of resources. It can be an individual host, a network segment, or a group of systems that support a specific line of business. Localized impact could also center around a specific geographic area, perhaps a branch or department or regional location versus the entire organization. In risk management, localizing impact can also mean minimizing impact in the event of an incident. Segmenting systems and networks, both logically and physically, can help to localize the impact to a single system or network segment, for instance, minimizing potential impact.

Immediate vs. Total

Another way of looking at impact is based on the immediate impact versus the total impact. The immediate impact again can be compared to a more localized or minimal level of impact. It can also be the impact measured while an attack is in progress, for example, versus the total impact, which may not be apparent until after the event. The immediate impact could include the cost to repair or replace a server or other equipment, labor hours, software applications, and so on. The total impact could also include measurements beyond those, including revenue lost, the total cost to mitigate the incident, and even elements that are not as easily measurable, such as loss of consumer confidence or reputation, for example.

In any case, measuring the impact, whether it is organizational or localized, and immediate versus total, is not a point-in-time process. It is more of a constant, long-term process that can be performed at various points during an incident. Understanding the impact along those various points of the spectrum can help an organization focus its resources and energy on specific pressure points, such as critical servers or processes, to minimize the overall total impact.

 NOTE Consideration of organizational impact versus localized impact, as well as immediate versus total impact, should be part of your risk management strategy.

Security Information and Event Management (SIEM) Review

Collecting all the data that we discussed so far does not do your organization any good at all unless you do something with it. In this case, that means categorizing, aggregating, correlating, and analyzing it. Beyond analysis, it also means taking meaningful action based on that information once you have it and are using it to secure your network. Remember that data is a singular piece of knowledge; by itself, it may or may not mean anything. But when combined with other data, and given context, it becomes information. Information is what is useful to you; it adds dimension to all the otherwise disparate collections of nonrelated data. Therefore, collecting the right data is important, as well as aggregating it into a useful form so that it can be analyzed in different ways. As we have previously mentioned, there are many ways to do this. Some of these ways, such as workflow orchestration, machine learning, and the use of automation protocols and standards, will be discussed in Objective 3.4.

With most of the data we have talked about in this objective, it's impractical to visit every system and go through all the built-in utilities, limited as they may be, to try to make sense out of the volumes of data you will have. It is more efficient and effective to send all the data you possibly can to a centralized security information and event management (SIEM) system. The system should be your go-to, one-stop solution for viewing all the disparate data in your infrastructure and making sense of it. Remember that the goal is not simply to collect and analyze it; it is to gain meaning from it that will help you make intelligent, risk-based decisions about the security posture of your network. While some of these critical and seemingly insurmountable tasks require a human touch, many of these data collection and analysis steps can be automated, delivering concise, relevant data to an analyst for further action. Depending on the complexity of the analysis engine, the SIEM system can be programmed to perform any of the data aggregation, signature, and behavior analysis for you. Of course, this is dependent on the rules you create for the system. Like all security devices, SIEM systems require well-written rulesets to process data. Each SIEM system may also have its own query language, enabling you to write detailed, complex query sets so you can further automate data transformation and analysis actions. In the next few sections, we will discuss some of the particulars of writing rules and queries for these systems, as well as discuss topics such as the usefulness of the SIEM dashboards.

Dashboard

The *dashboard* is the central nerve center of a security analysis tool for a cybersecurity analyst. It presents all the information the analyst needs to know, at their fingertips, as well as provides the interface to managing the different data that can be manipulated and viewed. Analysts can create queries, execute them, and view the results from the dashboard, as well as manage the different functions and options of the analysis software itself. This makes using the tool much simpler, more efficient, and effective. Otherwise, an analyst may have to use multiple different tools in different areas or systems, using different interfaces. This could significantly slow down the work of an analyst and render their efforts moot.

Rule and Query Writing

All network devices, whether routers, firewalls, intrusion detection/prevention systems, or SIEM systems, have their own built-in facilities for writing rulesets and queries. Rulesets are typically found more so in network devices that actually take action, such as routers and firewalls. Queries are more often found in more advanced devices where you need to analyze information coming from those devices, such as an IDS or SIEM system. We discuss firewall rules more in depth in Objective 3.2, so we will focus in this objective more on the rules and queries that are inherent to analysis devices, such as a SIEM system. Most popular SIEM systems, such as Splunk and the Elasticsearch, Logstash, Kibana (ELK) open-source system, have their own unique rule and query languages. Splunk has the Search Processing Language (SPL), while ELK uses its Kibana Query Language (KQL). Both are languages from different vendors; however, there are enough similarities that you can learn either of them easily if you are already proficient in the other. Many SIEM systems have the ability to import rules and queries created in other languages, such as Python and Perl.

The key to query writing is knowing exactly which data, under what circumstances, you want to derive from a large collection of aggregated data the SIEM system has at its disposal. Queries can be very simple or quite complex, depending on what type of specific data you are looking for, the volume of data stores you must search through, and the complexity of the criteria you are imposing on the search. Typical search parameters for queries include the following:

- IP or MAC addresses
- Domain names
- Protocol
- TCP/UDP port
- Inbound versus outbound traffic
- Traffic classified as allowed, denied, or dropped
- Username
- Action (for example, account creation, file deletion, or website accessed)
- File name, size, or contents
- Dates and times
- Bandwidth usage or volume of traffic

Note that these are only a few examples of basic criteria included in queries or rules. Many other, more detailed criteria and data characteristics could be included in the query to fine-tune the results returned.

Rulesets and queries can also take other devices' rules and query results as input into their own criteria. An example of this is the ubiquitous known-bad IP address rule. Almost all network security devices have a rule of this sort, either in the form of a deny rule or a deny list. In this type of rule, the administrator adds a list of IP addresses that are known by reputation sources or by experience to be malicious or undesirable in nature. These known-bad IP addresses are processed as part of deny lists or as part of a ruleset. While a SIEM is not a security device in that it can take action based on traffic that may be detected originating from or destined to one of these addresses, you can use these known-bad IP address lists as part of your rules and queries to search for and identify any traffic that matches one of these addresses.

String Search

One of the key elements of a query is the *string search*. Queries can look for characteristics of certain data elements, such as an IP address, that are frequently found in defined fields. However, sometimes elements you may want to search for may be, for example, alphanumeric strings that do not conform to any particular field or format. This is where string search is valuable. You can essentially search for any user-defined value or string, regardless of how the data is formatted or defined in fields. Using wildcards in your searches, as well as regular expressions (called *regex*), can greatly enhance and simplify your string and character searches.

Scripting and Piping

As part of the defined objectives for the exam, you should also know how to use techniques such as scripting and piping in your data collection and analysis efforts. As previously mentioned, scripting can take the form of built-in scripting languages that come with the security analysis tool, or various scripting languages such as Python and Perl can be used for creating rule sets and queries. Piping is a simple but useful concept and involves using the output from one command or script as the input for another. A script can execute certain tasks or manipulate data and produce an output that can be used as the parameters or input for another script. This is useful in chaining scripts together without making them monolithic and allows a more modular approach to scripting.

While scripting has practical limitations, it is perfect for ad hoc or smaller tasks that are repetitive and inefficient to manually perform on a routine basis. For larger, more complex tasks, although scripting could be used, it may be more efficient to use the built-in powerful query languages that are included as part of many Security Orchestration, Automation, and Response tools (referred to as SOAR tools), such as SIEM systems.

Cross-Reference

Scripting and its usefulness as an automation tool is covered in more depth in Objective 3.4.

E-mail Analysis

E-mail is one of the most commonly used services in the organization. It is also one of the most critical, since so much of the organization's communication, both internally and externally, takes place over e-mail. In addition to providing communications, e-mail is also a popular avenue of attack for malicious entities. The Simple Mail Transfer Protocol (SMTP), which most e-mail servers use, is older and inherently insecure. There are several methods used to secure e-mail, with varying degrees of effectiveness. Several e-mail attack vectors can be used against an organization, such as impersonation, malicious attachments, links, and phishing. We will talk about those in the upcoming sections. We will also look at analyzing e-mails for key elements that may tell you the legitimacy of the e-mail and if it has any malicious intent behind it. These include the digital signature, the e-mail header, and even the e-mail signature block. Finally, we will discuss three important security technologies recently implemented in e-mail systems that can assist in increasing e-mail security. These include Domain Keys Identified Mail (DKIM), the Sender Policy Framework (SPF), and the Domain-based Message Authentication, Reporting, and Conformance (DMARC) specification.

Impersonation

One of the more obvious ways e-mail can be used against an organization is through impersonation. E-mail is commonly used to attempt to impersonate a person or organization. More often than not, this is for random purposes in the form of phishing attacks but can also be used as a concerted effort from an advanced persistent threat (APT) to compromise an organization. Impersonation can be implemented using fake or slightly altered domain names and IP addresses, obfuscated URLs, and other spoofing techniques. Normally the impersonator will make the e-mail seem like it came from a legitimate source and is from an entity known to the user. Often, impersonation is not the end goal of the e-mail; instead, it is used to further attack the organization through other means, such as carrying malicious payloads, links, or phishing attempts. The impersonation part is simply to get the user to trust the sender of the e-mail so they will open it and execute a potentially malicious link or follow instructions that may be part of a phishing attack.

Malicious Payload

E-mail can carry malicious payloads in the form of attachments that the user may be tricked into opening, or even code that is embedded in the e-mail itself. The user does not necessarily have to click the payload to execute it; simply the act of opening the e-mail could execute malicious payload. If the organization has implemented good security measures at the perimeter and on the e-mail server, most malicious payloads should be detected and stripped from the e-mail, or otherwise alert an administrator. Many times, these malicious payloads are forms of malware, which can be detected through enterprise-level antimalware software.

Embedded Links

An embedded link is one that could be hidden in the body of the e-mail, behind a person's name, for instance, or address. If the user clicks the address thinking they are going to open it in Google maps, for example, it could actually redirect the user to another site of the attacker's choosing. As mentioned previously with malicious payloads, e-mail security mechanisms should strip or otherwise render harmless embedded links in e-mail messages.

Phishing

Phishing is an attack technique used through e-mail to trick the user into performing various actions, which may include clicking harmful links or even replying to an e-mail with a user's personal information, such as a password, credit card information, and so on. Phishing is a form of social engineering that is simply executed through e-mail. There are various forms of phishing, such as whaling and spear phishing, but essentially they are all focused on gaining the trust of an unsuspecting user and tricking them into performing actions that could result in compromised data or the installation of malware on the organization's network.

A phishing e-mail is typically designed to look exactly like a legitimate e-mail from a person or entity the user trusts. It may even contain embedded pictures or stationary that resembles a trusted organization, such as a bank. If the e-mail can establish some level of user trust, then it can use social engineering techniques to entice the users to perform potentially malicious actions, including clicking links, downloading attachments, or even replying to the e-mail with sensitive information. While there are many technical security controls that can help prevent or detect phishing attacks, ultimately user-level training is the best method for stopping them. If users are educated on various phishing techniques and their ramifications, they are better able to avoid these types of attacks.

Forwarding

E-mail forwarding can be troublesome in many different respects. First, users who continually forward potential spam or hoax e-mails are doing nothing more than using up network bandwidth and server storage space. However, this is the least of the organization's worries; this can be annoying and troublesome at best but can also be used to inadvertently spread malware throughout an organization. E-mail and acceptable use policies normally can be used to reduce this type of forwarding by simply enforcing the policies when users violate them. Some e-mail servers have configuration settings that can prevent the forwarding of potentially malicious attachments as well.

Another aspect of forwarding, albeit a bit older in nature, is a security misconfiguration that allows an attacker to use an organization's e-mail server as a potential forwarder. If configured improperly, the e-mail server could accept requests from an external attacker and forward e-mails on to yet another organization, becoming part of a potential attack. In this respect, external SMTP forwarding should be disabled on the organization's e-mail servers.

Digital Signatures

Digital signatures are implemented as part of a larger public key infrastructure (PKI) and are designed to verify that an e-mail is authentic and that the person who claims that they have sent it is actually the person who did. Digital signatures ensure authenticity and nonrepudiation. In other words, if an e-mail is digitally signed, a user cannot later deny that they sent it, assuming their public/private key pair has not been compromised.

Digital signatures can be verified using various means, including a certificate revocation list (CRL) published by the certificate issuer. If the e-mail sender's public/private key pair has been compromised, this, in turn, means that the certificate is compromised, and the issuer should publish an entry on the CRL that states such. This renders the key pair invalid, also invalidating any digital signatures used to sign e-mails. This is one way an organization can verify that e-mails are authentic.

Header

As part of our discussion on data analysis, e-mail headers provide useful information when analyzing an e-mail to determine if it has malicious intent and is authentic. The e-mail header can be easily viewed in most e-mail client applications or as part of e-mail server analysis tools. The header is supposed to indicate the identity of the user who sent the e-mail, the recipient, the originating e-mail server and organization, the destination e-mail server and organization, and possibly any intermediate hops the e-mail took on its way to the recipient. It may also include information on digital signatures as well as e-mail attachments.

E-mail headers cannot be fully trusted to indicate the authenticity of an e-mail. Headers can be forged, and they can also include information that is erroneous. The sender's e-mail client and server can be configured to put a variety of incorrect or false information into an e-mail header. However, when analyzing an e-mail to determine its authenticity, header analysis is usually the starting point.

E-mail Signature Block

Uninformed users often confuse the digital signature with an e-mail signature block. It is our job as cybersecurity analysts to make sure they understand the difference. Whereas a digital signature is a result of signing an e-mail with a private key, which is then validated by the corresponding public key, an e-mail signature block only contains what the sender intends for it to; this usually indicates the sender's name, title, and other relevant information. However, this information should not be trusted to verify the authenticity of an e-mail since it is so easily forged, and users need to understand that.

Domain Keys Identified Mail (DKIM)

The Domain Keys Identified Mail (DKIM) is a standard developed to detect e-mail spoofing, thereby preventing phishing and other impersonation attacks. DKIM uses a digital signature linked to an organization's domain name. The organization is issued a public/private key pair, and the e-mail is digitally signed by the organization, in addition to any user's digital signature included in the e-mail. The receiving organization can verify the digital signature because the public key has been published in the sending organization's DNS servers. This ensures that the e-mail was, in fact, sent by the originating organization and is authentic. DKIM is an Internet standard and was published in September 2011 in RFC 6376, with later updates included in RFC 8301 and 8463.

Sender Policy Framework (SPF)

Yet another e-mail authentication method is the Sender Policy Framework (SPF). It is not as effective as DKIM and works in a different way. Whereas DKIM uses digitally signed e-mails from the organization, SPF simply checks to ensure that e-mail has been sent from an authorized IP address, as published in the organization's DNS server. This is not as effective as using digitally signed e-mail, since the DNS server's record could be compromised and a false mail server (MX) record IP address inserted into it. Additionally, since IP addresses can be easily spoofed, an attacker could send an e-mail from a spoofed, yet technically valid IP address, which the receiving organization may be able to verify as one listed in the sending organization's DNS records.

Domain-Based Message Authentication, Reporting, and Conformance (DMARC)

Domain-based Message Authentication, Reporting, and Conformance (DMARC) is an e-mail authentication protocol designed to ensure the authenticity of e-mail sent from the organization. Rather than an authentication method itself, it specifies either or both of the previous two methods (DKIM and SPF). A DMARC entry is entered into the organization's DNS server records, which specify which is used (or that both are). The entry allows the receiving organization to check for authenticity and use the method specified by the organization. DMARC can also control what happens to the e-mail if it fails its authenticity check; the DMARC entry can specify that an e-mail can be rejected or forwarded under certain circumstances.

 EXAM TIP   Understand the differences between DKIM, SPF, and DMARC. DKIM uses organizational digital signatures to authenticate any e-mails sent from the organization and can be verified using the public key entered in the organization's DNS records. SPF verifies that the IP address of the mail server used to send the e-mail is a valid e mail server address authorized by the organization. DMARC is a policy entry in DNS that dictates which of the other two authentication methods should be used, and how the e-mail should be handled should it fail authenticity checks. All three of these authentication methods rely on an organization's DNS.

REVIEW

Objective 3.1: Given a scenario, analyze data as part of security monitoring activities   In this module, we discussed how to analyze the volumes of data that you will encounter on your infrastructure. We discussed identifying, collecting, storing, aggregating, and analyzing data from all the sources you have in your organization, such as hosts, networks, applications, and so on. We looked at different data analysis techniques, including signature and pattern analysis, behavior analysis, and heuristics. We also discussed the different types of trend analysis that data can help us perform.

Endpoint data is one of the key sources of data that has long been neglected but is recently becoming more important. You learned that we should create a baseline of known-good behaviors for both devices and users so that we have a basis for comparison when anomalous behavior is encountered. We discussed malware analysis in reverse engineering, as well as memory and file system analysis. We also discussed the particulars of system and application behavior. User and entity behavior analytics (UEBA) is a form of analysis concerned with user patterns beyond simply looking at user logs. We also briefly described the analysis of endpoint exploitation techniques.

Beyond endpoints, the network is the other massive source of valuable data. We discussed different types of traffic analysis, as well as URL and DNS analysis. We talked about how malware often uses domain generation algorithms to confuse security analysts by creating random and unique domain names. We discussed flow analysis, which looks at traffic in aggregate, as well as how to decompose traffic down to packet and protocol analysis. We also talked about the network characteristics that malware could exhibit, allowing you to further detect and track malware actions.

We discussed the value in reviewing the different types of logs you will find on hosts and network devices. These include generic event logs that cover a wide variety of events on different hosts, as well as syslog, firewall logs, WAF, proxy, and intrusion detection/intrusion prevention logs.

We also discussed e-mail analysis, since e-mail is a major critical system in most infrastructures, but it is also an avenue for many malicious activities, such as phishing attacks, embedded links, data loss, impersonation, and so on. When analyzing e-mail, there is much content to review, including the e-mail signature block, headers, and so on. We discussed the different characteristics of e-mail that are worth scrutiny, including malicious payloads that can be embedded in an e-mail. We discussed different technologies involved in securing e-mail, such as digital signatures, Domain Keys Identified Mail (DKIM), Domain-based Message Authentication, Reporting, and Conformance (DMARC), and the Sender Policy Framework (SPF).

Impact is one of the key pieces of information you should be trying to ascertain from all your analysis. You want to know not only the individual measures of impact on data and systems, but also the total impact on the entire organization, both point-in-time and over a long period of time. Impact can cause damage to the system, loss of data, financial losses, legal liability, or even loss of market share, consumer confidence, and reputation.

Security information and event management (SIEM) systems are concerned with serving as a central collection point for all types of data across the infrastructure. Their job is to collect, aggregate, correlate, and analyze data that would likely be too much for human analysts to do in a practical timeframe. They can discern different patterns of behavior and produce actionable information that you can use to make risk-informed security decisions. SIEMs provide a centralized dashboard that serves as the interface for cybersecurity analysts, allowing them to run queries, monitor systems, and manage functions of the SIEM itself. SIEMs can use built-in or external query languages to assist a cybersecurity analyst in locating and producing specific data. You can use these query languages to search on specific predefined data elements, such as an IP address, or free-flow strings that might not be in defined fields. In addition to the built-in query languages, you can also use scripting languages that are better suited for smaller, routine, repetitive tasks. Piping allows you to use the results from one script as the input for another script.

3.1 QUESTIONS

1. Rico is a cybersecurity analyst who is trying to perform analysis on unusual traffic patterns. The traffic does not match any known patterns and is not within the normal baseline of the organization's network traffic. Which of the following types of analysis would be best suited for Rico to use to match this abnormal traffic with characteristics of known attack methods?

    A. Signature-based analysis

    B. behavioral-based analysis

    C. Hcuristic analysis

    D. Trend analysis

2. Barney is a cybersecurity analyst who is attempting to configure network devices to prevent any potential malware from broadcasting outside the organization's network to an Internet command-and-control server. When he first analyzes a potential piece of malware, he sees that it is configured to send messages to a specific domain, which he promptly blocks. Several weeks later, he detects that same piece of malware on the network, as well as network traffic that indicates it is messaging a malicious server on the Internet. Which the following techniques did the malware most likely used to achieve this?

    A. User and entity behavior analytics

    B. Domain generation algorithm

    C. Sender Policy Framework

    D. Embedded links

3. You are a cybersecurity analyst who is looking at a large volume of network traffic data, collected over a period of two years, in an effort to determine why bandwidth usage increased over that time period. What type of analysis are you conducting?

    A. Historical analysis

    B. Traffic analysis

    C. User and entity behavior analytics

    D. Heuristics analysis

4. You are a cybersecurity analyst who has been tasked to review logs from over 200 individual hosts that make up your network. After two weeks of trying and failing to visit every single host to review their logs, you decide to come up with a better solution. Which of the following is the best solution for examining large numbers of logs in a central location?

   A. Syslog server

   B. SIEM system

   C. Web application firewall

   D. Proxy server

5. Amie is upgrading the organization's e-mail server and wants to include several security technologies in the implementation. She is looking at a specific technology that provides a method for recipients to verify messages by publishing the organization's public key to DNS records, which can be queried and verified by e-mail recipients. Which of the following technologies is Amie considering?

   A. Digital signatures

   B. Domain-based Message Authentication, Reporting, and Conformance (DMARC)

   C. Sender Policy Framework (SPF)

   D. Domain Keys Identified Mail (DKIM)

3.1 ANSWERS

1. **C** While not always highly accurate, heuristic analysis looks at abnormal behaviors and compares them to known characteristics of attack patterns.

2. **B** The malware is likely using domain generation algorithms to create random and unique URLs for the malware to communicate with Internet-based command-and-control servers.

3. **A** Historical analysis is a form of trend analysis where large amounts of data are examined to explain previous behaviors.

4. **A** The syslog server is the best solution for this scenario because it simply collects logs from multiple hosts and stores them in a central location.

5. **D** Domain Keys Identified Mail (DKIM) is an e-mail technology that creates a public and private key pair, publishes the public key into DNS records, and allows recipients of e-mail originating from the organization to verify the public key when they receive an e-mail. This allows them to verify that the e-mail was actually sent from the organization in question.

Objective 3.2 # Given a scenario, implement configuration changes to existing controls to improve security

By now, you should remember that security controls are measures taken to protect a system and its data. Controls are applied to a system, to data, to the operating and physical environment, and the organization as a whole to reduce risk, ensure privacy, and increase protection for sensitive assets. In this module, we're going to discuss several controls you need to know for the CYSA+ exam. We don't just limit our discussion to configuring and implementing controls in this objective, however. Every chapter in this book is concerned with implementing and managing controls in some form or another, whether they are technical controls such as encryption, managerial controls such as policy, or physical controls such as gates and guards. In this module, we will look at some more of the technical controls, including permissions, access control, firewalls and IPS, data loss prevention, endpoint security, network access control, malware rules, sandboxing, and port security. Before we get into these topics, however, we will also review some basic control concepts to refresh your memory and put you in the right frame of mind for addressing controls.

 KEY TERM   A **control** is a security measure or mechanism that is implemented to address a specific vulnerability and protect systems, data, and the organization.

Review of Control Concepts

We discuss controls throughout this entire book because review and repetition are always good for learning. In this section, we will briefly recap control concepts, including control categories, functions, and how controls are implemented with regard to risk.

Control Categories and Functions

Security controls typically fall under one or more of three categories: managerial or administrative controls, logical or technical controls, and physical or operational controls. Keep in mind that different texts may refer to these control categories and functions differently, but the meanings are still essentially the same. Also, remember that there are types of controls that are categorized by function: deterrent, preventative, detective, corrective, recovery, and compensating. As a refresher, Table 3.2-1 describes the three basic categories of controls, and Table 3.2-2 describes control functions.

A few items to note about control functions: Most controls do not cleanly fit into one control function or even a control category. Most of them overlap in some way. For example, a CCTV can be a deterrent control and a detective control at the same time. It can deter users

TABLE 3.2-1 The Three Basic Control Categories

Category	Description	Examples
Managerial (administrative)	Controls implemented by management functions	Policies, procedures, standards
Technical (logical)	Controls of a technical nature	Encryption, permissions, network security devices
Operational/physical	Controls regarding the physical environment, operations, and processes	Gates, fencing, guards, procedures

from committing a policy violation because they know they are being observed, and it can also detect malicious events or policy violations after the fact since it records video that can be reviewed later.

Sometimes people get confused about the difference between deterrent and preventative controls. A deterrent control is, in fact, also a preventative control; however, the chief difference

TABLE 3.2-2 Control Function Descriptions and Examples

Control Function	Description	Examples
Deterrent	Controls that must be known or visible so they can deter potential misuse or policy violations.	CCTV, guards, locked doors, warning banners
Preventative	Controls that help prevent misuse or policy violations; they do not have to be known by the user.	Firewall rules, resource permissions, locked doors
Detective	Controls that are used to detect or discover policy violations or misuse.	Audit logs, CCTVs, physical alarm systems, intrusion detection systems
Corrective	Controls that are used to correct an issue resulting in a nonsecure state; these are often short-term temporary controls until permanent controls are implemented.	Additional network security devices, temporary firewall rules, placing a guard near a hole in the fence until the fence can be repaired
Recovery	Controls that are used to restore the system, environmental, or organizational state back to a satisfactory secure state.	System backups, alternate processing sites
Compensating	Alternative controls that are used when more desirable controls are not feasible due to resource, environment, or technical constraints; these are more longer-term controls.	Using IPSec over otherwise nonsecure networking links; physical equipment locks when equipment can't be securely stored in a locked networking closet

is that in order to be effective, a deterrent control must also be known about. A warning banner on the screen can deter a user from committing a malicious act, as can a CCTV camera because the user knows they are being monitored. This requires the user to make a choice between committing the act or not. A preventative control, on the other hand, does not have to be known to be effective. A firewall rule that prevents the user from going to a malicious website will work regardless of whether or not the user knows about it. Both examples are preventative in nature, but only one is also a deterrent control.

One more item to note is the difference between recovery, corrective, and compensating controls. They all sound very similar; in fact, they can also overlap as well. A recovery control can be both a preventative control and a recovery control; consider a system backup, for example. It is a preventative control because it can help prevent data loss; however, in the event of an equipment failure, it can be used to restore lost data to a system, making it a recovery control as well.

A corrective control is temporary in nature; it is used to immediately correct an unsafe or insecure condition, possibly after an attack or some other negative event. With a corrective control, you know that the security issue is only temporary, and the deficient or missing control it is used to correct will either be back online soon, or a more permanent solution will be implemented. Expanding one of the examples listed in Table 3.2-1, suppose a fence has been cut or temporarily damaged due to weather. You know the fence will be fixed within a week or so, but for the moment, you must put a guard near it to make sure that no one goes in or out of the hole in the fence. That makes it both corrective and temporary. This is different from a compensating control, which is more long-term in nature. A compensating control is used as an alternative control when the preferred or desired control is not available or is infeasible to implement due to technical, environmental, or resource constraints. A longer-term approach may be needed; in the example where a guard is temporarily placed near the hole in the fence until the fence can be repaired, suppose the organization doesn't have the budget to fix it and knows that it will be quite a while before the fence is repaired. It's also not cost-effective or practical to permanently make a guard stand near the hole, so the organization may close off or barricade that entire area to prevent anyone from even approaching the fence. It also may set up CCTVs on a long-term basis to ensure that no one goes in or out of the whole in the fence. Note that compensating controls could still be temporary, as are corrective controls, but they are usually more long-term, of indefinite duration, and often consist of more resilient solutions.

Control Implementation and Risk

As mentioned before, security is in delicate balance with functionality and resources. Often you want more security, but it will come at the expense of functionality, and you may not have the resources to have as much protection as you want. This is where risk management comes in. You must decide if the impact of a negative event is more costly than the controls it would take to prevent the incident or lessen its impact. Consider this scenario: if all the controls necessary to protect a server from being stolen or damaged cost $10,000, for example, and the server and its data have been valued at $5000, then obviously the cost of security outweighs the value of the resource. This is where the balancing act comes in. Controls must be implemented that are cost-effective; in other words, they must be of a cost that is less than the value of the resource they are trying to protect.

When considering cost-effectiveness, you should look at the entire aggregate list of controls you must implement to protect an asset from a specific vulnerability or negative event. On the other hand, when considering the value of an asset, you should consider not only its replacement cost, but also the amount of revenue it generates for the organization, as well as intangible value, such as consumer confidence or business reputation. For example, the physical server may only cost $5000, and the data may be valued at $3000. However, if this server processes transactions that generate $5000 in revenue per week, you can quickly see that the value of this server is far more than its replacement cost. These are factors that must be considered when estimating the value of an asset. Then, you must determine if the cost for implementing controls to protect an asset is below, equal to, or exceeds the value of the asset.

In addition to the initial purchase of the control, you also have to look at longer-term issues, such as support contracts, upgrade costs, labor hours, personnel, and other costs involved in implementing and maintaining the control on a long-term basis. In the end, you simply must weigh whether the control is worth it or not. If it is, you should consider implementing it; if not, you should consider other (possibly less expensive) compensating controls that can help mitigate or lower the risk an asset incurs to an acceptable level. These can be controls that reduce vulnerabilities, add additional protection, or even reduce the likelihood or impact of the negative event.

 EXAM TIP Understand the balance that must be achieved in implementing controls; you must consider the cost of the control, the value of the asset it is protecting, and the risk the control mitigates.

Permissions

We've discussed the process of identification and authentication, and you already know that just because someone is authenticated to a network doesn't necessarily mean they have the authorization to perform any actions on a network resource, such as a file, folder, or printer. This is where rights, privileges, and permissions come in. These are assigned to a user (or, preferably, a group of users) to grant them the ability to access resources and perform actions with them. Without going into the more subtle differences between rights, privileges, and permissions, you should know that permissions are generally given to grant access to and determine actions that can be performed with resources. These include both local (on the host) and networked resources.

Permissions to resources are based on individual identity and business needs; an identified, authenticated user should have a valid business need (and sometimes clearance level) to access and interact with a resource. Permissions are routinely granted to users; however, it is a much better administrative practice to grant permissions to groups with similar requirements and then add users to the group. In addition to granting permissions to resources to groups, you can also impose other restrictions on members of the group as well, giving you even more flexibility to manage users.

Most operating systems manage permissions a bit differently; there are differences in the way Windows permissions work and the way permissions in Linux and other UNIX-based operating systems work. In the two following sections, we will discuss the permission structure of each.

Windows Permissions

Permissions for the Windows operating system have traditionally consisted of two types: file system permissions, which control access to local files and folders on a Windows box, and share permissions, which control access to a Windows share over the network. These are not mutually exclusive; you can implement both at the same time, which can sometimes have unintended consequences. File system and share permissions can often conflict; a person who has the Full Control file system permission for a file yet is explicitly denied access through a share permission will find that they are denied access to the file if attempting to access it remotely. For a user interactively logging in to the local box, share permissions are not an issue, however.

The following are the Windows file system permissions:

- Full control
- Modify
- Read and execute
- List folder contents (folders only)
- Read
- Write
- Special permissions

Note that special permissions aren't different from the permissions listed above it; they allow you to take additional actions such as change the creator/owner of a file or folder, view permissions, audit access to the file or folder, and view the effective permissions for the user, taking into consideration the groups they belong to.

Remember that Windows share permissions apply to folders, not files, and are only for users accessing the shared folder remotely across the network. Share permissions do not affect a user logged in interactively (locally) to the system. The share permissions for Windows folders are as follows:

- Full Control
- Change
- Read

Effective permissions are the actual permissions you have to a resource, after taking into account any individual permissions that have been assigned to you by the creator/owner of a file or folder, combined with any permissions you have as a member of a Windows group that may have permissions to that resource. Effective permissions also consider file system permissions versus share permissions you have been assigned. For example, if you are in a group that has been assigned only Read and Execute permissions, but the folder owner has assigned your user account with Full Control permission, you effectively have full control over the folder, including the ability to assign other users permissions. However, if you are assigned a deny for a permission, it takes precedence over other permissions. Denying you write access to a file for your individual user account means that you cannot write or change the file, even if you are in a Windows group that has been allowed write permission to the file. File and share permissions combined work in a similar manner. Permissions are accumulative except in the case of a deny permission for either type.

Figure 3.2-1 shows an example of Windows permissions for a file, and Figure 3.2-2 shows share permissions for a Windows folder shared across the network.

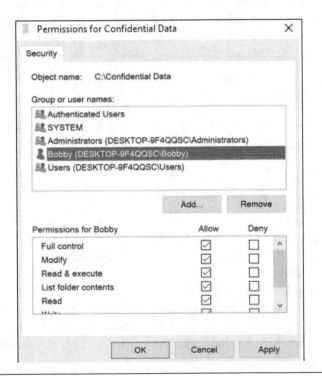

FIGURE 3.2-1 Example of Windows file system permissions

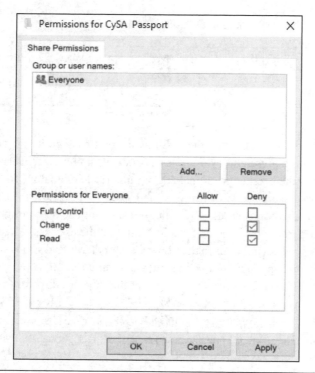

FIGURE 3.2-2 Example of Windows share permissions

Linux Permissions

Linux and other UNIX-like operating systems have a different permission structure than Windows. In some ways, it's not as complicated, but in other ways can be equally difficult to determine. There are only three basic permissions for Linux: read, write, and execute. However, these permissions can be assigned in different combinations to three entities: User, Group, and Others. Linux can use either alphabetic designations for its permissions (such as r, w, and x for read, write, execute, respectively) or octal numerals. The octal numerals representing the read, write, and execute permissions are 4, 2, and 1, respectively. The different combinations, when assigned to the different entities, can represent the total effective permissions for a file or directory. Permissions are additive, using the octal numerical representations. For example, the user who has read and write permissions but no execute (symbolized by the "-" for the execute permission, in this case) has permissions that, when added together, equal the octal number 6 (since read is 4 and write is 2, so the combination of read/write is 4+2, which equals 6). Note that the dash symbol (-) means there is no permission assigned and represents a numerical 0. Table 3.2-3 shows how this works.

TABLE 3.2-3   Alphabetic Versus Octal Notation for Linux Permissions

Entity	User	Group	Others
Alphabetic notation	rwx	rw-	r--
Octal notation	7	6	4

Using this representation, the most permissions any particular entity can get are read, write, and execute, which is represented by either rwx or the octal number 7. Permissions less than that are indicated by their respective alphabetic or numerical designators. In the example from Table 3.2-3, you may see permissions to this file listed as 764. You will frequently see these permissions listed together, such as 777, which means that all three entities have full read, write, and execute permissions, and 664 would mean that the user has read and write, groups that have been assigned permissions to the file or directory have read and write, and any others only have read permission. Figure 3.2-3 illustrates an example of Linux permissions. Note that the "d" at the start of a permissions entry means that the entry is a directory versus a single file.

 NOTE   macOS, while not specifically mentioned in our discussion of operating system permissions, is originally based on BSD UNIX, so it uses UNIX-style permissions as well.

```
                            CYSA+ Passport                    _  □  ✕

 File  Edit  View  Search  Terminal  Help
[bobby@localhost ~]$ ls -al
total 32
drwx------. 16 bobby bobby 4096 Aug 10 06:49 .
drwxr-xr-x.  3 root  root    19 Aug  9 13:06 ..
-rw-r--r--.  1 bobby bobby   18 Aug  8 2019 .bash_logout
-rw-r--r--.  1 bobby bobby  193 Aug  8 2019 .bash_profile
-rw-r--r--.  1 bobby bobby  231 Aug  8 2019 .bashrc
drwx------. 14 bobby bobby 4096 Aug 10 06:50 .cache
drwxr-xr-x. 14 bobby bobby 4096 Aug 10 06:50 .config
drwx------.  3 bobby bobby   25 Aug 10 06:49 .dbus
drwxr-xr-x.  2 bobby bobby    6 Aug 10 06:49 Desktop
drwxr-xr-x.  2 bobby bobby    6 Aug 10 06:49 Documents
drwxr-xr-x.  2 bobby bobby    6 Aug 10 06:49 Downloads
-rw-------.  1 bobby bobby   16 Aug 10 06:49 .esd_auth
-rw-------.  1 bobby bobby  314 Aug 10 06:49 .ICEauthority
drwx------.  3 bobby bobby   19 Aug 10 06:49 .local
drwxr-xr-x.  4 bobby bobby   39 Aug  9 12:56 .mozilla
drwxr-xr-x.  2 bobby bobby    6 Aug 10 06:49 Music
drwxr-xr-x.  2 bobby bobby    6 Aug 10 06:49 Pictures
drwxr-xr-x.  2 bobby bobby    6 Aug 10 06:49 Public
drwx------.  3 bobby bobby   17 Aug 10 06:49 .redhat
drwxr-xr-x.  2 bobby bobby    6 Aug 10 06:49 Templates
drwxr-xr-x.  2 bobby bobby    6 Aug 10 06:49 Videos
[bobby@localhost ~]$
```

FIGURE 3.2-3   Example of Linux permissions

Remember that permissions, regardless of the operating system in use, should follow the principle of least privilege; users should only get the permissions they need to perform their assigned functions, and no more. This is especially important to watch for in a complex network where users may be explicitly assigned permissions to their user accounts, but at the same time, they are members of groups that may also have different permissions assigned. In such an environment, it can be difficult to monitor effective permissions and ensure that users get only the cumulative permissions they need. *Permission creep,* where a user may get increasingly more (and excessive) permissions over time, can happen easily in complex environments.

 EXAM TIP   You will likely not be expected to know the specifics of Windows and Linux/UNIX permissions for the exam, but as a cybersecurity analyst, you should be familiar with these concepts.

Access Control Lists

Many security mechanisms use *access control lists* (ACLs). Access control lists essentially dictate rules for access to a particular resource or device. Access control lists can be found in different contexts. A resource, such as a folder, can have an access control list that lists users as well as their permissions to that resource. A network device can also have access control lists, which can dictate which ports, protocols, and services are allowed inbound to or outbound from the device, traversing the network.

Regardless of the context, the concept is essentially the same. Access control lists permit or deny actions based on a *ruleset.* Normally, each entry in the list is considered a rule, which establishes the item that is allowed or denied, the action to be taken (allow or deny), and a specific set of conditions that rule must meet in order to be implemented. Normally, in most access control lists, rules are read by the system sequentially. Once a rule is matched by a particular piece of traffic, content, or another item, rule processing for that particular content stops. ACLs can be used to control network traffic, actions performed on a resource, applications that users can run or install, and even access to a website. Regardless of the way ACLs are implemented, they all work in a similar fashion, but how it is implemented depends on the resource, the technology used, and what the overall goal is in implementing the ACL.

One use for access control lists that you must be familiar with for the exam is the use of *default deny and default allow* lists. Previously widely known as *whitelisting* and *blacklisting,* this security paradigm involves creating lists of allowed actions, network traffic, or content and then implementing those lists into a set of rules that specifically either allows everything that is on the list or denies everything that is on the list. We are going to talk about each one of these next.

NOTE As with everything in technology, concepts and terms change from time to time, based on newer technologies, the environment we live and work in, and even social change. And so it goes for, the terms *whitelist* and *blacklist*, which have been deprecated and are decreasing in use within our professional security community. For our purposes here in this book, I will use the terms *allow list* and *deny list*, respectively. However, be aware that because the exam objectives may not have caught up with social change at the time of this writing, you may still see *whitelist* and *blacklist* on the exam.

Allow Lists

An *allow list* is a list created that will be implemented into a ruleset that permits everything in the list to be used, transmitted, or accessed. Again, this can depend on context. For example, if you are centrally controlling applications a user is allowed to install or run (previously known as *application whitelisting*) on the system, then you would create a list of allowed applications and implement a security rule or mechanism that allows only those applications to run and no others. This process is preferred because then you have a known list of good applications that are allowed. Any application not on the list, is, by default, denied. This reduces the number of applications you must worry about controlling since only a small, finite number of applications are allowed to run and no others are allowed.

In the context of a network traffic allow list, the ACL would indicate only the network traffic that is permitted to traverse inbound to or outbound from a network interface.

Deny Lists

A *deny list* is the exact opposite of an allow list; in this list, all actions or content are prohibited. In the case of applications, any applications on the list are explicitly denied from being installed or executed. In the case of network traffic, the listed ports, protocols, and services are denied inbound or outbound through the network interface. There are situations where a deny list would be preferred; however, if you only rely upon deny lists, then you are limiting the number of actions or applications denied to a very small list. That means that anything not explicitly included in the list would be implicitly allowed, which is likely far too permissive for most environments.

EXAM TIP Although it appears to be a counterintuitive explanation, an *allow list* explicitly allows only items in the list and denies everything else (effectively a default-deny condition, where you only allow by exception). A *deny list* explicitly denies only items in its list, implicitly allowing everything else, making it a default-allow condition where you only deny items by exception.

TABLE 3.2-4	Explicit/Implicit and Default Deny/Allow Terms

Type of List	Stated in List (Explicit)	Not stated in List (Implicit)	Referred to as:
Allow list	Allowed	Denied	Explicit allow or implicit deny or default deny
Deny list	Denied	Allowed	Explicit deny or implicit or default allow

You may have also heard the terms *implicit* and *explicit* allow or deny. These essentially mean that any items in a list are explicitly stated, and any items not in the list are implicit (understood to be not included, without stating it). This can cause a lot of confusion between terms, such as allow or deny lists, default deny or allow, and implicit or explicit allow or deny. Table 3.2-4 should help clear these terms up, to ensure you have them straight for the exam.

One point that's worth mentioning is that you don't always have two separate lists—an allow and deny list—for security mechanisms. Most ACLs, in fact, include entries (rules) for both allowed items and denied items; the difference is that there is an action located within the rule for the list that specifically states whether the item is allowed or denied. It also often has qualifiers that further define the rule. For instance, in a router ACL, you could have rules for both allowed and denied ports and protocols. One of the rules in the access control list might be that all traffic inbound on port 80 is allowed, but only for a specific IP address, and denied to all other addresses. This would send all inbound HTTP traffic to a web server, and not to any other devices on the network.

You may also have heard of an explicit deny-all rule placed in access control lists, usually seen in network security devices such as firewalls or even routers. This is used as a catch-all just in case there is no rule written for a particular type of network traffic, application, or another context. Many cybersecurity analysts will place these in an ACL to prevent any unknown content from being allowed. However, use this type of rule with caution. In most ACLs, rules are processed sequentially until a match is made between the rule and the conditions it is processing. This means that if a particular type of network traffic is encountered, all rules will be examined in order until a rule is found matching the traffic and conditions that apply to it. If a rule is found that matches these conditions, the rule is processed, and no other rules are examined. In the case of a deny-all rule, *all* traffic would match. Therefore, as soon as this rule is processed, no traffic would be allowed to pass. This could have very undesirable consequences if the rule were placed before other valid rules since they would never get examined for processing. Therefore, if you use one of these rules, remember that it should be placed as the last entry in the list and should serve as a final arbiter for any traffic not matching an existing rule, where it will be denied.

 CAUTION   Remember that deny-all types of rules should be the last rule in an ACL so that any allowed content will not be inadvertently blocked.

Firewalls

A firewall can be a dedicated network security device, or it can be integrated into other devices, such as routers, which may include firewall functions. In its most basic form, a firewall filters traffic. That means, based on its configuration through a series of rules, it receives traffic into an inbound interface, examines that traffic for particular criteria, and then makes a decision, based on its rules, whether the traffic should be allowed to exit another interface, usually going into another network or out to the Internet. There are network-based firewalls that are dedicated appliances; some are all-in-one types of security devices that include firewall, proxy, VPN, and even DLP solutions, and there are also host-based firewalls, which focus primarily on traffic entering or leaving a single host. In any case, no matter whether it is a powerful dedicated network appliance or a host-based firewall, its job is to filter network traffic.

Firewalls can come in a variety of basic flavors. There are hardware firewalls, which are typically dedicated network appliances, as well as software firewalls, which are implemented as a software program on the host. Many people think of a firewall as something that is only a parameter device; however, firewalls can also be used internally to segment sensitive areas of an organization's network away from the general population of users. Firewalls also aren't typically the only device at the border in any event; usually, there are several security devices, including firewalls, VPNs concentrators, proxy servers, and border routers, that are deployed in layers and are responsible for inspecting and taking action on certain types of traffic. There are also many firewalls that, in addition to network appliances, are part of enterprise-level applications such as e-mail servers that could be deployed as part of an organization's e-mail services.

Firewalls operate their access control lists and rulesets just as described previously; there are entries that are written to handle a specific type of network traffic. The rule can specify what type of traffic and its characteristics, such as source and destination IP addresses, port, protocol, and service. There can be exceptions listed as part of the rule, and the rule will usually also dictate a default action, such as allow or deny.

Firewall deployment and architecture are very important; obviously, firewalls are usually placed at the perimeter of a network, but they can also be layered in different security zones, such as a DMZ, providing protection for different sensitive areas of an organization's internal network, or even an extranet set aside for business partners. The proper placement of firewalls can affect network security and performance, so careful network security design is important.

In the following sections, we will briefly describe the different types of firewalls and their functions.

Packet-Filtering Firewalls

Basic firewalls are simple packet inspection devices; these packet-filtering firewalls use very simple criteria to allow network traffic to pass. These criteria include the protocol, port, source and destination IP addresses, and domain names. For example, a simple packet-filtering firewall could decide whether to allow or deny FTP traffic inbound to a particular destination IP address, which originates from a particular source address.

Simple packet-filtering firewalls, however, aren't sufficient to stop attacks. You may use the packet-filtering functions of a border router to inspect and block basic undesirable traffic, but higher-level functions that would prevent modern, sophisticated attacks, such as maintaining state information or deep packet inspection, can usually be handled only by a more complex firewall.

Circuit-Level Gateways

A circuit-level gateway is also a simpler, older firewall type. In addition to packet filtering capabilities, it filters based on the TCP handshake between two hosts. This can help eliminate handshake attacks such as a TCP SYN flood. Although very efficient for allowing or denying traffic based on packet filtering criteria and TCP handshake, it has very few other capabilities and is therefore not in wide use any longer. Even most modern border routers can perform circuit-level filtering, in addition to other basic firewall functions.

Stateful Inspection Firewalls

Many types of traffic (HTTP traffic, for example) are stateless. This means that there is no built-in method for the protocol to keep track of the state of communications between two hosts. From a performance perspective, this can increase the efficiency of communications between a client and a server, for example. From a security standpoint, however, it could present some issues in that there is no way to track a back-and-forth communications session effectively. This could enable unsolicited communications from an untrusted network, like the Internet, to an internal host, disguised as an established communications session that was initiated by the client.

A stateful inspection firewall eliminates this issue by keeping track of different communication sessions and their states. It can track whether a connection originating from the Internet, for instance, was part of an already established communications session and then pass that response back onto the client. A stateful inspection firewall can also halt unsolicited communications that may be efforts to attack a system.

It works by maintaining an internal table in memory that keeps track of communication sessions that pass through it, by the internal client source IP address, the destination address, and the ports and protocols in use during that communications session. The table contains information about all requests and responses during the session until the session is terminated. It uses this information to allow requests and responses to flow inbound through and outbound from its interfaces, in addition to the other basic criteria that packet filtering firewalls use. One disadvantage to using stateful inspection firewalls is that they introduce some delay into the communications process because of the requirement to store and maintain session information and verify that before allowing traffic to pass.

Application-Level Gateways

Application-level gateways, sometimes referred to as proxy firewalls, work at the application layer. They filter traffic based on application and content. In addition to having the same capabilities as a stateful inspection firewall, an application-level gateway is able to perform deep packet inspection on traffic, checking the actual content of the traffic to ensure that it is legitimate and contains no malware or other suspicious content.

Web Application Firewalls (WAFs)

A web application firewall (WAF) is a more recent development that serves a particular purpose; it is designed to stand in front of web applications and their platforms to prevent various web-based attacks, such as cross-site scripting, injection, overflow attacks, and so on. WAFs can also perform authentication services for web applications and can connect to various authentication services, such as Active Directory, and third-party identity providers.

Next-Generation Firewalls

There's a bit of disagreement on what exactly constitutes a next-generation firewall. However, the consensus from the security community is that it includes all the basic functions that we previously described about other firewalls. It can do deep packet inspection, application-level inspection, content filtering, URL filtering, and stateful inspection, in addition to packet-filtering capabilities. Next-generation firewalls are also characterized by the fact that they are often integrated with intrusion detection and prevention systems, proxy servers, data loss prevention (DLP) solutions, network load balancers, and unified threat management systems (UTMSs). They use active threat intelligent monitoring capabilities and dynamically adjust their behavior based on that threat intelligence.

Cloud-Based Firewalls

Firewall services are now included in the service offerings from cloud-based providers. Many organizations, particularly smaller businesses, cannot afford the expense of network appliances or the personnel to maintain them. Firewall as a Service (FaaS) enables these organizations to minimize infrastructure and expense while at the same time providing resilient, robust, effective firewall solutions for both the cloud-based applications and their on-premises infrastructure. Cloud-based firewall services are especially effective for organizations that already have a significant presence with the cloud service provider and use service offerings such as Infrastructure as a Service (IaaS) and Platform as a Service (PaaS). Another advantage of a cloud-based firewall service is that it is easily scalable with the needs of the organization as it grows. Disadvantages of FaaS are the same disadvantages inherent to other cloud-based services: the organization is typically not in control of its own firewall and must rely on the cloud provider for rapid response for incidents and configuration changes. These concerns would need to be addressed in the agreement between the organization and the cloud service provider.

 EXAM TIP You likely will not be expected to know the different types of firewalls; however, you should be familiar with the basic functions of a firewall, such as packet-level filtering, stateful inspection, and so on.

Intrusion Prevention System (IPS) Rules

We discussed intrusion detection and prevention systems in Objectives 1.3 and 3.1. In this objective, we will specifically talk about rulesets for intrusion detection and prevention systems. Since we've already discussed default allow and deny rules, you've already learned some of the core concepts of rulesets for network devices. Most network devices follow a standard convention for rules. Rules are elements of an access control list and can be found on firewalls, routers, and intrusion prevention/detection systems. The basics of network security device rulesets are essentially the same: rules are read from top to bottom, sequentially. When traffic matches a rule, processing stops and then actions are taken based on the content of the rule. If traffic does not match a rule, it continues to be examined down the list. If there is no match for the traffic, the default configuration of allow or deny is invoked. Typically, there is a rule at the very bottom of the ruleset that specifies that anything else not explicitly allowed is specifically denied. This is called a deny-all rule and, as mentioned previously, should be placed at the very end of the rule processing for network security devices. In other words, if all else fails, and the traffic matches no other rule, then the device should invoke the deny-all rule.

Some rulesets can be very complex, as is the syntax of the rule. Intrusion detection system rules, particularly in the popular Snort IDS/IPS, require a little bit of knowledge to write and deploy. Simplistic rules are relatively easy to implement, but of course there are more complex rules that can be written. Here is an example of a Snort rule syntax:

```
<action> <protocol> <src IP> <src PORT> <direction> <dst IP>
<dst port> (msg:"Rule Description"; <optional
classtype> ;<optional snort ID (sid)>; <optional revision (rev)
number>;)
```

Examining the syntax for the rule, we can see the rule designates an action, such as an alert, the protocol in use, the source IP address and port, direction (inbound or outbound, for example), the destination IP import, the rule description, the class type, and other optional parameters. A complete Snort rule may look something like this:

```
alert icmp any any -> $NETWORK any (msg:"ICMP Alert"; sid:1000003; rev:2;
classtype:icmp-event;)
```

In this example, the rule is alerting the administrator if there is an ICMP (ping) scan from any source IP address and port to any destination IP address on the administrator's internal network. This rule would tell you if you are being scanned via ICMP. The `sid:1000003` value is the Snort rule ID; this can be assigned by the cybersecurity analyst for rules over 1,000,000 since all rule numbers below that are reserved by Snort. The `classtype:icmp-event` value is a predefined Snort event type. This is an extremely simple rule; Snort rules can be written to be very complex and handle all types of network traffic based on port, protocol, source and destination IP address, and other criteria.

 EXAM TIP   Understand the basics of intrusion detection systems as well as how rules are implemented.

Data Loss Prevention (DLP)

Data loss prevention (DLP) is the name given to a group of technologies and processes designed to prevent the exfiltration of sensitive data from an organization. DLP solutions are installed on hosts and network exit points, and they even can be used to prevent exfiltration of data through physical media devices such as USB memory sticks. DLP solutions can be installed as part of firewall solutions, proxy servers, and e-mail servers. For example, e-mails can be scanned to determine if they are being used to send predefined sensitive data outside of the organization. Any attempt to e-mail a Social Security number (SSN) or a credit card number, for instance, would be thwarted since DLP can identify and recognize patterns of data prohibited from leaving the confines of the organization's network.

Beyond simple pattern recognition, however, DLP works by labeling sensitive data with metadata that describes its sensitivity levels, as well as what can be done with the data. Data labeling enables specially configured network security devices and policies to flag sensitive data as it attempts to leave the network and prevent it from doing so. Of course, even before a DLP solution is implemented, the organization must determine its data sensitivity levels and designate data types appropriately in the policy. These written data sensitivity policies are then translated using DLP software integrated with network devices and host-based security. The software tags data with labels corresponding to the data sensitivity policy and can also be integrated with a variety of other line-of-business applications and databases. DLP is particularly essential in environments where there is a great deal of personal or medical information, such as hospitals.

Cross-Reference

DLP is also discussed in Objective 5.1.

Endpoint Detection and Response (EDR)

We have discussed many security controls and mechanisms focused on the network portion of the infrastructure. However, up until recently, one of the more neglected areas of security was the endpoint. Of course, we have antimalware solutions and host-based intrusion detection systems and host-based firewalls. These are all part of endpoint security. However, most of those solutions are designed to actively protect the host. They don't do much more in terms of discovering important information, such as what exactly happened to the host, how it happened, what indicators of compromise were present, and so on. That's why cybersecurity analysts began to look at more rigorous analysis of security information coming from the host.

Now there is a growing trend in treating the endpoint with the same depth and fidelity of analysis that we treat the network. Endpoint detection and response (EDR) is focused on enhanced monitoring and detection of activities that occur on the host. Like we do with networks, EDR brings in-depth data collection and aggregation facilities to the various endpoints. We can integrate all manner of data collected from the host into our network-based security information and event management (SIEM) system and look at more than just what type of traffic is coming into the host. Endpoint security is critical because that's where most of our security issues happen, whether it is a malicious event, user complacency, or malware. Since we know that a lot of malicious activity starts on the host, the idea is to collect data that could be an indicator of compromise early on and combine this with network data so that we get a more complete picture of what is going on in the infrastructure. The types of data we can collect and analyze include the following:

- Operating system and application logs
- Real-time memory usage
- Real-time process activity
- Registry settings
- Detailed user interaction data
- File and disk space data
- Enhanced network traffic data

All this information we collect from an endpoint, whether it is a desktop, server, or mobile device, may indicate malicious activity such as the following:

- Unusual network traffic activity
- Changes to the registry and file system by potentially damaging applications
- Excessive memory, CPU, network, and other resource usage
- Application and operating system configuration information, often as it changes

Data is typically collected through an agent-based solution and sent to a central collection server, such as a SIEM. As you can see, EDR collects a massive amount of data that must be considered in terms of storage and processor capability since it can create an additional workload for those resources.

Fully functional, robust EDR solutions are sold by vendors, but some of the major network analysis and monitoring systems also include EDR modules. Almost any strong network-based solution that purports to be a SIEM system has the capability to include EDR in its toolset.

 EXAM TIP Be able to understand the function of endpoint detection and response as well as how it enables in-depth data collection and analysis from various hosts.

Network Access Control (NAC)

Network access control (NAC) is a network-based security solution that protects the infrastructure from untrusted hosts connecting to the network. Most often, these hosts are connecting via VPN or wireless connections, or even may plug into a switch port. When they connect, their security status is generally unknown, even if they are corporate machines and have connected before. They may have malware or other issues that can harm other hosts. They might also not conform to the organization's baseline security configuration policy. NAC serves as a gateway when an unknown or untrusted host connects, and it ensures that the host is secure before it is allowed to connect. There are several aspects of network access control you should be familiar with.

A NAC is usually implemented as a network device, or as part of a larger integrated security solution. Many VPN servers and wireless access points have built-in NAC solutions. The idea behind NAC is that when the host joins, it receives a very limited connection to the network, usually only to the NAC device. The NAC initiates a series of health checks on the client, determining if it has antimalware software, if its signatures are up to date, its patch level, and other security configuration checks. Based on the security policies configured the NAC, the host may be denied a connection into the network, or the NAC may initiate remediation on the host, such as updating its antimalware signatures or its patch levels or reconfiguring its security settings. Note that updates and reconfiguration are typically only possible with a managed device; if an unmanaged device connects to the network, it will likely be denied a connection.

In addition to handling remotely connecting devices, NAC can also be integrated into the infrastructure as a system covering all connected devices, even the ones that are persistently connected to the network. There are integrated solutions that can provide NAC services to all hosts, including vulnerability scanning, patch management, and application deployment. These solutions can routinely scan all hosts on the network for security health and remediate issues whenever necessary. Most NAC solutions require an agent-based implementation, so all devices are centrally managed.

NACs can be configured to handle many different types of hosts and can create different policies for different groups of hosts, such as servers, user workstations, and mobile devices. Additionally, a NAC can further define network access control rules using factors such as time of day, the role the machine or user has on the network, the host's logical or physical location, and other specific rules that can be configured in the NAC policies.

NAC solutions can be resource intensive; scanning and remediating can take up a lot of network resources, so it's a good idea to have a strong, resilient network with plentiful bandwidth when implementing NAC. As with all network-based security solutions, any data collected by the NAC can be forwarded on to a centralized SIEM to be added to all other collected data for aggregation and analysis. This data can be used for historical or trend analysis regarding the health of client machines.

 EXAM TIP Understand the purpose of a NAC and how it protects the network from untrusted or unknown hosts connecting to the infrastructure. Be able to distinguish it from other types of network security devices.

Sinkholing

Sinkholing is a technique used most often to redirect traffic that could potentially be malicious to a different IP address. For example, let's say that one of your hosts is compromised and is trying to send data to a malicious command-and-control server on the Internet. Once you determine that this is the case, you could take the host offline or clean it of any malicious software. However, you could also leave the host up to determine the exact details of the malware that is causing it to send data to the remote server, without allowing it to do so. A simple way to do this would be to create an entry in your DNS server that redirects all traffic destined for the remote IP address to a local IP address or server, effectively keeping the traffic from going out on the Internet so that the host can't respond to instructions from the command-and-control server.

 KEY TERM **Sinkholing** is the process of diverting potentially harmful network traffic to a designated internal server or IP address, thus preventing it from exiting the network to a malicious entity.

Malware Signatures

Malware is a piece of software running on a machine with malicious intent. By malicious, we mean that it has the intent to disrupt the operation of the host and potentially compromise the confidentiality of data, making it available to unauthorized persons, changing the integrity of data or the operating system, and making the host unavailable for use by authorized personnel. Malware can do all these things. Malware is transmitted via network traffic, over e-mail, and through infected files on removable media.

Antimalware products are designed first to detect any instances of malware on systems, but also to eradicate that malware. Most antimalware products are very good at this, particularly for the well-known types of malware. It is the unknown types of malware that are of concern to us. These are the pieces of malware that may contain zero-day exploits, where there is no detection signature for them, and we don't know anything about their characteristics or how to eliminate them. Even without signatures, malware can be detected through behavior analysis. Some antimalware and host-based intrusion detection products can look at system behavior that is out of the ordinary and flag certain behaviors as suspect. This could be indicators such as excessive CPU or memory usage, high-bandwidth utilization, and so on. Users may also help detect potential malware through reporting inconsistencies in how the host operates, particularly if it is behaving out of the norm. In any case, malware detection is not an exact science; there is so much malware out on the Internet and on our systems that we still are unable to detect since malware authors are far more sophisticated than we may believe. They are constantly finding new and different ways every day to hide malware, change its signatures, and cause it to dynamically morph while running on a system. In the following section, we will discuss some of the particulars of creating malware signatures and how rules can be written for them.

Development/Rule Writing

Malware signatures are still the most used method for detecting malware. Most antimalware products are signature based, although most also perform some type of heuristic or behavioral analysis as well. Most malware signatures are written by the malware vendors, but cybersecurity analysts can also write their own custom signatures for their own environments. One such tool to write malware signatures is called YARA.

YARA is a popular open-source tool used to identify and classify malware. It can be used to perform rule-based detection of malicious files. YARA rules are made up of two parts: a string's definition and a condition. The string's definition defines patterns that will be used to search for in a potentially malicious file. The string consists of an identifier, a "$", and the name. The condition portion defines the conditions of the rule, using Boolean expressions. You can use an open source Python rule generation script created for YARA called yarGen, which can help create YARA rules by searching for strings found in malware files. Essentially, you call the Python script and specify the directory you would like to search in, and yarGen will search for potential strings that could be considered malicious. You can then add these rules to a database.

In addition to YARA, there is also an open-source project from Cisco's Talos threat intelligence group called BASS, which can generate antimalware signatures if you have the potentially malicious samples. BASS is a framework for developing a database of pattern-based signatures.

Sandboxing

Sandboxing is used to protect a system from unknown or untrusted software that could have malicious properties. Although antimalware is very good at detecting *known* malicious software and, to a degree, conducting a behavioral-based analysis of untrusted software to determine if it presents a threat to the system, it is not perfect. Sandboxing is a technique that cybersecurity analysts use to load and execute an untrusted application in a safe environment, where it cannot harm the host.

In earlier days, analysts had a special host (sometimes called a *detonation chamber,* copying the military term for a dedicated chamber to safely disarm or blow-up potential explosive devices) dedicated to running unknown and untrusted software to determine its safety. However, with the advent of micro virtualization, analysts can now execute untrusted software in a small, dedicated virtual machine host. This *sandbox,* as it is referred to, can isolate and execute the software in a secure environment to ensure that it does not interfere with or alter the underlying system in any malicious way. Sandboxes are also very useful for malware forensics so that the malware can be reverse-engineered and analyzed.

 KEY TERM **Sandboxing** is the process of executing a potentially malicious application in a controlled, secure environment for analysis.

Port Security

The word *port* has a lot of different meanings in information technology and security. You can "port" software from one platform to another, you can plug into a USB "port," and you can send information over a TCP "port." You can also have network ports, and although the term *port security* is tied to that context, it's more than that. Port security does not necessarily mean only securing a physical network port on the switch, for example, although it certainly can include that. Certainly, you can configure a switch to turn off certain unused physical network ports or enable them to be tied to only specific MAC addresses. This is more of a function of the switch itself than a formal port security standard. Port security can also involve placing different network ports in specific virtual local area networks (VLANs) so that when a host with a specified MAC address plugs in to the switch port, it automatically becomes part of a specific VLAN. *Port security* as a technology is a name given to various authentication and encryption technologies that can secure logical network connections, typically from remote users. The standard for port security that we often hear about is the IEEE 802.1X specification.

802.1X provides for port-based authentication, and although widely seen on wireless enterprise network implementations (for example, WPA/WPA2 Enterprise), it can also be used on wired networks as well. 802.1X can authenticate both users as well as devices to the network. Because it's more of a port-based security authentication framework than a protocol itself, it uses a wide variety of authentication and encryption protocols, including the classic Extensible Authentication Protocol (EAP) and its many variants (EAP-TLS, EAP-TTLS, and so on).

As mentioned, 802.1X is most often seen in situations where users and devices connect to the corporate network either through wireless means or remotely via VPNs or other remote access technologies such as RADIUS.

 EXAM TIP   Understand that port security is a collection of technologies that may include assigning specific hosts to a VLAN and dynamically disabling unused ports on the switch, and consisting of various authentication and encryption technologies. Understand the basic concepts of the IEEE 802.1X port security standard.

REVIEW

Objective 3.2: Given a scenario, implement configuration changes to existing controls to improve security   In this module, we discussed the fact that security controls are not static and must require changes from time to time since risk constantly changes. Controls may be replaced, upgraded, or even eliminated in some cases. First, we reviewed some important control concepts, such as the control category and function. There are typically three categories of controls considered by cybersecurity analysts: managerial or administrative, logical or technical controls, and physical or operational controls. There are also different functions each control performs: deterrence, prevention, detection, correction, compensating, and recovery. Many of these controls are extremely similar in function; in fact, some controls overlap and cover various functions.

We also looked at how controls are balanced with risk. The organization must look at the total cost of implementing a control versus the value of the asset it is protecting. Decisions and tradeoffs will have to be made about whether the resources are worth the expense of the control, based on the amount of risk that can be mitigated.

We also talked about different controls, including permissions and access control lists. We discussed how permissions are best assigned to groups versus individual users, and we looked at the different types of Windows and Linux permissions. We discussed access control lists, specifically allow and deny lists. Allow lists are used to allow the items in the list via entries called rules. Items could include software applications, network traffic, and even actions performed by an individual, depending on the context in which the access control list is used. Deny lists are used to deny the items in the list, and similarly contain rules to that effect.

We then discussed the various types of firewalls. We know that a firewall essentially is there to filter incoming and outgoing traffic through a network. There are different types of firewalls that perform progressively more complex functions. The simplest type of firewall is a packet-filtering firewall, which filters network traffic based on basic elements such as source and destination IP addresses, port, protocol, and service. We then looked at circuit-level gateways, which filter based on TCP handshake completion. More complex firewalls perform more in-depth filtering and analysis. Stateful inspection firewalls keep track of a connection session's state to prevent rogue sessions from being created and used to communicate with hosts on the inside of the network. Application-level gateways do deep packet inspection at the application level, and web application firewalls help protect web application servers. Next-generation firewalls typically are more robust and can perform all the functions that lesser firewalls can perform, but are also packaged as multiple function devices, such as proxies, intrusion detection systems, VPNs, and concentrators, and they are threat intelligence aware. Cloud-based firewalls are offered as a service by cloud-based providers.

We also briefly discussed intrusion detection rules and gave you an example of how Snort rules work and are created. We revisited data loss prevention solutions and how they can be deployed on the host or on the network and serve to tag sensitive files with metadata so they can be identified and prevented from leaving the network. We also looked at endpoint detection and response, which puts more focus on data collection and analysis at the host level in addition to the network level. Network access control is used to prevent insecure hosts from connecting to the network; a NAC conducts security health checks on the connecting host to ensure that its malware signatures are up to date, as well as its patch level and security configuration. It can also take remedial actions to correct these items. Sinkholing is a technique used to divert potentially malicious traffic from the host into an area where it can do no harm. It is often used to prevent compromised internal hosts from contacting command-and-control servers on the Internet. We also discussed malware signature development; malware signatures are still the most popular way to detect malware, except when there are no known signatures or patterns for new malware. We talked about two open-source utilities for creating malware signature rules: YARA and BASS.

We then discussed sandboxing, which allows us to execute potentially harmful software in a controlled environment to observe its effects. Sandboxing is also useful in malware forensics so that we can reverse engineer a piece of malware to see how it was created, what its effects are, and how we can develop a defense for it.

Finally, we discussed port security, which, in addition to physically protecting network switch ports, also means placing specific clients and MAC addresses in predetermined VLANs. Most of port security, however, involves port-based authentication and encryption, which ensures that random hosts cannot connect to the network without proper authentication. The IEEE 802.1X standard is the de facto standard for port security. 802.1X has the capability to authenticate both users and devices to the network; it's used widely in wireless enterprise implementations, but also used in wired implementations as well.

3.2 QUESTIONS

1. You are evaluating a set of recommended controls for implementation to reduce the risk for a system. The system is valued at $1 million, accounting for its replacement cost, data, and current revenue. The controls you wish to implement cost almost as much as the system but significantly reduce risk to almost a negligible level. Which is the most likely choice you should make?

   A. Allocate resources for the recommended controls since they significantly reduce risk and do not exceed the value of the system.

   B. Decline to spend the money on the controls since they cost almost as much as the system and effectively double its cost.

   C. Reevaluate the risk involved to see if it can be mitigated without spending money on the recommended controls.

   D. Reevaluate the risk involved to see what an acceptable level of risk is and allocate resources for the controls that will reduce the risk to that acceptable level.

2. Jared is a cybersecurity analyst tasked with determining which applications should be allowed to run on the company's network. Jared has selected a list of applications that should be allowed and determined that no one else should be able to run additional applications without going through an extensive approval process. Which of the following should Jared implement?

   A. Application allow list

   B. Application deny list

   C. Application exception list

   D. Jared should assign permissions to each application's executable that is allowed to run and not assign those permissions to any other application's executable. Jared should then create a group of users who can execute the applications.

3. Ethan is implementing a firewall solution for a sensitive internal network. The resources he is protecting contain sensitive web-based accounting applications that should not be accessible by any other users outside of the accounting department. Which of the following firewall solutions should he consider?

   A. Circuit-level gateway

   B. Stateful inspection firewall

   C. Web application firewall

   D. Next-generation firewall

4. Tala is a cybersecurity analyst who must analyze a suspicious application before allowing it to run on the network. She needs to make sure it does not interact with any other systems and cause any potential harm. Which of the following should Tala implement to examine the application?

   A. Endpoint detection and response

   B. Data loss prevention

   C. Sandbox

   D. Stateful inspection firewall

3.2 ANSWERS

1. **D** Even though the recommended controls will reduce risk significantly, that level of risk may not be the same as the acceptable level of risk, so you may be overspending for controls to get a near-perfect solution, rather than an acceptable solution. The amount of risk reduced should be reevaluated to determine if you should spend the money on a significant risk reduction or merely an acceptable level of risk reduction. This could determine the overall cost of the control in comparison to the system.

2. **A** Jared should implement an application allow list (previously called application whitelisting), which allows only those applications determined to be acceptable by the organization to run.

3. **C** Ethan should select a web application firewall since it is specifically designed to protect web-based applications and servers.

4. **C** Tala should implement a sandbox environment so that she can safely and securely run the suspicious application and observe its effects and interactions.

Objective 3.3 **Explain the importance of proactive threat hunting**

Most security processes are reactive in nature; the core of security is the defense of our assets, protecting them from various threats and attempting to mitigate risks. However, there are some proactive processes; penetration testing, for example, is one of them. Another critical proactive process is *threat hunting*, which is the process of actively looking for threats in your environment and on your systems. It is much more than a simple vulnerability assessment or penetration test. Threat hunting is a proactive process that assumes your systems are already targeted and may even have possibly been breached, even if you don't know about it yet. Threat hunting requires a great deal of analytical skill and experience; it relies on the knowledge and experience an analyst already has from a variety of other defensive security disciplines, such as vulnerability management, computer forensics, incident response, and other skills. Threat hunting involves using all these skills, plus the added benefit of threat intelligence, to enable you to actively seek out potential threats.

In this objective, we're going to examine the process of threat hunting, including the theory behind it, the tactics used, how to analyze the data you get from threat hunting, and how to integrate threat intelligence with various analytics you must undertake to improve threat detection.

> **Cross-Reference**
>
> Threat intelligence was covered extensively during Objectives 1.1 and 1.2; it's a good idea to review those objectives before studying threat hunting.

Establishing a Hypothesis

Because threat hunting is a defined process, it makes sense that you should use a proven methodology, such as the scientific method, as a foundation for your threat hunting processes. Therefore, the first step is forming a hypothesis. Remember that a hypothesis is an educated guess based on the observation of data. To establish a hypothesis in threat hunting, you must first gather enough data to make an educated guess about your threat.

The data you will use to form your hypothesis must be collected and analyzed in a defined, consistent, and defendable way. Often, the data you receive and the attention you give it will cause you to question what is going on in your network. This data will also serve as your initial driver for forming hypotheses and investigating potential threats. The genesis of your hypothesis can come via several different sources:

- **Situational**   Hypothesis comes from understanding your organization's unique situation in the threat landscape
- **Analytical**   Hypothesis stems from data received from analyzed data, such as machine learning (ML) analysis and User Entity Behavior Analytics (UEBA)

- **Experience**   Hypothesis is informed from your experience with previous threats
- **Intelligence**   Hypothesis driven by observation of indicators of compromise and threat intelligence

Essentially, you use the same data that you receive through one of these avenues to determine what your security posture and situation are. Some of the data might show unusual or simply unacceptable patterns of behavior, which would cause you to start looking for potential causes. While this may seem reactive rather than proactive, you are looking for threats based on data patterns, not because a threat has materialized. For example, increased bandwidth usage over time doesn't necessarily mean there is a threat; however, absent any other explanation, you should start looking for threats for which this could be an indicator of compromise.

Here's a scenario to help you understand the process of forming a hypothesis for threat hunting: Your company is working on a highly sensitive project for a new product that is to be released to the market in the next year. Based on data that may be available to you (for example, competitive intelligence), you learn that a competitor is working on a similar product. Also, the news media has been reporting about a recent flurry of alleged industrial espionage from your competitor. In this case, you may ask the question, could some of your competitors pose a threat of exfiltrating sensitive data from your infrastructure? Asking this question and observing any indicators that this may be the case could cause you to form a hypothesis that your company is being actively targeted by competitors to gain sensitive information about your products. From there, you would seek to prove or disprove this hypothesis by engaging in threat hunting.

 NOTE   Remember that a hypothesis is not the same thing as a theory or fact; it is merely a question, based on the observation of data. It is a beginning point for you to discover what threats may be on your network.

Profiling Threat Actors and Activities

Profiling means that you are looking closely at a potential threat actor and gathering as much information as you can about them. You want to know their tactics, techniques, and procedures as well as their patterns of behavior. It means gathering information about their potential motivations for attacking you. You should ask yourself what valuable assets you have that they may specifically be interested in. You will want to know if they have attacked similar types of organizations like yours, and what techniques they used. You will need to find out their characteristics. Are they a state-sponsored entity or merely a criminal actor in search of a profit? Could they be a competitor? Again, the idea is to gather as much information as you can about the potential threat actor and develop a set of characteristics about them. You should gather this information from a variety of sources, such as threat intelligence feeds, vendor security sites, government agencies, security organizations, and so on. Some of it may be generic in nature, but you may be able to get sensitive information regarding the threat actor that is very specific. This collection of information is called a *profile*. You would then compare potential malicious activities in your organization to their profile to see if there is a match.

Threat Hunting Tactics

There are many different tactics available to you as a cybersecurity analyst for hunting threats. Most of these are quite complex and involve gathering large amounts of data, looking for patterns, and being able to extrapolate to discover potential links between behaviors you observe on the network through data and potential threats. There are many different techniques you can use for threat hunting, and all involve first having good-quality, complete, and organized data. Threat data can be aggregated and analyzed to provide actionable processes you can use to focus your efforts on those that affect critical assets as well as on threats that pose the biggest risk.

Executable Process Analysis

Executable process analysis is a method of determining if there are potential threats to your infrastructure by constantly monitoring the applications that are executing on hosts to observe any abnormal behavior that might indicate potential malicious actions. Antimalware is one effective means of doing this in real time, but it only covers so much of the possible threats that could be present on the network. In-depth analysis of unknown or potentially malicious executables is important for you to have confidence that there are no threats from this vector. Reverse engineering of potentially malicious executables is a critical part of this analysis, and the use of sandboxing is an effective means of performing this task.

Reducing the Attack Surface Area

Attack surface is the term used to describe how much exposure your asset or your organization has to an attacker. At the system level, the attack surface may consist of open ports, protocols, and services, web or user interfaces, and connections with other applications or networks or systems. Ideally, you want to reduce the attack surface as much as possible. Reducing the attack surface can be accomplished through several means, depending on whether it is from a system, the network, the organization, or the operating environment.

System Level

At the system level, reducing the attack surface consists of ensuring there is a secure configuration on the system as well as ensuring the system is patched properly. "Locking down" or hardening the system is the goal here to reduce the system's attack surface. Hardening the system, at a minimum, should include the following actions:

- Reducing the number of open ports
- Ensuring there are no insecure protocols (such as FTP) running on the host

- Employing strong authentication mechanisms
- Using encryption for both data at rest and data in transit
- Implementing the principle of least privilege on the system
- Patching

These are general actions you should take to reduce the attack surface on any host, but there are many others, depending on the type of system, its function (for example, web server versus file server), operating system, and so forth.

Network Level

The network can provide a wide attack surface to a malicious entity bent on penetrating your infrastructure. There are two primary components of the network: the network media (wired or wireless) and network devices. Each has security controls that must be put in place to reduce the attack surface for the network:

- Reducing unnecessary ports, protocols, and services to only what is needed
- Physically securing network cabling and devices
- Ensuring strong authentication methods for network device access
- Employing strong encryption for data in transit
- Using only secure access protocols
- Limiting the number of personnel who have access to devices, both physically and logically
- Keeping network devices patched

As with the aforementioned caveat, these are only general methods used to reduce the attack surface; there are likely many more, depending on how your network is designed, the operating systems of the network devices on it, and their function.

Organization Level

Hardening the organization's attack surface focuses less on technical controls and more on managerial controls. There are technical controls, to be sure, but most of the actions necessary to reduce an organization's attack surface involve people. The more effective hardening techniques include the following:

- Strong policies for core security (for example, data sensitivity, acceptable use, encryption, data backups, and physical security)
- Frequent and comprehensive personnel security training based on user role and current threats
- Well-equipped and trained security personnel

- The commitment of resources to the security program
- Sound information security strategy and goals
- Defense-in-depth focus

Additionally, a strong risk management program will help an organization reduce both its attack surface and risk to an acceptable level. This requires sincere management commitment in terms of resources and organizational culture.

Operating Environment

The operating environment level of reducing the overall attack surface is the physical environment, but also the general business environment within which the organization operates. Although this may seem to be a strange level to focus on for reducing an attack surface, there are several key things the organization can do contribute to this effort at that level. For the physical environment, the organization should consider the following:

- Implementing strong exterior physical security controls such as fencing, guards, alarms, lighting, and so on
- Ensuring internal assets are segregated into security zones for limited access to the general user population
- Enforcing strict entry control to all facilities, both externally and internally
- Implementing secure locks, strong wall construction, and alarms for sensitive areas inside a facility
- Ensuring all equipment is physically tagged and secured to prevent theft

In terms of the business operations environment, the organization must control its interactions with external agencies, including customers, the media, regulatory or government agencies, business partners, and the public. To that end, the following actions can reduce that portion of the organization's overall attack surface as well:

- Controlling all outgoing information and data through single points (for example, media releases, websites, and social media)
- Requiring nondisclosure agreements with any party requiring legitimate access to sensitive data
- Implementing a data loss prevention (DLP) program and technologies
- Understanding and obeying regulatory compliance requirements
- Carefully evaluating any entity with whom the organization does business for risk and potential security issues (for example, business partners, contractors, and third-party service providers)
- Reviewing all service level agreements for potential issues that may impact the organization's security, compliance, risk, or its ability to do business

Many of the interactions you experience with entities external to your organization will not be completely within your control, but engaging in smart risk and security management can help reduce the amount of information an attacker can gather to use against you in an attack, as well as reduce your legal liability and preserve sensitive data.

 EXAM TIP The attack surface area could be for the system, network, or even the organization. It is the total of all potential attack methods used by an adversary. It includes items such as open ports, protocols, services, weak encryption algorithms, weak authentication, complacent people, and poor security processes, among many other things.

Bundling Critical Assets

Just as you aggregate data from various threat intelligence feeds, network sensors, audit logs, and so on, you can also aggregate assets for monitoring and management. The concept of *economy of use* is important here in that you can categorize assets together for detection and remediation processes as well as management of threats, vulnerabilities and risk for these bundled assets. You can apply different mechanisms to these assets for cost savings and effective use, such as common controls that protect multiple systems, for instance.

Attack Vectors

As discussed earlier in the objective, the attack surface is the sum of all the potential exposure an asset or organization could have that an attacker could take advantage of. An *attack vector* is a path or route an attacker takes to compromise the organization and its assets. Attack vectors are the methods of attack used against those attack surfaces. These are the various methods, processes, and tools the attacker could use; an attack vector also takes advantage of particular vulnerabilities. For example, if a system has a weak authentication mechanism and uses simple usernames and passwords with no password policies (password complexity, account lockout, and so on) enforced, an attack vector would be for an attacker to compromise the system via either a dictionary or brute force attack against user passwords.

Attack vectors are multilayer and involve varying levels of complexity, detectability, and preparation. There are a few general classes of attack vectors, including insider threat, phishing, lack of authentication, lack of encryption, insecure system configuration, malware, and a lack of patches. Note that these are only general categorizations; some cybersecurity analysts classify attack vectors in very specific detail, based on the specific vulnerability, threat, and attack method involved.

From a cybersecurity defense perspective, you should be looking at all vulnerabilities and determining what attack vectors could take advantage of those vulnerabilities. Mitigations are then determined for each potential attack vector. This includes reducing or eliminating vulnerabilities using various methods, including patching, secure configuration, and so on. While risk can never be completely eliminated, it can be reduced or mitigated by eliminating specific attack vectors as much as possible. For example, if an attack vector takes advantage of weak password authentication, then eliminating that vulnerability by implementing multifactor authentication will also eliminate that particular attack vector. If an attack vector takes advantage of a vulnerability due to lack of patching a system, applying that patch would then eliminate that specific vulnerability, rendering that attack vector ineffective. Therefore, it is important to understand what your vulnerabilities are as well as the potential attack vectors that could exploit those vulnerabilities.

EXAM TIP   Whereas the attack surface is the sum of all potential exposures of the system or the organization, attack vectors target those particular exposures in the attack surface. Although there is never really a one-for-one match, you should understand that the more you reduce your attack surface, the fewer attack vectors will be available to a malicious entity.

Integrated Intelligence

Integrated intelligence is nothing more than the coherent management of all your aggregated threat information, including threat intelligence from government, industry, and open sources. It is not enough to simply have all these feeds; you must be able to aggregate them, analyze them, and produce actionable intelligence from these feeds. Management software, including inputs from SIEM, machine learning, and intelligence-specific management utilities, can all help toward this goal. However, you must also have trained and experienced personnel with a background in cyber intelligence to make it all work.

Improving Detection Capabilities

As you perform your threat hunting mission, you are likely to uncover many aspects of your threat, vulnerability, and intrusion detection capabilities that need attention. Some of these will be minor in nature, such as the need to fine-tune your IDS/IPS or your threat management processes. However, you may also uncover flaws in your detection processes or mechanisms that need remediation or improvement. Threat hunting provides opportunities to discover shortfalls in your security infrastructure, whether it is in your protective, detection, or remediation controls.

REVIEW

Objective 3.3: Explain the importance of proactive threat hunting   In this module, we discussed proactive threat hunting. Threat hunting is a process where you examine all the data on your network to look for patterns indicating unusual or malicious behavior that could be tied to a threat. We also discussed developing hypotheses about potential threats, which requires a great amount of data. Profiling threat actors is the process of determining all available information and characteristics about a threat actor and any threats they can initiate. Threat hunting tactics include data aggregation and analysis as well as execution process analysis. Data can come from threat intelligence feeds, vulnerability scans, and other sources.

We also discussed reducing the attack surface. This can occur on several levels: the system, the network, the organization, and the environment. On the system level, this involves reducing the number of ports, protocols, services, and interfaces. In the network, this can be done by hardening network devices and physically protecting network media. At the organization level, this means reducing risks associated with program elements, management, and people. In the operating environment, this means controlling information that may leave the organization and fall into the hands of external entities. We discussed the effectiveness of bundling your critical assets just as you would aggregate threat intelligence data, for the purposes of economy of use.

We then discussed the various attack vectors that a malicious entity can use to infiltrate your infrastructure. These include common attack vectors, such as lack of strong authentication and encryption mechanisms, as well as many others. Attack vectors can be eliminated by secure configurations, patching, and many of the other security controls we have discussed in this book.

Finally, we talked about some of the advantages of threat hunting. For example, it can force you to integrate all your intelligence activities and feeds, making them more efficient and effective in determining which threats are actually on your network. Another advantage of threat hunting is that, as a consequence, you will likely improve your detection capabilities since threat hunting will often identify areas for improvement.

3.3 QUESTIONS

1. Emilia is a cybersecurity analyst who decides to undertake threat hunting on her network. She is looking at all the collected data from various sources, including endpoints, network devices, logs, and so on. Once she has enough data, which of the following should she develop regarding her observations about potential threats on the infrastructure?

   A. Hypothesis

   B. Theory

   C. Fact

   D. Process

2. Evie is a cybersecurity analyst who has discovered some potential threats on the network. She is trying to put together information about the characteristics of the threat and information about the threat actor as well as to discover some of their tactics and techniques. What is this process called?

   A. Threat hunting

   B. Threat modeling

   C. Profiling

   D. Risk analysis

3. Ben is analyzing different attack surfaces in his organization. Which of the following should he do on individual hosts to reduce their attack surface?

   A. Remove or disable all necessary ports, protocols, and services from the host.

   B. Add more administrative users on the host to ensure there are enough in case the host gets compromised.

   C. Open additional ports, protocols, and services to confuse a potential attacker.

   D. Install a honeypot on the host.

4. Sam is a cybersecurity analyst who has been performing threat hunting on his infrastructure and has discovered some disturbing issues with the ability of the organization to detect potential threats. Which of the following actions should he take?

   A. Install a honeynet in the perimeter to distract potential attackers, since they may not be easily detected with the organization's existing capabilities.

   B. Request additional funds for perimeter security for the infrastructure.

   C. Because those findings are peripheral to his objective of threat hunting, he should put those results aside for the time being.

   D. Use this as an opportunity to improve the organization's threat detection capabilities.

3.3 ANSWERS

1. **A**   Emilia should develop a hypothesis from her observations based on the collected data. Developing a hypothesis is the first step in the scientific method.

2. **C**   Evie is profiling threat actors to determine their characteristics.

3. **A**   Ben should reduce all ports, protocols, and services to only what is necessary to run on the host.

4. **D**   Sam should use these findings as an opportunity to improve and increase the organization's threat detection capabilities.

Objective 3.4 **Compare and contrast automation concepts and technologies**

Automation Concepts

The data that an organization produces every day is voluminous. Think about log data, transaction histories, network traffic captures, and so on. Considering all this data—likely terabytes of it daily from even a small organization—no one could hope to analyze or even view it all without help. Even scores of cybersecurity analysts could not get all of the work done in only a small-sized organization if they had to do everything manually; this would include log analysis, monitoring network traffic, risk analysis, threat monitoring, and all of the other detailed minutiae that infrastructure requires someone to watch over and act upon.

Fortunately, cybersecurity analysts do not have to do everything manually. Over the course of the years following the invention of the Internet and the development of sound cybersecurity engineering processes, IT and cybersecurity professionals have also built and honed their tools of the trade to make their work not only more efficient but more effective. These tools quickly handle the incredible volume of daily repetitive, tedious, and sometimes mind-numbing tasks that would take an analyst hours or even days to perform. This is especially advantageous for critical tasks that require precision and focus; human analysts may miss something important even in a simple pattern analysis task that can directly affect the security of the network; given the right set of criteria, automated methods of data manipulation and analysis don't miss as much as a human might.

This module is focused on those automated methods, processes, and tools that cybersecurity analysts use to collect, ingest, aggregate, analyze, and make decisions on data. It is also focused on methods we use to perform repetitive but critical tasks to save time and make us more effective. During this objective, we will discuss tools and methods such as workflow orchestration, scripting, interacting with software application programming interfaces (APIs), and automated malware management. We will also look at the processes that are more than just best business practices; they are critical to both the day-to-day and long-term infrastructure security management. These include data enrichment, threat feeds, machine learning, and automation protocols, as well as continuous integration and deployment.

Workflow Orchestration

Cybersecurity analysts often use a deep, multilayer cacophony of tools, processes, and methods for automating security tasks and managing security data. Many of these tools are stand-alone, and many of them do not necessarily allow themselves to be centrally managed. The ones that do may use different protocols or management interfaces; simply managing all these tools and processes that take care of task scheduling and performance or ingesting and analyzing data can be overwhelming. That's where workflow orchestration comes in. Workflow orchestration is the overall tactical and strategic management of all these automated (and sometimes manual) tools, methods, and processes. Picture having to spend all day inputting data for data analysis software, scheduling automated tasks, and so on. This would not be a very good use of your time and really does not remove inefficiency; it simply moves the inefficiency from performing all these tasks manually to managing all the automated tasks. Workflow orchestration helps you to manage all of this.

There are certainly homegrown solutions you can use to integrate all your various security tools and scripts; there also open-source frameworks that allow this. Some of the more robust commercial enterprise applications allow you to integrate compatible applications, such as security information and event management (SIEM) systems, intrusion detection/prevention systems, firewall management systems, and so on. None of them allow you to integrate every single tool you have; however, most use compatible protocols, messaging formats, languages, and other standards that can help integrate all these different tools. For example, most tools support XML input and output, so XML can be used to transfer data from one tool to another. Without a formal workflow management tool in place, there may be some programming involved to create an appropriate interface from an external tool if you have skilled programmers on staff who can facilitate this. Even with an enterprise-level workflow orchestration suite, there is still likely some setup or programming involved, but it will be much easier and efficient to implement.

Security Orchestration, Automation, and Response (SOAR)

Security orchestration, automation, and response (SOAR) is the name given to suites of tools dedicated to unifying your tools, processes, and methods used across the enterprise. These suites of tools can make it easier to ingrate all your efforts for collecting, aggregating, and analyzing data and then converting it to useful information used to make critical security decisions. SOAR primarily focuses on threat and vulnerability management, security operations, and incident response. Many of these tools are integrated as part of traditional network analytical tools, such as SIEM software. Many SOAR implementations come in the form of layered security software modules. These tools enable you, often through agent-based endpoints and various threat and vulnerability feeds, to gather all this information into a customizable dashboard, providing real-time metrics and performance data as well as alerting you to potentially malicious event patterns. Many of these tools can also accept plug-ins from tools such as Python scripts, for example, and schedule and manage the execution of routine security tasks.

 EXAM TIP   Workflow orchestration tools are used to provide overarching integration and management of all the disparate automated security tools, methods, and processes used by cybersecurity analysts.

Scripting

Scripting is a simple yet powerful way to automate tasks, particularly those that involve host or system-level tests. Scripting can also be used for network-wide tasks. Scripting at its basic level essentially involves taking commands you would normally run individually at the command line and including them in a file, called a script, so they can run sequentially and automatically. Occasionally, you must account for user input and either build that into the script or have a human being sitting there waiting for the script to ask for input.

Scripting can be quite simple or complex; most host-based scripts use the built-in operating system commands, but many use scripting languages such as Python, which must be installed on the system. Although scripts may be written and executed on the host, many scripts perform network-based tasks, such as collecting data, starting network backups, and so on. Scripts can be used to perform security tests as well, scheduled through the built-in operating system task scheduling mechanism (AT or cron, for instance) or as part of an overall management system that calls scripts on the fly when necessary, as certain conditions arise. You can have complex scripts that gather data from across the network and send it to a particular server for later analysis, and you can also use scripts to trigger a security alert if a predetermined condition occurs, such as a user being locked out of an account. Scripting can be useful when a graphical user interface for a particular security tool only provides limited or basic functionality. Scripting can allow an experienced security analyst to dig deeper and use more advanced tools than the graphical user interface permits, allowing more complex tasks to be performed.

Windows has various scripting facilities built in; for example, you can write and execute a simple command-line batch script consisting of operating system commands, or you can create powerful scripts using Windows built-in PowerShell feature. Linux also has built-in command-line scripting (called *shell scripting*) that can also be used to create both simple and complex scripts. For powerful, complex scripting needs that can be used to create cross-platform compatible scripts, many advanced cybersecurity analysts use scripting languages such as Python, which is essential to any analyst's toolkit. There is also a multitude of other scripting languages, such as Perl, JavaScript, and VBScript, that are used to create applications, utilities, and interfaces across systems. Scripting is a critical skill that all cybersecurity analysts should learn.

Cross-Reference

Scripting is also discussed in Objective 3.1.

Application Programming Interface (API) Integration

An application programming interface (API) provides a method for programmers to interface with an application's functionality. Through APIs, developers can create additional functionality for applications, or interface one application with another application completely. APIs enable the exchange of information between disparate applications if the data is in a similar or translatable format. This includes executing different processes and functions in one application initiated by another.

API integration involves automating API calls between applications and converting them to code that each system can use. This can include authentication between applications if it is required. Many different tools can assist in automating API calls, such as Insomnia, Codegen, and Postman. Automating API call interfaces between applications lends itself to further consolidating the various security tools under one orchestration umbrella.

 EXAM TIP   For this objective, you do not need to know the technical aspects of API programming; however, you should know how API integration is useful for automating security tasks.

Automated Malware Signature Creation

We discussed malware signature creation within Objective 3.2 and mentioned the popular YARA tool. YARA can automate the creation of malware signatures by creating rule-based detection signatures dynamically after analyzing strings found in malware files. Using tools such as YARA, along with scripts, as well as advanced methods such as machine learning (discussed in an upcoming section), cybersecurity personnel can automate the creation of malware signatures. This allows for malware signatures to be created based on the existing environment, as well as any external data the organization collects. This can also include threat intelligence, vendor malware information feeds, as well as other behavior analytics data from third-party sources.

Cross-Reference

Malware signature creation is also discussed briefly in Objective 3.2.

Data Enrichment

Data enrichment is an important yet simple concept. Rather than only working with singular pieces of data, data enrichment refers to combining related data from other sources, both automated and manual, to give data context. This can help you see different dimensions of a piece of data. Some of this data enrichment may come from threat intelligence feeds, open-source information, various security vendors, government agencies, and even professional organizations. Much of this information is presented in formats that are easily ingestible by security tools.

Data aggregation can also help with the enrichment process. The more data you have put in context, particularly related data, the more data will make sense, and you can look at other aspects of it, other than the facts that stem from the data itself. It can help you understand why something happened, how it happened, and other details that might not be obvious from the data itself. Data enrichment can help humans analyze data and form better hypotheses regarding malicious or unusual events as well as historical and trend analysis.

Data enrichment is as much data aggregation and correlation as anything else. Let's suppose that the piece of data you're looking at is as simple as an IP address and domain name. Collecting data from sources other than your log files from your intrusion detection system, such as threat feed, open-source intelligence, and so on, can give you insight as to who owns the domain, if it has been seen before in other potentially malicious attacks, and so on. Data enrichment can help you put the piece of data in the proper context.

 KEY TERM **Data enrichment** means to give existing data derived from sources across the infrastructure context by adding more data such as that from threat intelligence feeds, security agencies, vendors, and so on. This can help with analysis and generating hypotheses.

Threat Feed Combination

As we discussed in the earliest objectives of the book, there are various sources for threat data and intelligence. These can come from disparate sources, such as government agencies, vendor subscription services, and open sources. Because of the multitude of sources you have at your disposal, threat feeds can be overwhelming and sometimes confusing. That's where developing a process to aggregate or combine threat feeds and distill out the relevant data is important. Many of these threat feeds conform to some of the standards we discussed in Objective 1.2, but much of it is unstructured data. Enter automation, once again, which can be used to sort through various feeds, search for patterns that you specify as interesting, and efficiently look for context that can be used to combine relevant information from the different threat feeds.

Cross-Reference

Threat intelligence feeds are also discussed in Objectives 1.1 and 1.2.

Machine Learning

Machine learning (ML) is a discipline of computer science that can be used to expand data analytics significantly beyond simple pattern searching or correlation. Starting with predetermined criteria, including conditions that could expand beyond the patterns of data you're examining, machine learning can allow you to look past the obvious and explore avenues of data analytics you previously had not thought of. Intelligent software can extrapolate beyond its programmed pattern analysis and combine elements of behavior analysis with complex algorithms. Machine learning systems use methods known as algorithms. Algorithms improve over time with new data and previously developed patterns and relationships. Therefore, the machine "learns" from the data it gets and its previous analysis.

Machine learning models improve performance and efficiency by adaptively learning not only from patterns (signatures) and behavior analysis but also from historical and trend analysis. This can enable machine learning software and systems to search through terabytes of data to locate potentially malicious events with greater accuracy. Data is key to machine learning. The more data the system receives, the better it is at searching for patterns of data, classifying it, and predicting outcomes of possible actions based on the activities of the patterns.

Learning comes when the system can identify previously unknown patterns and relationships between data and sources. This makes it also able to detect anomalous behaviors as well.

Machine learning will not enable you to develop new hypotheses from data not already present. However, machine learning is especially useful when looking at the volumes of data produced by an organization and determining if there are potentially malicious activities going on, based on the relationships between data as well as the rules or patterns it is analyzing. Machine learning is also useful for things such as malware analysis, attack causality, and performance issues. It can be used to explain a historical analysis of data as well as predict potential trends. Machine learning is also good at recognizing patterns, such as network activity, facial recognition, and so on, if the algorithm can distinguish the data and analyze its behavior.

 KEY TERM   Machine learning uses complex systems and intelligent software to ingest massive amounts of data, look for predetermined conditions and patterns, discover potential matches to those patterns, and extrapolate additional behaviors based on interactions between data and its patterns.

Use of Automation Protocols and Standards

Systems security professionals use a wide gamut of disparate systems to do their job; there are many standards, protocols, connection interfaces, and data formatting methods as well as markup, scripting, and programming languages that security tools and applications use, thus making it difficult sometimes to interface and integrate them and their data sources. Sometimes this creates issues with data formatting, quality, sufficiency, and transference to or from different security tools. This may require security professionals to build a bridge or interface of some type to transform data and send it to another application. Although there is a wide push to standardize tools and data, such as using common network protocols, markup languages, and so on, there is still a need to develop automation-specific protocols and languages. Fortunately, there is also an effort toward that goal as well. One such effort, known as Security Content Automation Protocol (SCAP), is promulgated by the National Institute of Standards and Technology (NIST).

Security Content Automation Protocol (SCAP)

NIST, in conjunction with other major organizations, such as Carnegie-Mellon University and the MITRE Corporation, as well as federally funded research and development centers (FFRDCs), has developed a common set of languages and formats for expressing security data to be exchanged between tools. Also, NIST has led the way in efforts to standardize data formatting and interfaces. These different automated languages include those for expressing vulnerabilities, threats, assets, mitigations, and so on.

One of the major automation protocols to come from NIST over the past few years is the Security Content Automation Protocol, or SCAP. This is more of a framework than a protocol itself; it is used to assist in the overall risk management of systems by providing a consistent, open data format that can be used across different security tools and platforms. Most major security tools, including vulnerability scanners and so on, are SCAP compatible. NIST Special Publication (SP) 800-126, Revision 3, is the guiding document for SCAP. Table 3.4-1 lists the 12 standards in the five SCAP categories.

 EXAM TIP You should be familiar with the various SCAP languages and formats as well as their purposes for the exam.

TABLE 3.4-1 SCAP Specifications and Categories

Name	Category	Purpose (from NIST SP 800-126, R3, 2020)
Extensible Configuration Checklist Description Format (XCCDF)	Language	Provides standard vocabularies and conventions for expressing security policy, technical check mechanisms, and assessment results (NIST, 2020).
Open Vulnerability and Assessment Language (OVAL)	Language	
Open Checklist Interactive Language (OCIL)	Language	
Asset Reporting Format (ARF)	Reporting format	Provides the necessary constructs to express collected information in standardized formats (NIST, 2020).
Asset Identification (AID)	Reporting format	
Common Platform Enumeration (CPE)	Identification scheme	Provides a means to identify key concepts such as software products, vulnerabilities, and configuration items using standardized identifier formats (NIST, 2020).
Software Identification (SWID) Tags	Identification scheme	
Common Configuration Enumeration (CCE)	Identification scheme	
Common Vulnerabilities and Exposures (CVE)	Identification scheme	
Common Vulnerability Scoring System (CVSS)	Measurement and scoring	Provides for specific characteristics of a security weakness (for example, software vulnerabilities and security configuration issues) and, based on those characteristics, generates a score that reflects their relative severity (NIST, 2020).
Common Configuration Scoring System (CCSS)	Measurement and scoring	
Trust Model for Security Automation Data (TMSAD)	Integrity	Specification that helps to preserve the integrity of SCAP content and results (NIST, 2020).

Automating Software Integration, Delivery, and Deployment

Previously, in Objective 2.2, we discussed the principle of DevSecOps. DevSecOps was born out of necessity, due to problems inherent in the separation of the development, operations, and security communities. Prior to the integration of these three pieces of the software development process, software was often developed in a vacuum, with no input from the operational users for whom the software was intended or cybersecurity personnel. This sometimes resulted in software that not only did not meet its intended requirements or functions but also was not secure. With the merger of these three disparate communities into DevSecOps, the development of software has become more unified, and when properly implemented is able to produce secure, functional software that meets user requirements. Like all other efforts involving mass amounts of data, analytics, and security service delivery, the automation paradigm can be applied to software integration, delivery, and deployment.

Continuous Integration

Continuous integration refers to the ability to constantly produce quality software as it is being developed. In other words, changes to the software are made and rapidly integrated into the production code. Note that this does this doesn't eliminate the need for testing, but it does give the team the ability to rapidly move forward in the development cycle, from the necessity to integrate changes to those changes becoming part of production code. Continuous integration lends itself to automation since there are tools that can integrate and deliver code from the test environment to the production environment. Even with automated means, this does not take the human out of the loop as a decision maker in ensuring that the code is ready to be put into production.

Continuous Delivery and Deployment

Continuous delivery is the process of moving production code from the development environment into the production environment. This is after the integration process has taken place. This process can be automated, including the security processes that need to follow it (vulnerability testing, for example). Again, there still a human involved in the decision-making process to move the code from development to production. Automating this process could be something as simple as a script that moves the integrated code from a developer file share to a file share that is accessible by user applications or processes. Once the newly integrated code has been released from the developer and delivered into the user space, other automated processes, such as security testing, can take place before the software is actually deployed to the users.

Continuous deployment is the third step in this process; in this part of the automated software process, after software has been integrated and delivered to the central delivery point, it can be deployed out to the users through whatever means the organization chooses. Again, there are automated processes to do this; some are built in to software management applications and deployment points, such as app stores, and others are simple scripts that can be created to deploy software. Software can also be automatically deployed as part of a policy, such as the software policies created in Active Directory, or as part of user-directed action.

REVIEW

Objective 3.4: Compare and contrast automation concepts and technologies   In this objective, we discussed automation principles, methods, processes, and tools. These are necessary to handle the massive quantities of data that security analysts must deal with on a daily basis as well as to perform the multitude of tasks required to collect, analyze, aggregate, and use the data that's produced by an organization.

First, we discussed overall management of all these automated processes and tools, and how not all of them lend themselves to centralized management. Workflow orchestration is one method of doing that and can be implemented using a variety of commercial enterprise tools or individual tools such as scripting. We also looked at security orchestration, automation, and response (SOAR) systems and how they can provide centralized management for automated processes.

Scripting is a critical skill that cybersecurity analysts should develop to automate both small and large tasks. Scripts can be very simple or complex, using built-in operating system commands or complex programming languages. Application programming interfaces are used to connect applications together and interface them for data exchange or task performance integration. This allows security personnel to create a more unified management approach to multiple disparate applications. We also discussed automated malware signature creation, using tools such as YARA and scripts to search for patterns in existing files that may contain malware. Automation can take on much of the load in searching for and analyzing those patterns.

Data enrichment is essentially adding additional data and context to collected data from systems. This additional data context can help further analyze information to discern threats, unusual events, and undesirable trends in the infrastructure. This context can come from threat intelligence feeds, behavioral analysis, and so on. Machine learning is a powerful tool used to ingest large quantities of data, look for patterns of behavior, and use complex algorithms to discover and extrapolate potential malicious behaviors in the infrastructure.

There are several efforts to produce automation protocols used to exchange data in standardized, common formats between applications. NIST has developed several structured language and reporting formats for identifying assets, threats, and vulnerabilities and expressing other security data for exchange between security tools.

Automation can also be applied to secure software integration, delivery, and deployment. Tools can be used to seamlessly integrate new code into existing production code, deliver it for security testing, and finally deploy it out to the users. Automated methods of doing this include scripting, software management tools, and even software policies built in to enterprise-level services such as Active Directory.

3.4 QUESTIONS

1. Which of the following terms best describes an effort to manage and integrate multiple disparate security automation processes and tools?

   A. Data enrichment

   B. Workflow orchestration

   C. Scripting

   D. Machine learning

2. Which of the following automated methods is used to write interfaces between applications to exchange data and facilitate inter-application task management?

   A. Application programming interface integration

   B. Scripting

   C. Data enrichment

   D. Security Content Automation Protocol implementation

3. Joseph is examining raw data obtained from various log files and other sources within his network. However, it is very difficult for him to analyze what this data means without understanding why and how it was created and how it relates to various potential threats and vulnerabilities. Which of the following would allow Joseph to view this data in a much more productive way, allowing him to perform a more comprehensive analysis of the raw data?

   A. Continuous integration

   B. Machine learning

   C. Security orchestration, automation, and response

   D. Data enrichment

4. You are a cybersecurity analyst tasked with ensuring vulnerability scans begin at specified times of the night throughout the week. The vulnerability scanning software you are using does not allow for scheduled tasks. Which of the following would be the most efficient method for scheduling and executing the vulnerability scans at the prescribed times?

   A. Implementing a security orchestration, automation, and response (SOAR) to ensure that the vulnerability scans are scheduled.

   B. Creating a script that would execute the scans at specified times and dates.

   C. Installing a workflow orchestration suite to ensure that the vulnerability scans run when they are supposed to.

   D. Implementing machine learning software so that you can instruct it to execute the scans on a scheduled basis.

3.4 ANSWERS

1. **B** Workflow orchestration is the effort to provide overarching management and integration of various disparate automated security tools, processes, and methods.

2. **A** Application programming interface (API) integration is used to create interfaces between applications to facilitate data exchange and task execution between applications.

3. **D** Data enrichment allows cybersecurity analysts to add other data from various sources to existing data that they gain from network sources, to give it more context and allow for a more comprehensive analysis.

4. **B** Creating a script that executes the vulnerability scans at scheduled times and dates is the most efficient way of performing this simple task.

Incident Response

- **4.1** Explain the importance of the incident response process.
- **4.2** Given a scenario, apply the appropriate incident response procedure.
- **4.3** Given an incident, analyze potential indicators of compromise.
- **4.4** Given a scenario, utilize basic digital forensics techniques.

Objective 4.1 Explain the importance of the incident response process

Incident response (IR) is one area you must get right the first time. If an incident (a negative event) were to happen in your organization, you don't get a second chance to perform the response. Botched incident response can lead to data loss, financial loss, and loss of reputation, and can potentially even put your company out of business. That's why incident response processes are so critical for the organization to carefully plan, practice, document, and master. In this domain, we look at several critical incident response areas, such as incident response processes, procedures, indicators of compromise, and incident forensics. The processes for the incident response cycle include those needed for incident detection, response, containment, and recovery. In this domain, we will look at each of these in turn.

Critical Incident Response Processes

Several critical processes make up incident response. If any one of these processes fails, the entire incident containment and recovery effort could fail. Organizations must carefully plan for an incident and hope that they never have to use this planning for an actual event. Two of the most critical processes that are not focused on any given area in the incident response cycle are communications and coordination. You'll find these two processes are critical throughout an incident response, whether in the detection phase, the containment phase, or the recovery phase. Without effective communications and coordination, the incident response will fail.

Communications Plan

The communications process is vitally important during the entire response effort, but communications must be planned out; this does not happen dynamically or randomly, regardless of the hundreds of different possibilities that can be realized during an incident. The communications plan is an important part of the overall incident response plan. It details how communications will flow up and down the chain of command, laterally within the organization, and even how the organization will communicate with external agencies. The communications plan should be worked out and agreed upon by management and the incident response team in advance, and all parties involved in the response should be familiar with it. Key elements of the communications plan include items we will discuss in the upcoming sections, including limiting information to only those entities with a need to know, when you must disclose details of an incident to regulatory agencies, protecting information against unauthorized access, using secure methods of communication, and reporting the details of an incident.

Limiting Communication to Trusted Parties

Information about an incident should be closely guarded for the duration of the incident as much as possible. This is because an organization's adversaries, whether they are competitors or malicious external entities, might use this information against the organization. They may use it to destroy the organization's reputation or take advantage of an ongoing incident by attempting to cause further harm to the organization's assets. Adversaries aside, keeping information even from entities that don't have malicious intent is a good idea, particularly because it can cause a loss of faith in the organization by its customers, create unnecessary panic and second-guessing within the organization, and possibly expose the organization to additional risk, including legal liability. Additionally, any incomplete or inaccurate information that leaks before the organization has completed its investigation may cause unneeded speculation. The relevant information about an incident will be disclosed to the right people in due time, but the organization must carefully control information communicated during the early stages of an incident. This is especially true when the organization is trying to determine what happened and how to contain the incident, and until it has definitive facts to report to both internal customers and external stakeholders.

Information should be limited initially to only those personnel who have a valid need to know: senior management, incident responders, and only those other personnel who have a direct role in containing or recovering from an incident. Also, depending upon the nature of the incident, this could include the legal department, the security department, information technology group, human resources, and possibly even the organizational entity targeted by the incident. When required by the situation or regulations, obviously law enforcement or other regulatory agencies should be notified when the organization has enough facts to make a report.

Disclosing Based on Regulatory/Legislative Requirements

Some information about the incident will have to be disclosed, based on statutory or regulatory requirements. For example, if there is a data breach that involves health data, the Health Insurance Portability and Accountability Act (HIPAA) requires that individuals as well as the Department of Health and Human Services' (HHS) Office of Civil Rights (OCR) be notified if the number of records breached exceeds 500. Financial laws and regulations also require breach notifications for loss of financial data. Other laws require that individuals be notified in the event of a breach. Certain incidents may require that law enforcement officials be notified of an incident, particularly if it involves loss of life or jeopardizes public safety. The Federal Bureau of Investigation (FBI) may require notification if the incident involves suspected espionage or terrorism.

In addition to regulatory requirements that determine disclosure, organizations may have contracts or agreements with other entities that require immediate notification of a breach or other incident. To ensure that the organization is meeting its regulatory obligations with regard to incident disclosure, senior management should ensure the following:

- Governance requirements regarding incident notification are understood and complied with through policy.
- The legal department has a plan in place to notify legal or regulatory agencies in the event of an incident.
- All personnel are aware of their legal and ethical obligations to report details of an incident to senior management.

Preventing Inadvertent Release of Information

As discussed earlier, information regarding an incident must be kept confidential within the organization. If incomplete or inaccurate information were to be released, it may cause panic or unnecessary speculation. Even if the information is accurate or factual, it should be released only to certain individuals or entities within a certain time frame or order, and doing so outside of that order may expose the organization to legal or civil liability issues. To prevent accidental or inadvertent release of sensitive information about the incident, the organization should always do the following:

- Limit information to only those who need to know.
- Have an approved communications plan that details who in the chain of command and IR team is authorized to know details of an incident.
- Ensure a senior manager is appointed who is the focal point for the release of information.
- Vet and approve any information released to the public or external entities.
- Make sure that everyone understands how to handle sensitive information regarding the incident.

Using a Secure Method of Communication

As you probably already know, e-mail is not necessarily the most secure form of communication, and neither is the telephone. E-mails can be intercepted and read, particularly if they are not encrypted or there is no authentication mechanism built in. Telephone calls can be intercepted, overheard, and even recorded. These communication methods can still be used during an incident, however, provided the proper precautions are taken. Depending on the nature of the incident, the organization's communications infrastructure may be compromised, so Voice over IP (VoIP) telephones and unencrypted e-mail would be subject to further disclosure to a potential hacker.

The organization must take proper steps and plan for secure communications during the incident, particularly when it involves transmitting sensitive information to different parties.

The organization should take the following precautions when communicating sensitive information about the incident:

- Use encryption whenever possible, particularly when using nonsecure communications methods such as e-mail.
- Ensure that the recipient of the communications is authenticated; for instance, ensure that if you're e-mailing details of the incident, you use PKI certificates for positive identification and authentication.
- Encrypt sensitive data about the incident while it is in storage, with restricted permissions to files.
- Properly label sensitive data per your organization's data sensitivity and classification policies.

Reporting Requirements

The incident communications plan should detail requirements for the incident response team and other entities to report containment progress, as well as any other relevant information, to management periodically. In the early stages of an incident, this could be daily or hourly, depending on the severity of the incident. During the incident, this might be at regularly scheduled intervals or status meetings. Post-incident, this could mean simply developing and coordinating the final incident report for management. All personnel and departments involved in the incident should, at minimum, report the following:

- Labor hours involved with the incident response process
- Expenses incurred for incident response
- Any issues that would prevent an effective response
- Immediate threats to life or safety
- Threats to data or equipment
- Requests for information from any external entities or any other unauthorized personnel

 NOTE   The communications plan is likely one of the most critical processes before, during, and after an incident. Without a solid communications process in place, the incident response is likely to fail.

Response Coordination with Relevant Entities

When assembling an incident response team, the organization should include more experienced technical members of the organizational team. But the team is also composed of more than just technical personnel. Experts from a variety of areas within the organization should either be on or have representation on the team. These areas include the human resources, accounting, legal, security, and public relations departments, as well as any other personnel management deems as critical to an effective response. The team members, in addition to contributing their expertise, may also need to serve as a liaison to their respective areas, providing information and coordination with those areas. An incident response usually won't be limited only to interactions with internal organization personnel. Many different entities will be involved at various stages of the response, which we will cover in the upcoming sections.

Internal and External Entities

Regardless of whether an entity is internal to the organization or external, it may play a critical role in the response. In either case, effective, concise communications and coordination are critical. Senior management should appoint a spokesperson for the team who is responsible for coordination within the organization, possibly making use of team members from different areas as liaisons when the team requires assistance from those areas. Management should also appoint a point person for dealing with external entities—law enforcement, the media, regulatory bodies, customers, partners, and suppliers, for example. This should be someone with knowledge of the incident as well as laws and regulations, has excellent communication abilities, and can work well with external organizations to gain their assistance and trust. Additionally, the organization needs a public relations person to deal with the media, external customers, and even trusted partners. This person should be capable of passing on the right information to the right people, but only what they need to know and when they need to know it. Any coordination with external entities should be approved in advance by the senior manager in charge of the response.

Senior Leadership

Obviously, senior management must always be in the coordination chain. Often, a senior manager in charge of the response, if not the incident response team leader, will be the person tasked with coordinating all aspects of the response, both internally and externally. That person may appoint team members to different roles, such as public relations or dealing with law enforcement, as their expertise is needed. Senior management must be kept informed of all aspects of the incident promptly and given as complete and accurate information as possible. Typically, all decisions involving large expenditures of funds, excessive labor hours, or coordination with outside resources should be approved by the senior manager in charge.

Legal Department

The legal department has a critical role in incident response. While they may not be backing up or restoring servers, reverse-engineering malware, or dealing with user issues, their role is important because they deal with all the legal aspects of an attack. They are the primary office of responsibility when dealing with certain external agencies, such as law enforcement and regulatory agencies (discussed in upcoming sections).

They are also there to advise management on the legal and ethical aspects of the response. For example, they can provide solid legal advice on evidence collection, chain of custody, privacy issues, and so on. They can also assist human resources if there is an issue with an internal employee who may be responsible for the incident. The legal department can also advise management on potential liability issues associated with the event. And lastly, they can assist in negotiating or enforcing contracts with third parties regarding service levels during an incident, breach notification, and many other issues.

Typically, the incident response team will have a "go-to" person on the legal team who is qualified in law, ethics, and the particulars of incident response. That person will know what the legal responsibilities are of all internal and external parties and will facilitate coordination among them. They may also be the focal point of any law enforcement investigations that occur because of an incident.

Law Enforcement

The role of law enforcement during an incident should go without saying, but we will describe it here. Obviously, law enforcement would be considered an external third party to the incident response and would only be called in as a result of a decision by senior management and the legal department based on information indicating a criminal offense may have caused the incident or occurred during the incident. Law enforcement would be called to investigate any criminal aspects of an incident, and they would be expected to collect, secure, and analyze any evidence related to the incident.

The decision to call law enforcement in an incident response is not one to be taken lightly. Senior management and the legal department will consult with the incident response team to determine if there is the potential that a crime has been committed. The team does not have to conclusively rule out accident or negligence on the part of employees to consider calling in law enforcement. Once law enforcement personnel have been called in, the investigation and even part of the response may be taken over by that agency, as their requirements for investigation and response may be considerably more restrictive than that of the organization. For evidence of a crime to go to court, law enforcement must be involved in the preservation and collection of the evidence as well as the overall investigation. Cybersecurity analysts may be called in to assist law enforcement officers by providing detailed information about the infrastructure, how it is designed, and the particulars of the incident.

Regulatory Bodies

Compliance is a major issue in most modern organizations. Governance is often passed on to the organization from laws and regulations and monitored through regulatory agencies. The organization must comply with governance requirements, and frequently these require the organization to notify regulatory bodies in the event of an incident, particularly where it may involve a breach and unauthorized disclosure of protected data. Examples of such regulatory bodies might include the Department of Health and Human Services' Office of Civil Rights for healthcare-related data under HIPAA regulations, the Securities and Exchange Commission (SEC) for incidents involving financial information and business operations, and even the Payment Card Industry (PCI) regulatory body in the event an incident involves payment card data loss or the breach of a network that processes credit cards. Most regulatory bodies have specific reporting timelines and data loss thresholds that must be considered in the event of an incident or breach.

Human Resources

The human resources (HR) department has a key role to play if there is a possibility that an employee caused an incident, whether it was by accident, through negligence, or with malicious intent. The HR department would assist the response by determining if specific employees were properly trained, had the proper security clearance, and had a job position requiring access to any potentially compromised systems or data. They would also be able to provide any relevant information on the employee's background or disciplinary record. If there was sufficient evidence to determine that an employee violated any security policies that caused the incident, the human resources department would also be able to guide senior management on how an employee may be disciplined or terminated.

Another, more routine aspect of how human resources may be able to help during incident response is by providing senior management information on incident response labor costs and categories, managing overtime for the incident response personnel, and ensuring that exceptional performers get recognized for their actions during the incident.

Public Relations

The public relations team also has a vital role during an incident response. They are the direct liaison with the public, including media, customers, and other external entities. They provide information to external agencies and personnel based on the approval of senior management. In addition to providing an official source of approved information, they also are there to dispel any rumors and "manage" the organization's public image during and after the response.

The public relations team should be part of the incident response meetings and communication chain. Although they may know more detailed information than they can disclose, their job is to take whatever information senior management approves for public release and convey that information to the appropriate external entities, such as the media. Therefore, people on the public relations team should be highly trusted, cleared for all levels of information, and kept "in the loop" about the incident response.

 EXAM TIP You should understand the different internal and external entities that are part of the incident response team or will be useful in assisting in the response, and how they are used.

Factors Contributing to Data Criticality

As part of routine business operations, organizations should develop data sensitivity and criticality policies and procedures. These are likely also required due to external governance from regulatory agencies. Understanding which information in an organization is considered sensitive or critical is important to prioritize that information for both protection on a routine basis and response during an incident. Different types of data have different protection requirements, and as such may be protected at different levels and restored into operations based on criticality to business processes.

High-Value Assets

The organization must determine which of its assets (systems, data, equipment, and even personnel) are the most critical and most valuable to its business. Typically, this occurs using several different processes. First, a business impact analysis (BIA) can help an organization determine which systems and data are the most critical for specific business processes. The organization must identify its critical processes and then, in turn, identify the critical systems and data to support those processes. These are the systems and data that must be protected the most and restored the fastest during an incident. The organization can also perform risk management activities to determine which systems and data have a higher likelihood of being affected during a potential incident, as well as what the impact would be to the organization if they were affected by any negative events. Finally, another process that can help determine which of the organization's assets are the most critical is adherence to compliance requirements. Governance such as the NIST Risk Management Framework (RMF) requires that organizations undergo a system categorization step, where data types that are processed on systems are identified and rated based on criticality to the organization, using a scale of high, moderate, or low.

Regardless of how the organization determines its high-value assets, it must record these in its business continuity and disaster recovery plans and prioritize them for both protection and recovery during an incident. Examples of high-value assets often include critical servers, network infrastructure devices, and high-value data. High-value data may include competition-sensitive or proprietary data regarding formulas or processes, personnel data, customer data, and so on.

It goes without saying that any data considered critical or sensitive for any reason should be protected to the maximum extent possible. Protection mechanisms for certain sensitive or critical data include the following:

- Controlled access to data (only authorized personnel)
- Encryption mechanisms employed for both data in transit and data at rest to ensure confidentiality
- Redundant systems and data backups to ensure availability
- Integrity controls to ensure that the data has not been modified during an incident

In the following sections, we discuss some of these high-value assets.

Personally Identifiable Information (PII)

Personally identifiable information (PII) is a special categorization of data that relates to an individual. This is a legal designation for data that could be used to identify an individual and includes data elements such as Social Security number, passport number, taxpayer identification number, driver's license number, name, address, dates of birth, and other pieces of data. Most data privacy laws require that organizations make an effort to protect this information by masking the data, restricting access to PII to only authorized individuals who can be trusted to protect it from unauthorized disclosure, and implementing strong security controls such as encryption and authentication.

During the incident, the organization should, as with other high-value assets, ensure that PII is protected both during transmission and in storage and is available to authorized employees who process that data. The organization should take steps to ensure that during an incident this data is not inadvertently released to either a potential attacker or the public.

Personal Health Information (PHI)

Like PII, personal health information (PHI) is a legally defined category of information that is protected under statute. HIPAA is a regulation that requires organizations to protect PHI against unauthorized disclosure or loss. There are also certain other classes of PHI, such as those that deal with mental health, that are protected at even a higher level. Organizations using and storing PHI should ensure that their security controls are strong enough to protect PHI from inadvertent disclosure or a malicious attack. These controls include encryption for data at rest, strong access controls, strong authentication, and detailed auditing of access to PHI. During an incident, the organization must make sure that PHI is protected not only from a potential attacker or the public, but even from those members of the incident response team who may not have access to that information.

Special Protected Information (SPI)

Special protected information is a specific category called out in the General Data Protection Regulation (GDPR) from the European Union. It is also called out in other privacy regulations as well. Slightly different from PII, it does represent information about individuals, but not the types of information that may easily identify them. It's very personal information that could include sexual preference or orientation, religious or political affiliation, and so on. While by itself this might not be harmful, connecting it to an individual could cause harm through harassment by others, embarrassment, or even subject the individual to arrest in certain countries. This category of information is not necessarily protected in the United States, but you should be aware that if your organization does business with any European Union citizen, GDPR rules may legally apply to your organization. You should be aware that you must protect this type of information while it is in your possession, particularly during an incident that may result in the inadvertent release of it.

Financial Information

The need to protect financial information, for both individuals and the company, is obvious. This information should be considered a high-value asset, as well as proprietary and confidential. Inadvertent release of this information could subject the organization to serious legal liability as well as give competitors access to information that can harm the organization.

Corporate financial information includes revenue, profit, expenditures, asset valuation, contracts, labor rates, and so on. The organization would be also responsible for protecting financial information that belongs to individuals, such as payroll data, company stock information, 401(k) and other retirement data, and any other information that has to do with individuals' finances. Organizations suffering a loss of personal financial information that they have a duty to protect, including banks, stock brokerages, and other financial institutions, would violate several laws if that information were breached during an incident.

As with all the other types of high-value information, financial information should be protected against unauthorized disclosure or loss during an incident. Incident response team members from the organization's financial department should take special precautions to ensure that company financial records are secured and backed up in the event of a loss.

Intellectual Property

Intellectual property is a type of high-value asset that includes sensitive data relating to an organization's processes, methods, and ways of conducting its business. Intellectual property is developed by the company to participate in the market space and to maintain its competitive edge in that market. Obviously, if this data were inadvertently released, the company could suffer financial loss because someone else could use its methods and processes to develop competing products.

Several different types of intellectual property must be protected:

- Trade secrets are a type of intellectual property that is not known to the general public and relates to the organization's processes and methods of creating products or performing services.

- Patents are publicly known, but legally protected processes, methods, or designs that an inventor has registered with the government for protection.

- Copyright is a form of protection that covers original works of authorship—literary, dramatic, musical, artistic, and so on.

- Trademarks are names, slogans, or symbols used by the organization to identify its brand. Trademarks can be legally registered and protected.

In addition to these categorizations, intellectual property could be considered anything that the organization develops internally and uses for its business on a day-to-day basis. This could include media files, PowerPoint slide decks, policies and procedures, methods of writing contract proposals, and so on.

During an incident, these types of high-value data should be protected against unauthorized access, loss, or destruction. Without this data, the organization could suffer serious losses to its business.

Corporate Information

Sensitive corporate information could be considered intellectual property, but it usually doesn't neatly fall into the categories of trade secrets, copyrights, patents, and trademarks. Still, it should be protected to the level of sensitivity determined by data sensitivity and criticality policies. Examples of corporate information include the following:

- Human resources processes and procedures, such as employee evaluations and so on
- Internal reorganization plans
- Raises, promotions, and demotions
- Meetings with customers or suppliers
- Accounting or budget processes

While some of these types of information may seem unimportant or benign, they can still give a competitor, or even a potential attacker, an edge in understanding the internal processes of the organization.

 EXAM TIP Make sure you understand the different categories of information, particularly those mandated by governance, such as PII and PHI. Any information type that requires protection under the law should be protected to the maximum extent possible by the organization.

REVIEW

Objective 4.1: Explain the importance of the incident response process In this chapter, we discussed the importance of critical incident response processes, including communications, response coordination, and data criticality.

Communication is one of the most critical processes during a response. The communications plan should include provisions for limiting information regarding the incident to only trusted parties, keeping in mind any mandatory disclosures based on any regulatory or legislative requirements, ensuring the protection of information, and preventing the inadvertent release of information about the incident. The communications plan should also discuss using a secure method of communication that is both encrypted and authenticated. Additionally, the plan should discuss any mandatory reporting requirements, particularly those based on governance.

The incident response is not limited to only the incident response team in the server room. Several entities must be coordinated with regarding different aspects of the response. These include both internal and external entities. Senior leadership must be involved in all aspects of communications and decision-making. The legal department is the point of contact for any coordination with law enforcement or regulatory bodies. Law enforcement serves to investigate an incident if it is probable that a criminal act has occurred. Regulatory bodies get involved in incidents due to compliance requirements and must be informed in the event of an incident that results in a breach. The human resources department should be an integral part of the incident response team if an employee is being suspected of causing or being involved in the incident. The human resources team also provides management advice on labor categories and potential overtime hours for the team members. Finally, the public relations element of the incident response team is responsible for releasing approved information to the media and other external entities, as well as dispelling rumors and correcting wrong information.

Data criticality is of importance because the organization must categorize its information assets, based on asset value and criticality to its business and mission processes. High-value assets could include any number or type of systems and data but will typically be those types whose loss or unauthorized disclosure would harm the organization. Some data types, such as personally identifiable information and personal health information, are protected under regulations or statutes. Special protected information may also be required for protection under other regulations, such as GDPR. Corporate financial information could include data regarding revenue, profit, loss, asset valuation, and so on. Intellectual property typically includes trade secrets, patents, and trademarks. Even information that seems harmless, such as internal processes and procedures, should be protected from unauthorized disclosure during an incident.

4.1 QUESTIONS

1. You are the team leader of a corporate incident response team. You're helping to write the communications plan portion of the incident response plan. Which of the following parts of the plan must you ensure is included to prevent inadvertent data disclosure to internal employees?

   A. Details regarding who is authorized to release information to the public

   B. Details regarding which members of the incident response team have access to which information

   C. Details of the plan regarding the release of information to regulatory bodies

   D. Details regarding the use of PKI certificates in e-mail

2. You are the team lead for the corporate incident response team. During the containment phase of the response, you view evidence that indicates a crime has been committed. Which of the following is your best course of action?

   A. Immediately call law enforcement personnel, provide them with the evidence, and allow them to start an investigation.

   B. Preserve the evidence and relay your concerns to the legal department so they can decide about whether to contact law enforcement.

   C. Initiate an investigation into potential criminal acts, collect evidence, and forensically analyze it for potential presentation to law enforcement.

   D. Do not notify anyone about your suspicions, as you are not legally qualified to determine if a crime has been committed—this could be a false alarm.

3. You are the senior manager in charge of incident response for a large corporation. Your incident response team lead advises you that another employee is responsible for an internal hacking attack on a critical server. Which of the following actions should you take?

   A. Notify the legal department so they can initiate a law enforcement investigation.

   B. Immediately call the employee into your office and begin questioning them.

   C. Ask the human resources department for their advice.

   D. Notify the personnel security department to revoke the individual's badge and escort them out of the building.

4. Bill is a cybersecurity analyst in a small company that specializes in healthcare billing for insurance companies. As part of his official duties, he has access to all data on the network, including individual patient medical records and financial records. Which of the following would best characterize Bill's data protection responsibilities during a potential malware attack on the company's network?

   A. Ensure that all corporate financial information is immediately backed up.

   B. Give priority to protecting all corporate information regarding processes and procedures.

   C. Immediately clean all servers of the malware.

   D. Give priority to protecting all PHI and financial data on the network from unauthorized access.

5. Tim is responsible for writing data sensitivity and criticality policies and procedures. He must compose a list of personnel authorized to access sensitive information regarding the specifications and manufacturing processes for a proprietary aircraft part. Which of the following categories will this information fall under?

   A. Corporate information

   B. Special protected information

   C. Intellectual property

   D. Personally identifiable information

4.1 ANSWERS

1. **B**   Since you are trying to prevent internal leaks of information to unauthorized personnel, you should ensure that the plan includes details regarding which members of the incident response team have access to which information.

2. **B**   Unless you are a legal professional, you should preserve the evidence and relay your concerns to the legal department, so they can make a qualified determination about whether to contact law enforcement.

3. **C**   The manager should call the human resources department and ask for their advice on how to proceed, since it is an employee who is being accused.

4. **D**   Bill should give priority to protecting data regulated under statute, such as PHI and customer financial data.

5. **C**   Product specifications and manufacturing processes would be considered intellectual property, particularly a trade secret.

Objective 4.2 # Given a scenario, apply the appropriate incident response procedure

Incident Response Procedures

An incident is a negative event that occurs within the context of the organization. An incident could be the result of a malicious attack, employee complacency, accident, or even an environmental cause. Incident planning and response should be considered a subset of business continuity and disaster recovery planning, albeit on a more defined, narrow scale. Incidents have an impact on the organization, whether it be financial, reputational, technological, or even cultural. It can result in the loss of data, loss of equipment, and even sometimes a loss of life. Incident response is often viewed as a reactive process, but it is quite proactive if performed properly. Conducting an incident response successfully is a result of careful planning, which we'll discuss in this module. As with many other formal processes, incident response has a defined lifecycle and process. An example of this process is shown in Figure 4.2-1, taken from the National Institute of Standards and Technology (NIST) Special Publication 800-61.

Although this view of incident response is accurate, there many other lifecycle models as well, but all of them essentially focus in some manner on preparation, detection, containment, recovery, investigation, analysis, and post-incident activities.

EXAM TIP   You are not expected to know the particulars of the NIST incident response lifecycle; however, you should be aware of the general phases of incident response.

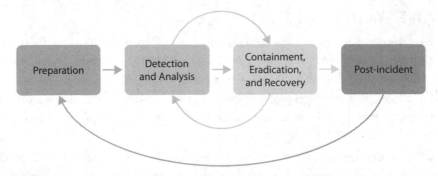

FIGURE 4.2-1   The NIST Incident Response Lifecycle (adapted from NIST SP 800-61)

Preparation

Preparation may be the very most important phase of the incident response lifecycle. During this phase, several activities must be carefully planned and executed. Without adequate preparation, the organization cannot expect to have a successful incident response effort. During this phase, the organization must take the following actions:

- Develop the incident response plan.
- Appoint incident response team members.
- Develop detailed incident response procedures for a variety of scenarios.
- Provision the team with the proper supplies and equipment.
- Ensure the team is adequately trained on incident response procedures.
- Exercise the incident response plan.
- Improve the incident response plan from lessons learned through testing and exercise.

Training

Ideally, the incident response team should be filled with people in the organization who are already trained, experienced, and well-versed in incident response procedures. Most of the time, however, there will be a core team of personnel who have had some level of training or experience with only some aspects of incident response, but usually only two or three who might be seasoned incident response professionals. In addition to incident response training, the team members must be trained in their areas of expertise, such as intrusion detection systems, firewalls, server administration, and so on. The overall incident response plan should include a section on training that details the different areas and tasks that team members should be trained on. This should be in addition to the technical training that they get to support their primary job function. Examples of topics that team members should be trained on include the following:

- Communication skills
- Public speaking

- Report writing
- Business continuity and disaster recovery procedures
- Forensics
- Relevant legal and governance considerations
- Emergency procedures

Testing

How do you know that your incident response plan actually works? Will you wait until an incident occurs to test it? That's generally not a good idea. An incident response plan should be tested annually, or at least at a prescribed minimum to meet governance requirements. However, a best practice is to test the plan when it significantly changes or when team members are rotated on or off the team. There are several ways you could test the plan, and you might even test it as part of larger business continuity or disaster recovery response exercise. The most used types of tests include the following:

- **Documentation review**   Individuals review copies of incident response plans and procedures.
- **Tabletop exercise**   Individuals perform a "paper" exercise with a written scenario without actually performing incident response tasks.
- **Walkthrough**   The team "walks through" the steps of an incident response without performing all the tasks or using all the necessary equipment.
- **Full test**   The team conducts a full incident response test, using all equipment and performing all relevant tasks.

 NOTE   If you are used to seeing additional types of tests, such as parallel or full interruption tests, keep in mind that these are unique to disaster recovery tests. For incident response, the types of tests you may encounter simply involve additional detail or depth of testing, versus the ability to determine if redundant equipment and processes can be activated, as during a disaster recovery exercise.

Documenting Procedures

No aspect of cybersecurity is without the requirement to document processes. This is true in procedures for handling sensitive information, procedures for changing the ruleset on a firewall, and definitely true for business continuity or disaster recovery programs. Incident response is no exception. For a successful response effort to occur, the organization must document all its processes and procedures. Without this documentation, any corporate memory of previous incidents or exercises is lost; there is simply no continuity without documentation.

Documentation is a formal process. Certainly, there will be drafts that are circulated for approval, but they must be written to be accurate, concise, and readable by the intended audience (the incident response team), and they must be vetted through members of the team with expertise in the relevant areas. They must also be approved by management. An auditor may encounter many very good incident response plans that are all these things, except they were not approved by management. Without formal management approval of the plan, there is no real plan because there would not be a requirement to follow those procedures with any kind of consistency. To document these processes and procedures, the organization should do the following:

- Use the relevant experts from the team to write the appropriate areas of the incident response plan.
- Vet the drafts of the plan among the different team members for editing and consensus.
- Ensure the plans are clear and concise.
- Ensure procedures are well organized and easy to follow.
- Get formal management support and approval for the plan.

In addition to the plan being written out, it must be updated periodically—at least annually is a strong recommendation. However, an update should occur any time there is a major change to the plan, a major turnover of personnel on the incident response team, or major changes in the organization's technical or operating environment, as well as when an incident response exercise or test has been conducted. Ideally, updates should be made on a regularly scheduled basis, even if none of these things occur.

The incident response plan and related documentation should be considered company proprietary or sensitive information, but all members of the incident response team and any other relevant stakeholders must be able to access and use the plan at any time.

Detection and Analysis

Although preparation is the first step of the incident response lifecycle, the response effort itself begins when the incident is detected. Detection can happen in many ways. An end user could notice some strange occurrences on their computer, such as sluggishness or applications doing "funny things." A system administrator could see some curious patterns in log files, or a cybersecurity technician could be alerted through an intrusion detection or prevention system (IDS/IPS) or a security information and event management (SIEM) system. No matter how the incident is detected, as soon as it happens, several things must occur very quickly. First, the frontline responder, typically a cybersecurity analyst, must determine whether or not this is a true incident. If they have insufficient information to make this determination, they should elevate the issue to management or even the incident response team. The incident response team, if provided with enough details, can determine as to whether this is an incident that requires a response or if it's something that a technician can simply resolve at their level.

One of the key issues with detection is response time. If there is an active attack in progress, the time span of detection to response is critical. The longer the incident is allowed to go unchallenged, the more damage can be done to systems and data. The following are examples of some of the considerations for the first responder who detects or is alerted to an incident as well as for the incident response team lead in determining whether or not to categorize the incident as requiring a response:

- Loss or corruption of a small dataset versus a large dataset
- Systems suddenly going offline or suffering degradation of performance
- Sudden, unexplainable increase in either inbound or outbound network traffic
- Widespread user complaints of system sluggishness, data loss, equipment failure, or departure from the normal baseline
- Unexplained events monitored by the SIEM, firewall, IDS, or other detection devices
- Otherwise known or predetermined incident response triggers

Once the incident has been detected and the event elevated to senior management or the incident response team, containment actions almost immediately follow. First, however, there is an initial analysis, where the team must determine the who, what, where, when, why, and how of the incident:

- What has happened (what is the nature of the incident)?
- To which part of the infrastructure has it happened (where did it happen)?
- What is the timeframe (start time, duration so far, and so on)?
- How did it happen (network attack, malware, massive file deletion, and so on)?
- Why did it happen (motivation of the attacker, failure of security controls, and so on)?

Most of these questions will have immediate answers, or at least incomplete answers until the incident has been contained and a thorough investigation and analysis have occurred. However, the team should try to gather as much information as possible going into the response so they can better contain the incident, preserve evidence, and understand what has occurred. In the next few sections, we'll discuss essential issues with incident detection and analysis.

Characteristics Contributing to Severity Level Classification

Once the team has determined that there is an incident that warrants a response, there must be an effort to determine the seriousness of the incident. As part of incident response planning, the team should have developed a severity scale that expresses the level of severity of the incident and the corresponding response. This should already have been approved by management in the plan, along with the measured responses for each level. Depending on the organization, its infrastructure, and how the team is postured on the response, those criteria could include the following:

- The scope of impact to the organization and its assets
- The volume of data loss
- The type of data loss (level of sensitivity)
- The level of degradation or destruction of systems
- The nature of the threat or attack vector
- Any specially defined criteria in the incident response plan

Downtime

System or business process downtime would be a consideration in determining the severity or scope of the incident. However, this may be unknown until the incident has been contained. The incident response plan should define levels of downtime association with incident severity. The organization should have a measured response for each of those levels, and this part of the plan should derive, to an extent, from the business continuity plan. You could develop a maximum tolerable downtime (MTD) measurement not only for each system but for the overall organization as well and its business processes. This measurement should articulate with the RTO in the business continuity and disaster recovery plans as well.

Recovery Time

Beyond the maximum tolerable downtime, recovery time measurements should also be included in the plans and would contribute to how severe the incident is considered. Again, interfacing with the business continuity and disaster recovery plans for these items just makes sense. Levels set for recovery time objective (RTO) and recovery point objective (RPO) should be considered when determining the severity of an incident.

EXAM TIP Remember that the recovery time objective (RTO) is the maximum amount of time the organization can tolerate being down without suffering catastrophic losses to the business. The recovery point objective (RPO) is the maximum amount of data (measured by time) that the organization can stand to lose. These two key measurements can be per system or even per business process. Organizational management sets these two measurements.

Integrity

Remember that integrity is one of the three goals of security, along with confidentiality and availability. In this case, data integrity refers to how much data (by volume or by defined sensitivity level) is determined to be exposed to unauthorized modification. In addition to a data breach, where data is exfiltrated or disclosed to unauthorized entities, another concern is the modification or destruction of data, which commonly occurs during an attack. Data sensitivity is probably the more important of the two since the volume of data doesn't necessarily mean that the data is critical to the organization. It can simply be an indicator of a serious attack. In any case, any indication that sensitive data is at risk should be sufficient reason for a credible response.

Economic Impact

It should go without saying that the economic impact of an incident should be a crucial factor in determining whether a response is warranted, and how large that response should be. Unfortunately, in the initial moments of the incident, the economic impact likely can't be measured. However, if systems that support critical business processes are seriously compromised, or critical data is lost, it's highly likely that economic impact will be significant to the organization. During the initial stages, based on the information a response team has at hand, senior managers must start to measure economic impact in terms of downtime of critical systems, loss of the ability to conduct business, and loss of critical information assets. Hopefully, the organization has already conducted a business impact analysis (BIA) during its business continuity and disaster recovery planning, so this information should be readily available. The organization can use criticality information from a BIA to determine exactly what the financial impact will be, which in turn may drive the level of response. Remember that it is not simply a matter of estimating the replacement cost of servers; it's the overall financial impact to the organization if the servers supporting critical business processes that generate revenue are lost, especially over long periods of time.

 CAUTION   If your organization has not already performed a BIA, that should be one of the top priorities it has as part of its overall risk management program. Without a BIA, the organization will have no way of knowing what its critical processes are, what its critical assets are, and how to prioritize their protection and recovery in the event of a disaster or other incident.

System Process Criticality

Following the discussion on economic impact, system and business process criticality is important in determining the level of response. In that same BIA, the organization should already have determined its critical processes that support its business, the systems and data that support those critical processes, and what the impact would be if either were partially or completely lost for an extended period. Once that has happened, the organization should be able to plan on which critical processes and systems to prioritize for response and recovery should an incident occur.

NOTE   You should already have guessed by now that incident response, business continuity, disaster recovery, and risk management are all interrelated parts of the same process, although they approach it from different directions. The goal of all these things is to preserve the critical assets that support processes that keep the business operational.

Reverse Engineering

Reverse engineering is an important part of the analytical process when it comes to gauging the intensity and severity of an incident, and later determining its root causes. We've already discussed reverse engineering in a previous module, but remember that essentially reverse engineering is decompiling unknown executables down to their basic assembly or machine language level to determine their function, operating characteristics, and potential malicious behaviors. On a higher level, reverse engineering can also be used to start from a known condition, such as the current state of the incident, and work your way backward to determine how an incident occurred, what attack methods may have been used, and how it affected the infrastructure. In either case, remember that reverse engineering is a critical part of the incident analysis.

Data Correlation

Data correlation essentially takes disparate types of data from a wide variety of different sources and consolidates them for analysis, looking for commonalities and connection points in the different data that can help develop and verify hypotheses as to how the attack occurred. You can correlate data using a variety of methods, but one critical way would be to use the data from a SIEM system, assuming you have one set up that ingests data from a variety of sources. These sources would include log data from systems, data from physical security systems, threat feeds, and so on. Some data doesn't necessarily lend itself to automated correlation, so you may have to gather that type of data (qualitative or subjective data) manually and pair it with electronic data to discover how an incident may have happened, as well as its timeline in progress. An example of this type of qualitative data might be interviewing your users or system administrators to determine what they observed on the system in question. Yet another type of data might be documentary evidence from previous incidents, both within your organization and others, that discuss attack vectors and how they materialized, what vulnerabilities they took advantage of, and so on. Correlating these two types of information, for example, with the information you can gather from your electronic sources (more factual or quantitative) in your security devices may help you develop answers to the who, what, where, when, why, and how questions that you are asking throughout the response.

Containment

Containment is the most immediate and highest priority for incident response. During this phase, the incident response team is focused on halting or minimizing any damage to systems or data and stopping an attack.

Depending on the nature of the incident, there are several ways to contain it. If the incident involves a network attack, someone may have to decide to shut off the external connection to the Internet; if it is malware, then the decision may have to be made to remove or isolate certain hosts or services. Other types of incidents will require other strategies. The key point here is to stop an incident and minimize its impact. Segmentation and isolation are two of the key containment strategies that are prevalent in most types of incidents, and the two we will discuss here.

Segmentation

Segmentation means that the infrastructure is broken up into different parts, such as a network into subnetworks or segments. This should be part of a good network design even before the incident. From a performance perspective, segmentation can reduce unnecessary network traffic by eliminating congestion that results from broadcast or collision domains. From a security perspective, segmentation can prevent hosts and different segments from communicating directly with each other. Segmentation can be achieved through either physical or logical means; networks can be physically separated through different cables or devices, and logically separated using virtual LANs, for example, or even through encryption methods.

During an incident, networks could be further segmented to contain outbreaks of malware or malicious traffic. This can help minimize the effects of the traffic or malware to only specific parts of the network. Part of the incident response plan should include procedures for rapid reconfiguring of network devices to logically or physically separate critical segments, and these procedures could be executed as soon as the team determines that segmentation beyond what is normally found on the network would assist in limiting the effects of the attack.

Isolation

Isolation, like segmentation, means separating parts of the network, or even individual hosts, from the rest of the infrastructure. However, isolation goes one step further in that it ensures that a particular network segment or host cannot communicate at all with any other part of the network or any other host. Isolation should be performed to quarantine a host infected with malware, so it won't spread, or even to segregate a specific network segment where one of the hosts is broadcasting malicious traffic. You may want to isolate either the host or the segment, versus simply shutting them down, to further gather data and analyze the attack without exposing other hosts or network segments to the attack. Removal goes one step further by not only physically and logically isolating a segment or host but actually shutting them down to prevent further damage to any data contained on them.

Eradication and Recovery

Once an incident is contained and there is significantly less risk of any malware or malicious traffic spreading across the network, the team must focus on eradicating the source of the attack and recovering systems and data. This can be a multistep process, and analysis is still going on during this phase of the incident response. The team must locate the source of the attack, such as malware, and completely get rid of it so that it does not continue to spread.

Recovery means restoring the infrastructure to its original pre-incident state as much as possible. In the next few sections, we will discuss different activities involved in eradication and recovery, as well as any potential issues you might encounter.

 NOTE Even as you contain the incident, eradicate the problem, and recover from it, you should always take care to collect and protect any evidence necessary for post-incident analysis and investigation. Even during time-critical incident response, make the time to collect the evidence before it is inadvertently destroyed during the response.

Vulnerability Mitigation

If the incident has been caused by a system vulnerability of any kind, the eradication strategy is to eliminate that vulnerability. This could include getting rid of malware, securing the configuration of the system, patching systems, and so on. Once you determine the cause of the incident, it's a good idea to run vulnerability scans that focus on that specific vulnerability to determine which systems may be susceptible to attacks that target that vulnerability. If time is of the essence, as it usually is during an incident, you may not have time to run a complete scan across all network segments and perform widespread mitigations. You'll likely have to focus on a few specific vulnerabilities that led to the attack and apply those specific patches or configuration changes that will mitigate them. If the organization has not been keeping up with vulnerability mitigation, this is going to take a long time, since the organization will have to update configurations and patches for many different vulnerabilities before it even gets to the one or two that caused the attack. In other words, prioritize your vulnerability mitigation for the most serious vulnerabilities that may have led to the incident. If your organization has already been keeping up with vulnerability management, this should make life much easier.

Sanitization

One key piece of eradicating the source of an attack is sanitization. Sanitization requires that the incident response team scrub and eliminate any traces of malware from media before a device is reloaded. Sanitization is necessary to keep the incident from reoccurring or malware from spreading to other systems. Because a system that is contaminated is likely to be reimaged with a clean, pristine operating system and backup, it only makes sense that you wouldn't want to reuse media that could be possibly contaminated with malware. There are several ways to sanitize media for reuse, including the following:

- **Reformatting/repartitioning media** This is not effective for completely making files unrecoverable, but it can be somewhat effective for eliminating certain malware.
- **Overwriting media (also called "wiping")** This entails writing patterns of ones and zeros all over the media, making it exceedingly difficult to impossible to recover existing data; this is the preferred method of sanitizing media.

Note that these two methods are used if you want to reuse the media, but formatting is not the most effective means of preventing data from being unrecoverable. If you do not intend to reuse the media, we will discuss methods in a later section that you can use when you intend to dispose of it.

Reconstruction/Reimaging

Once media on a device has been searched for evidence, and cleaned of the malware infection (sanitized), it may be necessary to reconstruct the system using known-good recent backups, assuming they exist. Hopefully, the organization has a good backup strategy in which critical data is backed up on a periodic and frequent basis, which should be based on the system's criticality. Without this, there is little hope of restoring a system to its pre-incident configuration, and there will be lost data and functionality. If good backups exist that are current, media that's going to be reused should be reimaged from a known-good master image (often called a "gold" master image, which is the official, up-to-date, secure baseline of the system) and restored from backup data. The organization's RPO metrics should drive how often the data is backed up in the event of a disaster, because that will determine how much data, in terms of time, is potentially lost.

Secure Disposal

For media that you do not intend to reuse, it is a best practice to destroy the media or at least render it unusable before you get rid of it. This would prevent any unauthorized person from reconstructing any data remaining on it. The two most popular methods for destroying media bound for disposal are degaussing and physical destruction:

- **Degaussing**   With degaussing, you subject to the media to a strong magnetic field to destroy any data on it as well as render the read/write heads unusable.
- **Physical destruction**   This method of media destruction can be performed by physically breaking the media using hammers, fire, destruction machinery, and so on.

Both of these methods render the media completely unreadable and therefore unable to be reused, which may be necessary for a serious attack in which you want to make sure no data is left on the media or if the media becomes physically damaged during an incident.

Patching

As mentioned earlier when discussing vulnerability management, patching is critical in containing an incident and eradicating the issues that caused it. If an attacker took advantage of a vulnerability in which there was a patch available but not applied, getting that patch or update installed is crucial. Because you may not know whether the attacker still has a foothold in the network, if you don't patch the vulnerability, the incident can start all over again. In the interest of time, focus on patching the specific vulnerabilities (if known) that allowed the attacker to compromise the network in the first place. But don't stop there. Once those are patched, continue to patch any other serious vulnerabilities that could be taken advantage of. Just because the attacker used one or two specific vulnerabilities during the attack, that doesn't mean they won't use additional ones to maintain their foothold once they are in the system. Prioritize patching along with tightening insecure configurations.

In the interest of time, you may not be able to test patches before they are applied, so it becomes a balancing act of delaying the response, so you can test a patch that may potentially break functionality, or quickly patching to stop an incident from becoming more widespread and damaging more systems and data. Make sure you record in detail all of your actions involved with patching because they are likely going to need to be reviewed post-incident for the configuration control board so that a new baseline can be established or updated.

Restoration of Permissions

One of the key factors in an attack may be that an attacker gained permissions they should not have had or was able to elevate permissions from a nonprivileged account. During your containment and eradication efforts, it's important to go and review rights, permissions, and privileges on systems and objects to determine if they have been changed. This is where having a document that details who should have which permissions is helpful. Often, organizations set permissions over time but don't necessarily record the reasons why different individuals have been given less-restrictive or elevated permissions. With a baseline document that details who should have which permissions and why, it will be easy to identify inconsistent permissions. Once these have been identified, you should make every effort to restore baseline permissions to their original pre-incident configuration.

While restoring permissions to contain an incident is your top priority, you will likely also run across instances where permissions were granted over time to people who did not need them. This is called *permission creep*, and it can occur as people change job positions or need permissions temporarily for specific instances and those permissions are never taken back. Make sure you record any instances of this that you find, but don't make it your top priority to fix them during the response itself. Just know that you will eventually have to go back and correct those permission issues to help prevent a future attack.

Reconstitution of Resources and Restoration of Capabilities and Services

Part of the recovery portion of incident response is reconstituting any resources needed to put the business back in operation. This means bringing servers back online, sharing out any network shares that were restricted during the incident response, restarting critical services, and so on. As the incident is contained, you might consider restoring critical services and capabilities first, and gradually phasing in other capabilities and services according to prioritization levels the organization (hopefully) set during its business impact analysis (BIA). A phased approach is a good idea when you can't bring all services back online at once and you want to make sure you eliminate the possibility of reinfection for malware or sanitize and restore a compromised network segment or host its original state. While there are specific restoration priorities you should prescribe within your organization, potentially these capabilities and services could include the following:

- Network communications (host and device connectivity)
- Security services (authentication, network encryption, malware detection)
- Internal communications services (VoIP, instant messaging, e-mail)
- Network file shares
- Network printer services
- Application services

You could break these down into their component services as well, as determined by your BIA as well as your business continuity and disaster recovery plans.

Verification of Logging/Communication to Security Monitoring

Once containment, eradication, and recovery processes are complete, you will need to make sure everything is functioning the way it should. There should be a period where you retain a heightened awareness after incident recovery and use this time to verify that the incident has been effectively dealt with. Activities that can help you do this include the following:

- Ensure audit logs are logging the appropriate activity on critical devices and resources.
- Make sure security services (such as SIEMs, IDS/IPS, firewalls, proxies, and so on) are correctly logging and monitoring activity across the infrastructure.
- Preserve any logs or artifacts generated before and during the incident as evidence.

Post-Incident Activities

Once the team has contained the incident, eradicated any malware or any other causes, and recovered systems back to the original pre-incident state, the work is still not done. There are many things to do after the incident to help analyze, investigate, document, and learn from it. The goal is to find the cause of the incident, remedy any factors that helped create it, and prevent the incident from occurring again. There's a temptation to disband or release the team back to their normal jobs, but this should be resisted until all post-incident activities have been concluded, as their expertise is still needed. Examples of these activities include preparation and analysis of evidence, writing reports, cleaning up after any changes to systems, and ensuring that any new data resulting from the response effort is used to prevent further incidents. We'll discuss many of these activities in the upcoming sections.

Evidence Retention

An entire objective of this domain is devoted to incident forensics, but it's a good idea to discuss this topic here in the current context as well. Collecting and preserving evidence is not only a function of post-incident activities but should also be performed from the very beginning of an incident when evidence is fresh, before it can be overwritten by well-intentioned remediation activities. The incident response team should be trained to identify evidence early on and make every effort to preserve it. Unless the evidence is needed immediately to determine the cause and resolution of the incident, it should be set aside for later analysis. Key evidence artifacts during an incident could include the following:

- Log files
- Malware binaries
- Disk or file system images
- RAM contents
- Physical media
- Infected files
- Network traffic captures

The incident response team must be trained in incident forensics procedures and techniques; otherwise, evidence could be contaminated, lost, or destroyed during a well-intentioned response. To ensure the best chance of identifying, collecting, preserving, and analyzing evidence, the team should focus on the following:

- Identifying potential evidence artifacts early in the response
- Using approved forensics techniques and tools
- Ensuring evidence is captured and preserved before media sanitization
- Documenting all aspects of evidence collection, including device names, IP addresses, timestamps, hardware, and so on
- Maintaining the chain of custody throughout the evidence collection process
- Analyzing evidence using only forensically sound copies, rather than original media
- Ensuring evidence is authenticated as true and accurate representations of artifacts discovered on devices and storage media

Lessons Learned Report

As part of the incident response report, discussed later, the incident response team should develop a "lessons learned" document that details what major lessons were learned from the response and how this information may be used to improve the response for future incidents, as well as prevent similar incidents. The lessons learned report should include the following:

- Information regarding the effectiveness of incident detection, notification, and team assembly
- Any identified shortfalls of personnel, equipment, training, or supplies
- Information on any identified vulnerabilities or control failures that helped to cause or worsen the incident

- Possible solutions for any incident response effort failures
- Suggestions for improving the incident response plan and effort

Additionally, the lessons learned document should not attempt to point fingers at anyone who may be to blame for any failures or shortfalls in the response effort. Rather, it should suggest who may be in a better position to address some of these deficiencies.

Change Control Process

For an organization that has a formal change control process, rapidly responding to changes in configuration for systems affected by the response may not be difficult. As part of the organization's change and configuration management plan, the incident response should have already been included in those documents and addressed as emergency change procedures. If this is the case, then those emergency change procedures should have been followed, which may have included quick testing of any critical patches or configuration changes, rapid and efficient review and approval by a senior manager, decisive implementation, and documentation. After the incident is over, the changes should be better documented and vetted by senior managers for consideration as temporary changes or as permanent adoption to the system baseline. Communication is important here; members of the team in charge of rapidly changing configurations to contain an incident should be in constant communication with senior managers who both understand and can approve these changes to mitigate the incident. If some changes must be considered provisional, then the full change control board should meet post-incident to consider them as permanent or to weigh the possibility of having to further change the baseline for a more permanent solution. In any event, changes should not be made off the cuff and without consideration of the long-term effects on the organization's baseline.

Incident Response Plan Update

During any type of incident response exercise or during an actual incident, issues will arise that possibly weren't considered when the incident response plan was originally written, or the environment may have changed to the point that the plan has to be updated. Even without incident response exercises or actual incidents, the plan should be updated periodically to ensure it is current and keeps up with the changing technologies and environments the organization works in. Any changes that are identified during an exercise or an actual incident should be seriously considered to improve both the plan and the response effort for future incidents. This may include items such as the following:

- Changing the team composition
- Reevaluating team member roles and responsibilities
- Determining any additional training needed by team members
- Increasing or decreasing supplies or equipment
- Changing the type or frequency of exercises or tests
- Changing incident response procedures

The plan should be reviewed and updated post-incident by the members of the incident response team, senior management, and other stakeholders. Ultimately, senior management must approve the new plan, and team members must be trained on its changes.

Incident Summary Report

After the incident, there must be an overall report submitted to management that describes the incident response effort. Writing the report should be a joint responsibility between the incident response team lead, the senior manager in charge of the response, incident response team members, and any other stakeholders whose input is deemed critical to the report. All available information about the incident should be collected, organized, and summarized in the report. The report should:

- Be concise, clear, and properly formatted for the organization
- Include an executive summary
- Fully describe the details of the incident in chronological and topical order
- Explain the results of the investigation and root causes of the incident
- Describe any recommendations or mitigations that could prevent or lessen the severity of a future incident
- Offer lessons learned regarding the incident or its response
- Reach a definitive conclusion about the incident

When writing the incident summary report, team members should keep in mind the technical level of their audience; the report is primarily intended for managers, so it should be written in understandable language. Any technical details required for the report should be included as attachments or appendices. In addition to the incident response team review, the report should be reviewed by other stakeholders before it is presented formally to management. The stakeholders could include the legal department, human resources, and IT. Any inputs from any external agencies, such as law enforcement, should also be considered for inclusion.

Indicators of Compromise (IOCs) Generation

As part of the post-incident response, the response team should generate and recommend a new list of indicators of compromise to the IT and cybersecurity teams for the organization. These IOCs will assist the respective teams in detecting future incidents by providing them with additional information that could help them identify any early warning signs of the incident. These IOCs can include specific log file entries, file system changes, network traffic anomalies, malware signatures, and so on. This is an important part of preventing future incidents or at least mitigating their severity.

Monitoring

Monitoring is also an important part of detecting and mitigating future incidents. Given the lessons learned during an incident or an exercise, the response team should be able to provide advice and IOCs to the cybersecurity and IT teams that will help them fine-tune their monitoring process and watch for traffic and other events that might indicate similar incidents. This should also serve to help the organization monitor events that they may not have been previously monitoring. Changes to the firewall ruleset, intrusion detection signatures, and SIEM event analysis, correlation, and rules may be necessary based on what was discovered during the incident.

REVIEW

Objective 4.2: Given a scenario, apply the appropriate incident response procedure In this module, we discussed a wide range of incident response procedures that are necessary to detect, respond to, contain, eradicate, and recover from an incident. The importance of preparation can't be overstated since the amount of preparation an organization undertakes directly contributes to its effectiveness in responding to an incident. Preparation includes training qualified personnel for the different roles and responsibilities on the response team, as well as testing a well-written incident response plan and updating that plan when necessary. In addition to the incident response plan, all procedures and processes should be documented as much as possible.

Early detection of an incident is critical to an effective response, and several quick decisions must be made early in the incident regarding how severe the incident could be and what its impact could be to the organization. Some of these factors in determining the severity or scope of an incident could include potential system downtime, how long the organization can afford to be offline from an incident (also known as the maximum tolerable downtime, or MTD), as well as data and system integrity. The economic impact to the organization due to loss or degradation of systems and data supporting critical business processes cannot be overstated. Loss of systems or data means that business processes will not function, which in turn means that the organization will be impacted by the loss of revenue, profit, and market standing. This directly relates to how critical systems and data are to business processes, and these are usually ascertained through a business impact assessment.

Incident analysis isn't just confined to post-incident tasks; the incident response team must continually analyze data during the event to determine its severity, scope, cause, and how the team must respond to it. Activities associated with incident analysis include reverse engineering of malware or higher-level events as well as data correlation from disparate sources, both quantitative (for example, electronic files such as logs) and qualitative (for example, interviews with critical systems personnel, documentation review, and systems observations).

Containment is the most critical part of incident response; unless the incident is contained, malware could spread throughout the entire infrastructure, data could be compromised, modified, or destroyed, and systems could be rendered unusable. Two important parts of containment are segmenting networks and hosts to prevent the spread of malware or malicious traffic and isolating or removing hosts from the network so that they will not compromise other parts of the network. Eradicating malware or any other cause of the incident is the first goal of containment, followed by recovering systems and data and restoring services. To eradicate the issues that caused the incident, the response team must mitigate any vulnerabilities believed to have caused the incident, sanitize any affected media, and rebuild data through the reinstallation and reimaging of media. Any media that is not intended for reuse or can't be reused should be disposed of securely, taking care to destroy any remnants of data through wiping or encryption. Another important part of eradication is patching systems that may have been compromised to mitigate the vulnerabilities that may have caused the incident. Investigating and restoring any permission issues to a secure state are also critical steps to prevent a malicious actor from using elevated permissions to continue the attack. Finally, after the source of the incident has been eliminated, the team must ensure that resources and services are restored. These can include network connectivity services, file shares, printer shares, and applications. Additionally, security services must be verified as fully operational, to include appropriate logging and auditing capabilities.

The activities the organization performs after an incident are equally as important. This includes collecting and preserving evidence and communicating any lessons learned about the incident or the response to the incident to management. Any changes that have been made to the baseline of affected systems should be documented and either approved as permanent changes to the baseline or considered temporary and additional mitigations put in place. The incident response plan will most certainly change after an exercise or an incident and must be updated to reflect lessons learned or additional information gained during the incident. The team members should also recommend any new monitoring strategies or indicators of compromise to the cybersecurity and IT teams. Finally, the incident report should be written, vetted, and submitted to management. It should be clear and concise, and detail all the different aspects of the incident and its response.

4.2 QUESTIONS

1. Emilia is a cybersecurity analyst who works in a security operations center. During a massive malware attack on the company's infrastructure, she needs to make sure that a group of critical servers stays online and is not infected due to the sensitivity of the data that resides on them. Which of the following is the best course of action to prevent the spread of malware to the servers?

   A. Sanitization

   B. Disposal

   C. Segmentation

   D. Reverse engineering

2. Evie is a cybersecurity analyst who works at a major research facility. As part of writing the incident response plan, she needs to determine the time frames for bringing systems back online after an incident. She does not know exactly which systems should be brought back online first. What is the best way for Evie to determine these time frames?

   A. Perform a business impact assessment for critical systems.

   B. Determine which systems were attacked first and bring those back online first.

   C. Bring systems back online in priority order based on user needs.

   D. Determine which systems are the costliest ones to restore or replace and bring those back online first.

3. Ben is a member of his company's incident response team. Early morning shift IT technicians noticed strange network traffic targeting several critical servers. Ben was the first incident responder notified, and he must make an initial decision on how severe the incident could be. Which of the following factors should Ben *not* consider when determining incident severity?

   A. System criticality

   B. Incident response team readiness

   C. Potential incident cost

   D. Possible business process downtime

4. Sam is a cybersecurity analyst trying to help contain a massive cyberattack on his organization's infrastructure. The incident response team discovered that the attacker took advantage of three known but uncommon vulnerabilities present on some of the organization's critical devices. How should Sam approach vulnerability management during this attack?

   A. Immediately isolate the company's entire infrastructure from the Internet.

   B. Apply the appropriate patches en masse to the entire infrastructure.

   C. Prioritize and scan for the target vulnerabilities to mitigate them first.

   D. Perform full scans on all devices and begin patching all discovered vulnerabilities.

4.2 ANSWERS

1. **C**   Segmenting the critical servers should be the first choice to prevent the spread of malware. Sanitization and disposal will render the servers unusable for the immediate future. Reverse engineering is used to analyze malware but will not prevent its spread.

2. **A**   Evie must perform a business impact assessment to determine the business process and system criticality. She must then use this information to determine which systems to bring back online on a priority basis.

3. **B**   Regardless of whether the incident response team is ready to respond, the severity of the incident depends on system criticality, the potential economic impact to the organization, and potential downtime.

4. **C**   If the team has determined which vulnerabilities were exploited to attack the infrastructure, those should be prioritized for scanning and remediation. Other critical vulnerabilities that may be found afterward should also be mitigated, but those are not the highest priority. Disconnecting the organization from the Internet may not stop the attack already in progress.

 **Objective 4.3** # Given an incident, analyze potential indicators of compromise

Analyzing Indicators of Compromise

Earlier in the book we discussed indicators of compromise (IOCs). These are individual pieces of data that indicate that the infrastructure has been attacked or otherwise compromised in some malicious fashion. These indicators could be specific events that are flagged in audit logs, unusual network traffic, permission changes, file integrity changes, or other types of events. Any of these, and many others, could be a clue that something abnormal is going on within the network or on a host. Rather than arbitrarily look for these indicators, organizations can determine their own IOCs based on historical and trend analysis, threat feeds, and experience. Also, professional and commercial organizations offer libraries of IOCs for organizations to include in their threat management programs. These IOCs can be very generic, such as a simple spike in network traffic, or very specific, such as an IOC for a Windows system indicating that a particular dynamic link library (DLL) has changed in a certain way.

Indicators by themselves don't necessarily mean the infrastructure has been attacked or compromised; this requires analysis and context. When you observe an indicator, through log file entries or system behaviors, you should attempt to track down the reason for the indicator. Perhaps there is a network performance problem caused, for example, by an equipment malfunction such as a chattering network card. A department may be installing some new software or engaged in a particularly intense business activity that could produce false network or system indicators. These can be tracked down and explained with a little work. The difference between an abnormal event that is innocuous and a true indicator of compromise is context. A cybersecurity analyst must ask questions such as the following:

- What could be the cause of this indicator?
- What changes occurred on the network or even within the business operations that can account for this indicator?
- What other data supports or disproves this is a true IOC?

Unfortunately, once the incident begins, there's very little time to ask these questions and get conclusive answers. We have to balance between a thorough analysis and a quick response. But throughout every stage of the response, we should be analyzing data so we can learn more about the incident, its true cause, and its true nature. We may get three or four hours into a response only to discover it was a false alarm. And truthfully, that's a much better alternative than discovering that we have a serious problem on our hands.

One key point that must be emphasized: if you do not monitor and audit your infrastructure, there will be no indicators of any type of compromise, because you won't see them. Indicators are like warning signs or malware signatures—to see them, you have to already have an idea of what you're looking for and be looking for them. Only those indicators you are actively monitoring for or auditing in your log files will show up. As you observe other new indicators, you should fine-tune your monitoring and auditing efforts to alert for those as well.

For the most part, we will examine indicators of compromise in this module that are fairly common and should be included in any organization's IOC library. We will discuss three key categories: network-related IOCs, host-related IOCs, and application-related IOCs. While we can't possibly cover every potential IOC for all operating systems and applications, the ones we will cover are both critical to detecting a potential incident and important to know for the CySA+ certification exam.

 NOTE   You must first develop your library of indicators of compromise and then set your monitoring of auditing evidence to detect those indicators.

Network-Related IOCs

Any potential clues that a system or infrastructure has been attacked or compromised in some way will likely show up as part of a network IOC. This might be unusual bandwidth usage, intermittent beaconing from a host, unusual or irregular communications between two hosts on a network, the presence of unknown network devices, and possibly network scans from an unknown host. Network IOCs can also present themselves as strange spikes in network traffic or traffic using unusual ports and protocols. In any case, these are IOCs any organization should look for by including them in their intrusion detection signatures, firewall rulesets, and security information and event management (SIEM) analysis.

Bandwidth Consumption

If an organization has done its job and developed a baseline for system and network performance, then any host that uses bandwidth outside of its normal usage should be noticed. Bandwidth consumption should be one of those performance indicators that is monitored and analyzed on both host-based performance utilities and as part of aggregated usage that is fed to and monitored by a SIEM system. During the normal course of business operations, hosts may occasionally send out or receive more data than normal; there could be a spike in usage or increased activity during certain business operations such as the end-of-year processing.

These can be expected and accounted for. But when hosts use bandwidth outside of their normal baseline, for other extended periods or during unusual hours or activities, this is something to pay attention to. Bandwidth consumption IOCs could include the following:

- Specific hosts that use excessive bandwidth beyond the norm on an irregular but frequent basis
- Excessive bandwidth usage after normal business hours of operation
- Short but large bursts of bandwidth usage

Beaconing

Beaconing is an indicator of compromise that's pretty cut and dry. If we discover that a host is sending out regular traffic (or irregular traffic, for that matter) to an external host for no good reason, there's a good bet we've been compromised by a botnet of some sort. The problem is discovering a beacon that may be hidden in innocuous traffic, such as HTTP traffic. We need to look at the traffic flow between the host and the destination to determine what kind of traffic it is, what port and protocol it uses, its regularity, the amount of data sent and received, and why the traffic is being sent at all. Some internal applications routinely send and receive traffic to external sites for license updates, automated patching, and so on. These need to be recorded as part of the baseline so they can be eliminated quickly when investigating potential beaconing traffic. It may be necessary to put a traffic sniffer on the wire to intercept traffic from the host and capture it for further analysis. In the end, it also may be necessary to isolate or remove the host from the network and sever its connection to the external command-and-control server it is contacting.

Irregular Peer-to-Peer Communications

Depending on how your network is constructed, larger networks probably use Active Directory or another Lightweight Directory Access Protocol (LDAP) structure. This enables file sharing and other services from a client/server perspective. This typically cuts down on the necessity for host-to-host communications. There may be occasionally a need for one host to contact another; for example, local file shares might be a reason, although that should be highly discouraged on a large network. On small networks, this may be more commonplace. Again, you should track down and determine why the two hosts are communicating with each other. Try to determine if there is a common application on both of them that needs to communicate, if there are any legitimate file shares that should be accessed between hosts, or if there is any other good reason for them to communicate. If you can't find a good reason that is recorded as part of the system baseline, then you may have to assume that there is an attempt to establish lateral movement by an attacker from one host to another. This also may be part of an automated bot system trying to establish lateral movement across the network. In either case, your best choice is to isolate the hosts, thus preventing their communications, and investigate the matter further.

Rogue Network Devices

Any unidentified or non-approved device connected to the network should also be an obvious indicator of compromise. Rogue network devices could take the form of unauthorized wireless devices that an attacker has inserted into the legitimate wireless network, or possibly a wired device that has been plugged into an open switch port by some malicious person. The indicators for such a scenario might be traffic from a previously unknown or unrecognized device. Unfortunately, the traffic may be lost in the general noise of the network, so this can be difficult to detect. If the organization has a very good inventory that it keeps up to date for all devices attaching to the network, as well as a network access control (NAC) solution, this should make it more difficult for a rogue device to connect to the network. Additionally, if devices must authenticate to the network to send and receive network traffic, such as authentication through Active Directory or an 802.1x protocol, this should also make it difficult for a rogue device to connect and communicate with the network.

Scans and Sweeps

Network scans and ping sweeps against a large organization by an external unknown entity are commonplace every day. Most of these are automated scans from a variety of actors—some of them malicious. Some scans are a prelude to a further attack, but for the most part, if your defenses are solid and multilayered, these scans are harmless. However, repeated scans of the same sort from the same origin are something that could be an indicator that an attack is imminent.

Unusual Traffic Spikes

In a well-run infrastructure, the organization knows what's going on in its network. Cybersecurity and IT personnel record and document baseline host configurations, device configurations, and, of critical importance, network traffic. Baselining network traffic means that analysts have recorded traffic throughout a variety of conditions:

- Time of day, day of the week, and so on
- Business process events (such as financial closeouts)
- Based on applications, such as those that might use higher-than-normal bandwidth at predictable times

A normal baseline is created by simply observing network traffic over time, during specific events, and taking into account routine consistent (and perhaps inconsistent or infrequent) types of traffic. As long as traffic can be explained, in the right context, it should be considered part of the baseline. All this is aggregated and analyzed to determine what "normal" traffic looks like.

Ideally, firewall rules have been created to allow permissible traffic and to deny traffic that is not part of the normal baseline. The same goes for intrusion detection signatures. SIEM systems have well-developed rulesets, queries, and analysis parameters so they can key in on all of this traffic and take into account what is part of the normal baseline. They should also be able to alert when unusual traffic happens.

Unusual traffic spikes could take many different forms:

- Spikes in the amount of traffic that a particular host sends or receives
- Spikes in the usage of a particular protocol or port
- Spikes in traffic originating from or going to a specific destination
- Increases in a particular file type or content of traffic

Any of these conditions is likely an indicator of compromise and should trigger alerts because the traffic is not normal on the network. In a well-managed infrastructure, these items will be brought to the attention of cybersecurity analysts through IDS alerts, SIEM analysis, log files, and other means.

Common Protocols over Nonstandard Ports

Closely related to spikes in network traffic would be spikes in unusual traffic over common ports, or common traffic over unusual ports. Either should indicate something abnormal and outside of the baseline. Seeing HTTP traffic over port 8080 might not necessarily be an unusual instance if a server has been configured to receive traffic over that port. That's why it's imperative that cybersecurity analysts record configuration settings for all devices, including those that may routinely send and receive traffic over unusual ports. Many organizations use nonstandard ports as a form of obfuscation—that is, "security through obscurity"—in the hopes that it will be less easily detected by attackers. A simple port scan would probably render this tactic useless, but there may still be merit to it, in that tactics like this would likely prevent an average user from accidentally finding an internal web server. As a general rule, however, organizations should probably stick to sending and receiving traffic over common ports, both for standardization purposes and to make it easier to troubleshoot and manage traffic.

As a baseline configuration, the organization should record ports and protocols used across the infrastructure. These can also be programmed into rulesets and signatures for all network security devices. This makes it easier for those devices to do their jobs when unusual traffic over a particular port or protocol is detected.

 EXAM TIP   Remember that network IOCs include excessive bandwidth consumption or use, beginning from one host to another, unusual or unapproved peer-to-peer traffic, any rogue devices you discover on the network, network scans, any type of unusual traffic increases, and unusual port and protocol usage. Only by baselining your system will you be able to see any of these unusual occurrences.

Host-Related IOCs

Indicators of compromise are also found on hosts. When you detect them on a network, you should immediately start looking at your endpoints. If the organization has been proactive with endpoint protection and monitoring, you should get a wealth of information regarding indicators that there is a malicious event going on. The keys to host-based monitoring include the following:

- Host-based IDS installed on all hosts
- Detailed logging with a centralized log collector
- Host logs and other information sent to a SIEM system
- Installed security agents for antimalware, vulnerability scanning, and so on

The information you get from the host that can indicate a malicious event includes information about processor utilization, hard disk or other media utilization, network bandwidth usage, security configuration, processes, any privileges on the host, and any potentially unauthorized software in use on the host. We'll discuss each of these indicators, and others, in the following sections.

Processor Consumption

High processor utilization is one indicator of a problem on a host. It might not necessarily be malicious; it could indicate a hardware issue with the motherboard or CPU, or it could indicate a performance problem with a badly written application. However, it can also indicate that the host has been compromised by a malicious program or entity. Malicious programs can create processor utilization issues during their efforts to exfiltrate large amounts of data from the system, communicate with a botnet or a command-and-control host on the Internet, or disrupt the system in a denial-of-service attack.

As with all other things, if you have properly baselined your system and are aware of what should be considered "normal" performance, detecting excessive processor utilization shouldn't be difficult. You can configure alerts on the system to notify the administrator when processor utilization gets too high. When you discover high processor use, you should try to determine what the issue is before you assume it's malicious. Again, more often than not it is a hardware fault or a badly written piece of software. Usually, through process and performance monitoring utilities, you can figure out which process is causing CPU utilization to spike. Then you would track down what this process is, what spawned it, and whether or not it could be malicious. We discuss malicious processes a bit later in the module.

Memory Consumption

Memory, as a resource, is subject to the same utilization issues as central processing units (CPUs). Excessive memory utilization can be caused by several factors. Hardware issues such as a bad memory chip or stick can cause problems since the system can no longer use that particular piece of hardware. Poorly written programs can access memory in inefficient and troublesome ways. Even an operating system that is poorly optimized can cause memory utilization issues. On the malicious side, however, memory consumption issues closely mirror CPU utilization issues; high memory usage could be caused by a malicious process that is attempting to exfiltrate data, communicate with an elicit host, or disrupt the system.

Detecting excessive memory usage by a malicious process will usually start with noticing performance hits on the system. The system will bog down, run slow, fail to start applications properly, and have other performance issues. The system may hang or abruptly shut down if memory utilization becomes too high. You may also see an effect called "thrashing," which means that the system has run out of memory and is trying to write to the paging file on the hard drive more than usual.

Tracking down the reason for memory consumption problems is similar to tracking down CPU utilization issues. You should look for processes that are using excessive memory, particularly for longer periods of time. If you have performance or process monitoring utilities on the system, these are usually good at tracking down processes that may be maliciously using the memory.

Drive Capacity Consumption

Yet another resource that could be the victim of a malicious process or software is media capacity consumption. One common tactic of an attacker's intent to carry out a denial-of-service attack is to rapidly fill up a hard drive with useless data in an attempt to disrupt or halt a system. Another reason for losing hard drive capacity might be that an attacker is staging data exfiltration by consolidating large amounts of sensitive data from different systems across the network to a single system to make it more efficient to send it out of the network. If you see a hard drive rapidly filling up with compressed or encrypted files, particularly large ones, this could be an indicator that this is happening.

As with other resource consumption, such as CPU and memory use, if you have performance monitoring utilities on your system, they could send you an alert or log an event that the hard drive is losing capacity by filling up with files. Your best course of action is to quickly triage to determine what could be the cause of this event; unlike memory and CPU consumption, however, there are not too many things that could unintentionally cause excessive hard disk space consumption. Almost always this is the direct result of a malicious attack. Balancing the need for collecting forensics evidence with the need to stop the attack, you might be tempted to shut the system down or at least isolate it from the network in case it is the victim of malware that may spread across the network.

Unauthorized Software

Unauthorized software can be an indicator of something bad in a couple of different ways. First, it could indicate that users have too many privileges on the network and can install unauthorized software that is not approved by the organization. This can be detected by routine software inventories and remedied through software restriction policies or application whitelisting.

Remember that application whitelisting enables only specific organization-approved software to be installed or run on the organization's systems. Second, and more sinister, is that it could be malicious binaries or software installed by an attacker. Software of this type usually is harder to detect and may be under the guise of routine programs, such as office productivity software or some other innocuous program. Unauthorized software can even take the form of Trojans or compromised binaries that are part of an authorized software package. This is where antimalware detection for malicious binaries comes in handy, as well as periodic integrity checking of critical binaries and application files. In any event, if you have unauthorized software, either in the form of an unapproved software package or an unknown, unauthorized, and possibly malicious binary, you should take steps to restrict user privileges as well as implement application whitelisting and file integrity checking.

Malicious Processes

Malicious processes are those that run on a system that perform unauthorized, and typically unknown, actions. Examples of malicious processes could be keystroke loggers, e-mail servers, FTP servers, peer-to-peer file-sharing services, and so on. Any of these should be considered dangerous to the organization.

Malicious processes can be difficult to detect; they can be hidden from ordinary view of a process monitor, they could be obfuscated by being named something similar to an authorized process, or they can be hidden, like a Trojan, in a piece of authorized software or binary. System integrity checking is one way to detect compromised system files that may spawn unauthorized processes. Antimalware software is another way to detect those malicious binaries. When monitoring for malicious processes, you should look for those that access files they normally wouldn't, use administrative privileges that they should not be allowed to use, excessively use CPU, memory, or network bandwidth, and so on. Essentially you are looking for processes that perform actions outside of the system's normal performance baseline. Process monitoring utilities can look for trends that would indicate a malicious process running, and they help you identify those same processes.

Unauthorized Changes

As a cybersecurity analyst, you already know about the value of change control in an organization. Unauthorized changes can result in damage to systems or breaking the configuration baseline. If your organization has a mature change and configuration management program that works well, detecting unauthorized changes might not be very difficult. If you detect that changes have been performed on a system that aren't logged or otherwise approved, this could be an indicator of compromise. Since the changes are unauthorized, you likely won't detect them, however, unless you audit changes to a system's configuration, critical files, and so on. If something changes on the system, it should be logged as an event, which may then feed into a SIEM system for alerting and analysis. There are also utilities you can install that will periodically check for the integrity of files to see if there have been any unauthorized changes or modifications to those files. This is particularly important for critical operating system files.

If you discover an unauthorized change, you should first look and see if there is any formal log of the change by whoever performed it, and if it was approved by the change control board. If it was an emergency change that was urgently needed before approval, there still should be some type of audit trail for it. These procedures should be built into your change management policies. If there is no explainable reason or context for the change, you start looking at other systems to see if similar changes have been made. You may need to quickly scan for vulnerabilities or malware to see if that could be the cause of the change. If necessary, you may need to isolate the system away from others so that potential malware can't spread and cause other unauthorized changes.

Some changes may not be because of malware; they may be the result of a malicious insider with elevated privileges. When you discover unauthorized changes, through logs and other means, you should determine the last person who had access to the system, what their level of privileges are on the system, and what they may have changed.

Unauthorized Privileges

Auditing can only tell you about an event once it has already occurred; that is, once it is "past tense." By this time, the damage may already be done, but at least you will know that someone has performed an illegal or at least questionable action. This is assuming, of course, that your organization audits privileged use of certain objects or certain actions. If you don't audit these actions, you'll probably never know whether someone is using unauthorized privileges on your network.

The other method of detecting unauthorized privileges is proactive; it involves periodically going through the properties of objects, usually the more critical ones, such as sensitive files and folders, to determine which user accounts have which permissions to perform certain actions on those objects. You also want to look at security configurations for hosts to determine which accounts have elevated privileges to perform specific actions on each host. This can be a painful aspect of security administration if you are looking at individual objects and hosts, one at a time. But there are utilities, some of them built into systems, such as Active Directory, that can actively monitor for privilege changes or dump an entire list of accounts and privileges in a file for you to examine.

In any case, a serious indicator of compromise is when you find, usually through the logs, that a user account has acquired new privileges or has used privileges that you were not aware they had.

Data Exfiltration

Data exfiltration is a problem itself during an incident, but it can also be an indicator of a bigger problem if you suspect that data is being slowly exfiltrated off of the network because this can indicate that your network has been compromised by an attacker. Data exfiltration can be difficult to detect, unless you have specific measures in place to do so, such as a Data Loss

Prevention (DLP) solution, or if you monitor potential indicators of compromise relating to unusual data movement. Such indicators might include the following:

- Excessive bandwidth consumption from a particular host
- Large files being sent across the network for no explainable reason
- Many files from the same data source, such as those that might be backed up from a particular database
- Compressed or encrypted files being sent across the network for no explainable reason
- Audit logs indicating attempted unauthorized access to sensitive files by persons

These are all indicators that someone could be stealing data through a network connection. However, other indicators could tell you that someone on the inside is stealing data by moving it to unauthorized media, such as removable USB sticks. In this case, you might look for log events that indicate the presence of a USB storage device on a system. In many environments, the use of external media is unauthorized, and USB ports have even been disabled physically or logically on a host. This should be done especially on hosts that process or store sensitive data, such as those in a hospital that might process medical information.

Abnormal OS Process Behaviors

It can be hard to describe or even detect operating system behaviors that are abnormal. Sometimes performance issues can cause an operating system, especially Windows, to behave in strange ways. Normal behaviors could include an abrupt system reboot, system hang-ups, abnormal application closing, applications starting up for no reason, quick screen flashes, and cryptic error messages. Routinely, most of these behaviors don't necessarily represent anything malicious going on with the host but could be because of faulty hardware, a bad network connection, or some other explainable reason. *Explainable* is the keyword here. When you're investigating abnormal operating system behaviors, you need to look at it in context. What could be causing the behavior? Has the system changed recently? Have there been performance problems that can be attributed to hardware? During routine host issue troubleshooting, you should be able to determine if the behaviors are caused by an explainable reason, or if there is no explanation for the behavior. If there is no good explanation, then you may have to look deeper at the security aspect of the behavior.

As we keep mentioning auditing, you should go back and look at the system logs to see what has been happening with the operating system. Look for activity from unusual accounts. Look for abnormal service or process activity. There many different tools beyond the log files that can also help you. There are real-time process monitoring utilities that can tell you if a process is taking up too much memory, using up too much CPU time, or writing abnormally to the hard disk.

When you can't explain abnormal system behavior as a performance or hardware issue, start looking for security explanations. Check your antimalware's event logs to see if it has detected or quarantined any potential malware recently. Make sure your signatures are updated. Look at your event logs for unusual activity. If you can't determine the cause of the abnormal behavior, collect forensic artifacts from the operating system, such as log files, lists of running processes, and so forth, for further analysis and then think about restoring the system from a backup. If an incident only affects a single host, that may be your best bet. However, if you're starting to get indicators of compromise such as these from a host, look at other hosts and the overall network as well for other indicators.

File System Changes or Anomalies

It is difficult to change some characteristic of the underlying file system without that event being logged. This is another one of those indicators of compromise that should be fairly easy to detect if you are paying attention to your baseline configuration and you audit changes to the system. File system changes could manifest themselves as changes to the file system itself; for example, changing from FAT32 to NTFS might be one to look at. Changed default file or folder permissions that are given to new objects would also be an indicator that something might be amiss on the system. When a new object is created, you should pay attention to not only its default permissions but default ownership as well. If someone created a folder or file on a file system that was not authorized, it should be logged.

It's also important to audit what is done to critical files on the system. If you have object auditing turned on, for certain files you may want to have attempted file deletion, file creation, or file change audited. This might prevent someone from making unauthorized changes in a file system.

Registry Changes and Anomalies

Any time-critical system files, such as binaries, dynamic link libraries, configuration files, and, in the case of Windows, the registry, have been changed, that could be a serious indicator of a compromise. Unless someone has a direct reason to edit or change the registry, or if it has been changed through an automated process, such as application installation, this is something you should be concerned about. Remember that the Windows registry is the central storage for all Windows configuration items. It is a hierarchical database that is very complex and very sensitive. Making any unauthorized changes to it or making any mistakes during editing the registry can result in serious system problems that may render the system unusable. Registry changes can be made by malicious entities to cause Windows to boot abnormally, hide malicious software or processes, run malicious binaries on startup, and so many other generally bad actions.

As part of a normal, healthy system backup strategy, the registry on your systems should be backed up on a routine basis. Normally the registry doesn't change very much, but during some routine events, such as installing an application, it is common practice to back up the registry before and after the change so you can restore it in the event the change causes system problems.

To prevent and detect registry changes, registry files are protected and only authorized for editing by an administrative-level user. Auditing of registry keys should be standard practice in an organization that is concerned with security. Any unauthorized changes, or any changes at all for that matter, would be detected and logged through auditing. Whenever you see a log entry for a registry change, unless you are sure it came from an authorized action, such as an application change, installation, or deinstallation, or some other good administrative reason, you should consider this an indicator of compromise on the host.

Unauthorized Scheduled Tasks

Automating tasks, especially those that are mundane, tedious, but routine, can save an administrator a lot of time and trouble. This could be a task as simple as copying event logs to a centralized backup location or running an automated script on a system every night. However, a malicious entity could schedule an automated task to run under the elevated privileges of an administrator, without them having to even be logged on to the system at that time. This is a common attack method that an attacker will use just in case they get kicked off of the system and need a script to run at a specific time.

As mentioned repeatedly, auditing is of vital importance to a cybersecurity analyst. If auditing is turned on and configured properly, it should be easy to detect if someone has scheduled automated tasks on the system. There are many different ways to automate a task on a system, including scripting or directly at the command line. There are also many different facilities used to enable automated, scheduled tasks. These include the AT command in Windows and the *cron* facility in Linux. Regardless of the method used, these events can be logged and reported to system administrators. When you see a scheduled task has been created, you need to investigate whether or not it's a valid task and determine what it does. Here are some questions you need to ask:

- Does the task execute a script at a specified time? Does it run a command or series of commands?
- Does the task set up communications with another host?
- Do the logs indicate who created the task?
- What time and date was the task scheduled to run? Is that an unusual time of day for normal operations?

Any of these might be indicators that a malicious user has created a scheduled job that may run under elevated privileges.

 EXAM TIP   Combined with network-related IOCs, host-related IOCs are strong indicators of an attack. They include resource consumption, unauthorized software, abnormal or malicious processes, unauthorized changes, unapproved elevated privileges, unapproved accounts, data exfiltration, unapproved scheduled tasks, and changes to the file system and registry.

Application-Related IOCs

Network and host indicators of compromise are not the only ones you should be paying attention to. Even application software can show indications that a potentially malicious incident is occurring. You must first rule out any unauthorized software or potentially malicious binaries that are on the system. This should be easy for an organization that implements application whitelisting and also scans for changes to an operating system and its binaries. Once a cybersecurity analyst determines that the software on the host is authorized, there's a possibility that it has been compromised in some way by an attack. Software can show signs of an attack through behaving strangely, throwing errors, and hanging up. But there are other indications that an application has been compromised that you should look for.

Anomalous Activities

What is defined as anomalous depends on the organization's configuration baseline. As mentioned repeatedly during this module and others, the organization has to baseline everything about the infrastructure, including bandwidth utilization, processor and memory utilization on hosts, patch levels, and many other critical elements on the network, hosts, and even applications. For application baselining, the organization has to determine what "normal" behavior is for an application. This is usually done by observing the application in process—that is to say, how it communicates with other hosts on the network or with a host outside the network, its common error messages, its speed, files it may access, and permissions it may require. As a cybersecurity analyst, once you have baselined your applications, as with networks and hosts, you should be able to determine what is considered "unusual behavior."

Introduction of New Accounts

So many indicators of compromise require that the organization has done its job in baselining configuration, understanding the traffic flow, and generally knowing what's going on in its network. The introduction of new accounts as an indicator of compromise is no exception. Unless the organization is auditing the creation of new accounts, their privilege levels, their group membership, and what those accounts are doing in terms of interacting with resources, then the organization likely will have no idea when a new account is added that could indicate a compromise of its network. That's one important point about indicators of compromise that you need to understand: without the proper preparation done in advance in terms of auditing, monitoring, baselining, and so on, most of the indicators of compromise we discuss in this module will never be detected.

Assuming the organization has full knowledge of the accounts that are supposed to be on the network and what they are supposed to be used for, any new accounts would be relatively easy to detect and would serve as an early indicator of a potential compromise of the network. Administrative accounts are something to monitor for—particularly their usage or the appearance of a new administrator account. But even new routine, normal user-level accounts should be monitored, because sometimes the first thing an attacker does is attempt to create an account and then later elevate that account's privileges. Even in an organization that does not have a complex security infrastructure, it's relatively easy to run a series of scripts every night that list new accounts created during the previous day's operations. In a more sophisticated network, it's relatively easy to have mechanisms such as Active Directory log and feed information to a SIEM system so that administrators can be alerted if a new account is created. There's almost no excuse for this indicator of compromise to go unnoticed.

Unexpected Output

What is unexpected output? It could be the output from an application that looks aberrant or strange, causes system crashes, or produces data that looks suspicious. It could be error messages or unusual events in the audit logs. It also could be unusual network traffic. No matter which form it takes, the unexpected output can be an indicator of a performance issue, an equipment or application malfunction, or even a malicious attack. In any case, unusual output is something that can be tracked using automated means to a certain degree; sometimes you must rely on the observations of users or administrators to notice unusual output from an application or device. Again, this is where baselining your system operations and network traffic comes into play. If you have an idea of what normal is, then detecting what is abnormal is so much easier.

Unexpected Outbound Communications

As with so many other indicators of compromise, unexpected communications from a host that attempts to exit the network to an external destination are relatively easy to detect if the proper processes-detection methods have been put into place first. If you know what normal traffic is supposed to look like, then detecting abnormal traffic can easily be accomplished by configuring rules on intrusion detection systems, proxies, firewalls, and other devices. An organization that has standardized and recorded all the ports and protocols used on the network can exclude those that are not used by denying them in the appropriate rulesets. Not only can attempts at outbound communications be detected, but they can also stopped before they cause harm to the network.

Indicators of unexpected and unauthorized outbound communications include the following:

* Traffic from a host that does not normally communicate outside the network
* Traffic on a port or protocol that is not in use by any standard applications on the network
* Any traffic destined for an unknown IP address outside the network
* Traffic destined for an IP address belonging to the network that may be spoofed; in other words, an IP address belonging to the organization's range but originating from outside the network perimeter or from a host that has not been recorded as a managed device on the network
* Excessive traffic beyond normal usage to an external point on the network by any host

Any of these can be easily detected and blocked if they are suspected as malicious traffic. Once this type of traffic is detected, it also might be useful to put a sniffer to work capturing the traffic for later analysis so the nature of the traffic can be determined, particularly if you feel you need to capture the traffic as evidence.

Service Interruption

A service interruption as an indicator of compromise could take several different forms. At the host level, it could be a service that is supposed to be running but has been paused, stopped, or keeps restarting. Often attacks on the host will change the start type of the service or stop the service for running.

Beyond the host level, service interruption could mean network-wide services, such as DNS or DHCP services. Services that are used across the network are often targeted by malicious entities in a denial-of-service attack. With appropriate logging and monitoring, service interruptions can be quickly detected and fixed. If the service repeatedly is disrupted or if the logs indicate any strange reasons for the service to be disrupted, you may have an indicator of an attack.

Application Logs

As a cybersecurity analyst, you can't underestimate the importance of logging. Host logs, security logs, and application logs of the most commonly used logs. Application logs in particular can be an indicator of compromise if an application is producing unexpected output, hangs up, stops abruptly, or otherwise malfunctions. If an attack is far more subtle, application logs can provide traceability of what has happened in the application at its lower levels, such as system calls, resource access, and so on. Application logs can indicate whether or not the application services were successfully started, if someone logged in to the application remotely, or if the application attempted to access a resource that was otherwise not permitted. Application logs, like other sources of information on the infrastructure, can be fed into a SIEM system for aggregation, analysis, and to alert administrators of issues. However, more often than not, application logs are analyzed after the attack has already been detected through another indicator of compromise, as part of an effort to trace the lifecycle of the attack and develop a timeline for it. In any event, application logs can be rich in information as indicators of compromise.

 EXAM TIP Application-related indicators should cause you to look further into issues on the host and network to discover if you have performance problems or an actual malicious event. They include strange application activities, creation of new accounts, unexpected output or communications with an external host, or service interruptions of any kind. View your application logs regularly to look for indicators of compromise.

REVIEW

Objective 4.3: Given an incident, analyze potential indicators of compromise   In this module, we covered the different types of potential indicators of compromise. We looked at three different areas into which indicators can be grouped: network-related IOCs, host-related IOCs, and application-related IOCs. Network-related IOCs include excessive bandwidth consumption, beaconing from a host to external unauthorized systems, peer-to-peer communications that should not be happening, potential rogue network devices, network scans that may be a prelude to an attack, unusual traffic spikes, and common protocols that are communicated over uncommon ports.

Host-related indicators of compromise include excessive resource consumption—CPU, memory, and drive space are all system resources that could be victims of excessive consumption by malicious processes or software. Unauthorized software in the form of non-approved programs that have been installed by ordinary users, malicious binaries, and compromised programs are the concerns here. Malicious processes are a chief cause of many of these IOCs. Unauthorized changes to the system could be in the form of changes to the configuration baseline, installation of unauthorized software, or other changes that could be either malicious or, at a minimum, unauthorized. Privileges should be monitored by the organization to detect unauthorized privilege elevation or use; these instances can frequently be determined by logged events. Data exfiltration is a problem unto itself, but it is also an indicator that the system or the network has been compromised by a malicious entity. Abnormal operating system problems include abrupt system reboots, halts, performance issues, and other issues that can't be easily explained or diagnosed. These issues may be the result of malware or an active attack. File system and registry changes should be monitored as potential indicators of attacks as well. Finally, any scheduled tasks, created by unknown or unauthorized users, that perform potentially malicious or destructive activities should be watched for and addressed as suspicious.

Application-related indicators of compromise include any anomalous activities by software, any new and unexplained user accounts, unexpected output in the form of error messages, any irregular or unauthorized outbound communications to external hosts, service interruption issues that might include sudden starting or stopping of services, and, of course, events that are logged as a matter of regular auditing in application logs.

4.3 QUESTIONS

1. Emily is a cybersecurity analyst who is in charge of monitoring the company SIEM system. Early one morning she notices alerts that several hosts on the network are utilizing a great amount of bandwidth, far more than they ever have. After examining logs and network traffic, she determines that they are all sending abnormally large files to an external host. Which of the following could be the cause of this event?

   A. Routine license updating for a common application on each host

   B. Data exfiltration

C. Normal patch updating for several hosts

D. A normal business application event that only happens quarterly

2. Lisa is a cybersecurity analyst who works at a major government think tank. She gets a call from a user stating that their computer is abnormally slow, stops responding for long periods, and won't open any applications. Which of the following should Lisa look at first to determine the cause?

A. Excessive resource consumption

B. A possible virus

C. Scheduled backups on the host

D. Faulty network connection

3. Tim has been asked to look into a user's computer that doesn't seem to be able to receive an IP address when they connect to the network. An administrator continually has to assign a static IP address to the host for it to communicate. After troubleshooting the host, Tim can find nothing wrong with it. Several other users begin to complain about the same thing. What should Tim look at next as a possible cause of the problem?

A. Malware attack on the network

B. Switch failure

C. DNS service failure

D. DHCP service failure

4. Bobby is a brand-new cybersecurity analyst and has been assigned to document all the organization's indicators of compromise for input into a database. What sources of information could give Bobby the existing IOCs the organization is already using?

A. Threat feeds

B. Vulnerability scanning

C. Monitoring and audit sources

D. Device configuration files

4.3 ANSWERS

1. **B** Since large files are being sent to an unknown host utilizing a lot of bandwidth from outside of the normal baseline, data exfiltration is a strong possibility that Emily should investigate.

2. **A** The host is a victim of excessive resource consumption. At this point, it could be memory, CPU, or hard disk utilization. It could be due to a hardware failure, an errant application, or even a malicious source.

3. **D** DHCP service failure would be the only choice that describes the problem at hand. Since troubleshooting the hosts indicates that there is no issue with them, troubleshooting the network-wide service that passes out IP addresses would be the next step.

4. **C** Monitoring and auditing tools should already be configured with what the organization is looking for. These will be the indicators of compromise. For example, if the creation of new accounts is audited, this is an indicator of compromise Bobby should document.

Objective 4.4 Given a scenario, utilize basic digital forensics techniques

Forensics Considerations

Forensics is an important part of an incident response. Using forensics, we attempt to discover what happened before, during, and after an incident; we are looking for the root causes of the incident. We are also trying to answer the questions who, what, where, when, and how.

During this module, we're going to look at various forensics considerations and issues, and we discuss the particulars of forensics as it relates to discovering the facts of an incident. Incident forensics can cover many different aspects, such as the network and hosts or other endpoints. Don't forget that these endpoints aren't always simply desktops or workstations. Mobile devices are also considered endpoints, and they present their unique challenges with information forensics. As a large majority of organizations are also using cloud-based services, cloud forensics has recently become an important part of incident response. And let's not forget virtualization; many organizations use virtualized systems, including servers and end-user devices.

Forensics is not as you see it on a one-hour television show. It often takes many hours and the work of a lot of different people with different skill sets to investigate an incident using forensic techniques. Information forensics involves the preservation, collection, security, analysis, and presentation of various types of electronic evidence. It requires skills that include advanced networking knowledge, in-depth knowledge and experience with operating systems and programming, and even knowledge of laws and regulations. For an incident response team, training on forensic skills is a must. Even if the team can quickly respond to, contain, and eradicate the cause of an incident, if they lack forensic experience and skills, they will not be able to effectively analyze the root causes of the incident and prevent a future one. Lack of forensic skills would also potentially enable a would-be attacker to go free from accountability or punishment.

In this module, we're going to discuss different aspects of forensics that you will need to know for the CySA+ exam. There's no way we can make you an expert on incident forensics, but you will gain the knowledge required by the exam objectives and more. We discuss network forensics, host and endpoint forensics, and how to apply forensic skills to cloud-based services and virtualization. We also cover some basic forensic skills cybersecurity analysts should be aware of.

Forensics Foundations

This book will not make you an expert on incident or information forensics. There are so many other books, training courses, and entire university degrees that are dedicated to that, as the amount of information, knowledge, and experience you need to be a fully qualified forensic examiner is so vast. However, you can conduct a very thorough, professional forensic examination on your organization's information assets by being trained and experienced in basic forensic techniques. You will need those skills and knowledge to be a functional and valuable part of your organization's incident response team. With that, you need to learn and understand several key foundations of knowledge, a few of which we discuss in the following sections.

Evidence Preservation

Evidence preservation is a key foundation you need to ingrain into your mind as a forensic investigator. This is probably the most critical part of an investigation. Even if you lack the skills to properly analyze evidence, you can save the investigation from failure by ensuring that the evidence is preserved and protected at all stages of the response and investigation. Evidence preservation involves aspects such as chain of custody, physical protection, and logical protection. Chain of custody is explained in the next section, and physical protection simply means that the evidence should be protected and preserved from the elements, such as weather, static electricity, accidental damage, fire, theft, and so on. Logical protection is a little bit more difficult; it involves taking some of the precautions that are outlined later on in the module, such as forensic duplication, hashing, and so on. All these steps are necessary to make sure that evidence is preserved and kept intact in its original form.

Chain of Custody

The concept of chain of custody is a critical part of preserving evidence. It essentially means that evidence is controlled, tracked, and documented from the moment it is seized or acquired, all through its lifecycle. A typical evidentiary lifecycle is shown in Figure 4.4-1. Note that securely storing and transferring evidence are part of each stage in the lifecycle and are prevalent throughout.

The lifecycle for a piece of evidence may not end until after the investigation, response, or even court case is concluded, which could take days, months, or even years. During the lifecycle, evidence has to be protected from contamination. When evidence is initially acquired or seized, the investigator or responder creates a chain of custody form. They are usually the first person to sign this form as having acquired the evidence and accepted it into the chain. Any subsequent person or entity receiving the evidence or performing any type of action on the

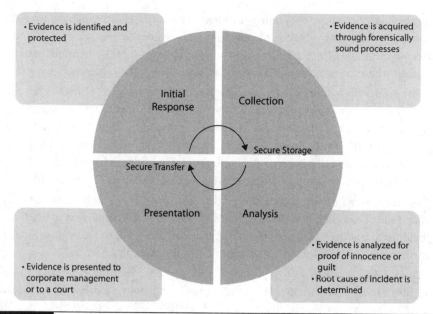

- Evidence is identified and protected
- Evidence is acquired through forensically sound processes

Initial Response

Collection

Secure Storage

Secure Transfer

Presentation

Analysis

- Evidence is presented to corporate management or to a court
- Evidence is analyzed for proof of innocence or guilt
- Root cause of incident is determined

FIGURE 4.4-1   The evidence lifecycle

evidence should also sign the chain of custody form. The chain of custody follows the evidence wherever it goes, even if it is transferred to another entity for storage or analysis. During the actual disposition of the case, either through the courts or corporate investigation, the chain of custody will be used for verification that the evidence has not been tampered with. When the case for investigation has been concluded, the chain of custody is kept and filed in case it is needed in the future.

Basic Forensic Procedures

Although this is not a book that focuses specifically on incident forensics, it is extremely helpful to understand some of the forensic procedures you may need to know for the actual investigation. Some of these seem like common sense, but unless you know them, you wouldn't necessarily think to employ them without training and understanding why they must be carried out. What follows are a few of the more critical forensic procedures that could potentially make or break a case:

- *Secure the scene of the crime or incident.* This could be an individual user's cubicle, an office, or even a data center floor. During the initial stages of the investigation when you are collecting and seizing evidence, no unauthorized person should be in the area. This includes people who normally might work in this area. If the area is necessary for critical operations and requires personal in the area, make sure they are observed at all times and do not attempt to disturb any potential evidence. Know what they are doing at all times.

- *Photograph the scene of the crime or incident before anyone disturbs any of the equipment or evidence.* This way, you can go back later and see how devices were set up and what items were around the equipment, and you can look for details you might have initially missed when you secured the crime scene and acquired the evidence.

- *Don't arbitrarily power off a device unless you absolutely have to.* Critical evidence could be lost from the contents of memory when you power down a device. Additionally, if an active attack is going on with the device, it may alert the attacker that they have been discovered, thus causing you to lose valuable evidence. You must weigh the value of keeping the device powered up to collect volatile evidence from it against the value of shutting it down and preventing an attacker from doing more damage to it.

- *Inventory every single item of evidence taken from the scene.* This includes any device, such as the computer, monitor, keyboard, cables, phones, media, and so on. It also includes any written materials that you believe are evidence or that you will need to further analyze a device (an operating manual, for example).

- *Place all evidentiary items in a protected container.* For electronic items that might be sensitive to static electricity, electrostatic bags are typically used. For items that may not be sensitive but should still be handled carefully, such as optical media, a strong storage container, properly labeled on the outside, should be used.

- *Maintain a strong chain of custody at all times.* Ensure that anyone who removes evidence for the scene has signed for it, and that any actions taken with the evidence, such as storage, transfer, removal for analysis, and so on, are logged.

- *Get written permission from the original owner (assuming the owner is not the suspect, as would hopefully be the case in a corporate investigation) before removing any evidence.* This can include the system owner, IT manager, or even the chief information security officer if necessary. It should be someone who has the authority to grant permission to remove an asset from its location and operations.

- *Have the proper tools at your disposal to perform an investigation.* Most tools, both software and hardware, have to be approved by some professional or legal organization as being tested and sufficient for use in information forensics. Some common, ordinarily used utilities, such as file copy utilities, may inadvertently change evidence and are not suitable for forensic use.

- *Don't perform any type of forensic action, such as analysis, if you do not have the proper training, knowledge, or skills.* Although you may mean well, you could inadvertently destroy or damage evidence to the extent that it cannot be used in an investigation, thus setting back the response and preventing the guilty parties from being held accountable for their actions.

- *Never perform any analysis on the original evidence.* Use forensically duplicated copies, as discussed later on in the module.

EXAM TIP You may not see questions on any of these procedures on the exam, but you should be expected to know them so you can answer more complex questions that may be part of the exam objectives.

Network

The network is the conduit for all information that travels throughout an organization. Because all data at some point touches the network in some fashion, that's the first place we should look for evidence during an incident. Volumes can be written on network forensics, but we will cover some of the very basic things that you as a cybersecurity analyst should know. Two primary skills include capturing network traffic with various tools such as Wireshark and TCP dump, as well as things you should look for during traffic analysis.

Wireshark

Wireshark is the ubiquitous traffic capture and analysis tool used by cybersecurity analysts. Wireshark is the graphical version; the command-line version, which makes it easier to script, is called *tshark*. Wireshark is available for Windows, Linux, and macOS platforms. It is open source and free to use but does exist as a commercial version as well. Wireshark can be used on both wired and wireless networks. For wireless networks, however, it requires a network card that has been put into monitor or promiscuous mode so that it can capture all wireless traffic on a network. For wired traffic, the machine serving as the host running Wireshark must be able to capture all traffic on a segment, including the ability to span a switch for switched traffic.

Wireshark uses a capture format called a PCAP (for *packet capture*) file. Note that this is a binary file and not a text-based (such as a CSV format) file. Wireshark can read files from other packet capture tools as well, such as tcpdump, discussed next. Note that packet captures contain huge volumes of data and can grow in size quickly, so organizations that perform a lot of packet captures must have a lot of space to store them. They can also be very unwieldy to analyze in large sizes.

Because of the volume of traffic that can be captured even during a short capture session through Wireshark, it can be overwhelming to try to sort through all the different protocols and IP addresses that flow through a capture. Wireshark can provide display filters that an analyst can use to narrow down the types of traffic captured and analyzed. Filters can be used to narrow down traffic based on the source or destination IP address, port, protocol, or any one of dozens of other characteristics.

NOTE Wireshark, as well as other packet capture tools, can capture traffic that occurs at all levels of the TCP/IP and OSI models, regardless of the layer.

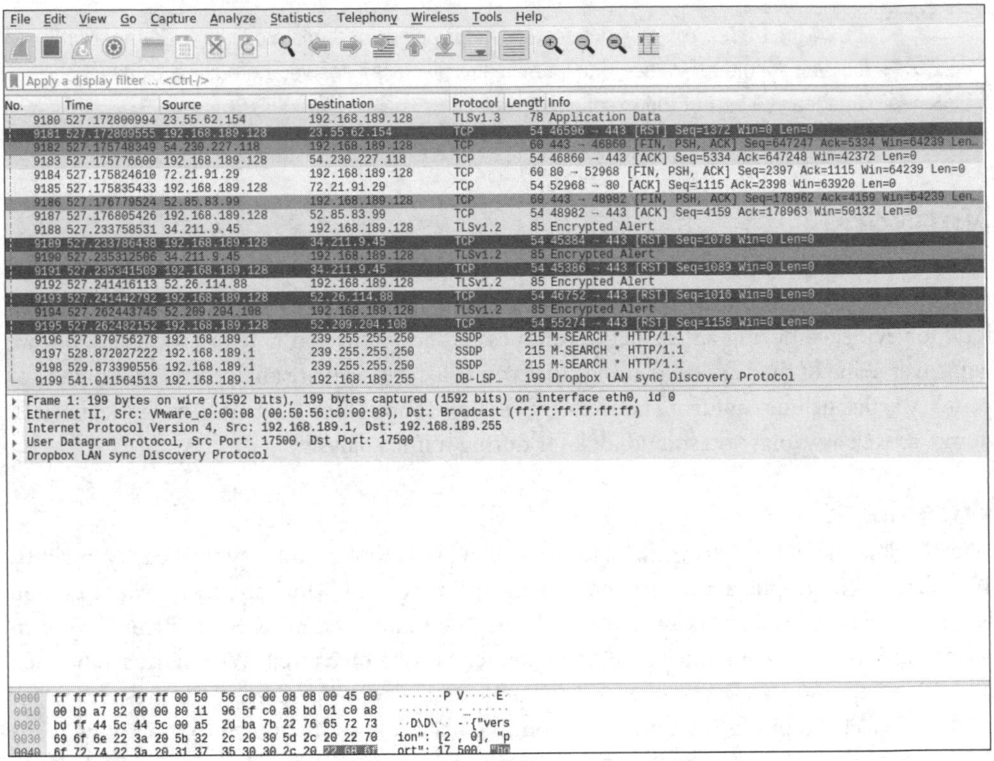

FIGURE 4.4-2 A Wireshark capture

Wireshark has a useful feature that allows you to look at TCP traffic, so you can follow its flow back and forth between devices. This feature is called *TCP streams* and can be very useful for both security and troubleshooting purposes. Using this feature, you can determine how traffic originated from a particular host and how it was received by the destination host, as well as the different traffic "conversations" both hosts engaged in during their communications session.

Like most of other network security programs, Wireshark cannot read or decrypt any captured encrypted traffic without being able to break the encryption. If an organization has the right infrastructure set up, this may sometimes be achieved through Secure Sockets Layer (SSL) or Transport Layer Security (TLS) inspection, but typically before the traffic is flowed through Wireshark. Most other types of encrypted traffic can be captured and stored but not interpreted by Wireshark.

Figure 4.4-2 shows an active capture from Wireshark.

tcpdump

tcpdump is a packet capture utility built into most Linux distributions and can also be found in some macOS and Windows ports. tcpdump essentially monitors all network traffic and sends it to a file or allows an operator to monitor it in real time on the screen. It is primarily used

```
File  Actions  Edit  View  Help                    Capturing from eth0
root@kali:/home/bobby# tcpdump
tcpdump: verbose output suppressed, use -v or -vv for full protocol decode
listening on eth0, link-type EN10MB (Ethernet), capture size 262144 bytes
20:12:42.228602 IP 192.168.189.1.17500 > 192.168.189.255.17500: UDP, length 157
20:12:42.230620 IP 192.168.189.128.40835 > 192.168.189.2.domain: 142+ PTR? 255.189.168.192.in-addr.
arpa. (46)
20:12:42.232961 IP 192.168.189.2.domain > 192.168.189.128.40835: 142 NXDomain 0/0/0 (46)
20:12:42.233160 IP 192.168.189.128.35195 > 192.168.189.2.domain: 52548+ PTR? 1.189.168.192.in-addr.
arpa. (44)
20:12:42.235933 IP 192.168.189.2.domain > 192.168.189.128.35195: 52548 NXDomain 0/0/0 (44)
20:12:42.236326 IP 192.168.189.128.51206 > 192.168.189.2.domain: 57542+ PTR? 2.189.168.192.in-addr.
arpa. (44)
20:12:42.238150 IP 192.168.189.2.domain > 192.168.189.128.51206: 57542 NXDomain 0/0/0 (44)
20:12:42.238314 IP 192.168.189.128.59596 > 192.168.189.2.domain: 42083+ PTR? 128.189.168.192.in-add
r.arpa. (46)
20:12:42.240171 IP 192.168.189.2.domain > 192.168.189.128.59596: 42083 NXDomain 0/0/0 (46)
20:12:47.404391 ARP, Request who-has 192.168.189.2 tell 192.168.189.128, length 28
20:12:47.404591 ARP, Reply 192.168.189.2 is-at 00:50:56:f7:2a:b5 (oui Unknown), length 46
20:12:47.279166 IP 192.168.189.1.17500 > 192.168.189.255.17500: UDP, length 157
20:13:27.751874 IP 192.168.189.1.59928 > 239.255.255.250.1900: UDP, length 173
20:13:27.752096 IP 192.168.189.128.35063 > 192.168.189.2.domain: 12902+ PTR? 250.255.255.239.in-addr.arpa. (46)
20:13:27.763632 ARP, Request who-has 192.168.189.128 tell 192.168.189.2, length 46
20:13:27.763650 ARP, Reply 192.168.189.128 is-at 00:0c:29:de:98:94 (oui Unknown), length 28
20:13:27.763794 IP 192.168.189.2.domain > 192.168.189.128.35063: 12902 NXDomain 0/1/0 (103)
20:13:28.752789 IP 192.168.189.1.59928 > 239.255.255.250.1900: UDP, length 173
20:13:29.754172 IP 192.168.189.1.59928 > 239.255.255.250.1900: UDP, length 173
20:13:30.755469 IP 192.168.189.1.59928 > 239.255.255.250.1900: UDP, length 173
```

FIGURE 4.4-3   tcpdump in action

at the command line. Because it cannot display and filter as elegantly as Wireshark, it's more useful as a capture tool rather than an analysis tool. Its output can be imported into a variety of packet analysis tools, including Wireshark. Because it is a command-line tool with a plethora of options, it's very useful in scripts that require very specific capture filters.

Figure 4.4-3 gives an example of a TCP dump in progress.

 EXAM TIP   You will not be required to know all the different options and switches for either Wireshark or tcpdump, but you should be able to understand when it might be appropriate to use either one and what the features are of both.

Endpoint Forensics Considerations

Endpoint or host forensics is a critical part of an incident investigation. Keep in mind that an incident doesn't only mean that an external malicious attacker has attacked the network. It can also mean that a malicious or complacent insider has performed actions on the host to steal or destroy data, or even simply to violate a policy (surfing to forbidden websites, for example). In any case, there will be plenty of forensic artifacts on endpoints that you must make every effort to obtain. You'll need specialized software and equipment in most cases, but you must also use good sound judgment and experience developed from your career as a cybersecurity analyst.

There are two key places you will obtain forensic evidence from: First, any permanent storage media that has been attached to the computer, such as the hard disk, CD/DVD/Blu-ray discs, USB drive, external drives, SD cards, and so on. Remember that not only are you looking for ordinary files, but you're also looking for file fragments from potentially deleted files, slack or free space on media, registry settings, running processes, and so on. Second, the other key source is from the volatile memory on the device, typically RAM. You will need specialized acquisition software, and in some cases hardware, to acquire evidence artifacts from either of these two sources.

Disk

For this discussion, we'll talk about hard disks in general, but understand that we also mean any type of permanent storage media, such as USB drives, SD cards, optical media, and so on. Most are fairly standard in how you would acquire forensic data from them.

To acquire forensic evidence from a media, you should go into an investigation with an understanding of the different types of media you might encounter, even older types, such as ZIP disks or even floppies. You also need to understand how file systems work, their characteristics, methods of indexing and accessing data, cluster and sector sizes, and so on. These will all vary based on the age and type of media. You need to know these things because they will help you use the right method to acquire the data and later analyze it.

As we discuss later in "Data Acquisition," you can use other software or hardware to acquire data from media. Software requires the use of a host with an operating system on it and is generally less efficient than hardware acquisition. However, software enables you to instantly preview potential forensic artifacts. Whether you use hardware or software, you must take special care not to contaminate the original media. By contamination, we mean to allow it to be written in any manner since this will disturb the integrity of the evidence (this topics is also discussed a little bit later in the module). The goal is to make a forensically sound exact duplicate of the media, capturing the state of it upon seizure, so that it will not be changed in any manner. This is important because if the evidence has been changed, it may not hold up in a courtroom or investigation since the argument could be made that evidence was changed to slant the guilt or innocence determination of a suspect. Your analysis of the evidence should be made on a forensically sound copy, meaning that it is an exact duplicate, right down to deleted files, rather than just a basic copy of all intact files on the media.

During the process of collecting evidence from media, you should take pictures of the media as well as record critical information about it, such as its type, manufacturer, make, model, serial number, capacity, and even information about the device from which it was seized. Chain of custody is of critical importance during this part of the investigation. Media can be at risk of exposure to static electricity, thus inadvertently destroying the data on it and rendering it unusable for the investigation. That's why you must take special precautions to protect sensitive media by using electrostatic bags, for example, and limiting the physical handling of the media.

Memory

Memory forensics is very similar to the actions performed on permanent storage media, with one powerful exception: memory, typically in the form of RAM, is volatile. In other words, power is required to maintain any data in memory. As soon as power is removed from the device, the contents of RAM are typically lost. There are, of course, exceptions to this, but for our discussion, you should assume that the contents of RAM could easily be lost if not acquired quickly and properly.

Unlike static files that you might acquire from permit storage media, the contents of RAM are important because they contain ephemeral data elements that will be lost when power is removed from the device. These include current system state information like running processes and services, unencrypted passwords stored in RAM, network connections and their state, and decrypted file information. Many types of malware only run in active memory rather than as a file executed from a file system. Additionally, some indicators of compromise of an attack only reside in running memory.

Normally, permanent storage media is acquired after power has been removed and it can be safely transported to a hardware or software device used to obtain the digital evidence. Because of the volatile nature of RAM, the contents of memory must be acquired using what is known as a "live" response. This means that the power for the host cannot be removed (shut down). The host is still online and processing during the memory acquisition process. There are risks involved with this because the contents of RAM are constantly changing, and even the acquisition process itself could change those contents. For the most part, this is an acceptable risk, as long as you document the process you used to acquire memory and record its state.

A cybersecurity analyst can use specialized utilities and hardware to obtain the contents of memory. Some of them treat memory as if it is a form of media; that is, the utility may "view" RAM as a device drive letter. Remember to document any software or hardware you use to acquire memory contents, as well as the detailed process you used since you are likely to change some of those contents. You have to be able to show that any changes made were part of the acquisition process and did not substantially affect the integrity of those contents.

 EXAM TIP Endpoint forensics involves collecting potential artifacts from two critical elements: permanent storage media, such as a hard disk, and volatile memory, such as RAM.

Mobile Forensics

Mobile devices are ubiquitous in today's business world. Smartphones, tablets, laptops, cameras, and other types of devices have both permanent and volatile storage. Mobile devices provide a wealth of forensic information, including e-mail artifacts, web surfing history, social media access, location information, and so on. Each of these devices also has a unique operating systems as well as unique forensic requirements.

Here are some considerations for mobile device forensics:

- Mobile devices require specialized software and tools to access the different manufacturers' storage methods, memory, and operating systems. These are often device or manufacturer dependent, can be quite expensive, and require a deeper level of knowledge and experience to use.

- Avoid turning off mobile devices for the same reason as other types of hosts: you may lose valuable volatile data from memory contents that cannot be recovered.

- Mobile devices may still communicate with other hosts and networks through wireless or cellular means. Since you should not arbitrarily turn them off, you must shield them from communicating with the outside world via a special container known as a Faraday bag. Because this container can block RF radiation and communications to and from the device, it can prevent the device from communicating with a potential suspect who may send remote commands to the device to wipe it, destroying valuable evidence.

- Mobile devices tend to have location data that should be preserved, in the form of GPS and other types of data. You should make an effort to preserve this data so the different locations where the device has been can be tracked.

- Privacy should be considered in cases where you have seized a device that is owned by the suspect instead of the organization but may have data from both. You might not be authorized to forensically examine a personal device and should check with your legal department before attempting to do so.

 EXAM TIP Two important considerations for mobile forensics are requirements for specialized software and hardware tools and the concern for privacy with personal mobile devices versus corporately owned mobile devices.

Cloud Forensics

Increasingly, organizations are moving resources to the "cloud." Although there is a lot of marketing hype and mystique about cloud structures, remember that a cloud is nothing more than a hosted data center to which an organization can transfer some of its resources and infrastructure. Third parties, called cloud providers, maintain the infrastructure of the data center in the form of high-speed network connections, robust servers, and other high-performance hardware needed to service their customers. Operating systems and applications specifically designed for cloud implementations are also included in this infrastructure. The different resources and services an organization can move to the cloud include applications, platforms, infrastructure, and even security, each with different variations of implementation.

Since cloud services are essentially "shared" models, the organization may find it difficult to conduct a full incident response or forensic investigation in conjunction with the cloud provider. Remember that the cloud provider owns a good majority of the resources used in the infrastructure, including the physical and virtual servers and the network devices. An organization can perform incident response and forensics on its on-premises devices, but may not be able to gather the information it needs from a cloud provider to complete the investigation. That's why contracts and agreements with providers are so critical.

Most of the larger cloud service providers, such as Amazon, Google, and Microsoft, have incident response teams and forensic technicians that can manage their part of an investigation.

However, information sharing between those entities and the organization can be limited to only what the provider wants to share, since it may consider this information confidential or even proprietary. The service provider contract should be written in such a manner that enables information sharing, at minimum, or access to the cloud provider's infrastructure, at best, to perform a full forensic investigation. With the larger providers, access to their infrastructure is going to be very rare. With smaller providers, you may be able to work language into the contract that allows your organization's personnel to have access to very specific parts of cloud provider infrastructure for very limited forensic data collection and response. It is more much likely that the cloud provider will gather the necessary forensic evidence it feels is appropriate and turn that over to your organization. Understand that this will all be at the provider's discretion, however. Keep in mind that if an attack has affected your cloud service provider, then the provider is naturally interested in keeping details of the attack closely held, such as any vulnerability information that may have caused the attack as well as any data loss resulting from it. The provider may not be able to conduct a forensic investigation until its incident response is complete and has restored any services that are down. Remember that you are likely not the provider's only customer. However, incident response and forensics considerations must be spelled out in any contract with a cloud provider, regardless of the types of services provided.

 EXAM TIP The key to cloud forensics is the agreement or contract between the organization and the cloud service provider. What the responsibilities and permitted actions are for both parties must be spelled out exactly.

Virtualization Forensics

In this modern era of technological wonders, hosts, servers, other unique devices, and even entire networks can be virtualized. Virtualization uses the resources of a host for a virtual machine, including virtualized operating systems and even virtualized applications. For the most part, virtualized devices and networks are stored as static files on a file system when they are not in use, but when they are active, they interact with their environment just as a physical system would. Because of this, they can be acquired and forensically analyzed just as any other physical host or device might. Although there are various types of files that different virtualization vendors create as proprietary formats, examples of the files a virtual machine might use include the following:

- **VMX** Configuration file
- **VMDK** Stores the virtual hard drive for the machine
- **NVRAM** Nonvolatile RAM; stores static virtual machine BIOS information
- **VMEM** For storage of volatile memory contents

Again, these are just examples of files a virtual host might use. The actual files used depends on the different types of virtualization technologies and hypervisors (discussed shortly) the organization is using.

Virtualization in the infrastructure, if properly implemented, can be quite helpful to a cybersecurity analyst performing forensic analysis on virtualized devices. In addition to all the benefits that virtualization offers the organization and its infrastructure, it offers several useful features during a forensic analysis. For example, when a virtual device is shut down gracefully, it can store all the contents of its running memory as a preserved file on disk, so when it is powered back up, it still has the same volatile contents in memory. A virtualized host can be transferred, through its files, to another media for analysis in a laboratory. It can also be easily forensically duplicated and powered back up for analysis, regardless of hardware needs. Finally, if damage is done to a virtual machine, it can be easily re-created from a backup.

Virtualization requires the use of a *hypervisor* to manage the resources on the physical machine and their use by a virtual machine. Remember that a hypervisor comes in two flavors: Type I and Type II. A Type I hypervisor, also called a *bare-metal* hypervisor, is a minimal operating system installed on a resource-heavy machine (multiple CPUs, a great deal of RAM, massive hard disk space, and so on) that does nothing more than creating and managing virtual machines. A Type II hypervisor, on the other hand, is merely a software application that is used on a host with an existing operating system to manage resources and to interact with a guest operating system, the virtual machine itself. Examples of popular Type I hypervisors include VMware's ESX and Microsoft's Hyper-V. Well-known Type II hypervisors include VirtualBox from Oracle and VMware's Workstation and Player products.

Most of the same forensic tools used for physical systems can be used with a virtual system. The same types of tools can be used to acquire disk images and memory contents as well as analyze them. There are some specialized tools, however, that are designed to work outside of the confines of the guest operating system. These are designed to locate artifacts that may be part of the hypervisor for the virtualized environment, as many specific attacks target the hypervisor itself in a virtualized infrastructure.

 EXAM TIP Understand the differences between the types of hypervisors and how forensics may be performed on virtual machines, using primarily the same types of tools and techniques.

Key Forensic Procedures

As we discussed earlier, there is key foundational knowledge you should have as part of your incident response training. A basic understanding of evidentiary procedures and legal processes is necessary. The actual hands-on experience of acquiring data and analyzing it is also needed. You will get this training and knowledge from incident response training courses as well as experience during an exercise or actual event, but there are also other key pieces of knowledge you need to have that we will cover here as part of the exam objectives. They include the concepts of a legal hold, evidence hashing, carving, and data acquisition. Understand that by no means is this a complete list of the skills you'll need for an actual incident response when it comes to forensic acquisition and analysis of evidence. If you're going to be a part of an actual incident response team, you'll have to move to the next level after the CySA+ exam to gain the necessary knowledge and skills to fully respond to an incident.

Legal Hold

Legal hold means that the organization must simply make every effort to preserve all sources of evidence for an incident, including any media on the host and the contents of RAM, log files from network security devices, and so on. This makes sense, but many organizations believe that after an incident, as part of their cleanup, they can simply reimage a drive or archive the logs. Additionally, during normal business operations, computers are retired, hard drives are destroyed, and the organization goes on with its daily business life. A legal hold is necessary to make sure that special efforts are made to preserve any evidence that may be relevant to the incident.

As part of the legal hold process, all evidence obtained from a host, as well as the host itself, its media, and any network-related evidence (even sometimes the network devices themselves), must be kept secured in storage, and access to the same must be controlled. All evidence items must be inventoried, and all documentation regarding evidence, such as evidence inventory, chain of custody, and so on, must be turned over to the legal department. Normally it is a legal department that will direct you to place evidence items under legal hold in the first place, pending an investigation.

Legal hold can sometimes have a serious impact on the organization, in that while evidence items, including devices, are on hold, they cannot be used as part of the infrastructure. For a single host, this isn't necessarily a large impact; you can simply issue out another machine to a user. If it involves several hosts, that could impact the ability of the organization to provide computers for its users. If the device is a network device, which may have to be removed from the network and stored under a legal hold directive, that could have a serious impact on the organization that must replace that device or re-architect the network around it. Another issue with legal hold is that in the event of a law enforcement investigation and subsequent court case, the hold could last for weeks or months, effectively making it so that the organization has to maintain secure storage for that evidence for an indefinite period, and not have that asset as part of its usable inventory.

Hashing

Remember from your cryptography studies that one of the primary uses of hashing is to prove the integrity of a file. Hashes are essentially fingerprints of a file, not the entire file itself, that are derived by a mathematical algorithm. A hashing algorithm computes a hash from a file that should be the same every time that hash is computed. If it is different at any point, then it can be assumed that the file has lost its integrity because it has been modified in some manner. Popular hashing algorithms include MD5 and the SHA family of algorithms.

Hashing is also used to determine the integrity of evidence. Digital files acquired as part of the evidence collection process are hashed when they are collected, and those hashes are recorded. During the process of analyzing, storing, and transferring evidence, those hashes are regenerated frequently at different points of the investigation to ensure that the evidence's integrity has been maintained and that those files have not been changed. You could hash a single file, a compressed set of files, an encrypted file, or even an entire disk image. Whatever hashes are generated with your hashing algorithm and utility must be the same every time that hash is generated, or it can be assumed that the evidence has been contaminated and is no longer useful for the investigation.

Data Acquisition

Data acquisition is a critical part of computer forensics. During this activity, digital evidence artifacts, such as files, are "acquired" for analysis. Assuming you have seized the physical evidence, such as a hard drive, the next step is to forensically duplicate the evidence. The reason for this is that you do not want to perform any analysis on the original evidence since you will likely change its integrity the second you plug the drive into a computer or access any of the files on the media.

Forensic duplication is called *imaging*, and you can image a hard drive or other media device through software or hardware. Software imaging requires a special program or utility that can take a bit-by-bit exact copy of the evidence item and forensically duplicate it in every way. This includes not only the obvious viewable files in the directories on the evidence item but also deleted files, file fragments, slack space (unused or unallocated space on the drive), directory structures, and file tables. Using software to image a drive requires that the imaging program reside on an operating system; unfortunately, during normal operations, data may be inadvertently written to the original media. That's where a *write blocker* comes in. Write blockers are devices that sit between the original media and the connection to the host you are using to image the media. Write blockers should be attached to the original media through a cable to prevent data from being sent to the media. Any data sent to the media, even if it is only control data that an operating system sends during routine activities, could change the original media.

Hardware imaging performs the same function but generally does not require software or a dedicated computer host. It performs its functions based on firmware embedded in the hardware imager, often offering a very limited user menu that performs specific functions. Hardware imaging is much faster and generally considered more efficient. It can also be safer in that most hardware imagers have built-in write blockers that can prevent any data from being written to the original media, ensuring that its integrity is not changed.

When you're imaging media, it's a best practice to make two forensically exact copies. The first copy is used to create other copies. It is never analyzed, and neither is the original media. A secondary copy is used to perform the actual analysis. If, for some reason, the analysis disturbs the integrity of the evidence on the secondary copy, or mistakes are made during that analysis, you can always make a copy of the first copy without going back to the original evidence and risking the possibility of changing its integrity.

NOTE   Data can be acquired not only from fixed media such as a hard disk or USB stick but also from the contents of RAM. For data acquisition, RAM can be treated just like fixed media, as long as its contents are forensically acquired and duplicated while there is active power to the host. This must occur during a live response before the host is powered down or removed from the crime scene.

Data Carving

Data carving is the science (and some would say, the art) of locating and pulling usable files or artifacts out of a large, otherwise unintelligible block of data. This would include deleted files, file remnants in slack space, and so on. Data carving is part of the forensic analysis process and is performed after an evidence item, such as a hard disk, is imaged. Remember that you do not want to perform any analysis on the evidence item itself; usually, this is done on a secondary copy. That way, if the evidence is disturbed in any way from its original integrity in a way that can't be justified, you still have the original copy of the evidence item to duplicate and start over with again.

There many different file-carving utilities out there; some of them are standalone utilities and some are part of a larger forensic analysis suite, such as those that come with the popular commercial forensic application Forensic Toolkit (FTK) by Access Data, or Encase, another widely used commercial forensic suite. You can also find native command-line tools in specific Linux distributions such as Kali. What all these have in common is that they allow you to locate characteristics of specific files, such as file headers and the logical beginning- and end-of-file segments. For example, if a suspect has deleted a JPEG file, as long as that file has not been overwritten during the normal course of file operations on the hard drive, a forensic analyst might be able to find the file, or even a partial segment of the file, based on the characteristics of a standard JPEG file. Most of this data is viewed in a hexadecimal format and translated into something that the analyst can visually see and use. The data-carving part comes from knowing where a file begins and ends in the massive unorganized block of data that may be remaining in the file system. Once an artifact has been located, it can usually be "carved out" with the carving utility and restored as a viable forensic artifact that can be used as evidence during an investigation.

EXAM TIP   Understand the different key forensic procedures from the objectives that you must know for the exam. They include legal hold, hashing, data acquisition, and data carving.

REVIEW

Objective 4.4: Given a scenario, utilize basic digital forensics techniques   In this module, we discussed a very important part of incidents response, which is forensic investigations and their processes and procedures. Although basic forensic knowledge and skills can be used to initially preserve and protect evidence, you must have more advanced knowledge and experience to become a full-fledged and qualified forensic investigator. The foundational knowledge you should have includes an understanding of evidence preservation and how a chain of custody works, and you should be able to perform basic forensic procedures, such as securing the crime scene.

Network forensics is very important because almost all data travels over the network at some point. The key to network forensics is observing and collecting network traffic for further analysis. There are several utilities you can use for this, including Wireshark and tcpdump, which are both indispensable utilities in traffic capture and analysis.

Endpoint or host device forensics is concerned with collecting forensic artifacts from either permanent storage or active memory. You must be careful not to disturb the integrity of either source of evidence. Memory must be acquired using live response techniques, typically with specialized hardware or software.

We also took a look at mobile forensics, which involves acquiring and analyzing data from a wide variety of mobile devices, including smartphones, tablets, laptops, and cameras. The key to mobile device forensics is that you will typically use specialized hardware and software tools due to the wide variety of manufacturers, operating systems, file systems, and hardware. You should also be careful to consider privacy with personally owned devices.

You learned about cloud forensics considerations, in that because the cloud is a shared infrastructure, you won't always have the ability to perform a full incident response or forensic investigation. Cloud forensics relies heavily on how the cloud provider contract is written, which will delineate the different responsibilities and allowed actions of both the organization and the cloud service provider.

Virtualization is a technology that requires special attention during incident response and forensics. Virtual machines run as guests on a host operating system, which can be a Type I or Type II hypervisor, depending on the scalability and hardware resources of the host server. For the most part, the same tools and techniques used to perform forensic analysis on physical networks and hosts are used with virtual devices, with the exception that some specialized tools might be needed to look at specifically designed hypervisor attacks. Virtual machines make forensic processes and procedures much easier, simply because virtual devices are typically stored as static files when not in use and can be quickly backed up, reconstituted, or forensically duplicated.

Finally, we discussed some key forensic procedures you need to know for the exam. These are not all the forensic procedures you will need to know to conduct an actual forensic analysis on data recovered from incident response, but they will help you on the exam and in the field. You learned about the process of a legal hold, where an organization is directed by the legal department to securely store and preserve potential digital evidence during an investigation. We discussed the concept of hashing and how it relates to maintaining the integrity of forensic evidence by producing a digital fingerprint of both files and images that can tell you if the integrity of those artifacts has been violated or disturbed. Data acquisition is the process of gathering digital evidence by imaging media as well as analyzing it. Data carving is a process where a forensic analyst attempts to "carve out" digital artifacts from a mass of unorganized or unrecognizable data, sometimes from the media's free or slack space.

4.4 QUESTIONS

1. Pete is a newly trained incident response team member. On his second day on the job, he receives an e-mail from a manager informing him that he must seize the computer of an employee the manager suspects is surfing for pornography on the Internet. Pete goes to the office of the employee, who is not present, and begins to secure the scene. What is the first thing Pete should do before he touches anything in the office?

   A. Power the machine down.

   B. Photograph the layout of the equipment and its location.

   C. Immediately acquire the contents of RAM.

   D. Pull the hard drive for imaging.

2. Greg is a cybersecurity analyst for a small company. He has received complaints from different users that the network is extremely slow, and several users have also experienced malware attacks in the past couple of days. Which of the following actions should Greg take to determine the cause of the network performance problems?

   A. Run a packet capture program and look for malware indicators of compromise in network traffic.

   B. Acquire an image of the hard drive contents from each user reporting problems.

   C. Shut down and reboot the switches that the users complaining about network performance are plugged into.

   D. Acquire the memory contents from the hosts of the users experiencing network performance issues.

3. You are a cybersecurity analyst for a medium-sized company that has recently moved some of its application services to the cloud. The organization experiences a potential hacking incident, where compromised office productivity software used from the cloud arbitrarily accessed sensitive data across the network using privileged accounts. You want to perform a forensic analysis of the application servers the cloud provider uses. Which of the following may impede that forensic analysis?

   A. The remoteness of the cloud provider's data center

   B. Lack of privileges and permissions to access the application servers

   C. Vague incident response roles and responsibilities in the service agreement

   D. Pushback from the cloud provider's cyber response team

4. Dawn is performing a forensic analysis on an image acquired from a large hard drive. Some of the data has been corrupted, and it's also obvious that the user attempted to delete several files several weeks ago, which may or may not be intact. What should Dawn do to collect as many intact forensic artifacts from the drive image as possible?

   A. Use a utility that can forensically wipe the drive before analysis.

   B. Use forensic application software to reconstruct the damaged or deleted files.

   C. Use a file-carving utility to locate potential files and fragments to determine their file headers and beginning and end segments.

   D. Use a hashing utility to generate a hash for each damaged and deleted file on the drive image.

4.4 ANSWERS

1. **B** Before touching anything, Pete should photograph the area so that he will have a record of where all the equipment was located and how it was set up.

2. **A** Since there are network performance issues so soon after the malware attacks, Greg should run a packet capture program and look for malware indicators of compromise in the network traffic.

3. **C** Even if there is pushback from the cloud provider's response team, if the contract is written appropriately, you will eventually get access to the application servers to perform a forensic examination, likely with the assistance of the provider's response team.

4. **C** For this scenario, Dawn should use a file-carving utility to collect as many intact file artifacts as possible.

Compliance and Assessment

DOMAIN
5.0

Domain Objectives

- **5.1** Understand the importance of data privacy and protection.

- **5.2** Given a scenario, apply security concepts in support of organizational risk mitigation.

- **5.3** Explain the importance of frameworks, policies, procedures, and controls.

Objective 5.1 **Understand the importance of data privacy and protection**

Privacy vs. Security

Privacy is the desire to control and the act of controlling information about *you*—information you consider personal. Privacy is concerned with keeping your personal information confidential and only allowing whomever you choose to access it and use it for whatever purposes you deem fit. Privacy information includes, but is not limited to, name, address, Social Security number (SSN) or social insurance number (SIN), gender identity, date of birth, age, race, medical information, financial information, and so on. Note that some of these data elements are defined and protected by laws and regulations, but this largely depends on the country you reside in. In other countries, different data elements of your personal information are protected, or not protected, depending on the laws and regulations of those respective countries. In certain countries governed by the General Data Privacy Regulation (GDPR), this also includes information about your religious or political beliefs, sexual orientation, and so on.

Whereas privacy is the belief that you should be able to control your information and use it or disseminate it as you see fit, *security* consists of the measures that go into protecting that information, as well as other types of information. While they are not the same thing, they are closely related. Measures that are used as part of security controls can also be applied to privacy. In this module, we're going to discuss different aspects of security and privacy and how they relate to each other.

What Is Privacy Data?

Most laws recognize specific pieces of data as *privacy data*. In the United States, this includes name, address, driver's license number, SSN, and any other data that can be specifically linked to an individual. This type of data is called *personally identifiable information*, or PII. Data related to an individual's medical conditions or care is referred to as *healthcare data* and is governed in the U.S. by the Health Information Portability and Accountability Act, or HIPAA. These are the two primary privacy data types recognized in the United States. However, other individual data, such as financial data, is also considered personal. Often you will find financial data intermixed with privacy or healthcare data, depending on how those data combinations are used. For example, if an individual is seeking medical treatment, there may be both medical data and financial data in their medical records because they must pay for any medical procedures performed, and those procedures are billed at certain rates. Individuals provide payment methods that are stored with their medical records. This could include credit card numbers or even insurance information.

Nontechnical Controls

You may remember from previous chapters, or even from the Security+ exam, that you have different types of controls. Remember that a control is a security measure implemented to protect data. Nontechnical controls typically come in the form of managerial (also called administrative) or operational controls, which are primarily policies and procedures. Those are the key controls that establish *what* you must do when it comes to protecting privacy information. The technical controls, discussed later on in the module, dictate a large part of the methods for *how* you must protect privacy information (in other words, the implementation of policies and procedures). We will discuss several nontechnical and technical controls throughout this module.

Data Types

The words *data* and *information* are frequently used interchangeably. Technically, data is an individual fact or piece of knowledge. Only when the context is given to multiple pieces of data is it referred to as information. Information is cohesive data. For our discussion, however, we will use these terms interchangeably as well. Keep in mind that even a small, singular piece of data can be sensitive, such as a Social Security number or phone number. When combined with other pieces of data, such as a name and address, this becomes privacy information. Data (and information) types are essentially descriptive categorizations of data; in other words, we are defining what the data relates to. As examples, data types could include privacy data, healthcare data, financial data, company proprietary data, legal data, market data, and so on. Data is defined as a type based on context and relevance. While there is no overarching formal taxonomy of data types, the National Institute of Standards and Technology (NIST) Special Publication (SP) 800-60, Volume II, "Guide for Mapping Types of Information and Information Systems to Security Categories," provides an excellent catalog that describes many different data types. Figure 5.1-1 shows an excerpt from SP 800-60 and examples of the various information types it describes.

Confidentiality

Remember from your earlier studies in cybersecurity that confidentiality is one of the three goals of security. Confidentiality essentially means that we want to keep information accessible only to authorized personnel and prevent access to those who were not authorized. Confidentiality can be ensured using strict access controls such as authentication, permissions, and encryption. Confidentiality can be applied to privacy because only those entities that have a valid need and authorization to access privacy information should be able to do so.

Data Sovereignty

Data sovereignty is a simple concept that means that any privacy data that is generated, stored, processed, transmitted, or received in a particular country is governed by the laws of that country. This actually can become complicated, as we'll see when we discuss the legal aspects of data privacy, since the laws of one country can extend into another country if the data relating to the citizens of one country is transferred or flows into another country.

Table C-1: Management and Support Lines of Business and Information Types[2]

Services Delivery Support Information

C.2.1 Controls and Oversight	**C.2.4 Internal Risk Management & Mitigation**	**C.2.8 General Government**
Corrective Action (Policy/Regulation)		Central Fiscal Operations
Program Evaluation	Contingency Planning	Legislative Functions
Program Monitoring	Continuity of Operations	Executive Functions
C.2.2 Regulatory Development	Service Recovery	Central Property Management
Policy & Guidance Development	**C.2.5 Revenue Collection**	Central Personnel Management
Public Comment Tracking	Debt Collection	Taxation Management
Regulatory Creation	User Fee Collection	Central Records & Statistics
Rule Publication	Federal Asset Sales	Management
C.2.3 Planning & Budgeting	**C.2.6 Public Affairs**	*Income Information*
Budget Formulation	Customer Services	*Personal Identity and Authentication*
Capital Planning	Official Information Dissemination	*Entitlement Event Information*
Enterprise Achitecture	Product Outreach	*Representative Payee Information*
Strategic Planning	Public Relations	*General Information*
Budget Execution	**C.2.7 Legislative Relations**	
Workforce Planning	Legislation Tracking	
Management Improvement	Legislation Testimony	
Budgeting & Performance Integration	Proposal Development	
Tax & Fiscal Policy	Congressional Liaison Operations	

FIGURE 5.1-1 Information types from NIST SP 800-60

Legal Requirements

Legal requirements for the protection of privacy data can be very complex. They also vary between countries, and indeed, even U.S. states. Legal requirements are based on the data type but also on the different laws and regulations governing that data. Since we are discussing privacy data in particular, it's useful to examine the legal requirements for the protection of privacy data in the United States and internationally.

Laws and regulations often include requirements to appoint personnel in the organization who are legally accountable for the protection of privacy data stored or processed by the organization. These roles may include a data privacy officer and other individuals designated to protect privacy data (called data processors and controllers in some regulations). Normally, organizations can face legal liability, including lawsuits, fines, or even criminal charges, if they do not protect privacy data as required by law.

In addition to appointing specific roles required by law, there are some elements of privacy policy that should be addressed (at least in the United States) to meet regulatory requirements, particularly in the financial and medical areas. These include the following:

- Legal authority to collect privacy information
- Purposes that collected information will be used for
- Data integrity and quality
- Minimization and retention of personal information
- Data breach reporting
- Audit of privacy systems and data access

- Privacy risk management
- Rights of individuals to be notified regarding data collection and use policies, to correct erroneous information, and for remedies against the collectors of such information

Some of these elements of privacy policy will be discussed later in the module.

Keep in mind that although many countries have privacy laws, privacy is not treated the same all over the world; there is no consistency between countries in law or practice. International privacy issues include the following:

- "Right to privacy" is different across the world.
- Use of encryption to protect private data is limited or prohibited in certain countries.
- Some data elements are not considered private in some countries.
- Search and seizure of potentially private data varies from country to country.

Here are just a few examples of laws designed to protect privacy data in their respective countries:

- **U.S. Constitution 4th Amendment**   Protects privacy to the extent that unauthorized search and seizure by government entities and law enforcement is prohibited
- **U.S. Privacy Act of 1974**   Protects PII used by the U.S. government
- **California Consumer Privacy Act (CCPA)**   Protects California citizens against privacy data misuse and gives more control to the individual
- **European Union's General Data Protection Regulation**   Protects individual EU citizens' ("data subjects") personal data
- **The Data Privacy Act of 2012 (Philippines)**
- **Article 13 of the Swiss Federal Constitution (Switzerland)**
- **Personal Information Protection and Electronic Documents Act, or PIPEDA (Canada)**

Some countries do not have specific laws or regulations that cover data privacy, but it is included as part of other laws. These countries include some Middle Eastern countries (Kingdom of Saudi Arabia, Kuwait, United Arab Emirates, Bahrain, and Oman) and the People's Republic of China (PRC).

Data Classification

As mentioned earlier, most of the nontechnical controls are policies and procedures. One of the most important policies you can have in your organization is *data classification*. Data classification determines to what level systems and data must be protected. This is based upon data sensitivity or criticality. How critical is the data to your organization? How sensitive is it? What regulations dictate the level of protection? You don't want to put a lot of time, money, and effort into protecting what would normally be ordinary public information or even company information that's of little importance, such as the details of the company picnic. That data would be

| TABLE 5.1-1 | Examples of Data Sensitivity and Protection Levels in a Policy |

Data Type	Protection Level	Explanation
Public	1	The lowest level. Data contains no sensitive information, requires no encryption during transmission or storage, and is releasable to the public after appropriate approvals.
Company Sensitive	3	Somewhat sensitive. Data could include company financial information, administrative processes, network diagrams, and so on. The organization should implement reasonable access controls, including restricted access to protect data from inadvertent public release.
Proprietary	4	Very sensitive. Data could include formulas or production methods that directly affect the company's ability to compete in the market. The organization should implement restrictive access controls, including role-based access and encryption.
Privacy	5	The highest level. Data could contain sensitive individual privacy information whose unauthorized release could subject the organization to legal liability. Requires highly restrictive access controls limited to only those personnel who have a need to know; requires role-based access and encryption during transmission and storage.

considered a lower sensitivity level and would not warrant very much protection. Other types of data, such as privacy data and other more sensitive data types, warrant a lot more protection. The organization should create a data classification policy to formally determine which data types are considered sensitive data and which are not as well as the level of protection those types require. Examples of the data types and protection levels you might find in a data classification policy are shown in Table 5.1-1.

Data Ownership

While, ultimately, the organization is the owner of data that is generated, stored, and processed on its systems, there may be a designated data owner by policy, such as the vice president of human resources, who is in charge of ensuring that all privacy data is protected at the appropriate level. The data owner is responsible for setting access controls, including determining who has access to it, ensuring that legal requirements are met, and determining who is accountable in the event the data is disclosed, lost, or modified through unauthorized means. While the data owner is ultimately responsible and accountable, typically, on a routine daily basis, a data custodian is directly responsible for implementing the security measures to protect data. The data owner makes decisions regarding the data, and the data custodian implements those decisions.

Data Retention and Retention Standards

Data policies should also include data retention standards. By and large, the more data an organization retains, the more difficult it is to maintain that data securely. Organizations retain data for various business reasons, including to develop and market products and services. Data is generated as a result of business processes and transactions. This could include financial data, product or process data, marketing data, and so on. This might even include privacy-related data. Sometimes data is retained for historic or continuity reasons. Depending on the data type, organizations also are required to retain certain data to meet legal or regulatory requirements. When organizations are required by regulation to retain data, typically requirements are imposed on the organization to retain it under certain conditions, such as for a specified length of time and under what protection conditions. These conditions could include the following:

- The requirement to keep the data for a specified time under the law
- The requirement to destroy data after that specified time in a specific manner
- The requirement to store the data in a secure manner
- Strict access controls for retained data

Data Minimization

Data minimization is a concept that essentially means that an organization will only collect the minimum necessary amount and types of data to fulfill its purpose of providing specific services to an individual. For example, during a credit application, a company might collect relevant financial data from an individual. However, there would be no reason the company would collect nonfinancial information, beyond superficial contact information. It could not, for instance, collect information on an individual's health. This would be collecting information beyond what is necessary to provide the individual financial services related to the credit application.

Purpose Limitation

Declaring a limitation of purpose serves to prevent an organization from using data, particularly privacy data, outside of an agreed-upon reason. For example, healthcare organizations may collect privacy data from individuals to support their medical care. Their privacy policy may state that they are allowed to exchange this data only with authorized healthcare providers or business associates and that it may be used to provide diagnosis, treatment, and billing for any healthcare the patient receives. The healthcare organization would be limited to only those particular uses of that data and could not use it outside of the stated purposes, such as for marketing.

Nondisclosure Agreement (NDA)

A nondisclosure agreement (NDA) is a legally binding contract between entities, such as two organizations, or even individuals and organizations. Essentially, one party owns or controls certain data, and the other party is agreeing that in exchange for access to that data, they will keep it secure and confidential under the conditions specified in the agreement. For example, an individual who begins work for an organization may be required to legally declare via an NDA that they will keep any data they encounter during the normal course of their work confidential, and not to release it to unauthorized personnel. An NDA could specify certain data types or could generally cover any data that an entity might be exposed to, including company-sensitive, proprietary, or even health and privacy data. NDAs can specify a certain period, or they can be written to last indefinitely. The NDA clearly states the individual's responsibilities in protecting that data.

Technical Controls

Nontechnical controls are the typical managerial or programmatic controls designed to establish requirements and policy; technical controls are typically the implementation mechanisms for those policies. If the policy says that a certain data type is confidential and must be protected at a certain level, then there should be technical controls to make that happen. You may see technical controls in the form of encryption, data loss prevention (DLP) devices, databases that perform data masking and deidentification, and so on. We're not going to go down to the heavy technical level in describing these technologies, but you should be familiar with technical controls and how they work to support data privacy and protection.

Access Controls

Access controls are security controls designed to manage who can read or write to sensitive data. Access controls help ensure the confidentiality of private information using the following elements:

- **Identification** An individual or entity asserting who they are via a username, smartcard, or another mechanism.
- **Strong authentication** Technologies that verify that an individual or entity is who they say they are.
- **Authorization** Once an individual is authenticated, they must be authorized to access specific data and perform certain actions with it.
- **Accountability** Holding an individual accountable for their actions with regard to data access.
- **Auditing** The ability to record and verify that an individual performed specific actions on a set of data, such as reading it, deleting it, or modifying it.
- **Nonrepudiation** The inability of an individual to claim that they did not access or perform specific actions on data.

Examples of technical access controls that support these elements are object permissions, role-based access, encryption mechanisms, multifactor authentication mechanisms, and audit logs.

Encryption

The technical aspects of encryption have been discussed elsewhere in this book, so here we will discuss the particular aspects of how encryption supports data privacy. As you should remember, encryption is used to transform data from human- and machine-readable format into a form that is not easily read by either to keep it confidential. Programs use encryption algorithms and keys to encrypt data during transmission from system to system, as well as to protect it while it is being stored. The same programs decrypt (or make readable) data so that it can be used by people and computers for its intended purpose.

Protected data classes, such as personal, healthcare, and financial data, use encryption to control access to that data. Only those people or machines that can access the appropriate algorithms and keys should be able to access the data once it has been encrypted.

Cross-Reference

Encryption is discussed in more technical detail in Objective 2.1.

Data Loss Prevention (DLP)

Data loss prevention is a group of technologies and practices designed to prevent sensitive data from leaving the confines of an organization's network, including via e-mail, file-sharing services, or even unauthorized removable media attached to hosts. DLP can be added as a separate module for certain network security appliances, as part of host-based security, and through data labeling. Data labeling enables specially configured network security devices and policies to flag sensitive data as it attempts to leave the network and prevent it from doing so. DLP is particularly essential in environments where there is a great deal of personal or medical information, such as hospitals. DLP starts with written data-sensitivity policies, of course, that are then translated using DLP software integrated with network devices and host-based security. The software tags data with labels corresponding to the data sensitivity policy and can also be integrated with a variety of other line-of-business applications and databases.

Data Masking

There are several techniques used to prevent unauthorized disclosure of privacy information. However, there are instances where authorized users need to access some portions of information that could be considered private, but not necessarily all the information. For example, a database could contain information on a person that includes identifying information as well as medical or financial information. A technician could require access to certain portions of the individual's record, but not all of it. One technique for limiting the information available to unauthorized personnel is *masking*. Data masking is simply the obfuscation of parts of certain data elements, such as a Social Security number. An administrative assistant might require access to the last four digits of a person's SSN to identify that person within the context of their work, but they don't need access to the entire SSN. In this case, the first five digits might be masked out with asterisks or blanks.

Other techniques of limiting the amount of information an otherwise authorized person might have available to them include allowing them to access only certain data fields in a record, restricting what they visually see from query results of a record, restricted user interfaces, and so on. In databases that contain a great deal of information, database designers often implement security controls that include role-based access so that a person in one role would not necessarily have access to all the information in a database that someone in another role would.

Deidentification

Mass amounts of data are often used for different but valid purposes than was originally intended; it could be required for use in historical or trend analysis, for research purposes, and so on. For example, suppose a medical researcher needs to examine 1000 records relating to cases of influenza to determine possible common factors for females over the age of 65. Most of the time, limitations on the use of such data would prevent this from happening, since the data could be linked to an individual and violate their privacy rights. This can be solved through the process of *deidentification*. Deidentification is a method used to remove any data that could indicate the identity of an individual from a record.

Normally deidentification involves removing names and other specific identifiers, such as geographical location more detailed than the name of the state or province, birth date (month and day), e-mail address, telephone number, and so on. The specific data that is removed may depend on the type of data and regulations that cover the data. For instance, HIPAA regulations require that data be deidentified using one of two methods: Safe Harbor, which requires removal of predetermined identifying data elements such as name, date of birth, and geographic location, and Expert Determination, which requires a recognized expert in the field of statistical analysis with a healthcare background who decides on the types of data to remove to reduce the risk of identifying an individual in a large dataset. The deidentification method can also be used by technologies to limit the amount of data that a normal authorized user can access for routine job functions, to prevent an individual from being identified through that data.

Tokenization

Tokenization is another method used to protect certain data elements from disclosure. Instead of displaying a user's credit card number, for instance, a unique hash value generated on the number might be substituted in a field displayed to an authorized user of that data. This number would remain unique and could still be used to identify the record, while the actual value (in this case, the credit card number) cannot be derived from it.

Digital Rights Management (DRM)

Digital rights management as a technology has been used for several years to prevent pirating of digital media files. Digital files can be tagged with specific information that can protect them in several ways, including limiting how many times or for how long they can be accessed, preventing their copying or alteration, and alerting the copyright holder if an attempt is made to illegally access or copy the files. The same technologies are also useful in protecting private data. DRM can work in a couple different ways. One way is through the use of *containment*, where the digital file is encrypted and can only be accessed by those with the correct encryption key, personal identification number (PIN), or password. More often than not, this is a function of the program and encryption mechanism being used to access the file, which can also be configured to securely authorize users for file access. A second approach is through *marking*, which means that there is a watermark (discussed in the upcoming section), flag, or electronic tag embedded in the file. In the case of an electronic tag, a signal can be sent to a reading device that the file is digitally restricted for access and can prevent opening or copying the file.

A potential drawback to the general use of DRM that's of interest to privacy advocates is the fear that it could be used to take advantage of a user's private information by changing the level of data access based on the user's information. For instance, a copyright holder could conceivably charge more money or restrict access to an otherwise available file based on a user's private data, such as their age, race, and so on.

Watermarking

Watermarking is a form of digital rights management where a file is visually or electronically marked to identify that it came from a certain location or is the property of a particular person or organization. Digital watermarking could be used to identify the source of a digital file containing privacy information, such as a hospital, clinic, or bank. Digital watermarking can also be used to embed a digital signature or other identifying information in a file to ensure its integrity.

Geographic Access Requirements

Yet another measure used to protect privacy information is the use of geographic restrictions on specific data. This can take many forms. First, it's not uncommon to restrict data to only certain hosts or IP addresses within an organization or network. This is relatively easy to do through technical access controls. To access a patient's medical record, for example, a health-care technician may be required to log in from a specific host or at a specific location, such as a records department. The problem with this is that in this increasingly mobile world we live in, doctors and other professionals frequently walk around to visit patients, or even travel to different departments or clinics that are geographically separated, using laptops, tablets, and even mobile phones. When privacy data is accessed on mobile devices, using technical controls such as network access control, encryption for data both in transit and in storage, strong authentication, the use of virtual private networks, and so on, is critical.

The second aspect of geographic access restrictions could even be the access of data between different countries. There could be nontechnical and technical controls designed and implemented to prevent access to data from an entity in one country on an individual in another country. In instances where an authorized entity must access data on an individual in another country, they must meet strict requirements, among them legal requirements imposed by regulations such as the GDPR. Such regulations impose additional requirements on the access and use of private data by entities in a different country.

This restriction not only applies to privacy or other sensitive data; it can be seen in other forms of information as well. For example, access to content protected under DRM, such as movies or other recorded media, is often restricted to certain countries. This practice is known as *geo-blocking*, and it limits the geographic locations in which digital content is available. The technologies used to implement this process are the same as those that help protect private information and include watermarking as well as implementing technology to prevent information from being accessed on untrusted devices, especially in certain countries or locations.

REVIEW

Objective 5.1: Understand the importance of data privacy and protection   In this module, we discussed the importance of protecting privacy data. Privacy data could cover a variety of personal data, including personally identifying information, medical data, and financial data. Privacy is the desire to keep and the act of keeping personal data from unauthorized access and controlling how that data is used. Security is the measures taken to protect privacy data. Security uses both nontechnical and technical controls.

Nontechnical controls include the creation and enforcement of policies protecting data at a level determined by its type and sensitivity level. Not all data is protected at the same level; it depends on the sensitivity of the data as well as any legal requirements to protect the data. Legal requirements for data protection vary across the world, as do the different data elements that define privacy data. A data classification or sensitivity policy should be developed and enforced by the organization. A data owner is someone who is legally held responsible and accountable for data protection. Organizational governance, including laws, regulations, and internal policies, should determine data retention policies and standards. Certain types of data are required to be retained for certain periods and using specified protection levels. Data sovereignty refers to subjecting any data created or processed in a specific country to the laws of that country. Data minimization refers to the practice of collecting and using only the minimum amount of privacy data required to fulfill a specific purpose. Organizations are often legally required to use data only for the purposes specified in their data protection policies or the law, and any use outside of those specified purposes is illegal. Nondisclosure agreements are typically required when employees or other entities access protected data, such as privacy information. These agreements state that employees or other entities may not disclose protected data to unauthorized personnel.

Technical controls include a variety of access controls designed to prevent unauthorized access to data. Access controls can include strong authentication, authorization through permissions, and encryption. Encryption is used to protect data both in transit and at rest. Data loss prevention technologies are designed to keep protected data from leaving the confines of an organization or its infrastructure. Data masking is a technique used to visibly hide certain data elements to prevent unauthorized disclosure. Deidentification removes certain data elements to prevent privacy data from being linked to an individual.

Tokenization removes sensitive data elements but replaces them with a hash generated from the data element. Digital rights management is used to protect privacy data by tagging or watermarking the data to determine its source, integrity, and identifying information as well as to prevent it from being copied in an unauthorized manner. Sometimes data is restricted to only being accessible from specific geographic locations, including specified hosts, IP addresses, or even countries.

5.1 QUESTIONS

1. You're a cybersecurity analyst who works for a large financial organization based in the U.S. You are working in a customer information database and must determine which data elements in the database are considered privacy information. Which of the following would be considered privacy data?

    A. A bank balance not connected to a customer name or account number

    B. A Social Security number and account number

    C. A check number and check amount

    D. A transaction identification number

2. Which of the following data types would be considered for the highest protection levels according to an organization's data sensitivity policy?

    A. Employee financial information

    B. Information regarding the company's financial portfolio available publicly via the Securities and Exchange Commission

    C. Marketing data for a new product

    D. HR information regarding the employee appraisal process

3. You are formulating a privacy policy and desire to include policy elements that will protect your company in the event of a regulatory audit. The primary information your company collects that would be considered sensitive is PII. Which of the following policy elements would you need to include in your policy to ensure that you are authorized to request this information from individuals per law or regulation?

    A. Breach notification

    B. Purpose limitation

    C. Nondisclosure agreement

    D. Legal authority to collect

4. Which of the following is the practice of replacing sensitive data elements with a unique number to identify them in the record without disclosing sensitive data?

    A. Tokenization

    B. Watermarking

    C. Deidentification

    D. Data masking

5. Tina is a cybersecurity analyst who works at Acme Industries. She is in charge of protecting sensitive employee information regarding financial compensation. She has been directed to configure access to that information such that only certain workstations in the human resources and accounting departments can be used to log in to the database containing sensitive employee financial data. Which of the following technical controls is Tina implementing to protect sensitive data?

   A. Strong authentication

   B. Data masking

   C. Geographic access controls

   D. DLP

5.1 ANSWERS

1. **B**   A Social Security number connected to an account number could be used to identify an individual.

2. **A**   Employee financial data should be considered at the highest sensitivity level and would warrant a protection level based on its sensitivity.

3. **D**   If you are authorized by law or regulation to collect personal data, you should include a statement in the policy regarding your legal authority to collect this data.

4. **A**   Tokenization is the practice of replacing sensitive data elements with a unique value to identify the data element in the record yet prevent disclosure of sensitive information.

5. **C**   Geographic access restrictions can help limit access to sensitive data by requiring that data only be accessed from certain hosts, IP addresses, or locations.

Objective 5.2 ## Given a scenario, apply security concepts in support of organizational risk mitigation

Organizational Risk Mitigation

This far in your career, you've probably already encountered the terms *risk, risk management, risk mitigation,* and other risk-related concepts. Risk management is one of the core principles of security. You can't make everything completely secure without turning all the network hosts off, unplugging them, and putting them in storage. Security is a balance between protection, functionality, and resources. While you can never completely remove risk, if you've ever heard anyone say that you can't have too much security, they're wrong. You *can* have too much security to the extent that you can't afford it, that the amount of resources you spend on it exceeds the value of the asset, or that the system becomes so limited in functionality that you can't use it. The trick is finding the balance.

Resources limit exactly how much time, money, labor, and effort you can put into securing systems and data. You also have to balance the value of the asset, such as information or systems, with what you are spending on protection for those assets. Functionality is typically inversely proportional to the amount of security you apply to a system: the more you secure it, the less functional it usually becomes. You don't want to apply so much protection to a system that it can't be used because that would negate the whole reason for having it in the first place. You will have to trade off on all three of those items to get the right balance of each. Essentially, this is what risk management is all about.

In this module, we're going to discuss trying to achieve the right amount of security, functionality, and resource management using risk management principles and mitigating risk whenever possible. We're going to discuss critical concepts such as business impact analysis, risk identification and calculation, risk factors, risk prioritization, assessing risk, training and exercises, and supply chain risk management. Understand that you're not going to become an expert on risk management or mitigation from this module, but we're going to cover the objectives and critical concepts that you need to understand for the exam.

Business Impact Analysis (BIA)

Organizations should ask themselves a few fundamental questions before embarking on any type of risk management process:

- What assets do we have?
- Why are they important to us?
- What business processes do they support?
- What would we do if we lost those assets or the business processes they support?
- What would be our priority for restoring assets and processes in the event of a disaster?

If an organization does not have the answers to these questions, then it can't figure out what assets it needs to protect and how much protection to give those assets. The organization won't be able to allocate the resources necessary for that protection.

That's where a *business impact analysis* (BIA) comes in. A BIA should be the beginning of all of your risk management activities. So much in risk management, and even security implementation, depends on knowing what you have, why it's important to you, and how much you should protect it.

A BIA is a process whereby the organization inventories all of its assets and business processes, to determine which of those business processes are critical to continuing its mission and reaching its goals. It also determines how its assets support those business processes. Based on how important those business processes and, by extension, assets, are, it determines the criticality of those assets (in other words, how important they are to keeping the business going).

Let's define assets: an *asset* is anything of value to the organization. This could be tangible items, such as servers, workstations, network devices, data, software applications, equipment, facilities, time, and even people. To a large degree, you could assign a monetary value to each of these assets. You can determine how much these items cost initially, how much they would cost to replace, and how much business, in terms of revenue or profit, you would lose if you lost those assets. There are also intangible items that are of value to the organization. These are hard to place a monetary value on, but they still impact the overall business financial posture. Examples of intangible assets include reputation and consumer confidence. Losing either of these intangible assets would also create a significant *tangible* business impact.

Assets are important, and our concern with cybersecurity risk management is to protect those assets. But keep in mind that assets support something even more important: business processes. Business processes are the activities and functions we perform to fulfill our business mission and goals. Ultimately, business processes are the most important aspect of a business. The assets we protect simply support those processes. Business processes can be critical to an organization being productive, competitive in the market, and surviving.

As part of our BIA, we need to identify assets and business processes and determine their criticality to the overall mission of the business. That is the central purpose of performing a BIA. We're going to discuss the critical activities of conducting a BIA in the upcoming sections.

Business Process Identification and Prioritization

Some business processes are critical to the survival of the organization. Depending on what type of business we are engaged in, these might include manufacturing, production, service management, and knowledge management, and so on. Each of these processes can be broken down or decomposed into many different subprocesses. Some of these processes may be critical to the overall business activity, and some less so. There are also support processes that can be critical to the business, including financial accounting, human resources management, research, marketing, and so on. Again, each of these business processes can be decomposed into smaller level processes, activities, and tasks.

The organization should break down its business processes into as much detail as possible, based on the function they perform and how they contribute to the overall business mission—whether that mission is manufacturing products or providing services. The organization should list these processes and describe them in terms of activity and criticality to the overall mission. Some business processes may be so vital to the business that to lose them even for a day would be devastating. Other business processes may be routine or noncritical, such that losing them for a week might be inconvenient but would not seriously degrade the ability of the business to operate. The organization should determine all of these business processes in as much detail as possible. It should also categorize these processes according to criticality or priority. In the event of a disaster, such as a tornado or terrorist attack, which business processes might the organization lose? Which ones could it restore, and what would the restoration priority be to get the business back into operation again?

These questions relate very much to business continuity and disaster recovery plans. Without a BIA, developing any kind of business continuity plan or disaster recovery plan would be impossible. A BIA is critical to those two plans, as well as the overall risk management strategy and operations of the organization.

Asset Identification

Asset identification is also an important step in conducting a BIA. You should inventory all assets, both tangible and intangible in the organization, again to as much detail as possible. Aside from the inventory, you should also map those assets to business processes. In conducting your inventory and mapping it to business processes, you should answer the following questions:

- Which business processes are supported by which assets?
- Are multiple processes supported by a particular asset?
- How critical is that asset to that process?

Asset identification is not only about counting servers or hosts. You should be determining and documenting details such as original cost, replacement costs, operating costs, how much revenue that asset generates beyond its cost to maintain, how much of it you could lose and still support the business process, and so on. You'll find that the value of an asset is frequently much more than its original or replacement costs. A critical server that cost $5000 but directly supports a business process that generates $10,000 in revenue per month is much more valuable than what it would cost to replace if it failed or were destroyed in a disaster.

Criticality Determination

Determining the criticality of both assets and business processes is where the BIA becomes valuable. Separately, knowing your business processes and what assets you have is important, but determining how critical both are to the business is the focus of a BIA. Once you determine how critical they are, you can determine your priorities for spending money and other resources on them for protection. Critical assets such as servers and sensitive data require more protection than other assets deemed lower in importance. This is the beginning of how you determine what you're going to spend on security. You want to spend the right amount of money on security to protect your assets, such that your expenditures don't exceed the costs of what the assets are worth to the business.

Another important result of a BIA is that you determine which assets and business processes have priority for restoration during a disaster or other incident. Both business continuity and disaster recovery plans are directly informed by the results of a BIA.

Risk management also benefits from a BIA, in that you now know what your critical assets are, so you can focus on determining what the risks are to those assets. You can focus your efforts on determining threats, vulnerabilities, impact to the business in the event a threat is realized, and what the likelihood of that threat materializing is. This information will also help you determine how much protection an asset needs versus the resources you can afford to put toward that protection. Again, that is what risk management is all about.

 EXAM TIP You should understand the fundamentals of a business impact analysis and how it relates to risk management, business continuity, and disaster recovery. You should also understand the basic steps in performing a BIA.

Risk Identification Process

Risk relates to the potential level of harm an asset could incur if something detrimental happened to it. That level of harm could be minor, or it could be major and destroy the asset or at least render the asset completely unusable. The level of harm to an asset is called the *impact*. Risk assessment and analysis activities are directly concerned with determining what that level of impact to an asset is, based on variables that affect the level of impact.

Just as identifying business processes and their supporting assets is critical to a business impact analysis, identifying risks is the critical first step in managing them. Several components of risk must be examined. Individually, they are not a risk, but they are part of it. Aggregated together, they present an amount of risk to an asset that you can determine to a degree. Once that risk is identified, you can determine the best way to mitigate or manage it.

Several factors feed into impact. You have to understand the factors that are attempting to harm the asset, such as a threat, and what weaknesses are in an asset that could cause it to come to harm, called vulnerabilities. We'll discuss threats, vulnerabilities, and other risk factors in the upcoming sections so we can determine how to identify potential risks.

Threats

Threats are negative events that affect assets or the organization. Threats are initiated by *threat actors* (sometimes also called *threat agents* or *threat sources*). Threats affect assets by exploiting vulnerabilities (weaknesses) in those assets. Threats can be classified as intentional or accidental, natural or man-made, internal or external, and various other classifications. For example, a natural threat event could be a tornado that strikes an organization's data center. A man-made threat would be a terrorist attack or a hacking attack on an organization's network. Keep in mind that the terms *threat, threat actor,* and *threat vector* are sometimes used interchangeably, but they are not the same thing. A threat vector is a method that a threat will use to exploit a weakness in an asset or the organization. To give a complete example, a hacker is a threat actor, the threat event is an attack on an organization's firewall, a threat vector might be sending large volumes of malicious network traffic to the firewall, and a weakness in the firewall that does not account for large volumes of malicious network track is what the threat takes advantage of. These weaknesses are called vulnerabilities and are discussed next.

Vulnerabilities

Vulnerabilities are weaknesses. Typically we look at vulnerabilities as weaknesses in an asset, but they can also be weaknesses in the effectiveness of security controls, or the lack of security controls altogether, weaknesses in a security program, or even weaknesses in organizational management. Vulnerabilities by themselves are not of concern unless there is a threat that can take advantage of or exploit a vulnerability. Threats and vulnerabilities should be paired whenever possible; if there is theoretically no threat that can exploit a vulnerability, then there is also, theoretically, no vulnerability. The same applies to threats; if you determine that a threat exists, but there is not a vulnerability that it can take advantage of, then the threat does not apply to your asset or organization.

Threat and vulnerability pairings are critical in determining the "what" and "how" that can happen to an asset. If you perform a vulnerability assessment on the asset and the organization, you can determine which threats apply to those vulnerabilities and, in turn, determine mitigations for those vulnerabilities, based on those threats.

Risk Calculation

Threats and vulnerabilities are what create the conditions for risk. However, they are not *directly* the factors that we use to calculate risk. Those are the probability and magnitude of impact. Risk cannot be defined in terms of only threats and vulnerabilities; if those threats never materialize, or if those vulnerabilities aren't sufficiently weak, and we have no other context, then we can't determine risk. We can only determine risk by calculating the probability of a negative event, and how serious that event would be if it occurred. We're going to discuss the two key factors in risk calculation—probability and magnitude of impact—next.

Probability

Although technically not the same thing, the terms *probability* and *likelihood* are used interchangeably within the risk community and in the various risk methodologies used to manage cybersecurity risk. We will follow suit here; for our discussions in this book, probability and likelihood are the same.

Both terms refer to the chances (expressed numerically or qualitatively) that a threat will exploit a vulnerability, causing a defined impact in an asset or the organization. Note that we are not saying that the likelihood of a threat occurring is a risk, because that probability could be 100 percent, but if the threat exploits a vulnerability and it creates very little impact on the asset, the risk could be negligible. You must frame risk in the context of all four of these elements (threat, vulnerability, likelihood, and impact) to completely define risk. Using only one or two of these factors does not adequately define risk.

Likelihood affects risk in that the higher the likelihood of a negative event (a threat) affecting an asset is, the higher the risk. Conversely, the lower the likelihood of a threat exploiting a vulnerability that affects an asset, the lower the risk. Likelihood can be expressed as a statistical calculation, provided you have the quantitative data to make that calculation, or it can be expressed subjectively or qualitatively, on a scale of very low to very high.

Magnitude of Impact

Impact is considered the level of harm to the asset or the organization should a threat exploit a vulnerability in the asset or organization. In other words, impact could be said to be how bad it would be if the threat happened. Impact can be measured in all sorts of ways. It depends on the context the organization wishes to frame it in. You can measure impact in terms of loss of revenue if a business process were interrupted due to the loss of an asset; you could also describe impact in terms of the cost of replacing or repairing that asset if it were lost or damaged. Just as likelihood can also be described in qualitative terms, such as very low to very high, impact can be described this way if it is difficult to place a monetary value on the impact. An example of this would be expressing the magnitude of impact to an intangible asset, such as damage to consumer confidence. The loss of customer confidence in the organization would be a very high impact in most cases. And it would directly affect the company financially, causing measurable impacts to revenue, profit, and so on. Most organizations tend to describe the magnitude of impact in multiple terms and aggregate it in some quantifiable fashion.

Impact is related to risk in that the higher the potential magnitude of impact, the higher the risk. And conversely, the lower the potential magnitude of impact, the lower the risk. Note the word *potential* in those statements. Once an impact has occurred because something has harmed an asset or the organization, it's no longer risk. It's called a fact. Remember that risk is related to the *possibility* that something bad will happen, so we have to describe risk in terms of *potential* impact.

Communication of Risk Factors

As mentioned earlier, risk is a product of both likelihood and impact. Threats and vulnerabilities cause the conditions for risk to be present, but the actual measurement of risk is solely based on likelihood and impact. Of course, there are mathematical methods of determining a more precise context of threats, as there are methods of determining how serious a vulnerability is in a system. But we only use likelihood and impact to truly determine risk. The relationships between threats, vulnerabilities, likelihood, impact, and risk can be expressed as follows:

- Threat actors cause or initiate threat events.
- Threats exploit vulnerabilities in an asset or the organization.
- Risk is a product of likelihood and impact.
- The higher the likelihood or impact, the higher the risk.
- The lower the likelihood or impact, the lower the risk.
- Likelihood and impact together inform risk, but likelihood and impact are generally independent of each other.

EXAM TIP Remember that risk is the product of likelihood and impact, based on a threat exploiting a vulnerability in an asset.

In addition to the threat, vulnerability, likelihood, and impact elements of risk, there are other influencing factors, called *risk factors,* that can affect each of these elements in different ways. In addition to communicating the different elements of risk, and the risk itself, you should also communicate to different stakeholders the various risk factors that could affect the risk to an asset or the organization. First, a discussion of risk factors is in order. Risk factors influence threats and vulnerabilities, in that they can make it easier for a threat to exploit a vulnerability, or increase the level of weakness of a vulnerability in an asset or organization. Risk factors can be both external to the organization and internal to it.

External Risk Factors

External risk factors could include the economy, market conditions, the political or social climate, and the regulatory environment. Most external risk factors cannot be controlled by the organization. They can only be managed in the context of reacting when those factors affect risks to their assets. Any of these factors could influence risk; for example, the economy could affect the organization's revenue stream, which could in turn determine how much money is allocated for cybersecurity management. The regulatory environment could change and require the organization to change the way it protects certain sensitive data. The organization cannot control external risk factors; it can only react to them. The key to reducing risk influence by external factors is to react to it in a way that reduces the effect of those risk factors on the organization.

Internal Risk Factors

Internal risk factors are those that are inherent to the organization. These are factors that the organization can control to a certain degree. These factors include budget, organizational factors (such as organizational climate, risk tolerance and appetite, and how the organization is structured), personnel qualification, network architecture and design, and anything else that is within the control of the organization to change or improve should it negatively influence risk. For example, the organizational budget could control how much money is allocated for security controls. How the organization is structured internally could affect the independence of the cybersecurity department from other departments that would wield influence over how they do their job. Both of these two internal risk factors could negatively impact the cybersecurity program within the organization, but both of these could be easily changed if necessary to reduce risk.

EXAM TIP External risk factors cannot be controlled by the organization; only the organization's response to them can be managed. Internal factors can be adjusted to reduce the negative influence they cause on risk.

Risk Prioritization

Once risks to assets and the entire organization have been determined, they are often aggregated for analysis. Individual risk scenarios, however, must be prioritized for mitigation or remediation. Remember that there are four basic ways to deal with risk:

- **Mitigation or remediation**   The organization attempts to reduce risk by the application of controls.
- **Avoidance**   The organization avoids activities that result in risk.
- **Transference**   The organization transfers risk to a third party, such as a service provider or insurance provider.
- **Acceptance**   The organization accepts what it considers to be minimal or residual risk that can no longer be dealt with through any of the other risk response methods.

Prioritizing risks for response is a factor of two things: the cost of the risk response and the criticality of the asset incurring the risk. The cost of responding to the risk involves how much it would cost to improve or implement security controls that would significantly reduce the risk to an acceptable level. This is where we go back to the business impact assessment—remember that it tells us how critical our business processes and the assets that support them are. We should expect to spend money and other resources on security controls that would reduce risk affecting critical processes and assets. The less critical a process or asset is, the fewer resources we might be willing to spend to reduce the risk associated with those processes and assets. It is typically not very cost-effective to spend a great deal on security measures to protect assets that are of low value. This is where we must prioritize risk response measures and ensure that only our most critical processes and assets are getting the bulk of our commitment of resources. For those assets that are not deemed as critical, the organization may elect to spend less on risk reduction measures, or simply accept the risk if it is already at a minimal level. The organization could also elect to outsource or transfer risk by purchasing insurance on its assets, thus reducing the impact if a catastrophic event were to happen to those assets, degrading its ability to operate its business. In any case, prioritizing risk is a function of management that relies heavily on accurate, complete risk assessments as well as a business impact assessment.

EXAM TIP   Risk prioritization depends on two factors: the cost of risk response and the criticality of the asset or business process it supports.

Security Controls

Security controls are the measures taken to protect an asset and reduce the risk to that asset. Examples of security controls might be strong authentication technologies, the use of encryption, well-formulated policies and procedures, and physical controls such as gates, guards, and CCTVs. Security controls should be implemented to meet a particular risk scenario, such as a concrete threat and vulnerability pairing. While some security controls might span and protect the entire organization, other security controls might be specific to a critical asset or process. Prioritizing resources for security controls involves understanding the value and criticality of those processes and assets.

Core foundations of cybersecurity state that there are essentially three types of controls: managerial (sometimes referred to as *administrative* controls), technical controls (also called *logical* controls), and physical or operational controls. Note that there is some disagreement on the categorization and definition of physical and operational controls. Typically, most security foundations state that physical controls are the measures put in place to physically protect an organization and its facilities, equipment, and personnel. These might include gates, guards, fencing, hidden cameras, alarms, barriers, and locked doors. Operational controls are often defined as the actual procedures in place that personnel must abide by to secure organizational assets. However, you will often see these two types of controls intermixed together, so it's important to look for context when either of these types of controls are described. The following further describes these three control types:

- **Managerial controls**   Administrative policies, procedures, plans, and management programs
- **Technical controls**   Technologies such as NAC, encryption, firewalls, IDS, anti-malware software, and so on
- **Physical/operational controls**   Fences, alarms, armed guards, gates, CCTVs, access badges, and so on

EXAM TIP   Although most classical security theories define control types as managerial, technical, and physical, the CompTIA CySA+ objectives state that the three control types are managerial, technical, and operational. You should be familiar with the definitions for all three of those control types.

In addition to the three control types, there are also control functions. These functions define how controls are categorized according to what they do. The following six different control functions are generally recognized in basic security theory:

- **Deterrent**   Controls designed to deter individuals from performing malicious acts or violations of policy
- **Preventative**   Controls designed to prevent malicious acts or violations of policy
- **Detective**   Controls implemented to detect malicious acts or violations of policy
- **Compensating**   Controls implemented to temporarily strengthen or supplement faulty or weak controls
- **Corrective**   Controls implemented to correct a condition resulting in higher risk
- **Recovery**   Controls used to recover systems, data, and equipment after an incident or disaster

If you are thinking that some security controls might span multiple functions, you are correct. For example, you could consider system backups a recovery control because they could help you recover a system after it has been attacked and compromised. You could also consider system backups a preventative control, so that data is not lost if something catastrophic were to happen to the server. Many controls span different areas, and it depends on the context you're referring to as to which function the control is fulfilling in a given instance.

Note that the difference between a deterrent and preventative control is that a deterrent control must be known for it to deter personnel from performing a malicious act or violating security policy. A preventative control, on the other hand, does not have to be known to perform the same function. Consider that a CCTV is a deterrent control if a would-be intruder is aware that it is there and decides not to break into a controlled access area because of it. A firewall rule, on the other hand, may not be known by someone who attempts to access a prohibited site, but it will still prevent them from doing so. In the examples given, a CCTV is not a preventative control because the would-be intruder may decide to still break into the controlled access area despite being seen by the camera. The firewall rule is not a deterrent control because the user doesn't necessarily have to know about it for it to still work.

> **Cross-Reference**
>
> Controls are discussed more in detail in Objective 5.3.

Engineering Trade-Offs

Risk management is not about absolutes. Managing risk is an effort to reduce the likelihood of a negative event occurring or the impact to the organization if it does happen. Risk can never be eliminated; there will at least always be some small level of risk. Because managing risk is a balancing act between reducing risk and still maintaining security and functionality, while applying the right amount of resources, there will have to be trade-offs.

Trade-offs mean that you must strike a balance between the right amount of security, the right amount of functionality, and the right amount of resources. It also means that to strike that balance, you may have a trade-off in the requirements, design, architecture, or implementation of a system. For example, to maintain functionality with existing systems, you may have to compromise on designing or architecting a system with the very latest technologies during the system engineering process. The same is true for security. If you need to maintain compatibility with legacy systems, you may have to allow for less than state-of-the-art security technologies in your engineering processes. Risk management is extremely important during the engineering process. With each compromise or trade-off you make, you will have to assess the risk of that trade-off. If you decide to include older or legacy security technologies, such as encryption algorithms, for example, then you have to assess the risk of that decision. Is increasing the risk necessary to ensure functionality with older systems? Can older systems be upgraded? If not, are there mitigations you could put in place to reduce the risk of using older technologies? As you can see, in every aspect of managing information technology and security, you must account for risk, even in the systems engineering lifecycle.

Systems Assessment

Risk can be assessed at different levels of the organization. You can assess at the top-level management tier by assessing program management risk, such as the risks incurred from budgeting, policies, governance, compliance, organizational structure, and so on. You can also assess the middle tier of the organization, where you are assessing the risk of processes used across the organization, such as human resources processes, security processes, training, and so on. Most cybersecurity analysts, however, more often than not assess risk at a lower tier—the system level. For this discussion, assessing risk at the system level also means assessing network infrastructure risk, security controls, data flows and usage, and so on.

There are many different risk methodologies that discuss assessing system risk. A few of the major ones, such as OCTAVE, ISO/IEC, and NIST, are explained in the following sections.

OCTAVE

The U.S. Government, in conjunction with Carnegie Mellon University, developed the Operationally Critical Threat, Asset, and Vulnerability Evaluation (OCTAVE) methodology to help organizations identify, assess, and manage cybersecurity risk. OCTAVE has several iterations, and its methodology essentially consists of four phases, divided into eight total steps, as follows:

- Phase 1: Establish Drivers
  - Step 1: Establish risk management criteria
- Phase 2: Profile Assets
  - Step 2: Develop an information asset profile
  - Step 3: Identify information asset containers
- Phase 3: Identify Threats
  - Step 4: Identify areas for concern
  - Step 5: Identify threat scenarios
- Phase 4: Identify and Mitigate Risks
  - Step 6: Identify risks
  - Step 7: Analyze risks
  - Step 8: Select mitigation approach

OCTAVE requires that an organization identify its assets, its threats, and its risks before selecting a mitigation approach. While OCTAVE is not specific about identifying vulnerabilities, these are considered as part of Phase 3 Step 4: Identify areas of concern. Typically, likelihood is also considered in Phase 3, as part of the threat scenario, since likelihood may be factored in as the likelihood that a threat will exploit a vulnerability in a given scenario.

ISO/IEC Standards

The International Organization for Standardization/International Electrotechnical Commission (ISO/IEC) are two organizations engaged in developing and implementing international standards for engineering, information technology, and many other endeavors. In this discussion, we are concerned with their standards for risk management. Two standards in particular are of interest here:

- ISO/IEC 27005:2018, "Information technology — Security techniques — Information security risk management" covers information security risk assessment and treatment.
- ISO 31000:2018, "Risk management — Guidelines" describes general risk management and processes.

Both of these publications, along with other ISO/IEC 27000-series standards, provide for cybersecurity controls implementation and risk management. Organizations using this methodology are typically required to be assessed and certified by an independent assessor qualified in those standards.

NIST Risk Assessment Methodology

The National Institute of Standards and Technology (NIST) is a comprehensive risk management and assessment methodology that is used in the U.S. federal government but can also be employed by public and private organizations. The NIST risk assessment methodology is found in Special Publication (SP) 800-30 and consists of four primary steps, broken down into a total of nine activities, as follows:

- Step 1: Prepare for assessment
- Step 2: Conduct assessment
  - Identify threat sources and events
  - Identify vulnerabilities and predisposing conditions
  - Determine likelihood of occurrence
  - Determine magnitude of impact
  - Determine risk
- Step 3: Communicate results
- Step 4: Maintain assessment

Note that most of the aforementioned risk assessment methodologies provide steps for identifying the basic elements of risk as part of the assessment: threats, vulnerabilities, likelihood, and impact.

While all these different methods provide a framework for assessing risk, there are certain methods you should use to gain a complete picture of system risk:

- Interviews with system personnel (system, network, and security administrators)
- Documentation reviews (operating procedures, security documentation, architecture diagrams, and so on)
- Technical testing (that is, vulnerability assessments)
- System observations (actually observing security controls in operation on a system)

These methods used together can give a more complete picture of system vulnerabilities, and by extension system risk, than any of the individual methods would.

EXAM TIP   You will not be required to know the steps of any particular risk assessment methodology; they are described here to give you a context and understanding of how risk assessments are generally conducted.

Documented Compensating Controls

Very often we assess risk and discover there are security controls that are not functioning as effectively as they should or that have controls missing. Our first impulse is to go ahead and improve our controls, upgrade them, or implement new ones. That's not always possible, for various reasons. There can be organizational constraints, time sensitivity, system criticality, budget issues, and even governance or compliance issues that prevent us from using controls we deem as ideal for the situation. As part of our risk mitigation strategy, however, we may determine that we can implement compensating controls to reduce the risk associated with ineffective or missing controls. Compensating controls are those that are not the ones we would like to use but rather those we must "settle for" to quickly reduce risk. Ideally, compensating controls are temporary, until we can overcome the constraints preventing us from using better solutions.

For instance, suppose you are trying to reduce the risk from a legacy financial database that can only communicate using an older encryption algorithm. Because that's the only way it can communicate with your other line-of-business applications, and it is a critical database the organization cannot afford to upgrade for various reasons, all other applications on the network must "talk down" to that encryption level. What could you do to compensate for this risk? You could isolate that database and limit the applications it communicates with. You do this either logically or physically, placing it on a dedicated subnet via a VLAN and then restricting access to that VLAN from other devices. You can also encrypt its communications via a tunnel with a stronger algorithm, if possible (for example, using IPSec), by sending its communications through another intermediary device before they are sent to any hosts with which it communicates. None of these situations is ideal, of course, but they might help compensate for the inability of the database to encrypt its communications using a stronger algorithm.

When responding to risk, you want to use the best mitigations at your disposal, such as the strongest controls. But when you can't do that, due to the constraints we previously mentioned, you may have to use compensating controls that might not be ideal. When this happens, you must document the use of these controls. Using less-than-ideal controls should be something that's approved by senior management, once you have communicated the risks to them. There should be a strong, well-thought-out justification for using compensating controls, and there should be a path forward for eventually finding a solution to use stronger, more permanent controls. You should document any processes and procedures used, as well as any unique requirements for the compensating controls.

The reason for documenting these compensating controls is that you might have to justify them to an auditor, an inspector, a customer, a business partner, or a regulatory agency. Documenting a control shows that you have done your due diligence and care and have assessed the risk of using the control. You must be able to demonstrate that it reduces risk while taking into account constraints that prevent you from using ideal controls. These constraints could include budget or other resources, backward compatibility, system criticality, time sensitivity, and so on.

 EXAM TIP Remember that compensating controls should be temporary, only until an organization can implement more desirable, permanent controls.

Training and Exercises

Personnel across the organization, including cybersecurity professionals, managers, and even end users, must be trained on proper security processes and procedures. Beyond that, the entire organization should adopt a culture that is focused on security. This can only come through intensive training and indoctrination. That's why training should be accomplished when individuals first join an organization, and periodically thereafter. It's also why training shouldn't focus only on general security procedures but should also target an individual's role and responsibility in the organization. Cybersecurity professionals, for example, should be trained on the security technologies they are required to support. Managers should be trained on topics such as due diligence and care, privacy, legal liability, incident response management, business continuity and disaster recovery, and investigations. Ordinary users should be trained on things like how to respond to phishing attempts and malware.

In addition to solid training, the organization has to produce detailed policies and procedures on security-relevant issues. This includes incident response policy and plans, business continuity and disaster recovery, and risk management. It is not simply enough to formulate these plans and put them on a shared drive or in a binder and declare them complete. These plans must be exercised so that the organization can determine if they are effective, if they address all issues, if they are properly resourced with personnel and equipment, and to ensure that personnel are well-versed on their responsibilities, processes, and procedures.

Red Team

Results from a vulnerability assessment are purely theoretical; those are weaknesses that could be exploited by a malicious entity such as a hacker. Exploiting those vulnerabilities, however, moves from the theoretical to the actual. An organization would rather not have a malicious hacker determine if their vulnerabilities are truly exploitable. That's why they hire a red team. A red team is composed of professional ethical hackers. Their job is not only to discover vulnerabilities on systems but to attempt to exploit those vulnerabilities. Of course, they do this with the full permission of the organization; typically that comes from a senior executive who is knowledgeable about the red team and their activities. The most important aspect of engaging a red team is that the team has legal authorization from someone in a position to grant it to attempt to exploit vulnerabilities on the target network. Without this authorization, they are simply malicious hackers.

While being "threat faithful" is the best way to perform a red team assessment, rules of engagement are understandably involved to prevent any permanent harm or damage to the network or its assets. Rules of engagement may include the following:

- Only attacking the network during specified hours or days of the week
- Only attempting to exploit certain vulnerabilities and ignoring others
- Only attempting exploits on certain systems
- Documenting all attempted and successful exploits
- Signing a nondisclosure agreement to keep any sensitive information about the security posture of the network from unauthorized personnel
- Agreeing to only use certain tools or tactics
- Assisting network defenders after the attack in mitigating any vulnerabilities that were exploited

Blue Team

If the red team is composed of cybersecurity professionals playing the role of the malicious attacker and attempting to exploit vulnerabilities discovered on an organization's infrastructure, then the blue team is the exact opposite. A blue team is composed of cybersecurity personnel who are network defenders. They are the ones tasked with detecting an attack, containing it, mitigating it, and responding to the incident. In some types of exercises, the blue team is aware that the red team is attempting to attack the network, so they are more vigilant in paying attention to intrusion detection and prevention systems in hopes of detecting evidence of an attack. In some exercises, however, the network defenders do not know that a red team has been employed to test the network. This is as much a test of their vigilance and ability to detect an attack as their ability to contain and mitigate it.

White Team

A white team (often called a *white cell*) is the group of cybersecurity experts in charge of conducting an exercise, acting as a liaison between the teams and the organization, enforcing the rules of engagement, and intercepting any problems that might arise from the exercise. They are also considered trusted agents, in that they are trusted with sensitive information regarding the red team's strategy and tactics as well as those of the blue team. They are also there to protect the overall interests of the organization. They serve as referee, subject matter expert, and arbiter as well as provide oversight for the exercise. The white cell team may consist of key experienced members of the blue team, red team, and organizational management, none of whom are playing in the exercise; instead, they are there to lend their expertise.

NOTE   Don't confuse a red, blue, or white team with the concept of a white, black, or grey hat hacker. These are completely different terms and concepts. Whereas the color of the team indicates their role in the exercise, the color of the hat denotes whether a hacker is an ethical hacker (white hat), a malicious hacker (black hat), or someone who could go either way, depending on the circumstances (grey hat).

Tabletop Exercise

While there are many different types of exercises, depending upon the overall goal of the exercise or test, the one conducted requires different efforts. A tabletop exercise is normally a paperwork type of exercise, where the participants sit around a table in a conference room and react to written scenarios by stating what the reactions or actions should be to meet the goals of the exercise. If it is a disaster recovery tabletop exercise, then the participants react to a natural disaster and each, in turn, participates by saying what they would do to respond to the disaster, saving lives and equipment, and recover from it. If the exercise is an incident response exercise, then the participants would respond to a scenario by putting forward different response actions appropriate to the scenario. In any case, no actual equipment is used and no actual activities are performed during the exercise; it is all theoretical and based on the organization's plans and procedures. A tabletop exercise is very effective in determining if your procedures are sound and if the plan covers all of the bases it should. A tabletop exercise can show any conflicts between activities or resources, prioritization issues, and organizational problems, and it can simply point out issues that may have been overlooked or forgotten.

Supply Chain Assessment

Risk assessments can span an entire organization, or they can be focused on a particular program, a set of processes used across the organization, or even a particular asset. Yet another type of risk assessment can be used to assess the risk involved with supply chain management. The supply chain is composed of many different elements, all focused on getting the organization the needed supplies, equipment, services, and other products it needs to perform its mission. However, malicious entities have discovered that sometimes it can be just as effective to attack an organization by subverting the same needed supplies and equipment with malware, counterfeit parts, and compromised firmware as it would be to directly attack the organization's infrastructure through the network. It simply requires a bit more planning and patience on the part of the attacker.

It should be noted that attacking the organization isn't always the goal of someone who poisons the supply chain. It could be just opportunistic criminals looking to sell cheap counterfeit parts to anyone who will buy them, to make money off of the purchasers. It can also, at the other end of the spectrum, be a calculated attack from an advanced persistent threat, such as the government of a nation-state, to subvert security hardware so that they may more easily attack a target undetected. No matter the motivation, supply chain risk is real and can cost organizations millions of dollars in equipment purchases and in implementing security measures that aren't effective because of compromised systems bought from a poisoned supply chain, never mind the costs of the attack itself in terms of lost data and systems.

Supply chain risk management looks at securing every link in the chain. This includes the purchasers, vendors, buyers, contracting functions, and any other entity involved in the acquisition process. A risk assessment of the supply chain looks at any possible risks at every stage of the process; purchasers may be required to buy from only certified sources, vendors may have to certify that their systems meet certain security standards, hardware components may have to have traceability by serial number right back to their manufacturers, firmware may have to be tested for integrity, and sources may have to certify that their equipment is genuine and has not been compromised. Two elements that we will discuss involving supply chain risk management include vendor due diligence and verifying the authenticity of hardware and its sources.

 EXAM TIP   Understand that supply chain risks must be assessed and mitigated throughout every link in the chain.

Vendor Due Diligence

Vendors and other providers must offer assurances that their equipment, supplies, and services are genuine, have not been compromised in any way, and meet full security and functional requirements specified by the organization. Often vendors are required to maintain a high level of insurance against potential issues with their products to help ensure that they are performing due diligence and due care in maintaining their portion of the supply chain. Third-party assurances and certifications may also be used to assure potential customers that their manufacturing processes, parts sourcing, and security assurance programs meet expectations. Most vendors offer warranties or guarantees against counterfeit products or any that may be found to be compromised. Additionally, vendors will often provide documented traceability of a product, particularly an expensive or critical one, for the customer to ensure that the supply chain has not been compromised in any way.

Hardware Source Authenticity

Hardware authenticity is particularly troublesome. Expensive specialized equipment, such as routers, switches, firewalls, and so on, have often been compromised with counterfeit components, which will fail more often than their genuine counterparts, or software or firmware that has been compromised in some way before it even arrives at the customer's facilities. Hardware traceability is important to a vendor so that they can provide their customers with some assurance that the hardware is genuine, secure, and meets all of its security and functionality requirements. Hardware is often traced by part and serial number for the overall assembly, but even the individual components, such as circuit boards and even chips, are also traced this way, typically by serial number, part number, and manufacturing batch. A vendor will offer documentation to support the integrity of the entire supply chain responsible for getting the product from the manufacturer to customer.

REVIEW

Objective 5.2: Given a scenario, apply security concepts in support of organizational risk mitigation In this module, we discussed risk concepts and their relationship to security. The organization has to navigate risk management along with balancing security, functionality, and resources to achieve the best risk reduction possible.

One of the first things organizations should do is perform a business impact analysis. A BIA can tell an organization what its critical business processes are, as well as the assets that support them. Then the organization can prioritize these assets and processes for protection, restoration, risk reduction, and resource expenditure.

As part of the risk management process, the organization should identify its risk elements, including threats, vulnerabilities, and assets. The organization also has to determine what the probability is that a threat will exploit a vulnerability in an asset. The magnitude of impact is the level of harm that is done to an asset when this happens. Risk is a product of both the probability of occurrence and magnitude of impact.

Risk factors can influence the different elements of risk in different ways. There are external risk factors that the organization cannot control, including the economy, sociopolitical environment, market conditions, and so on. Internal risk factors are those the organization can exert some control over, including internal organizational structures and allocation of resources.

Risk prioritization is what the organization must do when it assesses risk and determines how it will respond to different risks. Organizations can respond in different ways, including risk mitigation, risk acceptance, risk transfer, and risk avoidance. Prioritization is a decision based on the criticality of assets and the number of resources the organization is willing to commit to reducing risk for those assets.

Security controls are measures the organization takes to protect assets and reduce risks. Generally, there are three categories of controls: managerial, operational, and technical. There are also different types of functions the controls fulfill, sometimes concurrently. These can include detective, deterrent, preventative, corrective, compensating, and recovery.

Risk management is a balance struck between reducing risk and security, functionality, allocation of resources. Trade-offs have to be made during the entire systems engineering lifecycle, particularly in the requirements, design, architecture, and implementation phases of the lifecycle. Any engineering trade-offs should be documented and justified. Risk assessments also have to be performed on security control trade-offs, and any increased risk incurred should have a plan for mitigation.

Assessing risk to the system can use one or several different standard methodologies, including OCTAVE, ISO/IEC standards, and the NIST risk assessment methodology. Four key ways an organization can get a complete picture of risk are interviewing key personnel, reviewing system and security documentation, technical vulnerability testing, and observing system security controls in operation.

Compensating controls are used when a more preferred control cannot be implemented for various reasons, including system and organizational constraints. These constraints could be resource constraints, system criticality, or even governance constraints. The use of compensating controls should be justified and documented accordingly.

Training personnel and exercising response capabilities are important ways not only to ensure that personnel understand their roles and responsibilities with regards to various security issues but also to perform tasks in the event of an incident or disaster. Different types of tests and exercises are performed to assess the security of an organization as well as its resiliency. Three particular types of teams involved in assessing an organization's security posture are the red team, the blue team, and the white cell team. These teams are concerned with participating in an adversarial assessment exercise, whereby vulnerabilities are not only discovered but also exploited. Tabletop exercises are documentation-based exercises where participants answer various written scenarios with proposed documented action plans and procedures. These exercises serve to ensure the adequacy of response plans and improve an organization's response capability.

Supply chain risk management involves examining every link along the chain that provides organizations with services, equipment, supplies, and systems. This includes vendors, purchasers, contractors, and the technical processes used along the way. Supply chain integrity depends on the due diligence of vendors who must document their processes and ensure that they are providing genuine systems and parts that have not been compromised in any way. Hardware source authentication means that a piece of hardware must be able to be traced back to its component manufacturers, via part number, serial number, and even batch number. The end user must have an assurance that the hardware has not been compromised in any way and that it is not counterfeit.

5.2 QUESTIONS

1. Adam is a cybersecurity analyst who is performing a risk assessment on a system. His supervisor insists that once the organization understands its threats, risk can be understood as well. Which elements of risk should Adam tell his supervisor that risk is derived from?

   A. Probability and magnitude of impact

   B. Threat and vulnerability pairings

   C. Threat, vulnerability, and assets

   D. Internal and external risk factors

2. Sarah has been tasked with identifying internal risk factors that could increase the risk to a critical system. Which of the following would be considered an internal factor that increases system risk?

   A. Economic downturn causing a recession in the organization's region

   B. Civil unrest in the organization's area

   C. Reduced organizational budget for implementing security controls

   D. Streamlining the organizational structure to give the cybersecurity department more independence and authority

3. Greg is a cybersecurity analyst who must select a risk assessment methodology to use within the organization's cyber risk management program. He needs a methodology that considers all of the basic risk elements. Which of the following elements must be included in the methodology?

A. Threats and vulnerabilities only

B. Threat actors, vulnerabilities, likelihood, and impact only

C. Likelihood and impact only

D. Threats, vulnerabilities, assets, likelihood, and impact only

4. You are a cybersecurity analyst assigned to participate in a test of the organization's cybersecurity posture. You are to monitor intrusion detection systems for indicators of an attack during the exercise. Which team are you most likely assigned to?

A. Red team

B. Blue team

C. White team

D. Grey team

5.2 ANSWERS

1. **A**   Risk is a product of the probability that a threat will exploit a vulnerability and the magnitude of the impact if this happens.

2. **C**   A reduced organizational budget for security controls could mean that needed security measures will not be implemented, thus increasing risk to critical assets.

3. **D**   Threats, vulnerabilities, assets, likelihood, and impact must all be considered in a risk assessment methodology.

4. **B**   If you are assigned the task of monitoring the network for signs of an attack, you are likely assigned to the blue team as a network defender.

 **Objective 5.3** # Explain the importance of frameworks, policies, procedures, and controls

Organizational Governance Flow

Organizational governance can be a complex mechanism within an organization. As a reminder, governance imposes requirements on an organization for compliance with certain rules. Governance can be external to the organization, in the form of laws, regulations, and standards. Governance can also be internal to the organization, taking the form of internal policies and procedures. Also, remember that the internal governance of an organization exists primarily to support and articulate external governance. For instance, if a law or regulation requires that a specific data type be protected to a certain level, then internal policy should be written to support that requirement and require all organizational personnel to comply with it.

Very often governance can establish the rules, methods, standards, and processes an organization must use to perform certain tasks, engage in certain activities, or support policies. These are typically mandatory in an organization and are considered as part of governance. In this module, we will discuss the various governance vehicles used to enforce compliance with laws, regulations, and policies. We'll discuss frameworks, policies, procedures, and controls.

Frameworks

A framework is an organized methodology used to establish processes and activities that an organization may employ to create or manage a program. For example, the NIST Risk Management Framework (RMF) establishes a phased lifecycle approach to managing risk throughout a system's entire useable life. The RMF provides for detailed steps and processes that an organization can use to categorize its systems, select security controls to protect those systems, implement those controls, assess control effectiveness and risk, gain approval to operate a system, and continuously monitor risk. The RMF is a useful framework that an organization can tailor and use iteratively to meet its needs.

There are other examples of frameworks designed to be used in various security or risk-related scenarios. There are management frameworks, control frameworks, risk frameworks, and so on. Each of these provides the overarching roadmap used to develop, implement, and manage a security-related program. Frameworks can be either risk-based or prescriptive.

Risk-Based

A risk-based framework allows for some level of modification or tailoring, depending on the needs of the organization. It also allows for a certain level of subjective decision-making regarding risk in the organization and risk of the program in question. A risk-based framework does not necessarily require a lockstep, by-the-numbers approach, although there is a formal structure provided that can be used as a guide whenever possible. Examples of risk-based frameworks include the NIST RMF, OCTAVE, and ISO/IEC standards (discussed previously in Objective 5.2)

Prescriptive

Conversely, a prescriptive framework is very much a sequential, by-the-numbers approach to a program or process. It requires strict adherence to rules, requirements, phases, and steps to be accomplished to achieve the objectives of the activities using the framework. It normally does not allow for subjective measurements or decisions. Examples of prescriptive frameworks include laws and regulations, strict standards, go/no go compliance assessments, and quality control models.

EXAM TIP   Understand the differences between risk-based and prescriptive frameworks. Risk-based frameworks are structured but allow some leeway in their interpretation and implementation, due to the dynamic nature of risk. Prescriptive frameworks are stricter and should be followed exactly. Examples of prescriptive frameworks are laws and regulations, compliance frameworks, and so on.

Policies and Procedures

As previously mentioned, policies and procedures are internal governance, which is created to support external governance, typically in the form of laws and regulations. Policies and procedures articulate the requirements handed down from external governance, such as ethics, legal liability, due care and diligence, data protection requirements, organizational structure, privacy, employee rights and responsibilities, and so on.

Policies are directive in nature and normally cover a wide range of security programs and issues. Examples of policies might be data sensitivity and protection policies, backup policies, equipment care and use, acceptable use policies, onboarding policies, termination policies, and so on. Policies are typically short and to the point, and they plainly point out what the requirement is that members of the organization must comply with. Policies may also assign responsibilities and provide enough details to support the requirement. This may include stating what the ramifications of noncompliance with the policy may be.

Procedures support policies in describing in detail the steps that must be taken to comply with the policy. Whereas a policy will tell you what the requirement is, the procedure will tell you how to carry out that requirement. Senior management normally develops policies, often with input from lower-level technicians or managers, but line managers and knowledgeable employees typically develop procedures that are approved at the senior management level.

In the sections that follow, we are going to discuss an example of the policies you will find in an organization, including code of conduct, acceptable use, password and account management, data ownership, and several others. Understand that these are only a sampling of policies you need to be aware of for the exam; organizations can and do produce many other types of policies that are specific to the organization or the requirements laid out by other governance.

EXAM TIP   Remember that policies are directive in nature and tell you *what* you must do. Procedures support policies by dictating the details of *how* you will do it.

Code of Conduct/Ethics

A *code of conduct* or *code of ethics* dictates to individuals how they must carry themselves from a legal, moral, or ethical perspective. Typically, an individual agrees to this code when they join an organization and voluntarily chooses to abide by its behavioral requirements.

Organizations have codes of conduct, whether it's an employer or a professional certification organization, such as CompTIA, for example. In agreeing to a code of conduct, you accept the consequences of behaving according to the code, as well as the consequences if you do not. An employer may state that failure to adhere to the code of conduct may result in punitive measures or even termination. The human resources and legal department should jointly manage this aspect of employment.

A code of conduct normally requires that members of the organization behave ethically, honorably, and responsibly, that they practice due care and due diligence, that they observe and obey all policy requirements of the organization, and that they operate legally in all aspects of their professional career. All persons desiring to test for or who have achieved a CompTIA certification must abide by CompTIA's Code of Ethics, detailed here: https://www.comptia.org/testing/testing-policies-procedures/test-policies/continuing-education-policies/candidate-code-of-ethics.

Failure to adhere to this code may result in the revocation of your certification.

Acceptable Use Policy (AUP)

An organization will have many different policies, but none is probably more critical than the acceptable use policy. An acceptable use policy is the core policy the drives what individuals, such as employees, contractors, and even business partners, are allowed to do on the corporate network. The AUP typically covers anyone who legitimately accesses the network. Employees typically sign and accept the policy when they are first hired. There may also be periodic reviews of this policy where employees have to acknowledge any changes or updates to the policy.

The AUP drives what employees are allowed to do and not do on the corporate network. In draconian organizations, this could include prohibitions on web surfing to other than approved websites, as well as no expectations of privacy on the network, forbidding private data to be processed or stored on the network at all. The AUP also covers the typical restrictions against prohibited content, such as pornography, hate speech, terrorist or criminal sites, and so on.

The AUP, like all policy documents, should also declare what the consequences are for violating the policy. This could include censure, loss of pay, suspension, criminal prosecution, and even termination. The policy should be administered by the information technology department but informed and supported by the cybersecurity, human resources, and legal departments. It should be promulgated across the organization, and all authorized users of the network should be aware of its contents. They should also be required to read and sign the policy, acknowledging that they have read it and understand it, ideally annually.

While it's best to keep the policy confined to the authorized use of network resources and the Internet, the policy could be very broad and account for other issues, such as e-mail use and installation of unauthorized software, for instance. In a less-restrictive environment, organizations could allow their employees some limited personal use of corporate IT assets, such as allowing them to engage in off-duty online education, view medical appointments and banking information, and so on. Normally the policy provisions allowing these behaviors would take place after on-duty hours.

Password Policy

A password policy is also a critical policy in the organization. In the "old days," a password policy was sufficient and directed how authorized users would create and protect passwords. Today, organizations are finally using a wide variety of stronger authentication methods (multifactor authentication, for example). Usernames and passwords are still present, unfortunately, so it's necessary to still have a password policy that is probably part of a larger authentication policy.

If you still use passwords in your organization, you should make every effort to minimize their use and implement stronger user identification and authentication methods. These would include multifactor authentication technologies. Multifactor authentication involves the use of different *factors* to authenticate, including the following:

- Something you know (such as a password)
- Something you are (such as a fingerprint)
- Something you have (such as a token or smartcard)
- Your location (from where you are attempting authentication)
- Other characteristics (time of day, authorized host, and so on)

Remember that for multifactor authentication to work, you must use at least two of these factors together. Many people think that the username and password combination is multifactor, but those are two things you know, so they comprise only one factor. Examples of multifactor methods include the use of a smart card (something you have) and a personal identification number, or PIN (something you know), or biometric authentication methods, such as a retinal scan, fingerprint, and even DNA (something you are) and a password or PIN. A common example of multifactor authentication is the use of automatic teller machine (ATM) cards.

In the event you're forced to use passwords for the network or even certain specific applications, here are the guidelines that should be included in your password policy:

- Use complex passwords consisting of each of the following: uppercase letters, lowercase letters, numbers, and special characters.
- Use longer passwords, ideally 8 to 20 characters, depending on the technologies you use. This increases your possible *keyspace,* or numbers of combinations of characters, you can use.
- Do not use dictionary words or any word that can be derived from any number of different types of dictionaries, such as an ordinary language dictionary, foreign word dictionary, and medical, sports, and technical dictionaries. Avoid using common things such as your spouse's name, child's name, pet's name, or special dates, and, obviously, passwords should not contain any part of the user's name.

Passwords should expire after a certain amount of time. In days long past, six months might have been the limitation. For passwords these days, with the rapid increase in computing power and the ability of malicious entities to crack passwords much faster and much more efficiently, it's not uncommon to see 90 or even 60 days' expiration time, particularly for critical systems and applications.

Passwords should be recycled so they cannot be reused for at least several password change cycles. The default for Windows is 0 passwords remembered, but it can be set for up to 24 previously remembered passwords. This makes it so users cannot revert to a previously used password in any reasonable amount of time, assuming your password policy requires a maximum password age (expirations) and minimum password age (discussed next).

Just as there's a maximum password age, there should be a minimum password age. This prevents users from having to change their password at the normal expiration time but then changing it back to something else immediately. The theory is that if the users are required to keep a new password for a certain amount of days, it becomes a habit to them and they get used to it, so they are less likely to change it. This also prevents them from quickly recycling through the number of passwords in the password history file to reuse an older password. The password policy should also discourage users from compromising passwords by writing them down in an easily accessible place, sharing passwords with another user, and so on. Finally, the password policy should state that the users' organizational passwords be unique from personal passwords, such as personal e-mail and social media. This will help prevent the situation where a password is exposed in, say, the LinkedIn breach of 2012, where nearly 170 million credentials were leaked. If the user's password was the same as their organizational password, it would be easy for an attacker to then go try it against the organization's systems.

Passwords for critical systems and accounts, such as the true administrator or root account, should be secured in a locked area, and they should require two-person integrity to access them. This is if an emergency happens and the administrator password must be used. Hopefully, if your account management policies and procedures are written correctly, this should never happen, since ordinary users who should need administrative rights will have separate accounts for that purpose.

Data Ownership

Organizations are responsible for the data they generate, store, process, transmit, and receive. Even in cases where there is no overall regulation or law that prescribes this, which is rare, the organization has a responsibility to itself to take care of its data. This includes protecting it from unauthorized access, ensuring its integrity is maintained, and making it available for the authorized users who need it. One of the most critical policies that an organization can create is a data sensitivity policy. This typically defines what an organization considers to be sensitive or important data and how it must protect that data. An element of this policy, or even as a separate policy, is that of data ownership. The data owner is responsible for and accountable to the organization for protecting certain data types. This data owner may be responsible for several data types, or just one specific type. Typically, the data owner is a senior leader or manager in the organization designated in writing to be the responsible data owner.

The data owner determines data sensitivity, provided that the law or other regulations don't already prescribe this, to what level it should be protected, and who is responsible for implementing the protections. The data owner also determines who has authorized access to the data.

Similar to a data owner, a *data custodian* is responsible for the protection of designated data types as well. However, whereas the data owner makes decisions regarding data and its protection, a data custodian implements those decisions at the functional level. This is usually a lower-level cybersecurity or IT technician who is responsible for implementing permissions on data objects, such as files and folders, as well as performs the technical aspects of giving individuals access, as directed by the data owner. This person is also responsible for the day-to-day maintenance of the data, including backing it up, checking for integrity, reviewing audit trails related to the data, and so on. Ultimately the CEO or CIO is responsible for all data in the organization, but this ownership, as well as responsibility and accountability, can be delegated down to another legally authorized entity. In fact, certain regulations, such as the European GDPR, require the appointment of such persons, such as a data privacy officer, a data processor, and a data collector.

Data Retention

Data retention is yet another policy-driven element of data security. You should probably have a data retention policy because of any legal requirements imposed by external governance, such as laws and regulations. Data retention essentially tells an organization which sensitive data it should keep, and for how long, and how it must be protected in storage. The data retention policy can be a part of a larger data use or data sensitivity policy if needed, as long as it can be articulated back to a legal requirement to retain data. As a general rule, organizations do not keep large amounts of data unless legally required; the storage requirements alone can be unsustainable. In addition to storage requirements, the organization has to ensure that it can quickly access this data when required, typically during an audit, inspection, or investigation.

If no laws or regulations are requiring an organization to retain data under specific circumstances, the organization should carefully consider whether or not it actually needs to retain the data. It may need to keep data for business purposes; this might include data such as business records, financial data, plans, proprietary data that it uses to conduct its daily business, and so on. Even when not required by regulation, if an organization decides that certain data is sensitive enough to retain, there should be a policy that dictates this, by describing the data type, the justification for keeping it, and the specific data retention requirements. These would include the amount of time data is retained, and how it must be protected during retention.

As part of data retention policies, the organization should also describe how it disposes of certain data when its retention requirement time has expired. This can include destruction by secure means, such as a high-grade document shredder, mulching, or incineration. It could also describe how to destroy, or even reuse, media that the data is stored on. Keep in mind that the methods for destroying data no longer needed on media include wiping, physical destruction, burning, and degaussing.

Work Product Retention

Part of the data you may retain for business purposes includes work products, which are those products that contain information as the result of doing business. You'll hear this sometimes referred to as an organization's "intellectual property." It could mean financial products, process products, human resources products, or any other type of product created as a result of the organization performing its primary mission or from the different programs and processes that support the mission. These products should be evaluated for retention per the organization's retention policy. This information should be assigned a specific data type and protected according to policy. As a general rule, the more data an organization retains, the more difficult it is to protect that data, in terms of allocating resources for protection as well as for retention. That's one of the reasons an organization should carefully consider retaining only the most important data it needs for care and diligence, legal liability, and to maintain business continuity.

Account Management

Account management includes the processes and activities associated with managing accounts during their lifecycle. The account management lifecycle typically is composed of account verification, account creation, provisioning, authorization change, account validation, and, finally, termination or disposal. Account management is a complex process within an organization that seriously affects the security of the organization. As such, there should be definitive policies and procedures created for it.

Remember that not only people (employees, contractors, business partners, customers, suppliers, and so on) have accounts, but also machines and other entities. Also keep in mind that these various entities don't only have internal network accounts; they have accounts for extranets, specific databases and applications, and specific systems. Part of account management means segregating all these different accounts for different resources in the organization both logically and physically.

Different functions may provide different account management functions in the organization. For example, the help desk may be in charge of routine account maintenance, while there could be a dedicated section of IT or IS (information security) focused on verifying and validating accounts, changing permissions to resources, and even provisioning administrative-level accounts.

To begin with, having an account in the organization should mean that a person has the following:

- The proper clearance to access the organization's network
- The appropriate need to know based on their job duties
- The approval of someone authorized to grant such approval in management

The organization must develop, as part of its procedures, steps to verify the need for an account through a supervisor or manager, the identity of the person or entity requesting the account, and the resource access needed by the account. In general, account management procedures and policy elements should include the following:

- Everyone should have a normal user account at minimum, even administrators.
- Normal user accounts should not have administrative access to any types of applications, shares, systems, network devices, and so on.
- There should be no guest or common use accounts.
- Administrative-level accounts should be granted only to those personnel who have a valid need, based on their duties and verified by a manager.
- Administrative account holders should only be using their administrative-level account for specific duty-related tasks, and not everyday activities, such as surfing the web or e-mail.
- All accounts should be periodically audited for necessity or to make sure they are not performing any functions they should not be.
- Administrative-level accounts, in general, should be audited daily for any access to resources or use of special privileges.
- All accounts should be periodically validated with a supervisor or manager.
- Any time an administrative account is created, there should be a paper trail or other documentation to back it up.
- At any given time, a cybersecurity analyst should be able to look at an audit trail to see what a particular account has done in every instance from the day it was created until the present. This is useful for security, nonrepudiation, and establishing usage trends for administrative-level accounts.

Always ensure that account management operates on the premise of least privilege. In other words, you should have only those privileges or permissions necessary to be able to perform routine daily job functions. Privilege creep occurs when an account, over time, acquires privileges that it should not have because it has not been properly monitored or validated regularly. That's why part of the account management lifecycle includes occasional periodic account validation.

Account management procedures should be separated by job function, enforcing the separation-of-duties concept. For example, users who create accounts, such as account operators, should only be able to create and/or delete accounts. They should not be responsible for giving account permissions to resources. There could be another function tasked with placing user accounts in the correct resource or permission groups or roles. Typically the data owner will decide who has access to which resource, so that should be a function of the data owner versus an account operator, for example. Furthermore, the individuals who audit account usage should not be the ones to create or delete accounts or assign resource permissions. Again, this enforces the concept of separation of duties. What you want to avoid is a situation where someone could create an account, assign permissions to it, perform some illegal task, delete the account, and then delete the audit trail associated with the account.

Continuous Monitoring

Continuous monitoring is a concept promulgated by several risk management frameworks, including NIST. Continuous monitoring means several things. At a lower system and infrastructure level, it means to consistently gather data from a variety of sources and be able to perform historic and trend analysis on it, as well as to be able to view data in real time and get alerts in case something happens. Monitoring your network is the best way to ensure you can detect incidents when they happen and respond to them. From another perspective, continuous monitoring means continuous risk management. This means monitoring for changes in risk and responding to them when they happen. This also means monitoring the organization's environment, both internal and external, to detect changes in risk factors that may affect the system or organizational risk.

When monitoring for risk, the organization should look for changes in threats, vulnerabilities, impact, and likelihood. Threat modeling is one way to monitor threats. This looks at threat scenarios and how that might affect the organization. Vulnerability assessments performed periodically are a component of continuous risk monitoring. Factors that affect the likelihood or impact are also carefully monitored. This could mean changes in infrastructure, resource allocation, and both external and internal risk factors that may affect impact and likelihood.

As we are discussing policies and procedures, you should ensure that the organization has a policy for continuous risk monitoring and management. Risk doesn't only occur one or two times a year when you do a risk assessment. Risk is ongoing and changes constantly; therefore, risk management should change with it. Ensure that you have a policy for continuous monitoring, at the systems and infrastructure event level as well as at the organizational risk level.

 EXAM TIP   Understand that policies are required for implementation, and examples of common policies in organizations include account management policies, password policies, and, probably the most critical one, the acceptable use policy.

Control Categories

The exam objectives call for you to understand the different categories of controls. For the CySA+ exam, these are managerial, operational, and technical. Traditional security foundations typically refer to these as administrative, technical, and physical, but we will use the CompTIA terms here, albeit with some additional guidance on the use of these terms, as they depart from traditional security thinking somewhat. In the next few sections, we will discuss what each of these categories of control means. We will also discuss the different control types or functions, which, again, can be a little bit different from what we see in traditional security texts.

Managerial

These controls—sometimes referred to as administrative controls—are those that are implemented as policies, procedures, standards, and guidelines. Managerial controls typically tell you what security requirements are and how you should implement them. As their name suggests, managerial controls are created and implemented by the management of an organization.

Examples of managerial controls might include acceptable use policies, privacy policies, and backup procedures. Typically, for each managerial control, there is a roughly corresponding technical or operational control that implements the requirements of the managerial control. For example, an encryption policy, as a managerial control, would direct that you use a particular type of encryption method, algorithm, or strength. A technical control would complement that using the prescribed encryption method, such as AES-256.

Operational

Operational security controls are typically physical controls and other operational procedures. These include processes or procedures performed by people. This might include cameras placed throughout the facility, gates, guards, guns, locked doors, alarm systems, and so on. These controls are designed to protect personnel, equipment, and facilities from a physical or operational threat. Note that there can be significant overlap between managerial, operational, and technical controls, thus making discerning the control categorization a bit difficult sometimes.

Technical

A technical, or logical, control is a control implemented with technology, such as firewalls, intrusion detection/prevention systems, encryption, audit logs, object permissions, and so on. Typically a technical control is the implementation of a corresponding managerial control that issues a requirement, and the technical control implements that requirement.

EXAM TIP Previous CompTIA exam objectives for both the Security+ exam (SYO-501) and the CySA+ exam (CS0-001) categorizing the types and functions of controls have changed significantly since these two previous exam iterations. CompTIA, for both the new SY0-601 and the CySA+ CS0-002 exams, has reclassified control types and functions. Although the practical day-to-day definitions have not changed, be aware that they are now classified differently on each exam, so you should know the new categories and types.

Control Types

All controls are designed to perform one or more overall functions: to prevent a malicious act or a violation of policy, to detect either a malicious act or a violation of policy, or to make up for a deficiency in or lack of a control. More often than not, a control can overlap in function and perform several different functions at one time. It's not unusual to see a control be both a deterrent and a preventative control, for example, or to be both a compensating and corrective control. We will discuss the different control functions next.

Deterrent

A *deterrent control* is one that deters a person from performing a malicious act or violating policy. An example of a deterrent control might be a closed-circuit television camera (CCTV). Its mere presence lets a would-be intruder know that their actions are being monitored and recorded. Just knowing the control is there might be enough to deter anyone who might violate policy by entering a restricted area, for instance. The key thing about a deterrent control is that the person who may perform the act or violate the policy must *know* that the control exists for it to be a deterrent to them.

Preventative

A *preventative control* does exactly what its name indicates. It prevents someone from violating a policy or performing a malicious act. Note this is almost the same definition as a deterrent control. However, there is a critical difference between the two types of controls. A preventative control will do its job regardless of whether someone knows about it or not. An example might be a firewall rule that blocks video chat. Regardless of whether a person knows it exists, it will still prevent someone from violating a policy that prohibits video chat outside the organization. As mentioned earlier, the key difference between that and a deterrent control is that a deterrent control must be known about to be effective. Referring back to the example of a CCTV, it would not be effective as a deterrent if a person did not know it was there. It still might be effective as a detective control, discussed next, but not as a deterrent control.

Detective

A *detective control* is one that detects an incident or can provide information about the incident. Good examples of a detective control would include CCTVs, an alarm system, and an audit log. Note that detective controls are reactive: they do not prevent or deter malicious acts or policy violations; instead, they only serve to alert someone after the act or violation has occurred, even in the case of real-time monitoring and alerting.

Compensating

The *compensating control* is used to temporarily strengthen or take the place of a missing or ineffective control. Consider a section of fencing that has been damaged due to a break-in. Until that piece of fence is repaired, a compensating control might be for a guard to be placed at the break in the fence. Obviously, it's not as effective as the fence being there, but it will serve to deter people from entering the break in the fence as well as prevent that from happening. It also serves to reduce risk, which is one of the main functions of security controls.

Another example may indicate that compensating controls are not always as temporary as we would sometimes like. Consider a smaller organization that does not have enough people to adequately separate security duties, such as reviewing audit logs. The organization may outsource some of its security functions, such as security device monitoring, to a third party that also reviews audit logs. While log review should be performed normally by a trusted security administrator within the organization, until the organization can hire someone to do that, it must rely on an outsider to perform that task. This is then not an ideal control but rather a compensating one in this case.

Corrective

A *corrective control* is used to temporarily correct a nonsecure condition caused by a malfunctioning, ineffective, or missing control. This typically happens due to an incident, and something must immediately correct the nonsecure condition caused by a control failure. A corrective control is considered temporary, and it is also not an ideal control solution. Therefore, in these two ways, it is very much like a compensating control. The key difference here is that a compensating control may be more long term, proactive, and planned in nature, whereas a corrective control is usually reactive due to an incident or obvious failure of a previously functioning control.

 EXAM TIP On the exam, if presented with a scenario that causes you to have to choose between a corrective and compensating control, look at the context of the scenario. If the control is reactive and short term in nature, it is usually a corrective control. If it is proactive, longer term, or planned to make up for a known ineffective or missing control, then it is a compensating control.

Recovery

A *recovery control* is traditionally one that is used to take a system or organization from a nonsecure or unsteady state to a secure one after an incident. For example, backup tapes that are used to restore a server whose operating system has been damaged due to an attack would be considered a recovery control. As control functions sometimes overlap, you might also consider this control to be preventive in nature (preventing data loss by performing backups) or even corrective (restoring the data from backups corrects a nonsecure condition—that is, data loss), although considering it a corrective control might be a stretch.

 EXAM TIP For the exam and its objectives, the recovery control type/function is no longer listed on CompTIA's exam objectives. However, traditional (and current) security thinking and teaching still acknowledge this classification of control function. For the exam, recovery controls are typically categorized as compensating or corrective controls.

Physical

Physical controls are normally considered a category of controls versus a control function, but their categorization for the exam objectives doesn't make too much of a difference in understanding them. A physical control, as mentioned earlier, is a control designed to protect the physical environment of the organization—its people, equipment, facilities, systems, and data.

Physical controls include the obvious: gates, fencing, guards, CCTVs, and so on. But they also include environmental controls, such as those that protect against temperature fluctuations and excessive or insufficient humidity, since significant variations in those two measurements can be detrimental to sensitive equipment.

> **EXAM TIP**   The physical control type/function is no longer listed on CompTIA's exam objectives as one of the three main types (categories) of controls. Traditional (and current) security thinking and teaching still acknowledge physical controls as being one of the three main types (managerial/administrative, technical/logical, and physical/operational). For the exam, physical controls are categorized as a subtype of control, not a main type.

Audits and Assessments

We've already discussed assessments in Objective 5.2 and touched on the topic elsewhere in the book. For our discussion on frameworks and policies, you should definitely have an audit policy as well as an assessment policy.

An audit policy essentially states what the organization will audit in terms of specific resources, such as systems and data, and how it will audit them. This policy could be connected to your data sensitivity policy somewhat, in that once you know your data sensitivity levels and how they must be protected, you should audit those particular data types accordingly. Your audit policy should restate this. It should state how often sensitive data types are audited and what information you need from the audit trail. Information from an audit trail could include the following:

- Which user or entity accessed the data
- The time and date the data or system was accessed
- What actions were performed on the data (read, changed or modified, deleted, and so on) or system
- From what host the data was accessed

You would audit sensitive data so that in the event of an incident or investigations into unauthorized access of data, you would be able to trace those actions back and show what happened as well as hold someone accountable for the incident. You should implement your audit policy by assigning the proper audit configuration items, such as read or write success or failure, for example, to systems, folders, and files that contain sensitive data.

An assessment policy should detail what types of assessments the organization routinely performs, how often and why, and what the organization expects to have as a goal from the assessment. For example, the assessment policy may require that vulnerability assessments be required once per month. This vulnerability assessment policy or element may state that vulnerability assessments should be performed once per month, or weekly on certain subnets if the network is very large, and what types of vulnerabilities should be looked for. The policy may also dictate what kind of software is used for vulnerability assessment assessments, and the day of week or time of day they are conducted. It will probably also require that the department in charge of performing vulnerability assessments develop detailed procedures for them.

Other assessments might include penetration testing assessments, tests and exercise of the incident response plan, business continuity and disaster recovery exercises, and so on. These types of assessments may also be separate and included in the appropriate response plan policies. In any event, policies should set forth requirements for the different types of assessments, as well as who will conduct them and, to a small degree, how they will be conducted. Two different types of assessments you may be required to perform that your policy may address include compliance assessments and regulatory assessments. These are discussed next.

Cross-Reference

Tests and exercises, also forms of assessment, are also discussed in Objective 5.2.

Regulatory and Compliance Assessments

Regulatory agencies often require specific assessments be performed periodically to ensure that organizations comply with their requirements. These assessments could take many forms, although typically you would see a unique version of a risk assessment or a controls assessment. Any so-called risk assessments do not necessarily produce a picture of true risk; they are assessments to determine compliance with controls or other strict requirements. This is particularly true in U.S. government agencies, such as the Department of Defense, or with certain types of data, such as HIPAA assessments.

Controls assessments perform two important functions: First, they can provide an organization with the knowledge that the controls selected for protecting assets are the correct controls and are functioning effectively. Second, they can assure an auditor that the organization is complying with control requirements. Control requirements alone do not provide a picture of risk. Unfortunately, however, that is often what you'll see with regulatory or compliance assessments. The theory behind this form of assessment is that if you are using the correct controls, and they are effective, then you have taken steps to reduce risk. This is by and large true, but a control assessment does not take into account other factors, some of which can't be measured by verifying and validating controls. These include threat scenarios, vulnerabilities, the impact to an asset or the organization if a negative event occurs, and the likelihood that a negative event will occur at all.

In the best scenario, a regulatory or compliance assessment will not only look at controls but also risk to the asset or organization. A complete end-to-end assessment should consist of several parts:

- Full threat modeling
- Vulnerability assessments
- Controls assessments
- Adversarial simulations (or penetration tests)

- Incident response, business continuity, and disaster recovery exercises
- Thorough risk analysis of likelihood and impact
- Consideration of external and internal risk factors
- Continuous monitoring

REVIEW

Objective 5.3: Explain the importance of frameworks, policies, procedures, and controls

In this module, we discussed organizational governance, both internal and external. Remember that governance is the legal and ethical requirements imposed on the organization by laws and regulations as well as by the organization itself in the form of policies.

Frameworks are very important in that they establish a methodology and process for performing risk and security management functions. The two primary types are risk-based frameworks, which are a little bit more flexible, and prescriptive frameworks, which are very strict.

Organizations typically have many different policies and procedures that are established to guide and regulate the organization's behavior and activities. A policy is a requirement; all employees and others accessing organizational resources must obey them. Policies explain the particulars of what must be done. Procedures support policies by providing detailed steps of how to perform a task or activity. Common policies that an organization develops and implements include the acceptable use policy, account management policies, password policies, data ownership and retention, and continuous risk monitoring. Other typical policies you might see include data sensitivity, backup policies, equipment control and care, and encryption policies.

We discussed controls at length, including categories and types. CompTIA provides for three different overarching control categories: managerial, operational, and technical controls. Managerial controls are those established by management and include policies and procedures. Operational controls include processes and procedures performed by people as well as physical controls. Technical controls, also known as logical controls, are those that are implemented using various technologies. Examples include encryption, authentication mechanisms, antimalware, and so on.

Control types determine what function a control serves, and controls can span several different functions at one time. Deterrent controls must be known in order to be effective, and preventive controls help to stop malicious acts to prevent policy violations, regardless of whether a person is aware of them. Detective controls are used to detect, discover, or investigate violations of policy or malicious acts. Compensating controls are put into place when the control is known to be ineffective or missing. Corrective controls are more immediate and temporary and usually put into place after an incident to correct a serious security issue. Physical controls include physical barriers and measures to protect people, facilities, and equipment. Environmental controls are those that detect and regulate environmental changes, such as temperature and humidity.

The organization must have strong audit and assessment policies. An audit policy details which different types of sensitive data may be audited as well as what should be included in an audit trail. The assessment policy should dictate what types of assessments the organization routinely undergoes, including vulnerability assessments, penetration tests, and scheduled tests and exercises of response programs. Regulatory and compliance assessments are designed to determine if the organization is compliant with various regulations, policies, and standards. These types of assessments are normally prescriptive and may not take into account the broader risk picture.

5.3 QUESTIONS

1. Charles has been tasked with writing policies for an organization that has never really had any formalized internal governance structure. He needs to write a policy that covers the requirements for getting an administrative account since the organization wants to reduce the number of users with administrative accounts in the organization. Which of the following policies should he write to address this issue?

   A. Data ownership policy

   B. Authentication policy

   C. Acceptable use policy

   D. Account management policy

2. Quiana is writing a report for customers for whom she has just completed a risk assessment. She is describing controls that are ineffective or missing, and she is making recommendations for controls the customers could implement if they cannot implement ideal controls due to resource constraints. Which of the following describes the types of controls Quiana is suggesting in place of the preferred controls that could also help reduce risk?

   A. Compensating controls

   B. Corrective controls

   C. Preventative controls

   D. Deterrent controls

3. You are a cybersecurity analyst who has been assigned the task of recommending controls that have been determined as deficient during a recent risk assessment. Your organization uses effective technical encryption methods on the network, but there is no direction that states which encryption method must be used and how it must be used. This written direction must be developed for compliance purposes. Which of the following control categories and written directions should be developed to dictate what the requirements are for use of encryption within the organization?

   A. Managerial controls; encryption policy

   B. Managerial controls; cryptography procedures

    C. Operational controls; encryption policy

    D. Technical controls; cryptography policy

4. Shawn is a cybersecurity analyst who has just written the organization's audit policy. Which of the following should he ensure is included in the policy?

    A. The list of prohibited actions that may be discovered during an audit

    B. The type of assessment that must produce the audit

    C. The data sensitivity type that must be audited, as well as particulars of the audit event

    D. The punishment for misuse of data discovered during an audit

5.3 ANSWERS

1. **D** An account management policy is likely the best policy to address the requirements for getting administrative accounts.

2. **A** Quiana should recommend compensating controls for the organization if they cannot implement the preferred or ideal controls due to resource constraints. Compensating controls can help reduce the risk for controls that have been identified as inefficient, ineffective, or completely missing.

3. **A** Since the method used on the network is a technical control, a corresponding managerial control should be developed to dictate the encryption requirements for the organization. This is best developed as an encryption policy, which will detail what those requirements are.

4. **C** Normally, an audit policy should include details about the different sensitive data types that are to be routinely audited according to policy as well as the particulars about the events that will be audited, such as username, time and date, the action performed on the data, and host or location from which the event occurred.

About the Online Content

This book comes complete with TotalTester Online customizable practice exam software with more than 200 practice exam questions including ten simulated performance-based questions.

System Requirements

The current and previous major versions of the following desktop browsers are recommended and supported: Chrome, Microsoft Edge, Firefox, and Safari. These browsers update frequently, and sometimes an update may cause compatibility issues with the TotalTester Online or other content hosted on the Training Hub. If you run into a problem using one of these browsers, please try using another until the problem is resolved.

Your Total Seminars Training Hub Account

To get access to the online content, you will need to create an account on the Total Seminars Training Hub. Registration is free, and you will be able to track all your online content using your account. You may also opt in if you wish to receive marketing information from McGraw Hill or Total Seminars, but this is not required for you to gain access to the online content.

Privacy Notice

McGraw Hill values your privacy. Please be sure to read the Privacy Notice available during registration to see how the information you have provided will be used. You may view our Corporate Customer Privacy Policy by visiting the McGraw Hill Privacy Center. Visit the **mheducation.com** site and click **Privacy** at the bottom of the page.

Single User License Terms and Conditions

Online access to the digital content included with this book is governed by the McGraw Hill License Agreement outlined next. By using this digital content you agree to the terms of that license.

Access To register and activate your Total Seminars Training Hub account, simply follow these easy steps.

1. Go to this URL: **hub.totalsem.com/mheclaim**

2. To register and create a new Training Hub account, enter your e-mail address, name, and password on the **Register** tab. No further personal information (such as credit card number) is required to create an account.

   If you already have a Total Seminars Training Hub account, enter your e-mail address and password on the **Log in** tab.

3. Enter your Product Key: **d97g-tr54-p2gp**

4. Click to accept the user license terms.

5. For new users, click the **Register and Claim** button to create your account. For existing users, click the **Log in and Claim** button.

   You will be taken to the Training Hub and have access to the content for this book.

Duration of License Access to your online content through the Total Seminars Training Hub will expire one year from the date the publisher declares the book out of print.

Your purchase of this McGraw Hill product, including its access code, through a retail store is subject to the refund policy of that store.

The Content is a copyrighted work of McGraw Hill, and McGraw Hill reserves all rights in and to the Content. The Work is © 2021 by McGraw Hill.

Restrictions on Transfer The user is receiving only a limited right to use the Content for the user's own internal and personal use, dependent on purchase and continued ownership of this book. The user may not reproduce, forward, modify, create derivative works based upon, transmit, distribute, disseminate, sell, publish, or sublicense the Content or in any way commingle the Content with other third-party content without McGraw Hill's consent.

Limited Warranty The McGraw Hill Content is provided on an "as is" basis. Neither McGraw Hill nor its licensors make any guarantees or warranties of any kind, either express or implied, including, but not limited to, implied warranties of merchantability or fitness for a particular purpose or use as to any McGraw Hill Content or the information therein or any warranties as to the accuracy, completeness, correctness, or results to be obtained from, accessing or using the McGraw Hill Content, or any material referenced in such Content or any information entered into licensee's product by users or other persons and/or any material available on or that can be accessed through the licensee's product (including via any hyperlink or otherwise) or as to non-infringement of third-party rights. Any warranties of any kind, whether express or implied, are disclaimed. Any material or data obtained through use of the McGraw Hill Content is at your own discretion and risk and user understands that it will be solely responsible for any resulting damage to its computer system or loss of data.

Neither McGraw Hill nor its licensors shall be liable to any subscriber or to any user or anyone else for any inaccuracy, delay, interruption in service, error or omission, regardless of cause, or for any damage resulting therefrom.

In no event will McGraw Hill or its licensors be liable for any indirect, special or consequential damages, including but not limited to, lost time, lost money, lost profits or good will, whether in contract, tort, strict liability or otherwise, and whether or not such damages are foreseen or unforeseen with respect to any use of the McGraw Hill Content.

TotalTester Online

TotalTester Online provides you with a simulation of the CompTIA CySA+ CS0-002 exam. Exams can be taken in Practice Mode or Exam Mode. Practice Mode provides an assistance window with hints, references to the book, explanations of the correct and incorrect answers, and the option to check your answer as you take the test. Exam Mode provides a simulation of the actual exam. The number of questions, the types of questions, and the time allowed are intended to be an accurate representation of the exam environment. The option to customize your quiz allows you to create custom exams from selected domains or chapters, and you can further customize the number of questions and time allowed.

To take a test, follow the instructions provided in the previous section to register and activate your Total Seminars Training Hub account. When you register you will be taken to the Total Seminars Training Hub. From the Training Hub Home page, select **CompTIA CySA+ Passport (CS0-002) TotalTester** from the Study drop-down menu at the top of the page, or from the list of Your Topics on the Home page. You can then select the option to customize your quiz and begin testing yourself in Practice Mode or Exam Mode. All exams provide an overall grade and a grade broken down by domain.

Performance-Based Questions

In addition to multiple-choice questions, the CompTIA CySA+ (CS0-002) exam includes performance-based questions (PBQs), which, according to CompTIA, are designed to test your ability to solve problems in a simulated environment. More information about PBQs is provided on CompTIA's website.

You can access the PBQs included with this book by navigating to the Resources tab and selecting the quiz icon. You can also access them by selecting **CompTIA CySA+ Passport (CS0-002) Resources** from the Study drop-down menu at the top of the page or from the list of Your Topics on the Home page. The menu on the right side of the screen outlines all of the available resources. After you have selected the PBQs, an interactive quiz will launch in your browser.

Technical Support

For questions regarding the TotalTester or operation of the Training Hub, visit **www.totalsem .com** or e-mail **support@totalsem.com**.

For questions regarding book content, visit **www.mheducation.com/customerservice**.

Glossary

acceptable use policy (AUP)   A policy that dictates which actions users may and may not take with regard to resources on an organization's networks

access control list (ACL)   A list of containing actions, network traffic, or software that can be used to allow or deny actions based on criteria such as user, IP address, port, protocol, service, or executable

Address Resolution Protocol (ARP)   Protocol residing at the network layer of the OSI model that maps media access control (hardware) addresses to logical addresses

Advanced Encryption Standard (AES)   National encryption standard published by NIST for encryption suitable for all commercial and government applications; it is a block cipher based on the Rijndael algorithm, having key sizes of 128, 192, and 256 bits with 128-bit block sizes.

advanced persistent threat (APT)   Threat actor characterized by unlimited resources, advanced attack techniques, and the ability to engage a target for long periods. Typically seen as nation-states or large criminal organizations.

allow list   List of entries containing network traffic ports, protocols, services, applications, users, and other subjects to grant permissions. Replaces the outdated term *whitelisting*.

anti-tamper   The management program and set of technologies used to ensure hardware authenticity and integrity along the supply chain

application programming interface (API)   Method of interacting with and accessing software code between applications, including interfaces and data exchange

application stress testing   Method of testing application resilience by sending large volumes or unusual traffic to an application to determine how it reacts

asset tagging   Software and hardware method of embedding inventory information into an asset

atomic execution   A method for controlling program run so that processes must execute in a specific sequence and cannot be interrupted between the time the process starts and when it ends

attack surface   Level of exposure of an asset to potential attacks from various means

attack vector   Method of attack that takes advantage of specific vulnerabilities

attribute-based access control   Access control method that determines resource access based on specific characteristics or attributes of the subject or object, such as group membership, role, time of day, location, and so on

blacklisting   An outdated term used to describe a deny list, in which the elements of the list are denied access to the network, a resource, or security privileges. See also *deny list.*

blue team   Name for the team of cybersecurity professionals charged with network defense during a security assessment

bring your own device (BYOD)   Method of infrastructure management where users can bring personally owned devices and connect them to the organization's network

buffer overflow attack   An attack where the memory contents of an application are overwritten, causing the application to behave erratically or unexpectedly

bus encryption   A method for encrypting/decrypting data at the CPU, rather than on a storage media, to prevent data from being intercepted and decrypted as it traverses between the media and the CPU

business e-mail compromise (BEC)   Compromise of an organizational e-mail infrastructure through direct attack or phishing attempts

business impact analysis   Process in which an organization's business processes, as well as the information technology assets that support them, are inventoried and prioritized for criticality in the event of an incident

carving   The forensics process of locating and removing files, artifacts, or other usable data from deleted or damaged data

Center for Internet Security (CIS)   A community-driven nonprofit organization that produces and promulgates cybersecurity standards, including the CIS Controls and Benchmarks

central processing unit (CPU)   The primary processing chip and associated circuitry responsible for all logic, arithmetic, and control functions within a computer system

Certificate Authority (CA)   Entity granting a digital certificate and public/private key pair to another entity based on validated identity and other requirements

change management   The process and associated activities of carefully planning and executing authorized changes within an infrastructure

closed source intelligence   Information that is unavailable to the general population and only obtainable by being a member of a closed group authorized access to such information

cloud access security broker (CASB)   An intermediate layer of security management technology used to consolidate and communicate with an organization's cloud services

code review   The process of reviewing and validating software code to ensure that it is functional and secure

commodity malware   Malware produced and sold as a commodity to various malicious actors

Common Vulnerability Scoring System (CVSS)   Provides for specific characteristics of a security weakness (for example, software vulnerabilities and security configuration issues) and, based on those characteristics, generates a score that reflects their relative severity

community cloud   The cloud model used when multiple organizations have similar infrastructure requirements and may need to share data at some level

compensating controls   Controls used on a short-term basis when preferred controls cannot be implemented.

confidence rating   A ranking of how confident an organization is that a threat rating is accurate. This rating is often measured on a scale of 0–100, with 100 representing the highest level of confidence

containment   Process of curtailing an incident in preventing further damage to an organization's assets.

continuous integration/continuous delivery (CI/CD)   Concept describing the continuous integration and delivery of secure, functional software code to the production environment

Control Objectives for Information and Related Technology (COBIT)   Control framework published by ISACA that covers business management of IT resources

controller area network (CAN)   A standardized architecture protocol used in vehicles to facilitate communications between internal components

corrective controls   Controls that are implemented in a temporary and possibly urgent situation to strengthen existing weak or faulty controls

credential stuffing attack   An attack technique that allows an attacker to make use of credentials previously compromised in another data breach

cross-site scripting (XSS) attack   A web-based attack involving the injection of malicious scripts into a vulnerable website. These scripts are then run by a victim who visits the website.

customer relations management (CRM)   Unified processes, activities, and tools designed to manage all aspects of customers and their data

cyber intelligence   Aggregated cyber threat information, including threat intelligence from government, industry, and open source sources

cyber kill chain   A framework that identifies the various stages of a cyberattack

data enrichment   Process of adding additional context to a single piece of threat data, enabling an analysis of all aspects of the threat

data loss prevention (DLP)   Collection of policies, programs, and technologies that allow an organization to prevent sensitive data from leaving the organization through the network, storage media, and other means

data masking   Obfuscation of parts of certain data elements (such as a Social Security number) from a record in order to ensure that authorized individuals can see only the data required for their job

deidentification   Removal of specific identifiers from a dataset so that the subjects of that data cannot be identified

demilitarized zone (DMZ)   Security zone within an organization's network that isolates and controls access to specific hosts and network segments

deny list   A list containing entries of network traffic, applications, or subjects used to deny permissions or actions to those elements. Replaces the outdated term *blacklisting*.

detective controls   Security controls designed to detect malicious actions or violations of policy

deterrent controls   Security controls designed to be known to a potentially malicious actor to deter them from performing a malicious act or violation of policy

DevSecOps   Integration of the development, security, and operational personnel and processes to develop software that is more usable, meets functional requirements, and is more secure

Diamond Model of Intrusion Analysis   An analytical methodology for cybersecurity analysts to utilize prior to, during, and after cybersecurity intrusions. The model demonstrates the relationships and characteristics of an attack's four main components: adversary, capabilities, infrastructure, and victim.

digital rights management (DRM)   Processes designed to integrate mechanisms into digital media to prevent its unauthorized access or use

directory traversal attack   An attack in which the attacker can navigate through sensitive directory structures on a server or network that they should not usually be allowed to access

discretionary access control   Access control model allowing the creator or owner of a resource, such as a file or a folder, to grant access to others based on their own criteria

distributed denial of service (DDoS)   Denial-of-service attack characterized by multiple, simultaneous attacks on a host from various other hosts

Document Object Model (DOM)   A standard dictating how client browsers interact with HTML presented from a web server

domain generation algorithm (DGA)   Method of dynamically generating random domain names and URLs. Primarily used to obfuscate malware command-and-control servers.

Domain Keys Identified Mail (DKIM)   A standard developed to detect e-mail spoofing, thereby preventing phishing and other impersonation attacks. DKIM uses a digital signature linked to an organization's domain name.

Domain Name System (DNS)   Internet-wide system that allows Internet Protocol (IP) addresses to be translated to a common human-understandable name

Domain-based Message Authentication, Reporting, and Conformance (DMARC)   An e-mail authentication protocol designed to ensure the authenticity of e-mail sent from the organization. DMARC uses either Domain Keys Identified Mail (DKIM) or the Sender Policy Framework (SPF) as its method to ensure authenticity.

dynamic analysis   Method of code analysis that requires the software code to be executed in a secure environment to observe how it interacts with the operating system and other elements of the network

Dynamic Host Configuration Protocol (DHCP)   TCP/IP protocol responsible for issuing IP addresses and other critical network information dynamically to hosts on a network

Elasticsearch, Logstash, Kibana (ELK)   Open source, comprehensive security information and event management (SIEM) solution

endpoint   Individual device on a network; typically, an end-user host or individual host dedicated to a single function

endpoint detection and response (EDR)   Process focused on detecting and responding to malicious events on an endpoint device

enterprise resource planning (ERP)   Comprehensive management of primary business processes through carefully orchestrated processes, tasks, activities, and dedicated software tools

Extensible Markup Language (XML) attack   Attack in which the attacker manipulates an XML application or service logic by injecting XML content or structures into a web application to bypass the program logic of the application

false negative   A result from an assessment tool that neglects to indicate a specific vulnerability that is in fact present

false positive   A result from an assessment tool that indicates a vulnerability that actually does not exist

federated authentication   An authentication model in which multiple organizations either trust each other so that authentication mechanisms and credentials are transitive across organizations or they all use a centralized authentication provider

field-programmable gate array (FPGA)   An improved version of a system-on-chip configuration used in a wide variety of electronic devices, including medical devices, automotive electronics, industrial control systems, and consumer electronics. FPGA is more flexible and allows programmers and end users to install firmware updates to reconfigure the hardware so that new software functionality, as well as security mitigations, can be implemented on it.

File Transfer Protocol (FTP)   TCP/IP protocol used to transfer basic files from one host to another. FTP is inherently insecure, as it offers no encryption or authentication mechanisms and transmits all data in cleartext. It uses TCP port 21 for control and port 20 for data.

Firewall as a Service (FaaS)   Cloud-based service offering that provides firewall and other perimeter security services for client organizations

Forensic Toolkit (FTK)   Comprehensive commercial forensics application available from AccessData

frameworks   Overarching architecture of processes, activities, and tasks that provide a method for implementing a program

Function as a Service (FaaS)   Cloud service that offers customers a serverless architecture that only provides specifically defined functions abstracted from a server infrastructure

fuzzing   Method of software testing where large volumes of a random or unexpected input are sent to the application to observe its reactions for the purposes of gauging its resilience, functionality, and security

hacktivist   Activist individual or group that conducts cyber attacks on organizations as part of a self-defined moral or ethical cause

hardware security module (HSM)   Hardware device responsible for generating and storing cryptographic keys. It is often implemented as an add-on card or device installed separately from the computing device.

heap overflow attack   An attack in which the attacker attempts to exhaust the memory dynamically available for the application in the heap portion of system memory

heuristics   Method of detection and analysis that offers a best guess of behaviors based on characteristics of previously known attacks

honeynet   A network of honeypot devices

honeypot   A networked host designed to be inherently insecure to attract an attacker for the purposes of observing the attack without the attacker's knowledge. Honeypots are also used to distract an attacker from an organization's sensitive network.

host-based intrusion detection/prevention system (HIDS/HIPS)   A software intrusion detection/prevention system installed and focused on a single host

hybrid cloud   A cloud solution having combined characteristics of other cloud deployment models, such as private, public, and community clouds

impersonation attack   An attack that attempts to impersonate a specific user or host

indicator of compromise (IoC) A piece of data or other artifact that may indicate that a system or the network has been attacked or otherwise compromised

Information Sharing and Analysis Center (ISAC) A nonprofit organization that collects, analyzes, and distributes threat intelligence to public and private sector organizations with critical infrastructures

Information Technology Infrastructure Library (ITIL) A library of practices and standards used for IT service management that focuses on aligning IT services with business needs

Infrastructure as a Service (IaaS) Cloud service model in which the cloud provider offers the hardware, network, and storage assets so that the organizational user can install and use its own operating system and applications

Infrastructure as Code (IaC) A functionality offered by cloud service providers that allows developers to dynamically change the infrastructure based on changes in their code rather than relying on servers and networks

integer overflow attack Attack method in which an attacker creates a mathematical operation using a numerical value that is larger than the application's memory space assigned for it and injects it through invalid input

International Organization for Standardization (ISO) Organization (often seen in conjunction with the International Electrotechnical Commission, or IEC) engaged in developing and implementing international standards for engineering, information technology, and many other areas

Internet Message Access Protocol (IMAP) TCP/IP application layer protocol used by e-mail clients to retrieve e-mail messages from an e-mail server and defined by RFC 3501. IMAP uses TCP port 143 (non-secure) or TCP port 993 for the secure version (IMAP over SSL, called IMAPS).

Internet of Things (IoT) Name given to the paradigm of Internet-connected end devices that have very minimal resources and operating systems and serve very specific functions, such as consumer electronics devices and industrial control systems

Internet Protocol (IP) TCP/IP protocol responsible for logical addressing, routing, diagnostics information, and troubleshooting

intrusion detection system (IDS) Network- or host-based system designed to detect an active attack in progress. An IDS is often combined with an intrusion prevention system (IPS).

intrusion prevention system (IPS)   Network-or host-based system designed to prevent or stop an active attack in progress. An IPS is often combined with an intrusion detection system (IDS).

Lightweight Directory Access Protocol (LDAP)   Primary protocol used in directory services infrastructures to enable integrated resource location. LDAP is an X.500-compatible protocol and uses TCP and UDP ports 389, or port 636 for LDAPS (LDAP over SSL).

local area network (LAN)   Network infrastructure that uses locally routed resources and does not traverse a wide area network (WAN) link

machine learning   A discipline of computer science that can be used to expand data analytics significantly beyond simple pattern searching or correlation. In addition to predetermined criteria, machine learning can allow an analysis to extrapolate beyond its programmed pattern analysis and combine elements of behavior analysis with complex algorithms.

magnitude   In risk management, the level of impact that a negative event has on the organization or an asset

managerial controls   Controls focused on security management measures, such as policies and procedures

mandatory access control (MAC)   Access control model based on a subject's clearance and objects labels. Access can only be assigned by an administrator.

man-in-the-middle attack   An attack characterized by a malicious entity who intercepts communications from both the sender and receiver and impersonates both parties to access, alter, and redirect communications

measured boot and attestation   Measured boot is the process of collecting hashes of startup or boot files when booting in a mode other than secure boot. Attestation is the process of comparing those same hashes to known-good ones to validate the startup or boot files.

memorandum of agreement (MOA)   An agreement between two entities, usually within the same organization, that specifies levels of service or other commitment

memorandum of understanding (MOU)   An agreement between two parties, usually within the same organization, that outlines specific points of understanding or agreement, such as guaranteed service levels, between the two parties. See also *memorandum of agreement*.

Message Digest 5 (MD5)   Deprecated hashing algorithm that produces a 128-bit hash in the form of a 32-digit hexadecimal number

microservices A popular service-oriented architectural method that consists of individualized deployable application services that are focused on business transactions and perform very specific functionality

MITRE Adversarial Tactics, Techniques, and Common Knowledge (ATT&CK) framework A public knowledge base of threat tactics and techniques developed by the nonprofit MITRE Corporation. The ATT&CK framework describes the tactics, techniques, and procedures threat actors use to penetrate networks, move laterally across the network, escalate privileges, and evade the target defenses.

mobile device management (MDM) The overarching management infrastructure for all mobile devices, such as smartphones, tablets, and laptops within an organization to integrate their interoperability and security functions

MODBUS A widely used communication protocol originally developed in 1979 by Schneider Electric for use in industrial electronic automation systems

Monitoring as a Service (MaaS) A cloud service model that allows for monitoring systems, networks, devices, users, and other aspects of an organization for security, function, and performance

multifactor authentication (MFA) An authentication model that uses more than one factor, such as a smartcard and PIN, to authenticate a user to a system or facility

Multi Router Traffic Grapher (MRTG) Cross-platform network traffic monitoring and measurement software that allows the user to see traffic in graphic form. MRTG is written in the Perl scripting language and can be run on Windows, Linux, and macOS platforms.

National Institute of Standards and Technology (NIST) U.S. government agency under the Department of Commerce tasked with developing formal U.S. standards and technologies

network access control (NAC) Method of ensuring that any host joining the network is subject to inspection and required security measures, such as antimalware, secure configuration, and patching

network address translation (NAT) Method of mapping private Internet Protocol (IP) addresses to public IP addresses for the purposes of security and efficiently using the limited IP version 4 address space

network interface card (NIC) Hardware attached to a system through an external interface card, USB device, or chip on a motherboard that allows communications between the host and a network

network intrusion detection systems (NIDS)   Network-based system designed to detect potential network attacks or compromises; often combined with an intrusion prevention system

nondisclosure agreement (NDA)   Agreement signed between individuals or organizations requiring each signatory to maintain confidentiality of any sensitive or proprietary information exchange between the agreeing parties

open source intelligence   Intelligence derived from public or nonproprietary sources, such as the Internet, public directories, and so on

Open Source Security Information Management (OSSIM)   A Linux-based, open source security information and event management system

Open Web Application Security Project (OWASP)   A nonprofit organization focused on software and web application security. OWASP has developed several open source software projects, including Zed Attack Proxy (ZAP) and the OWASP Top 10 Web Application Security Risks.

operational controls   Controls focused on the physical and operational environment and associated procedures

original equipment manufacturer (OEM)   The manufacturer or vendor who originally provides a device or software application

packet capture (PCAP)   File containing network traffic capture, typically generated from a network protocol analyzer such as tcpdump or Wireshark

passive footprinting   Process of gathering all available information about an organization, its personnel, structure, network, and other characteristics. Passive footprinting uses techniques that allow someone to gather information without actively interacting with the organization or its infrastructure.

password spraying attack   Attack in which the attacker uses one or only a few passwords across many different accounts in an organization in hopes of compromising an account

Payment Card Industry (PCI)   Professional trade industry composed of the major credit card issuers, including Visa, MasterCard, and American Express. PCI publishes the data security standards that are levied upon credit card merchants.

personally identifiable information (PII)   Personal information that can be used to uniquely identify an individual; this includes information such as name, address, driver's license number, passport number, Social Security number, and so on.

physical controls   Security measures that apply to the physical environment, such as fencing, gates, guards, closed-circuit television cameras, and environmental controls

platform   Term describing the architecture of a computing device and includes elements such as the operating system and CPU

Platform as a Service (PaaS)   Cloud-based service in which providers offer computing platforms on which an organization can run their applications

pluggable authentication module (PAM)   A mechanism that allows multiple authentication schemes to be used in an operating system or application. PAMs allow concurrent use and management of authentication mechanisms such as username/password and multifactor authentication and are primarily seen in Linux systems.

port security   Term used to describe the authentication mechanisms used in the IEEE 802.1X standard

preventative controls   Security measures used to prevent a violation of policy or malicious action

privacy   The exercise of control of personal information by an individual, to include its use, distribution, and disposition

private cloud   Cloud computing resources dedicated to the sole use of an organization

privilege escalation attack   Goal of an attacker in which a compromised user account is used to gain higher privileges on the host or network

privilege management   Processes and activities used for comprehensive management of user accounts and their authorized access to resources

probability   In risk management, the likelihood of a threat exercising a vulnerability

processor security extensions   Specialized components found in modern CPUs that work together to create a trusted execution environment by setting up a reserved area of memory for the application's process to execute securely and through dynamic memory encryption/decryption

protected health information (PHI)   Specific personal health information protected under statute such as the Health Insurance Portability and Accountability Act (HIPAA)

public cloud A cloud model in which the cloud provider owns all of the resources, including hosts, network infrastructure, and applications, used to provide services to any organization. Each organization has its own unique piece of the public cloud infrastructure and therefore is logically separate from other organizations' portions of the infrastructure.

public key infrastructure (PKI) The management infrastructure involved in controlling the secure lifecycle of public and private key pairs, including identity verification, issuing, maintaining, and retirement of digital certificates

real-time operating system (RTOS) A specialized operating system, sometimes developed from an existing operating system such as Windows or Linux, that is installed on an electronic chip and run on a variety of special-purpose devices, such as system or industrial controllers and Internet of Things devices

red team Team of cybersecurity specialists tasked with exploiting found vulnerabilities during the security testing of an organization's infrastructure

Remote Authentication Dial-in User Service (RADIUS) A TCP/IP protocol that provides centralized authentication, authorization, and accounting (AAA) services to remote hosts accessing a network. RADIUS uses TCP and UDP ports 1812.

remote code execution A goal of an attack in which the attacker can remotely execute any arbitrary code of their choosing on a compromised system

Remote Desktop Protocol (RDP) TCP/IP protocol used to remotely access and control the resources and user interface of a system. RDP uses TCP port 3389 by default.

Representational State Transfer (REST) An architectural method used to overcome some of the limitations with the older SOAP protocol. REST is designed to allow stateless communications between services, applications, and web-based resources.

reverse engineering The process of decomposing a piece of hardware or software down to its component elements to understand how it is constructed, its underlying functions, and its security mechanisms

role-based access control Access control model that assigns privileges, rights, and permissions to a specified role rather than an individual. Individuals must be assigned to the roles in order to gain access to the resource or be able to perform the specified actions.

rootkit Sophisticated malware that replaces an operating system's critical files with compromised copies, allowing an attacker to control all aspects of the system and potentially go undetected.

sandboxing The process of executing unknown or suspicious software in a controlled and secure environment to prevent its interaction with the underlying operating system or network

Secure Hash Algorithm (SHA) A family of hashing algorithms published as a set of standards by the National Institute of Standards and Technology (NIST)

Secure Shell (SSH) A TCP/IP protocol designed to secure remote sessions between hosts by offering encryption and authentication services. SSH uses TCP port 22.

Secure Sockets Layer (SSL) A deprecated TCP/IP protocol designed to protect communications across networks using encryption and authentication services. SSL was replaced by Transport Layer Security (TLS) and used TCP port 443.

Security Assertions Markup Language (SAML) A markup language that has specific tags in its structure that allow applications to use formatted information about the user, including their identity and other authentication and authorization information

Security Content Automation Protocol (SCAP) A framework developed by NIST used to assist in the overall risk management of systems by providing a consistent, open data format that can be used across different security tools and platforms. SCAP includes various languages and formats to describe security vulnerabilities, exposures, and assets, as well as reporting formats, identification schemes, measurement and scoring, and data integrity.

security information and event management (SIEM) The centralized collection, aggregation, correlation, and analysis of disparate forms of data from across the network infrastructure. SIEM devices typically use agents to collect data for consolidation analysis.

security operations center (SOC) A centralized security operations center that serves to consolidate security personnel and management activities for an organization

Security Orchestration, Automation, and Response (SOAR) The name given to suites of tools dedicated to unifying your security tools, processes, and methods used across the enterprise

security regression testing A type of test that integrates new application code with existing infrastructure and tests for security issues that may result from the new code, including incompatible security technologies

segmentation The process of separating sensitive hosts and network segments from nonsensitive ones using physical and logical means, such as virtual LANs, encryption, and physically separated networks

self-encrypting drive Permanent storage media implemented as a hardware-based cryptographic solution, as a cryptographic module is part of the drive hardware and is typically built into the disk controller itself

Sender Policy Framework (SPF) E-mail authentication method that checks to ensure that e-mail has been sent from an authorized IP address, as published in the organization's DNS server

sensitive personal information (SPI) Information of a personal nature that could include PII and PHI but also may include information beyond the two categories

Server Message Block (SMB) A TCP/IP application layer protocol primarily used in Windows networks for file and print sharing. SMB is considered deprecated.

service level agreement (SLA) An agreement between two organizations, typically a customer and a service provider, where defined levels of service are agreed upon and included in the contract

service set identifier (SSID) The human-readable name of a wireless network that uses common security protocols and credentials

service-oriented architecture An architecture describing software components that interface and interact with each other to provide services via standardized components. These components include application programming interfaces (APIs) and markup languages.

session hijacking attack An attack that interrupts an established communications session between two parties and effectively takes over the session. This often includes a man-in-the-middle or impersonation attack.

signature-based detection An attack detection method that looks for known patterns or signatures

Simple Object Access Protocol (SOAP) A messaging protocol used to facilitate communications and interactions that take place between different services and applications, and allows clients to access services over HTTP, regardless of the application server platform

single sign-on (SSO) A method of authenticating to multiple disparate resources using a single set of credentials. SSO is designed to make security administration and authentication processes simplified and streamlined.

sinkholing   A method for sending potentially malicious traffic, such as botnet command-and-control traffic, to an internal host rather than to an external Internet address.

Software as a Service (SaaS)   A cloud model where customers access and use common or line-of-business applications provided by a cloud service provider

Software Development Lifecycle (SDLC)   A process that describes how software is planned, designed, created, tested, implemented, and maintained throughout its useable life. SDLC is a formalized framework consisting of steps, tasks, and processes that drive all activities associated with software development and use.

Secure File Transfer Protocol (SFTP)   A method of securely transferring files by using ordinary FTP over SSH.

static analysis   A method of software code analysis that uses predetermined libraries of issues to automatically check for in code, examining it line by line, looking at different objects, checking their properties, references, and so on. Static analysis tools can check for a wide variety of known issues, such as input validation weaknesses and code injection.

Structured Query Language (SQL) injection attack   An attack using invalid input in the form of SQL statements that can access an underlying database and return or update data that the attacker does not have access for

Structured Threat Information eXpression (STIX)   STIX is a standardized language developed by MITRE, now maintained by the OASIS Cyber Threat Intelligence (CTI) Technical Committee, for describing characteristics of threat data, such as threat motivations, capabilities, and response.

supervisory control and data acquisition (SCADA)   Automated information systems that control a wide variety of geographically separated systems, including critical infrastructure and utilities such as transportation systems, power grids, water treatment plants, and nuclear power plants

supply chain attack   An attack on an organization's producers, vendors, warehouses, transportation companies, distribution centers, and retailers to steal or destroy data or to compromise an organization's infrastructure

system-on-chip (SoC)   An embedded system in which software and hardware are integrated into a single computer chip. The chip is self-contained and consists of a processor, system RAM, and other critical components miniaturized into a single integrated circuit.

tabletop exercise   A paper-based exercise that presents scenarios to which participants state how they would conceptually respond.

technical controls   Security measures that apply to the technical aspects of an organization's infrastructure; examples include authentication and encryption mechanisms, network security devices, and access control lists.

Terminal Access Controller Access Control System Plus (TACACS+)   A Cisco-proprietary extension to the original TACACS remote access and authorization protocol, which provides for authentication, authorization, and accounting (AAA) services for remote hosts. TACACS+ uses TCP port 49.

threat   An event that takes advantage of a vulnerability and has negative consequences for an asset or organization

threat actor   An entity that initiates a threat event

threat hunting   The activities involved with actively searching for potential threats in the infrastructure

threat modeling   The process of using available threat capability and motivation information combined with comprehensive information about the organization, its assets, and its vulnerabilities to accurately determine the existence of specific threats acting against the organization

threat rating   A ranking of a threat's potential danger level on a defined scale

tokenization   A method used to protect certain data elements from disclosure by substituting a value generated as a placeholder to take the place of that information

Transmission Control Protocol (TCP)   A protocol in the TCP/IP suite that operates at the transport layer of the OSI model and provides connection-oriented sequencing and acknowledgment of data

Transport Layer Security (TLS)   An application protocol in the TCP/IP protocol suite designed to protect communications over a network through encryption and authentication. TLS replaces its outdated predecessor, SSL, and uses TCP port 443.

trend analysis   The process of examining a broad range of data to determine causes, patterns, and behaviors; two important types of trend analysis are temporal analysis and spatial analysis.

Trivial File Transfer Protocol (TFTP)   Simplified version of the File Transfer Protocol suitable for moving small files, such as configuration files, between hosts and network devices. TFTP uses UDP port 69.

true negative   Results verifying that a vulnerability does not exist

true positive   Results verifying that a vulnerability does in fact exist

Trusted Automated eXchange of Intelligence Information (TAXII)   A cyber threat standard that describes how threat data can be shared. TAXII uses a flexible communications API to make it compatible with multiple cyber-threat-sharing models such as hub and spoke, peer-to-peer, and source/subscriber models.

trusted execution/secure enclave   An environment in which a software abstraction layer creates containers where several applications can run protected from the underlying operating system and any potential vulnerabilities inherent to the OS (and vice versa)

Trusted Foundry   A Department of Defense program for vetting and approving vendors of trusted hardware

Trusted Platform Module (TPM)   A specialized chip embedded in a device that handles cryptographic functions, such as key generation and storage

unified endpoint management (UEM)   Term given to the collective processes, activities, tasks, and tools used to exercise comprehensive management over all end users and devices

Unified Extensible Firmware Interface (UEFI)   Firmware implemented on a host used for handling its hardware, security, and integration with its operating system. UEFI replaces the older Basic Input/Output System (BIOS) firmware used on legacy devices.

unified threat management (UTM)   Comprehensive process and software solution spanning network security devices and processes, including threat intelligence management, firewalls, proxies, and intrusion detection/prevention systems

Uniform Resource Locator (URL)   An identifier that helps locate an Internet resource based on its hostname and location

Universal Serial Bus (USB)   A technology allowing peripherals such as printers, cameras, and external media to be easily plugged into a host device based on a set of standardized interfaces

user acceptance testing   Software test in which the end-user community tests the performance and functionality of a software application against its stated requirements for possible acceptance

user and entity behavior analytics (UEBA)   A method of analysis that focuses on end-user behavior patterns

User Datagram Protocol (UDP)   Connectionless protocol that works at the transport layer of the OSI network model. UDP is appropriate for transporting network traffic that does not require an establish connection, sequencing, or acknowledgment of receipt, such as audio and video protocols.

virtual desktop infrastructure (VDI)   Virtualization method that allows users to have a desktop running VDI software to make remote connections to shared network resources without requiring intense computing power for the client

virtual local area network (VLAN)   A local area network infrastructure implemented at the software level, typically on layer 3 switches, which allows connected hosts to join specific virtual networks. VLANs are used to segment and segregate sensitive hosts as well as eliminate the need for separately routed subnets.

virtual private cloud (VPC)   A set of cloud-based dedicated resources, set aside for one organization's use, either in their own data center or in the service provider's infrastructure

virtual private network (VPN)   Two private networks separated by a larger public network, such as the Internet, implemented so that users can logically connect to a private network using a secure tunneling protocol

virtualization   The name given to a variety of technologies allowing organizations to create and manage multiple dynamic instances of hosts and networks through software

vulnerability   A weakness inherent in an asset, or a lack of security measures implemented to protect an asset

watermarking   Process of embedding an identifying piece of information, such as a logo, into a media file or document

web application firewall (WAF)   Network security device designed specifically to protect web application servers from potentially malicious activities

white team A team tasked with providing exercise support, liaison, and oversight between offensive and defensive teams during a security assessment

whitelisting An outdated term for a list that contains entries of allowed traffic, applications, or subjects. See also *allow list*.

wide area network (WAN) Network characterized by using wide area network protocols and devices. A WAN typically spans larger geographic areas and connects multiple local area networks together.

workflow orchestration Method of unifying security processes, tasks, activities, and tools for centralized management, scheduling, and data flow

Zed Attack Proxy (ZAP) Web proxy tool developed by OWASP that allows an analyst to send and receive carefully crafted traffic to and from a web server for security testing purposes

zero day Name for a previously unknown attack that has not been addressed by a software vendor or for which there is no known patch or mitigation

Index